T0279596

SLAVES OF SATAN

A Catholic Study of Perfect Possession, Diabolical Subjugation and the Enemies of Jesus Christ

PATRICK R BELL

Published by:
Trine Day LLC
PO Box 577
Walterville, OR 97489
1-800-556-2012
www.TrineDay.com
TrineDay@icloud.com

Library of Congress Control Number: 2024933169

Bell, Patrick.
–1st ed.
p. cm.

Epub (ISBN-13) 978-1-63424-486-2
Trade Paperback (ISBN-13) 978-1-63424-485-5
1. RELIGION / Christian Theology / Angelology & Demonology. 2. RELIGION Christian Life Spiritual Warfare. 3. RELIGION / Demonology & Satanism. 4. Demoniac possession Social aspects. 5. Demoniac possession Psychological aspects. 6. BODY, MIND & SPIRIT Parapsychology General. I. Bell, Patrick. II. Title

CREDOS is an Imprint of TRINEDAY

FIRST EDITION
10 9 8 7 6 5 4 3 2 1

Printed in the USA
Distribution to the Trade by:
Independent Publishers Group (IPG)
814 North Franklin Street
Chicago, Illinois 60610
312.337.0747
www.ipgbook.com

Publisher's Foreword

One of the artifices of Satan is, to induce men to believe that he does not exist:
– John Wilkinson, *Quakerism Examined*, 1836

One of the most striking proofs of the personal existence of Satan, which our times afford us, is found in the fact, that he has so influenced the minds of multitudes in reference to his existence and doings, as to make them believe that he does not exist; and that the hosts of Demons or Evil Spirits, over whom Satan presides as Prince, are only the phantacies of the brain, some halucination of mind.
– Pastor William Ramsey, *Spiritualism, a Satanic Delusion, and a Sign of the Times*, 1856

My dear brethren, never forget, when you hear the progress of wisdom vaunted, that the cleverest ruse of the Devil is to persuade you he does not exist!
– Charles Baudelaire, *Le Joueur Généreux* 1864

Baudelaire, that old flower of evil, was right: The Devil's cleverest wile is to make men believe that he does not exist.
– Whittaker Chambers, "The Devil," *LIFE*, 1948

The greatest trick the Devil ever pulled was convincing the world he didn't exist.
– Kevin Spacey (Verbal), *The Usual Suspects*, 1995

… and what doth the Lord require of thee, but to do justly, and to love mercy, and to walk humbly with thy God?
– Micah 6:8

Jesus said unto him, Thou shalt love the Lord thy God with all thy heart, and with all thy soul, and with all thy mind. This is the first and great commandment. And the second is like unto it, Thou shalt love thy neighbour as thyself. On these two commandments hang all the law and the prophets.
– Matthew 22:36-40

I do not believe in the Devil or Satan/Lucifer or whatever you care to call the personification of evil. I do believe in God. Belief is an interesting thing. A dictionary definition: *an acceptance that a statement is true or that something exists; and a trust, faith, or confidence in someone or something.*

I consider myself a "red-letter Christian." In that I enjoy the sentiments of Jesus as related in the Gospels, but find that throughout history priests have used religions to befuddle us and used their positions for control and power.

Patrick Bell and his book *Slaves of Satan* is an exhaustive look at the subject of "Demonic" possesion and the beliefs of many Christians and other religions. There is a lot of excellent research, information and writing in this book.

I did tell Patrick: "I am not a believer in Satan. I find that evil is done by men [mankind], I do not believe that the devil makes folks do things. I do believe in incarnate 'spirits,' basically groupings of vibrations that can attach themselves to a person." And that I believed in the Holy Trinity. Patrick's answer was: "Ok, fair enough."

From a 2009 article titled "The Biochemistry of Belief":

> The biochemistry of our body stems from our awareness. Belief-reinforced awareness becomes our biochemistry. Each and every tiny cell in our body is perfectly and absolutely aware of our thoughts, feelings and of course, our beliefs. There is a beautiful saying "Nobody grows old. When people stop growing, they become old." If you believe you are fragile, the biochemistry of your body unquestionably obeys and manifests it. If you believe you are tough (irrespective of your weight and bone density!), your body undeniably mirrors it. When you believe you are depressed (more precisely, when you become consciously aware of your "Being depressed"), you stamp the raw data received through your sense organs, with a judgment – that is your personal view – and physically become the "interpretation" as you internalize it. A classic example is "Psychosocial dwarfism," wherein children who feel and believe that they are unloved, translate the perceived lack of love into depleted levels of growth hormone, in contrast to the strongly held view that growth hormone is released according to a preprogrammed schedule coded into the individual's genes!

In my mind it boils down to belief. And as the Good Book says:

> *Do not be deceived: God cannot be mocked. A man reaps what he sows. The one who sows to please his sinful nature, from that nature will reap destruction; the one who sows to please the Spirit, from the Spirit will reap eternal life. Let us not become weary in doing good, for at the proper time we will reap a harvest if we do not give up.*
> –Galatians 6:7-9 NIV MIT

Onward to the Utmost of Futures,
Peace,
R.A. Kris Millegan
Publisher
TrineDay
March 1, 2023

This book is dedicated to Ed Warren (1926-2006) and all the other brave souls
on the frontlines in the battle between good and evil

CONTENTS

"The **ultimate danger**, though, would be to allow your human spirit to **absorb** the reprehensible, blasphemous characteristics of the demonic"
– Ed Warren

"I could actually feel Satan consuming me, **absorbing me** into his very being, as though this was the deepest possible initiation and bonding, and the deepest and yet most horrible union"
–Thomas Altizer, infamous heretic who declared "God is dead"

"The life you live would not be your own, but instead one **directed** by another"
– Ed Warren

"It was like another person was in me, doing a lot of **directing**"
– David Berkowitz, the Son of Sam

"The soul that has lost divine grace is **driven** by Satan"
– Father Francis Spirago

"I can't stop it… it controls me, you know, it's like in the driver's seat… it is **driving** me."
– Dennis Rader, BTK (bind, torture, kill) Serial Killer

INTRODUCTION

This book is going to deal with a topic that admittedly is somewhat obscure, but also extremely important to all Christians. At its core the topic of this book deals with evil on a scale and magnitude rarely written or spoken about. It deals primarily with evil people who have given themselves, body and soul, voluntarily, to the source of all evil, who is Lucifer. These people are servants of the devil, exercising their free will they have chosen to give their allegiance to him who was the first rebel, the first sinner, the first angel, the light bearer. They have completely rejected God and all his ways and have chosen to serve, with all their being, the fallen archangel, the discarnate entity who is "princeps," prince and king of the dark and diabolical kingdom, Satan. They are, in effect, slaves of Satan.

Satan has often been called an "ape" of God. Satan seeks to copy, and mock Gods works. Catholic saints are completely and totally committed to the love of God, to the service of God and his people. They are completely committed to Jesus Christ and his church, and they spend their lives bringing the light of Christ and love into the world. Lastly, they are in the state of sanctifying grace and indwelt by the Holy Spirit. The diabolic mockery and aping of a Catholic saint are those people who have committed their lives to serving the devil and his angels. These people look forward to the time when they will die and be in hell with their prince, some even intentionally ending their own lives for this desired result. They spend their lives bringing the darkness of Satan, hatred and evil into the world. Most importantly, which is the primary topic of this book, they are indwelt by the presence of evil spirit, who collaborates with them in various ways for the working of evil on this planet and among mankind.

This topic is extremely important for several reasons. The first is because it is through the people I will be talking about in this book that some very grave evils are perpetuated throughout the world. I believe that modern society, formed by Hollywood and the modern printing press has a skewed view of what true evil actually is. There has of late been an explosion of books and movies dealing with traditional extraordinary dia-bolical activity. That would be local infestation of places, material objects and animals; diabolic oppression; diabolic obsession; and diabolic pos-session. These movies and books can give the impression that evil only works in an extraordinary manner. That the devil's activity does not ex-ceed the bounds of what is portrayed. That true evil is only present when a doll named Annabelle levitates and oppresses its owner[1]; that true evil is only present when Regan McNeal projectile vomits green slime and caus-es Father Karris to be thrown down a staircase to his death[2]; that true evil is only present when Emily Rose sees horrid devil faces and undergoes terrifying exorcisms in the middle of the night during electrical storms.[3]

The three movies I just mentioned were all based on real cases[4], and di-abolic evil was present in all of them. However, the evil present in them is certainly not the most serious or pressing concern to the common Chris-tian. There is a level of diabolic activity that goes above and beyond what is portrayed in these movies. Extraordinary diabolic activity is spectacu-lar and frightening. There is no question it negatively effects peoples lives and is dangerous. And there is also no question this activity is the primary concern of the exorcist and should be addressed by him for the good of the souls so afflicted. It could also be said that these books, movies and tv shows serve a certain purpose to alerting people as to the existence of the Devil where previously they did not believe in his existence whatsoever.

Extraordinary diabolic activity, however, also catches the attention of people and then they only concentrate on it as if this is the only evil that exists in the world. As if true diabolic evil only manifests itself in the ex-traordinary, preternatural displays depicted in these cases. As if abortion is not a much graver evil, as if gay marriage is not a much graver evil, as if organized pedophilia and the pornography industry are not a much great-er evil, as if totally debauched movies and music purveyed to our youth is not a much graver evil, as if the flooding of dangerous narcotics into our societies that destroys countless lives is not a much graver evil. When people believe that the devil only works in the extraordinary manner as portrayed in the movies or on tv shows, then he and his servants are free to do real damage throughout society. In addition, people are ill-informed

---

1   John R. Leonetti, *Annabelle*, New Line Cinema

2   William Peter Blatty, *The Exorcist*

3   Scott Derrickson, *The Exorcism of Emily Rose*, Lakeshore Entertainment: In addition, the plethora of tv shows having to do with ghost hunting and demonic activity are another perfect example.

4   See Warren, *The Demonologist*; Allen, *Possessed*; Goodman, *The Exorcism of Anneliese Mi-chel*; Fortea and LeBlanc, *Anneliese Michel A True Story of a Case of Demonic Possession*

and not prepared for the more wide-ranging and far more destructive activities of the devil and his followers.

The activity that is the primary topic of this book could be classified both ways. It is no doubt an extraordinary activity of the devil, it goes way above and beyond what is normally called the ordinary activity of the devil which is temptation. We are dealing here with diabolical possession, but in a completely different sense than what is normally considered or talked about. Because the phenomena at hand is technically diabolic possession it can be classified as an extraordinary activity of the devil, albeit the most serious form. In my opinion it can also be classified as an ordinary activity of the devil, although not in the traditional sense, because the phenomena that we will be talking about in this book is one of the ways in which diabolic evil, diabolic ideas, ideologies, doctrines, strategies and plans are ordinarily and ultimately introduced into the world. I am speaking of events in the course of the history of humanity that have been perpetrated by thoroughly evil people, servants of the devil and inspired by this same devil. The human sacrifice of any number of ancient civilizations[5], the murder of Christians by the Romans, the introduction of destructive heresies into the early church, the holocaust, the genocide in places like Soviet controlled Ukraine, Cambodia, and Rwanda:

> "During the exorcism Zago boasted of being the captain of the world, claiming that everything moved as he wished, **that he had instigated the civil war in Rwanda himself**, relishing and taking satisfaction from the spilled blood of brothers"[6]
>
> "The thing sat on a throne of bats, spewing fire everywhere. Death was on its mind. It told the boy how it was **personally responsible for the torture and killing of thousands of people during World War II.**"[7]

The murderous evils that take place in the abortion mills, in the blood-soaked drug wars in Mexico and other places, organized pedophilia among elites, organized crime or the mafia, the organized campaign to destroy traditional marriage, the pornography industry and other powerful structures of sin in modern society and finally organized satanism and devil worship on a worldwide scale. Everything I just listed are things

---

5   And for that matter the human sacrifice still perpetrated today by radically evil underground, sometimes multigenerational devil worship cults.

6   Gabriel Amorth, *Memoirs of an Exorcist*

7   Brittle, Warren, *The Devil in Connecticut*

that I believe were and are inspired by the devil and then collaboratively carried out by his servants, who are the people I will be writing about in this book. The phenomena of *perfect possession*[8] is one of the ways in which Satan uses his human servants to run and further his kingdom on this earth for the destruction of souls.

The second reason I believe this topic to be of the utmost importance is because it is a virtually ignored topic in the modern literature of demonology, possession, and exorcism. If it is dealt with it is only with a few sentences or a few paragraphs at the most. Being that this form of diabolic activity among men is the most serious and the most dangerous, this is a pretty glaring oversight in the books of modern authors.

Being that we are about to undertake the discussion of the most serious and dangerous form of diabolical activity, a brief statement on the lesser forms will suffice. Diabolic activity has generally been divided into two distinct categories, the *ordinary* activity of the devil, which constitutes *temptation*, and the *extraordinary* activity of the devil which comprises the four general forms that I listed above. A very brief word on each of them will suffice.

Diabolic Temptation: Human beings are tempted in various ways, these temptations coming from three principle sources: our flesh or concupiscence, the world around us, and the devil. Diabolic temptation is when an evil spirit, rarely Satan himself, suggests evil to us in a multitude of different ways. Theologians have generally agreed that diabolical spirits are free to use our material senses, but not move our will or intellect. Meaning the devil can use our senses, our imagination, memory, and sensitive appetites to tempt us or suggest evil to us. It has also been speculated that the higher a person climbs the ladder of perfection the higher level of demonic agency is assigned to tempt the person[9] and as a result the temptations become subtler and harder to

---

8   There are only five reputable books where the actual term "perfect possession" appears; see Martin, *Hostage to the Devil; Euteneuer, Exorcism and the Church Militant*; Davies, *Exorcism from a Catholic Perspective and Peck, Glimpses of the Devil*; and the very recent work by Jesse Romero, *The Devil in the City of Angels*. And another recent work by Father Chad Ripperger titled Dominion: The Nature of Diabolical Warfare. I would note that this book was released after I had finished the manuscript for the current book and the work by Father Ripperger actually contains the most information about Perfect Possession and Diabolical Subjugation than any other work up to this point. Ripperger devotes an entire 13 pages to the topic of Diabolical Subjugation, Perfect Possession and Pacts with the Devil which is substantially more than any other author writing in the same genre. Perfect Possession has also been mentioned at the Mundelein Conference over the course of several years, as well as by Father Ripperger in various talks he has given, and Father Lampert in an interview he gave to the U.K. *Telegraph*.

9   Joseph F Sagues, S.J., *Sacrae Theologiae Summa: On God the Creator and Sanctifier, On Sins*, P. 213

recognize or become extremely intense, violent and almost rising to the level of *diabolic obsession*.

EXTRAORDINARY DIABOLIC ACTIVITY[10]

*D*iabolic Infestation*: Also called *Local Infestation*[11]. This is when an evil spirit or spirits have for whatever reason applied their power to a certain place, object or animal and as a result can be actually said to be *present* in the place. A place can become infested for many different reasons. These would include the practice of grave evil in a place such as pedophilia or necrophilia, drug dealing and use, the practice of black magic, satanism, or witchcraft, the direct invocation of diabolic entities, a curse or cursed object present in the place, murder, abortion, or even playing with a Ouija board. Generally, this activity consists of banging, pounding, doors slamming, objects flying around or being flung about the residence, foul smells, objects materializing or dematerializing, spontaneous combustion's, black shadows or masses seen, religious objects being destroyed, people becoming terrified and other phenomena that can be dangerous and extremely frightening. The general nature of a haunting that is caused by the diabolic is destruction[12]. If evil is involved there will invariably be some kind of destruction in the place, both destruction of material things, relationships and people's lives in general.

Diabolic Oppression: This constitutes a diabolic attack on the exterior of a person. Balducci called this *personal infestation* that is *external*. It should be noted some exorcists break this up into even more categories and call this vexation and external pain. Much older authors have labeled this as *circumcession*. The absolute best examples of this type of diabolic attack can be found by studying the lives of certain saints. The lives of St. Anthony of the desert, Hilarion, Martin of Tours, Catherine of Siena, Teresa of Jesus, Ignatius of Loyola, Paul of the Cross, Gemma Galgani, John Vianney, John Bosco, Padre Pio and many more are especially profitable for study. Oppression can take many different forms, including a person

---

10   It should be noted that some exorcists use up to six categories to classify extraordinary diabolic activity (Amorth, Ripperger) and some, especially older authors use three or less. Older authors would usually classify just obsession and possession (Tanquerey, Garrigou LaGrange, Royo Marin, Delaporte) or at the most, circumcession, obsession, and possession (Sagues S.J., Pohle-Pruess, Blackmore S.J., Houck). The classification I give here has been given by other authors (see Warren, Balducci, Bamonte) but most importantly has been consistently used by the International Association of Exorcists, subsequently approved by the Italian Bishops Conference and included in the new Rite of Exorcism, Exorcisms and Certain Supplications.

11   Balducci, Gli Indemoniati; Bamonte, *Diabolical Possession and Exorcism*

12   Father M, Mundelein Conference; Ed Warren, *The Demonologist*

being slapped, beaten, scratched, bitten, burned, pulled by the hair, and whipped. To quote Bamonte, some saints have been,

> "showered with rocks or feces falling on them from some unseen source, while still others have been thrown out of their beds, down stairs, tossed into the air and thrown to the ground... Others have been transported to places far away."[13]

Saudreau notes that oppression, which he calls "external obsession" can be inflicted by itself, or in the context of possession. Saudreau goes so far as to say there is never possession without external obsession.[14] Another form *oppression* can take is when someone's finances, relationships, health, or work is disrupted or destroyed by diabolical action. To find reputable Catholic descriptions of oppression one can consult a number of works.[15]

Diabolic Obsession: Balducci uses *personal infestation* that is *internal*[16] and avoids the term *obsession* specifically because it has been used in a psychiatric context.[17] This form of diabolic attack is more serious than oppression because instead of focusing on the exterior of a person, it is an attack directed on the interior of a person, on their internal faculties rather than just on their exterior senses as in oppression. Some authors like Garrigou LaGrange note that *obsession* is like an enhanced form of temptation. However, it should be clearly noted that the attack itself is still directed from outside the person[18], which specifically differentiates

---

13   Bamonte, *Diabolical Possession and Exorcism*

14   Saudreau, *L Etat Mystique, Les Faits-*

15   See Warren, *The Demonologist, Saudreau, El Etat Mystique, Ribet, La Mystique Divine Tome 3*, All the works of Amorth, Bamonte, Balducci, and Syquia, and the mystical theology manuals of Garrigou Lagrange, Royo Marin, Tanquerey, Devine, Aumann, Poulain S.J., and Arintero O.P. There is also an abridged translation of Scaramelli's *Il Direttorio Mistico* available. In addition, the lives of the above-mentioned saints as well as case studies on hauntings can be good resources for studying actual cases of oppression. The reader could consult *An Unknown Encounter: A True Account of the San Pedro Haunting* by Barry Conrad, or *Sallies House* by Debra Pickman, or *The Haunted* by Robert Curran or *The Demon of Brownville Road* by Bob Cranmer or *An Authenticated History of the Famous Bell Witch* by M.V. Ingram. Additional resources can be found in the bibliography and recommended reading list at the back of this book.

16   Balducci, *Gli Indemoniati*

17   Balducci does this to avoid confusion because in Gli Indemoniati he devotes a whole section of the book on psychiatric diseases that can mimic diabolic attack and then goes into the specific modalities of each disease and how they specifically differ from diabolic attack. Gli Indemoniati is possibly one of the best books ever written on diabolic possession, it unfortunately has never been translated into English.

18   Tanquerey in *A Manual of Dogmatic Theology, Vol 1* clearly defines this difference between diabolic action that occurs from without or from within, however, Scaramelli S.J. believes that in obsession the devil sometimes "enters in from time to time for the purpose of arousing temptations and causing pain." See *Il Direttorio Mistico or A Handbook of Mystical Theology* P.148

it from *possession*.[19] The old version of the *Rituale Romanum* classified all demonic attack as *obsession*. Some older authors like Blackmore S.J.[20] define *obsession* as essentially a lesser form of *possession*. Other older authors claim that *obsession* is more dangerous than even *possession* because *obsession* has as its goal the corruption of the soul, whereas in *possession* the corruption of the body is at state. This position was put forward by Ribet and taught by Royo Marin.[21] Contemporary authors define *diabolic obsession* as a diabolical attack directed at the imagination and memory in which obsessive, foul, sinful, or evil thoughts bombard the mind of an individual, the individual being powerless to stop them. For instance, Father Garrigou-LaGrange notes:

> The direct action of the devil on the imagination, memory, and passions, may produce obsessing images, which persist in spite of energetic efforts and which lead to anger, to very lively antipathies, or to dangerous affections, or again to discouragement accompanied by anguish.[22]

Likewise, Father Arintero notes:

> Not a single idea occurs to them, nor any good thought. Instead, they are tormented by many horrible ideas of blasphemy, despair, and every kind of evil which is suggested to them by the enemy.[23]

Bamonte notes that obsession can take the form of a person being obsessed by the idea of making a pact with the devil or the idea of committing suicide or even the idea that they are going insane. Saudreau notes that a soul under *obsession* can believe itself to "hate God and to love blasphemy"[24]. Likewise, Dom Vital Lehodey writes:

> Temptations to diabolical wickedness; execrable blasphemies seize upon the imagination, and they are **so strong and vivid** that we almost believe we have uttered them.[25]

Ed Warren gives additional examples of obsession that can take the form of terrifying and violent demonic images in one's mind to wear the

---

19   See Johnson, *Apparitions: Mystic Phenomena and What They Mean*, P.325
20   Blackmore S.J., *The Angel World*
21   Ribet, *La Mystique Divine*, quoted in Royo Marin, *The Theology of Christian Perfection*
22   Reginald Garrigou-Lagrange, OP, *The Three Ages of the Interior Life*
23   Fr. John Arintero O.P., *The Mystical Evolution in the Development and Vitality of the Church,* Vol 2
24   Saudreau, *El Etat Mystique*, Chap 22, authors own translation
25   Dom Vital Lehodey, *The Ways of Mental Prayer*

person down with fright and dread in a process leading ultimately to possession.[26]

Diabolic Possession[27]: The traditional definition of diabolic possession is when an evil spirit enters into the body of a person and controls that body and its faculties from within, but not the spiritual faculties of intellect and will, which are only affected indirectly. Traditionally, possession has been defined by two factors: First the presence of the devil or devils in the body of a possessed person and second, the action of the devil on that body. All authoritative authors distinguish between two states in a possessed person; a state of calm and a state of crisis. The state of crisis is when all the violent, blasphemous, insalubrious, and de-humanizing phenomena occur, although sometimes in the state of calm the person can have certain maladies always present or there can also be paranormal or poltergeist phenomena occurring around the person even when they are in a state of calm. The state of crisis can leave the person totally unconscious or in a trance state, where when they come out of it, they remember nothing of what has happened. A much rarer state is the "lucid state"[28] when a person is actually awake and aware during the crisis manifestations. A couple important notes on possession: First, possession does not go as far as animation[29], meaning the demon does not take the place of the soul in the body. The human soul continues to be the principle life force of the human person. The diabolic spirit acts directly upon the members of the body and controls them "despotically"[30] at his whim. Saudreau notes that during the crisis state the demon's own personality comes across, "his emotions, his anger, his pride, he seems to look with the eyes of the possessed."[31] Both Saudreau and Poulain believe possession is a direct diabolic mockery of the incarnation. Saudreau and many other authors state that one of the factors in the *intensity* of the possession has to do with what demons are actually present. Saudreau notes that true "princes of hell"[32]

---

26   The best description of obsession is probably in Saudreau, *L Etat Mystique*, Chap. 22 and Scaramelli, *A Handbook of Mystical Theology*, P.147-152 However, all the previously mentioned authors in footnote 14 (especially the mystical theology manuals) as well as the lives of the saints will all be profitable for study.
27   Some authoritative Catholic authors on this topic would include: Thyraeus S.J., Del Rio S.J., Suarez S.J., Scaramelli S.J., Schram, Ribet, Saudreau, Waffelaert, Gorres, Poulain S.J., Lagrange, Royo Marin, Tanquerey, Bruno de Jesus Marie et al in Satan; and in more recent times Balducci, Bamonte, Amorth, Fortea, Syquia, Laurentin, Cristiani, Nicola, Rodewyk S.J., Warren, Martin, Ripperger, Ermatinger, Blai, Lampert, Gallagher and Rossetti.
28   See Oesterreich, *Possession and Exorcism, and Lhermitte, Diabolical Possession*, True and False
29   Saudreau, *L Etat Mystique*
30   Balducci, *Gli Indemoniati*
31   Saudreau, *L Etat Mystique*
32   Ibid

have been present in the worst and most violent cases. For the purposes of this study I will close by saying traditional diabolic possession is largely characterized by the extraordinary manifestations of preternatural power that occur in the possessed person. It is these very phenomena that allow the exorcist to discern between true cases and frauds. And it is also partly these phenomena that differentiate cases of partial and *perfect possession*,[33] and lastly it is these phenomena that the exorcist is strongly advised to ignore lest he take his focus off the power and work of Jesus Christ.

All of the extraordinary diabolical activity that I just described, despite being characterized by different modalities and phenomenology, all usually have one thing in common, which is the will of the demonic conflicts with the will of the victim, meaning these are cases of diabolic *attack*, and not willing collaboration. Regardless of the fact of whether the person originally opened a door[34], developed a relationship with a diabolic agency or initially consented with their will, the fact remains that the extraordinary psychological, medical, behavioral, and paranormal phenomena are occurring is precisely because the will of the victim is in *conflict* with the will of the demonic, they are nonconsensual. Where they once consented, opened a door or developed a relationship, the victim of diabolic attack cries out for help and now wants to extricate themselves from the illicit diabolic relationship that they have been a part of. This conflict of wills or *struggle* is normally how the case gets noticed for what it is and is eventually brought to the attention of church authorities. Malachi Martin writes:

> "Some area of revolt arises against the control originally accepted. The possessed become revolters; and insofar as they do revolt, they are attacked with increasing ferocity by the invading spirit, who, in its turn, protests any attempt to dislodge it from its "home." It is that strange and terrible struggle between the rebelling victim and the evil spirit protesting the rebellion that, in a strange way, begins to produce the repulsive, disquieting, and frightening events so often associated with the possessed and which lead their families or friends to seek help on their behalf."[35]

---

33   That is because cases of perfect possession do not display violent and preternatural phenomena that occur in cases of partial possession.

34   Almost all authors agree that some kind of door or entryway must be opened for the demonic to come into one's life, in an extraordinary fashion.

35   Malachi Martin, *Hostage to the Devil: The Possession and Exorcism of Five Contemporary Americans*; Also see the story of the Gerasene Demoniac. The Gerasene demoniac displays all the classic violent phenomena of possession, yet when he encounters Christ, with what free will he has left he runs up to Christ and prostrates himself before him. This was a cry for help and the violent phenomena are a symptom of that cry for help.

Similarly, Dr Scott Peck writes,

> "possessed people are not evil; they are in **conflict** between good and evil. Were it not for this conflict we could not know there is such a thing as possession. It is this conflict that gives rise to this "stigmata" of possession. Thoroughly evil people are not in conflict; they are not in pain or discomfort. There is no inner turmoil… Malachi believed that thoroughly evil people were that way because of demonic involvement and because of their **complete cooperation with the demonic.** Hence he calls such people the **perfectly possessed.**"[36]

In the rest of this study we will be discussing the persons mentioned above who have given their "complete cooperation" to the diabolic. This class of person intentionally invites the diabolic spirit into their life or accepts the invitation of a diabolic spirit to come into their life. This class of person wishes to be possessed, to spend eternity in hell, and forever be a servant, vassal, and slave of the devil. This class of person, once they have invited and consented with their will to the diabolic in their life, do not usually revoke the initial invitation, they persist in it. They do not intend to change their mind and they revel in it and like it. Eventually they make one clear, final, definitive decision to accept the devil, serve evil, and become its slave. Even so it is usually a process, a process of a human being slowly ceding parts of their will, intellect, and body to a diabolic force, step by step, until a point is reached where they have made a definitive decision for evil and the devil.[37] They essentially give themselves, body and soul, over to the devil to be *used* by him as he wishes. *'I can't stop it… it controls me, you know'.*[38] Furthermore, they fully cooperate with their will in the overall mission of the diabolic kingdom to destroy the Catholic Church and make sure as many human souls as possible end up in hell.

This diabolic phenomenon and this class of person exhibits very different phenomenology and symptoms than what I just described above regarding the traditional four forms of extraordinary diabolic operation and assault. This type of person and this diabolic action that we will be

---

36   M. Scott Peck M.D., *Glimpses of the Devil: A Psychiatrist's Personal Accounts of Possession, Exorcism, and Redemption*

37   This definitive decision for evil and the devil sometimes takes the form of some horrific and violent attack in which people are brutally murdered and often the possessed then immediately commits suicide, also by violent means.

38   Quote by Dennis Rader, the BTK serial killer, speaking about something that he claims possesses him that he calls both demons and Factor X. This statement by Rader shows clearly the deplorable state of those perfectly possessed. Completely and totally in slavery to the devil and being essentially controlled but collaboratively controlled by the devil or a devil.

describing, are the most dangerous, terrible and frightening of all the diabolic phenomena at work in the world. Such people in this condition are
not only *extremely* dangerous and destructive in society[39] but they are also
in grave spiritual peril of being damned to hell.[40] As I stated earlier, they
have freely given themselves completely over to the devil for service in
his kingdom. Their wills and souls are so blackened by sin and given over
to the practice of evil that it is Satan that is their master and Satan that is
in control and uses these people to further his own interests, which they
have fully consented to.

The most popular contemporary terminology for this phenomenon is
either *Perfect Possession* or *Diabolical Subjugation*[41]. Because the term *"Perfect Possession"* seems to be the most widely used and accepted of these
terms, especially in the United States, I will use it throughout this study
when referring to this phenomenon. This phenomenon is spoken of briefly by many authors, some however, do not use the terms *Perfect Possession*
or *Subjugation*. It has been called different things by different authors and
is talked about not only in the modern literature on possession and exorcism but also in much older books on mystical theology and moral theology. In mystical theology it has been spoken of in the context of those
who make pacts with the devil and in the context of the most serious and
deplorable type of mortal sin, those committed through obstinacy, malice[42] and hatred of God. In moral theology it is spoken of in the context of
the "sin against the Holy Spirit," which sin sometimes ends in the practice
of devil worship and "compact with Satan."[43]

In some books it is called *invisible possession*[44], *latent possession*[45], *voluntary possession*[46], *constantly possessed*[47], *permanent possessions*[48], *fully pos-*

---

39   Father M, Mundelein Conference, 2010
40   One author even called them "the walking damned"
41   In note 8 I listed the five authors who have used the term perfect possession. Likewise, the authors who have actually used the term Subjugation in their work would be Amorth,
An Exorcist Tells His Story; An Exorcist More Stories; Bamonte, *Diabolical Possession and the Ministry of
Exorcism*; Syquia, *Exorcist A Spiritual Journey*; Ripperger, *Introduction to the Science of Mental Health*; Syquia, *Exorcist A Spiritual Journey*
and Bolobanic, *An Exorcist Speaks*.
42   Royo Marin, *The Theology of Christian Perfection*; Saudreau, *L Etat Mystique*
43   Preuss-Koch, *A Handbook of Moral Theology*; Davis S.J., *Moral and Pastoral Theology*
44   Cristiani, *Evidence of Satan in the Modern World*, "Far more terrible than these extreme
cases are the cases of invisible possession, cases where Satan has no need to reveal himself, although he is more than ever present, and whispers his diabolic suggestions into the ears of those
who are already his own."
45   Saudreau, *L Etat Mystique*; See P.34 of this study for the full quote
46   Cristiani, *Actualite de Satan*; Corte, *Who is the Devil*; See P.33 of this study for the full
quote
47   Baglio, *The Rite*; See P. 60-61 of this study for the full quote
48   *Mary Crushes the Serpent,* ed. Theodore Geiger, trans. Celestine Kapsner, "They admit
that they have won over a large number of souls whom they keep as their slaves and whom they

sessed[49], active possession[50], full and unquestioned possession[51], the most severe form of possession[52], formal union with the powers of darkness, mystic marriage of the human mind with Satan[53], diabolical scandal and compact with Satan[54], integral possession or diabolic integration[55], an extreme form of possession[56]complacent possession[57], freely chosen possession[58], total possession[59], demonic dependence[60], willed satanic subjugation[61], and demonic bondage.[62]

There are also some authors who speak briefly about what could be construed as perfect possession but do not actually give it a formal name like the authors I just mentioned. Two such authors are Ed Warren and Laurent Volken. In his very good book, *The Demonologist*, Ed Warren states:

> "What would you say is the **ultimate danger** in dealing with the demonic? "On the transitory level," Ed replies, "the life you live would not be your own, but instead **one directed by another**. **Throwing your will open to the demonic is to allow yourself**

regard as their permanent possessions. In their battle against the Church the demons use the wicked people as their allies."

49   Cruz, *Angels and Devils*; also, In a talk Father Ripperger gave in which he mentions diabolical subjugation and perfect possession he uses the term "full possession" to describe perfect possession.

50   Giuseppe Ferrari, *Phenomenon of Satanism in Contemporary Society*, "The possible cases of diabolical possession, found in those who participate deliberately in satanic activities, are to be classified as cases of an active rather than passive type, since it is the persons themselves who offer themselves voluntarily to the devil."

51   Scaramelli, *Guide to the Spiritual Life or Directorium Asceticum, Vol 2*, "St Gregory is of the same mind as St Jerome, since he says, that the devil cares not to disturb those unhappy souls of whom he has gained full and unquestioned possession."

52   Rodewyk, *Possessed by Satan*, "By making such a pact, the man or woman denies himself God's grace and support, opens himself to the Devil's whim and may experience the most severe form of possession."

53   Preuss-Koch, *A Handbook of Moral Theology*; See page 62. Of this study for the full quote

54   Davis S.J., *Moral and Pastoral Theology*; Many authors have linked compacts with the Devil with perfect possession.

55   "Integral possession" was first mentioned by Father M at the Mundelein Conference in 2009; Father Gary Thomas, *What You Need to Know About Exorcism*, "a person that accepts the demon, we call that integration, whereas a possession would be involuntary."

56   Bishop Julian Porteous, *Manual of Minor Exorcisms*, "An extreme form comes about because the person has, in some way, surrendered their freedom to the Evil One."

57   Fr. Jeremy Davies, *Exorcism from a Catholic Perspective*, "We speak of the possessed as 'the afflicted' but this is because we are usually speaking of those who are seeking to be free and that is why the Devil is afflicting them. The far more terrible state is that of the possessed who are complacent, who have the peace of this world."

58   Euteneuer, *Exorcism and the Church Militant*, "We speak here about the freely chosen possession of people who have given themselves over to devil worship."

59   Euteneuer, *Exorcism and the Church Militant*, P.124, Euteneuer uses "total possession" interchangeably with perfect possession; Ravenscroft, *The Spear of Destiny*, "total possession" is used by Ravenscroft to denote the type of diabolic possession present in Adolf Hitler

60   Amorth, *Get Out Satan*

61   Bamonte, *Diabolical Possession and the Ministry of Exorcism*

62   Syquia, *Exorcist A Spiritual Journey*, P. 53

to be its stooge. The ultimate danger, though, would be to **allow your human spirit to absorb the reprehensible, blasphemous characteristics of the demonic** – the enemy of being. For when this happens, the individual runs the potential risk of sharing the fate of these spirits of darkness: separation from the source of being. That would be the sobering danger of **allowing yourself to be taken over by these negative spirits of perdition.**"[63]

Ed Warren here speaks in the context of the most serious threat posed by the demonic, the "ultimate danger" as he calls it. It should be noted this passage is near the end of the book and is talked about last, only after all the other forms of extraordinary diabolic activity have already been discussed. In response to the question of what the ultimate danger is with regard to the diabolic, Mr. Warren is clear that it would be to "allow yourself" to be "taken over" by a diabolic spirit. When *perfect possession* is written about it is always in the context of being the most serious form of diabolic affliction or it is spoken of as being the worst and most terrible form of possession, both Monsignor Cristiani and Father Davies both use the qualifier *"far more terrible"* when describing *perfect possession* in relation to partial possession. Additionally, it is usually spoken of in the context of a human being voluntarily giving oneself to the devil, allowing oneself to be "taken over" as Ed explains.

Laurent Volken is another author who writes about what seems to describe *perfect possession*, however, he only devotes two sentences to it, and he does not give it a formal name or cite a source for his assertion. In his book, *Visions, Revelations, and the Church*, Volken writes:

"**The entire man with all his faculties may even fall wholly under the devil's domination,** that is, if **he freely gives himself to the devil.** He cannot then withdraw himself even if he wants to; he becomes truly the possession of the devil; as a possessed person he is **totally at the disposal of the devil:** he is the "prophet" of the devil who speaks through him"[64]

Volken, like Warren, speaks to the essence of what *perfect possession* is, which is as Volken puts it, to *freely give* oneself to the devil. Volken, like Warren, makes this statement after he had already discussed traditional diabolic possession, leaving the most serious form (freely giving oneself to the devil) for last. I stated above that the devil exorcises complete control over these people, they are totally enslaved to him. Some readers may

---

63   Ed Warren, *The Demonologist*
64   Volken, *Visions, Revelations, and the Church*

question that concept, however even the two authors I just quoted (there will be more later) were very clear that these people's lives are "directed" by the devil as Ed Warren puts it and "totally at the disposal" of the devil as Laurent Volken notes.

There is an additional author I was able to locate that speaks of *perfect possession* but also does not give it a formal name, except to say that it is a form of *obsession*. This author defines *obsession* in the classical terms of *possession* and then defines another form of *obsession* as other authors have defined *perfect possession*. The author I am referring to is Alois Winklhofer, a German theologian, who is the author of a book titled *Traktat Uber Den Teufel*. Adolf Rodewyk quotes Winklhofer in his classic book *Possessed by Satan*, and what Winklhofer writes is probably one of the best descriptions of *perfect possession* I have been able to find. Winklhofer writes:

> We differentiate two forms of obsession: one is the abuses of man by Satan and his angels for a longer or shorter period... and a second type, which does not actually eliminate personal freedom of the victim nor seize his body as a field of operation for demonic power but exercises **constant psychological and spiritual-ethical guidance**. This, too, may last for varying periods of time... **It is based on sin, on a pact,** which leads to **increasingly uninhibited collaboration with Satan,** enabling him to encircle the human person and **influence him inspirationally**, so that he becomes more and more **dependent**[65] **and obedient**... We must recall that Satan entered Judas (John 13:27); but the same applies to people who suddenly, without evident prehistory, **turn into criminals, attack children, and later kill them and who, when arrested, commit suicide**. When something as horrible as all that suddenly emerges from previously peaceful and apparently levelheaded personalities, there can hardly be any explanation but the impact of alien forces which in some uncanny manner have brought about **the dissolution** of an established personality structure.[66]

There is a lot to unpack in this paragraph, and I will have occasion to speak to different aspects of it throughout this study. For now, we can be content in noting that Winklhofer's description in is line with all the other definitions of *perfect possession* given by various authors, Winklhofer just goes into more detail. Rodewyk quoted Winklhofer near the end of his book and did so in the context of new definitions of diabolic posses-

---

65   I noted above that Amorth has labeled subjugation as "demonic dependence."

66   Alois Winklhofer, *Traktat Uber Den Teufel*, quoted in Adolf Rodewyk, *Possessed by Satan*, P.183

sion and obsession. Rodewyk was investigating different authors and how they differed amongst themselves in how they exactly defined possession and obsession. As Rodewyk notes, Winklhofer defines possession in two ways, the first is the classical case of possession in which a person comes under the attack of an evil spirit, Winklhofer calls these cases "abuses of man by Satan and his angels"; the second type of possession however, which is separate and distinct from the previously mentioned cases is a much more serious form where a human being becomes a willing collaborator and participant in all the works of Satan and his kingdom.

I said above that *perfectly possessed* persons introduce various forms of evil into the world working in collaboration with the Devil. Winklhofer notes this when he says the possessing demon "exercises constant psychological and spiritual-ethical guidance," and influences the possessed "inspirationally," which does not "actually eliminate personal freedom"[67]. This is caused by a "pact" that results in what Winklhofer calls an "increasingly uninhibited collaboration with Satan," which can also result in criminality, attacks on and the murder of children, and finally suicide. Needless to say, the ideas and concepts of Winklhofer duly cited will be found throughout this study, which is why I felt it important to quote him in the introduction. Adolf Rodewyk then in commenting about the above quote by Winklhofer also speaks of perfect possession in the clearest terms possible he just does not give it a formal name. Rodewyk notes,

> "We noted at the outset of this chapter that the obsessed person is weaker than the possessed. Thus, when Satan wants to **unleash his powers**[68], he must seek to use a possessed rather than an obsessed person. **The Antichrist and his predecessors**[69] **would have to be possessed human beings**. One tends to resist this concept, because of the **common misconception that a possessed person is forever ranting and raving, completely out of control, and so violent that his condition can be easily recognized**[70]; thus it is falsely assumed, he could not have any effect on the world around

---

67   This concept will become important later in this study as I argue that perfectly possessed people are in fact conscious of their actions, they are not in a state of trance and not aware of what they are doing, the following makes them responsible and liable for crimes they commit, despite being possessed.

68   I have already noted multiple times above that it is through perfectly possessed people that various forms of evil are introduced into society or committed against society.

69   The predecessors of Antichrist would be people like Herod, Nero, Caligula, Marx, Stalin, Hitler, Mao, and Pol Pot.

70   As I stated above this is a very important concept towards a full understanding of perfect possession. The fact that the perfectly possessed do not display the normal traits or symptoms of possession is one of the main factors present in every case of perfect possession. See Chapter 4, No. 6, for a full explanation of this concept.

him… In reviewing Winklhofer's ideas, it is necessary to point out that a "criminal on the worldwide political scene" might very well be possessed. This need not show in his daily work, except that he would display an unusually great capacity for work, unusual energy, and a virtually uncanny feeling for interrelations and dangers in his daily activities. The speech of such a man might easily and imperceptibly be invaded by the Devil, up to the point where he could finally speak directly through this individual. In such a person, the unique excitement of the possession crisis might very well be camouflaged by strong emotions and much shouting. Such a man might command uncanny suggestive powers, his knowledge and his grandiose plans might well be impressive. He could **exercise nearly irresistible power- and yet, all his actions would lead to destruction and death.**"[71]

The above quote by Rodewyk contains many important points, the first is that Rodewyk notes that when Satan wants to introduce evil into the world, he uses possessed people, perfectly possessed people. Rodewyk also notes that it is a common misconception that possessed people are forever ranting and raving. This is very important to understand because perfectly possessed people indeed do not show any of the normal signs of possession. Finally Rodewyk notes that a person like this may be so taken over by the devil that the devil would be able to "speak directly" through this individual, and that this individual's actions would lead to nothing but death and destruction, which will become important in chapter 12, signs and symptoms of perfect possession.

The oldest explicit mention of what we know to be *perfect possession* that gives it a formal name that I have been able to locate is from Father Auguste Saudreau, a prolific writer on the spiritual life, in 1907[72]. I have been unable to locate any reference or any work older than 1907 that cites the specific topic of *perfect possession*. The older works that I have studied do not speak to the specific topic of *perfect possession* but rather speak to the possibility of certain persons entering into formal compacts with the devil.

There are works and writings going all the way back to the time of Christ, including the scriptures, that speak of some type of slavery to the evil one through mortal sin and also works that speak of diabolical possession in the traditional sense. Some of these works, like the old witch

---

71   Rodewyk, *Possessed by Satan*, Rodewyk is clearly referring to Adolf Hitler in this paragraph.
72   Saudreau, *L Etat Mystique*

hunting manuals and even St. Thomas speak of the possibility of pacts with the devil. They do define the difference between an explicit pact and an implicit pact and even admit this can lead to diabolical possession[73], however, they do not take it a step further and define the nature of what has been called *perfect possession* or *subjugation*. There are also a few biblical passages and incidents that would seem to speak of this, but in no way is it defined or given any kind of substantial treatment. One example is in the book of Wisdom where it says:

> It was the **wicked** who with hands and words **invited death, considered it a friend**, and **pined for it**, and **made a covenant with it**, because they deserve to be in its **possession**.[74]

Additionally, the Book of Isaiah states of the same people:

> "Because you have said, "**We have made a covenant with death**, and **with Sheol we have an agreement**"[75]

There is also the case of Judas, who we will have occasion to speak of at the end of chapter 1, and the cases of other evil personages in the Old Testament who worshiped demons, performed human sacrifice, committed murder, and ruthlessly persecuted the Israelites. People like Cain, Jezebel, pharaoh and many more. In the New Testament we find the same, people like Herod and his summary murder of possibly hundreds if not thousands of children, Pontius Pilot who condemned the son of God to a horrible, demeaning and torturous death, the chief priests and Sanhedrin who subverted Christ's work and planned his murder in secret[76], Simon Magus, Elymus and more. In fact, Jesus himself declared that the Pharisees who were trying to kill him could count the devil as their "father" and that they were "full of all uncleanness."[77] Father Bamonte describes this as *paternity*[78], meaning Jesus labeled some of the evil people around

---

73   Thyraeus, *Hoc Est Daemoniaci*
74   Wisdom 1:16
75   Isaiah 28:15
76   The people who subverted Christs work and planned his murder in secret were exceedingly evil individuals. These people knew about and witnessed all the miracles being performed by Christ, they even plotted to murder Lazarus after Christ raised him from the dead! Despite seeing this they were consumed by hatred and jealously and successfully petitioned Pilate to execute their Messiah, the Son of God.
77   Matthew 23:27; Jesus also said they were like whitewashed tombs, beautiful on the outside but full of death on the inside. This concept is essential to understanding perfect possession. As I said above perfectly possessed people do not display the normal traits of possession, they may look and act like completely normal human beings and even be powerful, wealthy, and well respected, yet on the inside they are utterly devoted to the practice of evil and are fully and completely possessed by the devil.
78   Bamonte, *Diabolical Possession and the Ministry of Exorcism*

him and that were trying to kill him as being sons of Satan. All of the supremely evil characters in the bible have one thing in common, they all in some perverse way opposed God and his people. The bible is clear that the intelligence behind these attacks is Satanic. Yet Satan does not appear personally in some angelic form to conduct the attack[79]. He attacks through his human servants who have given themselves fully to him, who are totally beholden to him, and enslaved to him, some of whom may be *perfectly possessed.*

In addition to the scriptures the general concept of *perfect possession* was written about in various ways in the old witch hunting manuals of the 15th, 16th, and 17th centuries, it just was not defined or named. The primary form that it took was speaking of witches who were servants of the devil and in formal league with him. The authors of this time believed that the witch entered into a formal covenant or pact with the powers of darkness and intentionally served the devil and opposed God. Some of the writers of this time admit these witches to be possessed by the devil but do not delve into the topic and explain why this type of possession is more serious than the other traditional cases except to say that because they have intentionally made a pact and intentionally serve the devil their condition is more deplorable. For example, in a classic Catholic book about angels, devils, and diabolic activity, Father Frederick Houck noted:

> "Witchcraft implies an explicit surrender of oneself to Satan. The witch or wizard becomes Satan's human agent"[80]

We also find mention of this phenomena in the writings about spiritualism in the late 19th century and early 20th centuries. These writers also speak of people, (specifically mediums and spiritualists) practitioners of the black arts, who have given themselves fully to the devil, or who have voluntarily invited possession based on the "mental passivity" that is required for those involved in the practice of spiritism. For example, Jesuit Father Simon Augustine Blackmore S.J. in one of the best books written on the subject writes:

> "Mental passivity, even in its mildest form, implies the weakening of ones will power. At first it may be only a condition similar to a listless day dream; but, growing by degrees, it assumes a serious form, something akin to hypnotic trance, in which with conscious-

---

79   The only exception is of course the temptation in the desert.
80   Houck, *Our Friends and Foes or The Angels, Good and Bad*

ness and free will in a temporary total eclipse, one **offers unimpeded access** to invisibly roaming spirit agencies."[81]

In an even more explicit passage about what happens to people who are serious practitioners of the occult Jesuit Father Devivier writes:

"Paralyzing the energy of the will, whose power is gradually **weakened** and is finally **surrendered to the control** of invisible agencies."[82]

And finally, A.V. Miller in *Sermons on Modern Spiritualism* writes:

"As the power of the spirit will has **increased** over theirs, so they find that their power over their own will has diminished to such an extent that they are **reduced to slavery and unable to resist**."[83]

Lastly Cardinal Lepicier states:

"these practices result in a **considerable weakening** of the natural energy of the **will**. Persons accustomed to be under the influence of the spirits insensibly acquire such a **passive mental** disposition as to be in the end **helpless** and **unable to initiate any decided act of the will**. This, then, is an evident sign that these practices do not take place without a **person giving up**, to some extent at least, the use of **the free-will** and **surrendering** it to those mysterious agents, who may thereby be said to **take possession of the entire man**."[84]

The same can really be said for any occult practice, not just spiritism. In any occult practice, like witchcraft, divination, sorcery, necromancy, and devil worship, the energy of the will is weakened, the person consents with their will to commerce with evil spirits, they "surrender" their will to these entities, who then "take possession of the entire man."

When A.V. Miller states that they are "unable to resist" it sounds strikingly similar to Volken when he says "He cannot then withdraw himself

---

81   Blackmore S.J., *Spiritism: Facts and Frauds*
82   Rev W. Devivier S.J., *Christian Apologetics, Vol 2*
83   A.V. Miller, *Sermons on Modern Spiritualism*
84   Lepicier, *The Unseen World*; When Lepicier states that the spirits "take possession of the entire man" he is essentially referring to perfect possession. The diabolic possession of an "entire man" is a possession of both the body and soul. This is coupled with the fact that this very state is brought about due to the person intentionally "surrendering" their free-will over to the demonic world. The above quote by Laurent Volken also confirms this when he states: "the entire man and all his faculties may even fall wholly under the devil's domination, that is, if he freely gives himself to the devil." The entire man and all his faculties being possessed and dominated by the devil due to the person intentionally giving himself to the devil is basically the definition of perfect possession.

even if he wants to"[85], of which concept will be covered in the last chapter. It could be said that *perfect possession* could be renamed as diabolical slavery, which is essentially what demonic *subjugation* means. The most important keywords, which will become important later in this study, from the above four quotes are "unimpeded access," "surrendered to the control," "reduced to slavery," and "take possession of the entire man." This is really the crux of the whole subject. The people I will talking about in this book have given themselves fully to the devil, either intentionally through practices like those mentioned above or unintentionally through a long life of very serious mortal sin. One of the primary factors in *perfect possession* is that ones will power has been so weakened and so pummeled that the person is no longer in control of themselves, they have "surrendered to the control"[86] of demonic agencies and they are "reduced to slavery and unable to resist." They have intentionally and voluntarily "surrendered" their free-will to the Devil. Because they have been so enslaved to diabolic agencies they are now, like any slave, forced to obey the will of their master who is Satan. The scariest aspect to this is that these people choose this state, either implicitly or explicitly, they choose to be slaves of Satan, they are happy and content with their state of life and their slavery and despite being so enslaved they still retain a measure of their free will that they use to continually consent to the devil being in control of themselves.

Like many of the time periods and subjects I researched for this book, the books on spiritism do not give a formal name to this phenomenon, they do not call it *perfect possession*, but some authors do admit that this type of *possession* is different and more serious than the forms of possession spoken about in the *Ritual Romanum*. Jesuit Father Heredia writes:

> "One does not have to be a scientific observer to discover that there is a wide difference between the condition of the medium and the condition of the victim attacked by the devil.... **But I do say that such possession is not of the kind which the church describes in the Ritual and of which we have many examples in the history of the church** .... There is reason to believe that the devil consents to act with **those who directly or indirectly call upon him.**"[87]

The first author to my knowledge who gave this a formal name and labeled it as a form of possession was the above mentioned Father Saudreau

85   Volken, Visions, *Revelations, and the Church*
86   Devivier S.J., *Christian Apologetics, Vol 2*
87   Heredia S.J., *Spiritism and Common Sense*

who used the term *"latent possession."*[88] Fr. Leon Cristiani, also known as Nicholas Corte, who was extremely knowledgeable on the topic of the devil, picked up on[89] Saudreau's teaching and spoke about it in three of his books[90] and called it *"voluntary possession"* and *"Invisible possession."* These books by Cristiani were mostly published in the late 1950's. The above quote from Winklhofer, in which he describes *perfect possession* but does not label it as such appeared in 1961. Then in 1976 Malachi Martin's famous work *Hostage to the Devil* was released and this is the first time, as far as I can tell, that the term *perfect possession* was used. In *Hostage to the Devil*, Martin writes:

> "The **perfectly possessed**, a person who at some point in his career made one clear, **definitive decision** to **accept possession**, who never went back on that decision in any way, and who came under the **total control of an evil spirit**."[91]

Everything Martin wrote about *perfect possession* in 1976 lines up perfectly to what Saudreau, Cristiani, and Winklhofer wrote before him, their descriptions of *perfect possession* are basically identical to Martin's. After Martin called it *perfect possession* in the 1970's, modern authors, post 2000, began using the term as well. One modern author that does so is Father Jeremy Davies, an English priest and exorcist. In his book, *Exorcism from a Catholic Perspective*, he writes:

> "when a person has freely given himself totally to evil ('perfect possession')"[92]

In later chapters I will have occasion to quote every *reliable* author I have been able to locate that has actually used the term of *perfect possession* and *diabolical subjugation*.

I cannot state unequivocally where Malachi Martin got the concept of *perfect possession* from as he does not cite any source for his teaching. He does not call it *voluntary possession* as Cristiani does, or *latent possession* as Saudreau does, he calls it *perfect possession* and he even goes on to say that "the condition *commonly* called perfect possession may result"[93], the

---

88   Saudreau, *L Etat Mystique*
89   Both Saudreau and Cristiani are French authors and Catholic theologians, further, Cristiani states in *Evidence of Satan in the Modern World* that there is no better guide to understanding possession than Saudreau.
90   *Actualite de Satan; Who is the Devil; Evidence of Satan in the Modern World*
91   Martin, *Hostage to the Devil*
92   Davies, *Exorcism from a Catholic Perspective*
93   Martin, *Hostage to the Devil*

issue with this is according to my research I have been completely unable to locate any source whatsoever that used the term *perfect possession* before Malachi Martin did. So, I am not quite sure why he claimed that the condition was "commonly called" *perfect possession*. The fact is that as far as I can tell, Malachi Martin was the first person ever to call it *perfect possession*.

It is possible that Martin's mentor in exorcism taught him about this, his mentor being an unnamed Irish priest who he worked with in Cairo, Egypt where Martin had his first encounter with diabolic possession and exorcism. What the reader must understand is that there is a very large body of knowledge on diabolic phenomena that is never written about in any book. This knowledge is always passed down from priest exorcist to priest mentor and sometimes very rarely to lay people who have a special calling.[94] I know Malachi Martin was associated with many different priest exorcists and was at least for a time an exorcist himself. It is very likely this is where he learned the concept of *perfect possession* from.

As far as the term *diabolical subjugation* goes, it would seem it originated from Fr. Gabriel Amorth or possibly from his mentor Fr. Candido Amantini. This would seem to make the most sense as Father Amantini was responsible for training Father Amorth and many other priests for that matter. There is a foot note in Father Bamonte's book that would seem to point to this being the case. The context of the footnote is a discussion on satanism and those who immerse themselves in it reaching a so called "point of no return," which would be akin to *perfect possession*, at which point the footnote states:

> "According to some exorcists (among them the Servant of God Candido Amantini, who died in the odor of sanctity in Rome on September 22nd, 1992), sorcerers and Satanists can reach a point in which **conversion is impossible**, becoming something akin to **slaves of Satan** who find it impossible to turn back."[95]

From there the term *subjugation* was used in books by Father Bamonte and possibly some other Italian exorcists, as well as Father Bolobanic[96], Father Syquia[97] as well as Father Chad Ripperger.[98] At the 2010 Munde-

---

94   Additionally Ed Warren noted in his book *The Demonologist* that the Vatican archives probably contain one of the biggest stores of knowledge on the diabolic but that it is most certainly never been opened to the public and very rarely to even priests for that matter.

95   Bamonte, *Diabolical Possession and the Ministry of Exorcism*

96   A Croatian exorcist who wrote a book titled *An Exorcist Speaks*

97   A Filipino exorcist who penned a four-volume set on exorcism, just as good if not better than Amorth's works.

98   An American Exorcist who wrote, *Introduction to the Science of Mental Health*. Ripperger

lein Conference on Healing, Deliverance and Exorcism, Father M[99] (as I will call him throughout this book) spoke of *perfect possession* at some length. After his discussion he got a question from another priest in the audience who asked if what he was talking about was the same as what Father Amorth called *Subjugation*. Father M stated that yes, they are essentially the same thing, just two different terms. I bring this up so that the American reader can understand that the two terms are the same thing, they describe the same thing and that this was confirmed by one of the most well-respected priests in the exorcism ministry in the U.S. Father Bamonte also confirms this in his book, *Diabolical Possession and the Ministry of Exorcism*, where his description of *Diabolical Subjugation* is identical to how *Perfect Possession* is described in other sources. Additionally, Father Ripperger, in a talk he gave mentioned both *subjugation* and *perfect possession* to describe the same phenomena, the sixth form of extraordinary diabolic activity according to his classification.

The purpose of this book however is not to discuss the history of this teaching or where it exactly came from. It is to endeavor to discuss at length the state known as *perfect possession*; its nature, its causes, its dangers, why it occurs, who it affects, signs and symptoms of it, whether it is reversible, and some probable examples from history. There has never been a whole book written on *perfect possession*, there is only small tidbits of information on it throughout many different sources spanning many years. There is also no definitive teaching on this topic or body of literature like there is for traditional *possession*. I will admit that this surprises me a great deal. What is known as *perfect possession* is definitely the most severe form of demonization known to man and also the greatest threat posed to humanity by the diabolic. This will become clear later in the book when I profile people who very likely were *perfectly possessed*. All of these people have caused inestimable damage and harm to the church and the souls and bodies of mankind in general.

The reason the bookshelves abound with books about traditional *possession* is because that is the type of *possession* that displays all the extraordinary phenomena, and that sells books. In addition, the frequency of demonic attack and the number of exorcists needed has exploded, leading to many of these exorcists to write their own books. Levitations, head spinning, crucifixes flying off walls, throwing up huge quantities of

---

cites Amorth in the section on diabolical subjugation.

99   I have chosen not to reveal his name for various reasons, but it will suffice for now if I say that Father M is one of the most well respected, and senior most figures of the exorcism ministry in the U.S.

slime and filth[100], speaking in ancient and sometimes dead languages[101], and superhuman strength are all things that are truly extraordinary, and they peak people's interest and they quite frankly sell as books and movies. *Perfect possession*, on the other hand displays no such phenomena and I guess is not as entertaining, not as glamorous. *Perfect possession* is still *diabolical possession*, but it is a different form of it, as Father Adolf Rodewyk has stated, it is the "most severe form of possession."[102] *Perfectly possessed* people only display a cool, calculating, seductive and pervasive evil that spreads through societies like a cancer destroying the bodies and souls of man and subverting the work of the Church.[103]

As I will have occasion to say later in this book, the real evils of our day are not to be found in the bedroom of Regan McNeal, but right around the corner at Georgetown University where the Sandra Fluke's of the world spew their false teachings and errors to modern society.[104] Or in Albany, NY where late term abortion, the murder of children, is enshrined, argued for, protected, celebrated, applauded, and toasted with champagne.[105] Back in 1961 C.S. Lewis, one of the greatest Christian thinkers of our time, wrote:

> "The greatest evil is not now done in those sordid 'dens of crime' that Dickens loved to paint. It is not done even in concentration camps and labor camps. In those we see its final result. But it is conceived and ordered (moved, seconded, carried, and minuted) in clean, carpeted, warmed and well-lighted offices, by quiet men with white collars and cut fingernails and smooth-shaved cheeks who do not need to raise their voice."[106]

---

100   People have also vomited nails, glass, toads, leeches, etc...
101   Aramaic, Syriac, Phoenician, Latin, Greek, Hebrew and Ancient Egyptian have all been noted.
102   Rodewyk, *Possessed by Satan*
103   Father Cristiani in his book *Actualite de Satan* while speaking in the context of perfect possession states that "life offers us examples of true diabolical possession: cold perversities, calculating and reasoning hatreds, systematic corruptions, and cynical immoralism." Please see the beginning of chapter 3 for the full quote.
104   Fluke argued that Catholic Colleges should be forced to cover contraception for students despite the fact that Catholic teaching is clear on the grave immorality of using artificial contraception. She is also an abortion apologist and radical feminist.
105   A recent law signed by Catholic New York Governor Andrew Cuomo, allows for unimpeded late term abortions. When the law was passed the politicians stood up and applauded it. The Freedom Tower was subsequently lighted in pink to celebrate the passage of the law. This whole series of events, from a so-called Catholic governor signing the bill to the freedom tower, which replaced the twin towers which may have been allowed to have been destroyed as a chastisement for America's immorality, being lighted in pink was a grave insult to God, a blasphemy and mockery of his sovereign law. It was utterly diabolic in nature, "ghoulish" according to Cardinal Dolan and a "scene from Hell" according to Bishop Strickland.
106   C.S. Lewis, *The Screwtape Letters*

Similarly, an excellent article written on diabolical activity from the author of the traditional Catholic web site Fisheaters.com states:

> "The *perfectly possessed* are typically Satanists and people who make pacts with the Devil in exchange for earthly power… there are those who actually do sell their souls, who make a pact with the Evil One for some form of temporal success or another. As with true magic (the art of performing actions beyond the power of man with the aid of powers other than the Divine), these pacts with the devil may well work! Satan is the Prince of this world (e.g., John 12:31, 14:30, 16:11) and does have power that is passively allowed to him by God for a time. **Don't doubt that for a minute! Look around you and see the evidence of what spirit dominates this world, what allows for the fact that 1% controls almost all of the world's wealth and media, the power of the "banksters," the oily, power-mad types who end up in Congress and the Oval Office, the "stars" who make filth, the thugs with "hot chicks" hanging on their arms.** Those who enter into such pacts give up their immortal souls for a bit of temporary, temporal power and "success" as the world defines it. **They may, if the demons find something useful in them, become "stars" or "winning" politicians**"[107]

Therein lies one of the most important concepts of this study. Namely that traditional extraordinary diabolic activity, while evil, while dangerous, while destructive, is not the most serious form of evil in our society. I would even go as far to say that it may even in some cases be a flashy distraction, meant to get people to concentrate on the extraordinary, while real, true evil is being carried out in all its banality. Real evil is being carried out in offices, boardrooms, political bodies, courtrooms, medical clinics, invitro fertilization clinics, bio-research facilities, stock exchanges, prestigious universities, newsrooms, video game, music and film studios by people who may be well respected and who appear to be completely normal human beings on the outside but in reality are far more possessed than Regan McNeil and Emily Rose. I give full credit to C.S. Lewis for the originality and utter truth of his observation, and while it is his observation others have noted the same thing much closer to our own time.[108] My goal is to attempt to add to Lewis' idea the hypothesis that this evil that is being perpetrated in the above mentioned places is being carried out by

---

107   https://www.fisheaters.com/praeternaturalworld4.html
108   Two of the best examples is Euteneuer in the introduction to his book and Malachi Martin in an interview he gave entitled *The Kingdom of Darkness*

people who are servants of the devil (some explicit, some implicit), some of whom are no doubt *perfectly possessed.*

Before I conclude this introduction, I would like to state that researching this book was at times easy, at other times frustrating, and yet other times draining[109]. Easy in the sense that many modern authors devote a few sentences of their books to this topic and those I have been able to locate without much effort, frustrating in the sense that almost none of the authors I researched who explicitly talked about *perfect possession* provided any reference whatsoever for their teaching. Almost none of the authors I am about to highlight have given a specific source for their teaching on *perfect possession* or *subjugation.* The primary offender is Malachi Martin, the first person to label this state as *perfect possession.* Another is Father Adolf Rodewyk, a very learned Jesuit and demonologist. Rodewyk, in his classic book *Possessed by Satan* says that *pacts* with the devil can result in "the most severe form of possession," clearly a reference to *perfect possession.* However, he provides absolutely no reference at all for this teaching nor does he investigate or define what "the most severe form of possession" is. Another is Saudreau. He is the oldest writer who speaks of this and gives it a formal name (*possession latente* = latent possession) yet gives no reference or source for his teaching.

Also frustrating was the fact that for months I scoured Catholic theology manuals; Dogmatic, Moral, Mystical, as well as books on witchcraft and Eschatology[110], for references to this obscure topic. I will say I was able to find a few references but largely came up totally empty. For instance, the books on witchcraft[111] all admit the witch to be an explicit servant and agent of the devil who has given himself/herself totally over to evil and entered into a pact with evil forces. This being said, these books almost never take it a step further and define what this actually means, what the actual state of the witch is, whether possessed or not. Moral theology manuals[112] all admit the same possibility of a human being entering

---

109   Researching people who are totally and utterly evil and what they have done to their fellow man is draining to say the least. I would recommend being fortified with prayer before continuing this book.

110   I was especially searching for references to the Antichrist and the specific condition of his body and soul when he comes. We know this will be a man who will come with all the power and working of Satan, what we do not know is what this actually means; will Antichrist be perfectly possessed or just morally possessed or just be a wicked person. The scripture is clear that it will be a man, but in exactly what manner the satanic power will operate through this man is yet to be determined.

111   Robbins, *Encyclopedia of Witchcraft and Demonology*; Russell, *Witchcraft in the Middle Ages*; Haining, *The Anatomy of Witchcraft*; Summers, *History of Witchcraft and Demonology* and *A Popular History of Witchcraft*, Henry Charles Lea, *Materials Towards a History of Witchcraft*

112   Slater S.J., McHugh-Callan O.P., Prummer, Davis S.J.

into formal pacts with diabolical forces, but these likewise do not elaborate on the subject except to say it is a grave sin of superstition and contrary to the first commandment. Dogmatic theology manuals[113] all speak to the possibility of diabolical possession, obsession, and infestation and some even go further and define magic and divination; however not one of these theological manuals has even a passing reference to *perfect possession*.

Because of my limitations in foreign languages I was unable to conduct an in-depth study of some of the more important historical works on diabolic phenomena that very well may have references to *perfect possession*. The authors I was unable to examine in depth were Peter Thyraeus, Martin Del Rio, Brognolo, Schram, Luhmkull, Marechaux, Mirville, Van Noort (*De Deo Creatore*), Scaramelli, Gorres, Noldin, Ribet (*La Mystique Divine*) Tonquedec, Waffelaert and many others.[114] In addition I also spent countless hours in a local seminary library examining all the dogmatic theological manuals that are in Latin for possible keywords that would indicate the existence of the topic of study I was searching for. I searched through manuals by Herve (*Manuale Theologiae Dogmaticae, De Angelis* Vol 2), Mancini (*Theologia Dogmatica, De Angelis*), Pesch (*Praelectiones Dogmaticae*, Vol 3, De Angelis), Jungman (*Institutiones Theologiae Dogmaticae Specialis, Tractatus De Deo Creatore*), Graun (*Compendium Theologiae Dogmaticae Specialis*), Eduardo Hugon (*Tractatus Dogmatici* Vol 1), Mazzelle (*De Deo Creante*), Suarez (De Angelis), and Petavius (De Angelis). Needless to say, I was unable to find anything that would indicate these authors treated of the subject at hand.[115]

I would be willing to bet that if the works of Thyraeus, Del Rio, Schram, Scaramelli, Gorres, Ribet, and Suarez were analyzed closely, one would find some reference or mention as to the type of diabolic possession we will discuss in this book.[116]

My only hope in writing this book is to be able to contribute to a sort of intelligibility in this matter, to clarify some things and to define some things as new, to put this subject and the various authors that have treated it into *one source material*. While I will be quoting some sources in an

113   Van Noort, Tanquerey, Murphy-Cunningham, A.M. Henry, Chetwood S.J., Smith, Brunsman-Preuss, Farrel O.P., Pohle-Pruess, Wilhelm-Scannell, Hunter S.J. and the *Sacrae Theologiae Summa* by Joseph Sagues S.J. now in English.
114   Smit, *De Daemoniacis in Historia Evangelica*; Fortea (Summa Daemoniaca and Exorcistica) Laurentin, *Le Demon Mythe ou Realite*
115   This is probably due to my utter ignorance of foreign languages, some of these authors may very well have treated of this subject, however I did search pretty extensively.
116   I say this because all these authors came before Saudreau who may have gotten his idea of (latent possession) from one of them.

effort to show the reader what the various authors have said about *perfect possession*, much of the material in this book is new and has never been put together as a whole concept before. I quote the various authors only in an effort to put the whole subject of *perfect possession* together into one whole or intelligible teaching that can be used by the Christian faithful as information for their life in Christ but also be used by priests and others working in the exorcism ministry as a reference to this somewhat obscure topic. By directly quoting these authors it was in no way my intention to take away from the originality of their works but rather to put them all together into one source. My deep hope is that those priests and lay people who are much smarter than this author and have a much more scholarly background will pick up where I left off and write about this topic further and investigate and research it much more thoroughly.

To give a summation of the entire contents of the book I could say that the first part of the book will be used to demonstrate that *perfect possession* does indeed exist, demonstrated by the writings of various theologians and exorcists, many of which were already given in this introduction. As part of this discussion we will investigate the three ways the literature teaches cases of *perfect possession* can be brought about. We will also define the nature of *perfect possession* and the seven elements present in all cases of it.

I will then move into the question of why perfect possession exists. The most important reason from the diabolic perspective is that *true evil*, occurs in the banal way described above. The next four chapters will then be spent detailing the people who perpetrate this evil, giving examples from history. There will then be a chapter on the probable signs and symptoms of *perfect possession*, signs that people, who I believe to possibly have been perfectly possessed, have exhibited. The last chapter will be a discussion on whether the state of *perfect possession* is reversible or not and the reasons why. Finally, in Appendix a I will highlight what I would call multi-generational *perfect possession*, otherwise known as multi or trans-generational satanism or witchcraft. Finally, I would like to provide an extensive bibliography and recommended reading list. I think my reading recommendations could be greatly helpful to anyone who because of ministerial needs is undertaking study in this subject.

CHAPTER 1

THE IMPLICIT FORM OF PERFECT POSSESSION

O ne of the best descriptions of the topic of our current chapter can be found in the classic book *Who is the Devil* by Nicholas Corte. He states the following:

> "**The most serious, deplorable**, and common form of **diabolical possession** is that which is **voluntary**; it consists either in **intentionally worshipping Satan**[1] and performing satanic ceremonies of the type discussed in the previous chapter, **or else occurs unconsciously by an indifference to, and neglect of, all religious faith and all compliance with the obedience due to God**"[2]

Father Cristiani outlines for us here that the condition of *perfect possession*, which he calls *voluntary possession*, is the most serious, deplorable and common[3] form of *possession*. I stated in the introduction that *perfect possession*, when written about in the literature is always claimed to be the most serious form of possession, and this is exactly what Cristiani labels it as. He also states two of the ways in which it can happen; that is through an *explicit invitation* in the form of some type of devil worship or black magic or through an *implicit invitation* through a life of total neglect of God and the commission of constant mortal sin. It is the latter (*implicit invitation*) that is the topic of this current chapter. As I said in the introduction, Father Cristiani's source for this teaching is Father Auguste Saudreau. Saudreau wrote of this in two of his books, one of which was trans-

---

1   This is the explicit form of perfect possession and the topic of chapter 2.
2   Corte, *Who is the Devil*
3   Father Euteneuer states in his book that there are probably many more possessed people out in the world than we will ever know about. He states this in the context of perfect possession. Because perfect possession displays none of the traditional crisis states of partial possession, it can be very difficult if not impossible to determine if an actual case of this is present, furthermore perfectly possessed people may appear to be utterly normal, their success in introducing evil into the world and influencing people to commit evil depends heavily on their camouflage and their ability to blend in with modern society, therefore it is entirely possible perfect possession is the most common form of possession as Cristiani states.

lated into English, and both of which I will quote here. In *L Etat Mystique: Les Faits Extraordinaires de la Vie Spirituelle,* Saudreau states the following:

> "Latent Possession:[4] So far we have spoken about demonic posses-
> sions that exhibit violent phenomena, where the demon applies his
> tyrannical power to a poor creature who groans to suffer it; how-
> ever, there is **another type of possession** in which the demon can
> enter into a miserable **person who calls to him**, **who gives him-
> self to him**; the demon enters into him to add its hellish forces to
> the human forces and so increase the power of evil. Possession is
> then latent and is all the more deplorable. It is a contest more than
> a possession.[5] **It does not seem necessary for this type of pos-
> session to exist that man invokes the devil explicitly; do not
> certain faults of exceptional gravity give Satan the right to en-
> ter a miserable man who sinks into the last abysses of vice and
> hardens himself stubbornly? Is there not is this desired hard-
> ening, an implicit call to Satan, who's obstinate sinner wants
> to remain at all costs the obedient slave? The example of Judas
> would lead us to believe it."[6]

Like many of the other authors I have quoted, Saudreau saves this passage as the last paragraph in his chapter on extraordinary diabolic phenomena.[7] In this passage Saudreau clearly differentiates between *partial*
and *perfect possession.* He says there is another type of possession, which
he calls "latent" or that is *hidden*[8], that is separate and distinct from other
forms of possession that display violent phenomena. This *other* form of
possession is caused when a person "calls" or invites the demon (explicit) or "sinks into the last abysses of vice" (implicit) and which is more
"deplorable" than the other type of possession he had discussed prior.
Saudreau teaches us, like Corte, that not only is this form of possession
the most serious but that it can occur in two ways, *explicit invitation* and
implicit invitation. He states clearly that an explicit invitation is not necessary for this type of possession to exist, that certain persons who commit
faults of "exceptional gravity" or who sink into the "last abysses" of sin

---

4   The definition of latent, is hidden or concealed.

5   This particular sentence may be a mistranslation on my part.

6   Saudreau, *L Etat Mystique*, authors own translation.

7   That would be Chap 22 of *L Etat Mystique*: Les Faits Extraordinaires de la Vie Spirituelle

8   Latent or hidden meaning the possession is not recognizable by the normal means of
discernment. There are no symptoms of the possession, the person appears to be normal or at least
normal according to the definition of our modern society, which may have been totally immoral
in times past. It seems that the perfectly possessed have no problem blending in with our modern
society which is totally corrupt morally. This is an essential factor in understanding perfect possession.

and vice and harden their hearts, can also be possessed in this way. This is very important to note because there is a difference between being in a state of grave mortal sin which Saudreau calls "sinking into the last abysses of vice" and stubbornly hardening one's heart, and actual bodily possession. As far as this chapter goes the most important thing Saudreau and Cristiani teach us is that the state of moral enslavement to the devil can and does sometimes lead to actual possession[9] and not just any type of possession, a type of possession that is far more serious and hidden, that displays no violent phenomena, but instead displays signs of moral depravity which takes various forms. This is *perfect possession.*

A natural extension to the above quotes would be to ask the pertinent question: Is there a specific type of sinner that Cristiani and Saudreau are referring to? Saudreau writes that the people who succumb to this *other* form of possession are those that fall into the last abysses of vice and "harden" themselves. In *The Degrees of the Spiritual Life Vol 1* Saudreau writes about the same topic, the same type of sinners, the same type of possession, and this time goes into more detail on the type of sinner that he was referring to in *L Etat Mystique*. In his *The Degrees of the Spiritual Life*, Saudreau writes:

> "Finally, there are the sinners who sin out of mere wantonness, **knowing and perfectly understanding the gravity of their disorders, their irreligion, or their vices**, and **cheerfully making up their minds to do evil**. We can place in the same class those that commit sin from vexation or wounded pride. They began going wrong through weakness, then when their disorders drew on them well-merited humiliations, their self-love was wounded, and they avenged themselves by plunging further into the abyss. Both classes are not merely indifferent, like those of whom we spoke before, **but actually hostile**; they feel a **repugnance for virtue** and a **hatred for the good**. If they willfully cherish this hatred of good, it in time **assumes frightful proportions**, and they end up by displaying the furious rage of demons and lost souls. Such are the initiates in those higher grades of the secret societies, those energumens of whose frightful orgies, blasphemies, and Satanic acts we cannot read without a shudder. **They have allowed the evil spirit to assume such a power over them, they follow out his suggestion with such readiness and promptitude that we can**

---

9   Saudreau notes this clearly when he says the demon "enters" into the person to add its hellish forces to the human forces and so increase the power of evil, he also clearly calls it possession when he states "there is another type of possession" and then goes on relate what this other type of possession consists of.

say of them, in reversing the words of St. Paul, that it is no longer they who live, but Satan who lives in them"[10]

In this passage Saudreau again speaks of both the implicit and explicit forms[11] of *perfect possession*. In the first part of the paragraph he describes the type of sinners that he was referring to in the first quote. Specifically, those that are not merely indifferent but totally "hostile" towards God. They actively "hate" the good and this ends up assuming "frightful proportions." It is those souls who sin out of pure malice and hatred, rather than weakness or ignorance, or indifference. Such souls are essentially the walking damned[12] and display the characteristics of demons and damned souls.[13] In a passage strikingly similar to the above quote from Saudreau, Father Royo Marin O.P. writes about the same type of sinners, those that sin out of pure malice. Royo Marin goes into even more detail and does a great job explaining what happens to a man over time when he commits mortal sin perpetually and never repents. Father Royo Marin writes:

> "This class of sinners is the most culpable and the most horrible. These people do not sin through ignorance, weakness or indifference, but through a **refined malice** and **diabolical obstinacy.** Their most common sin is blasphemy, **which is pronounced strictly out of hatred for God.**[14] They may have begun as good Christians, but little by little they degenerated. Having yielded more and more to their evil passions, these passions gradually assumed gigantic proportions, until the moment came when their souls were **definitively conquered.** Then in the arms of despair, came the inevitable consequence of defection and apostasy. The last barriers which kept them from falling over the precipice have been broken and they are hurled, by a kind of vengeance against God and their own conscience, into **every kind of crime and moral disorder. Fiercely they attack religion; they hate the good; they may enter into a non-Catholic sect and propagate its doctrines with zeal and ardor,** until finally driven to despair

---

10   Saudreau, *The Degrees of the Spiritual Life, Vol 1*
11   When he writes about people involved in secret societies who partake in blasphemous orgies, he is referring to devil worship, which is the explicit form of perfect possession.
12   Euteneuer calls the perfectly possessed the walking damned.
13   This topic will be discussed in detail later when I describe signs and symptoms of perfect possession. Some of these signs and symptoms have to do with human beings who display diabolic traits such as inordinate pride, hatred, a murderous attitude, and the desire to be venerated or worshipped.
14   *The Catholic Encyclopedia* article on "hatred" describes the hatred of God as the worst of all sins and also calls this attitude "diabolical."

by the accusations of their own conscience, which speaks to them in spite of everything, they fall more and more deeply into sin."[15]

Unlike the passages from both Saudreau and Cristiani, Royo Marin does not explicitly state that this type of sinner or sinning necessarily results in actual possession. However, he does link it with the diabolic when he states that these people sin through a "diabolical obstinacy." In addition, this passage is so similar to the above quote from Saudreau it could be speculated that Royo Marin's source for this passage is in fact Saudreau, who he cites in a number of different places in his book. Of course, Saudreau absolutely links this type of sinning and sinner with a specific type of possession when he says, "it is no longer he who lives but Satan who lives in him."[16]

There are three additional authors I would like to highlight who have in some way written about perpetual mortal sin as leading to *subjugation*, *possession*, or it being a certain type of *implicit invitation*. The first is Father Francesco Bamonte, who specifically states that the state of enslavement of the soul to the devil, is a form of "total subjugation." Father Bamonte writes:

> "Can the devil possess a soul? No, if possession of souls means the devil living in it. On the other hand, **yes, if possession means "external imprisonment" of the soul through sin**, which might be better defined as **enslavement of the soul to the devil**, "**total subjugation**" brought about by consent to that which goes **gravely against the divine order**. We define such a phenomenon as **mortal sin**. The devil is incapable of inhabiting the soul. Demonic possession of the soul is impossible in the physical order. Mortal sin does not make the evil spirit enter the human soul but rather brings about a **moral dependence of the person on the devil**. This dependence increases **and becomes ever more oppressive depending on the nature, gravity, and frequency of mortal sin committed.** Such a state is **more dangerous** than diabolical possession since it can lead to eternal damnation... In fact, at least **implicitly**, such a person wishes to be **with the Devil** and has opened the door to the state of moral dependence on the devil which Jesus describes as "paternity."[17]

---

15   Royo Marin, *The Theology of Christian Perfection*

16   Saudreau, *The Degrees of the Spiritual Life, Vol 1*

17   Bamonte, *Diabolical Possession and the Ministry of Exorcism*

Now Father Bamonte like Royo Marin does not say that the state of moral enslavement to the devil automatically leads to actual bodily possession and he does differentiate the two in the subsequent paragraphs of his book.[18] However, what Bamonte writes about is basically the implicit form of *perfect possession*, that is a human being living a life of total depravity, which leads to an enslavement of the soul which eventually can lead to bodily possession as well, which both Saudreau and Cristiani note. This implicit invitation brings about a "moral dependence" on the devil caused by a "consenting to that which gravely goes against the divine order"[19] or as Cristiani puts it, by an "indifference to, and neglect of, all religious faith and all compliance with the obedience due to God."[20], or even as Saudreau noted "by committing faults of exceptional gravity" and "sinking into the last abysses of sin and vice and hardening oneself stubbornly"[21]. Furthermore, Bamonte does note that the state of "enslavement of the soul" is a form of *total subjugation,* in and of itself. This is significant because the only other time Father Bamonte uses the term *subjugation* is in the context of satanism and devil worship and the state of those involved in such activities, which is the explicit form of *perfect possession* and the topic of the next chapter. Probably the most important thing Bamonte notes is that it is indeed possible for a human soul to be diabolically possessed "externally" due to the intentional decision of a man to live a life of unrepented moral depravity.

It also needs to be pointed out that the above passage from Father Bamonte is substantially similar to the above quoted passage by Saudreau from his *L Etat Mystique*. Both passages speak of some type of implicit invitation to the devil in the form of serious, unrepented, and habitual mortal sin. Saudreau states this implicit invitation leads to what he calls "latent possession"; Bamonte states this implicit invitation leads to what he calls "total subjugation." The question is do both authors speak of the same thing? Based on what is written I am fairly confident in stating that both Bamonte and Saudreau speak of the same thing, just in different terminology.

In the introduction I mentioned that *perfect possession* could be thought of as a kind of caricature of someone who is a saint. Saints being people who have intentionally devoted their lives to the service of God, and the

---

18   He notes that the state of moral enslavement to the devil and bodily possession are two separate and distinct states and that only some people have both a moral or soul enslavement and bodily possession together.

19   Bamonte, *Diabolical Possession and the Ministry of Exorcism*

20   Corte, *Who is the Devil*

21   Saudreau, *L Etat Mystique, Les Faits*

perfectly possessed being those who intentionally devote their lives to the service of the devil. One author looks at people who have intentionally given themselves over to evil in the form of persistent and continual mortal sin as a kind of de-consecration, a consecration in reverse if you will. Jesuit priest, Father Louis Monden S.J. writes:

> "Now it is conceivable that, on the other hand, **a man long given over to evil doing, may become obsessed by a wish to remain in this path of life by a basic act of choice. This would be a hardening of the human heart, a consecration in reverse, a vow made unto Satan**… Is it not to Satan's advantage if, in such a case, he cast aside his anonymity and show his agreement to the explicit offering of his client by a sensible sign?[22] Does it not increase his status as anti-God if he then, in a kind of caricature of the sacraments, **deconsecrate the man in question as his vassal, his instrument, his ambassador, his priest**? Soloviev, in his well-known Legend of the Antichrist, describes how the spirit of Satan takes possession of the Antichrist, deliberately caricaturing the giving of the Holy Spirit to the apostles after the Resurrection."[23]

Here again is a passage that accurately describes the *implicit* form of *perfect possession*. Monden describes a certain type of sinner, specifically a man "long given over to evil doing" that is "obsessed" to stay in this state by his own free will and who also undergoes a "hardening of the human heart, a consecration in reverse, a *vow* made unto Satan." This "vow" made unto Satan results in a man becoming a "vassal," "instrument," "ambassador," and "priest" of Satan, in other words a servant of the devil. Furthermore, Monden also equates such people with the Antichrist and speculates that they are possessed by Satan in a kind of caricature of the giving of the Holy Spirit to the apostles after the Resurrection.

In his chapter on *Diabolic Pseudo Miracles*, Monden delineates between three distinct forms of diabolical influence. The above quote is taken in the textual context of the first kind of diabolical influence that Monden describes, which according to Monden is a kind of possession of the human soul or will brought about by the intentional, although implicit decision of a man to live a life of unabashed and unrepentant grave mortal sin. As stated above Monden equates such people with the Antichrist and speculates that they are possessed by Satan in the same way that Antichrist will be.

22   This sensible sign can only mean actual possession or some form of possession. He confirms this when he says such people become a vassal, instrument, ambassador, and priest of Satan.
23   Monden S.J., *Signs and Wonders*

To Monden, the *most serious* form of diabolical influence is a kind of possession of the will or soul, externally as Bamonte describes, brought about by habitual, unrepented, grave mortal sin, which then leads to Satan taking actual possession of the person so that the person is a "vassal" or "priest"[24] of Satan. However, most importantly, Monden is careful to note that Satan is,

> "not able to make himself master of the human soul at choice unless it be **surrendered to him** in one way or another by a free act of man's will."[25]

I will also note that Monden specifically differentiates this type of freely giving oneself to the devil in the form of constant mortal sin from the type present in cases of devil worship. After Monden discusses this certain type of implicit diabolical possession he states:

> "Let us not be too quick to equate this perversion with those "bargains with the devil" or "sales" of the soul to Satan"[26]

Therefore, like other authors he distinguishes between the *implicit* and *explicit* forms. Monden describes the implicit form as a "man long given over to evil-doing" that is "obsessed" to stay in this state and "give itself over to Satan" which Monden says is a "lucid choice of a satanic pride, a fundamental option." Monden then carefully notes again that "such a manifestation is not of necessity linked to that kind of Satanism associated with devil-worship" and black masses, but that he is rather thinking of,

> "a more secret involvement of the will."[27]

Monden gives the impression that he is thinking about people who have implicitly given themselves over to the devil and are totally but secretly dedicated to serving the devil.

---

24   The word vassal means "someone in a subordinate or subservient position" or a "slave." Monden noting that this can lead to someone being a "priest of Satan" is significant because Monden himself is a Catholic priest and we can be certain he fully comprehends what it means to be a priest. A Catholic priest is someone who works in persona Christi. Christ actually acts through the priest, additionally the priest is indwelt by the Holy Spirit. In the diabolic reverse of this, a priest of Satan means Satan is actually working through a person and this person is indwelt by the presence of Satan. A Catholic priest normally displays signs that indicate he is indwelt by the Holy Spirit, likewise those that are perfectly possessed and a "priest of Satan" also display their own signs, namely, certain forms of moral depravity and Satanic pride. Monden also notes these people become an instrument of Satan, meaning Satan uses them to introduce evil into the world and influence people to do evil.

25   Monden, *Signs and Wonders*

26   Ibid

27   Ibid

Finally, after describing how the human will can become dominated by Satan due to man intentionally giving himself over to Satan in the form of blatant lifelong moral depravity, Monden goes on to note that this state can eventually lead to a human being becoming totally and completely possessed by Satan. Monden seems to say that the people whose souls have been possessed and dominated by Satan due to the intentional decision of a man to subjugate his own will to Satan can also be possessed then in a bodily way which leads to the total diabolical possession of "the entire man"[28] as stated by other authors. Father Monden in describing how this is possible notes that it is,

> "by Satan's direct grasp of a man who, by **repeated acts of his own choice,** has been brought to such psychological weakness, to such total susceptibility to suggestions of evil that his **soul is transformed** into a **completely subservient instrument**, fit to be led and directed at the whim of whoever grasps his hand… the **Satanic dominance** can be attained in the case of a soul which is weak by nature or as a result of sin, when another man who has **surrendered to Satan** exerts psychological pressure and communicates his own will to him"[29]

The last sentence in the above quote is very important to note because Monden seems to be confirming that one of the things perfectly possessed people do is try and influence other people to commit evil by exerting psychological pressure and communicating "his own will" to the person they are trying to corrupt and turn towards evil.

It is also very important to note that Monden specifically separates and distinguishes this type of possession that he describes in the above quotes from the more traditional cases of possession we find in the scriptures. Monden calls these more traditional cases "evangelical cases" of possession that display the normal phenomena of possession and which are found in the New Testament. Monden also describes what would be traditional obsession or oppression as the third form of diabolical phenomena that he states are mostly to be found in the lives of the saints. I strongly believe that Father Monden provides us with one of the best descriptions of the implicit form of perfect possession.

Father Corrado Balducci, an expert in demonology and the author of one of the greatest books ever written on diabolical possession also has

---

28   "The entire man with all his faculties may even fall wholly under the devil's domination, that is, if he freely gives himself to the devil." *Volken, Visions, Revelations, and the Church*; "use of the free-will and surrendering it to those mysterious agents, who may thereby be said to take possession of the entire man." Lepicier, *The Unseen World*

29   Monden S.J., *Signs and Wonders*

written about a certain type of implicit invitation in the form of grave mortal sin that leaves a wide open "door" to Satan who is ready and willing to "enter" and according to Balducci "make the person another self." In his classic book *The Devil*, Balducci states of such people,

> "Then the **soul** that was meant to be the temple of the Trinity ends up as **the dwelling-place of the devil**. After that, the individual can eventually become **a child of Satan, a bearer of evil, a devil incarnate**. It is not easy to discern the precise cause of this openness to Satan, this possibility of being **transformed into something like him**. However, **constant resistance to the promptings of grace until they are silenced and can no longer be felt; the progression of religious indifference and incredulity to a state of hostility; the abandonment of known truth or the tendency to deny it and even attack it** – all these are clear signs that a person does not want to know about God. They represent not only a crack in the wall but a **door** that **is wide open** to Satan, who wants to **occupy the empty place** that is left for him. These symptoms are an **implicit invitation** to him who is willing and ready to **enter and make the person another self**"[30]

Here again is a passage that accurately describes the implicit form of *perfect possession* and which is also very similar to many of the quotes I have listed above. Balducci speaks of a certain type of sinner, specifically those that constantly resist the "promptings of grace" until they are silenced completely, which basically means the person has definitively chosen evil. Those that progress from a state of religious indifference to a state of total "hostility" towards religion, those that not only abandon known religious truth but who go on to actively deny it and "even attack it." Balducci states clearly that this type of lifelong mortal sinning, this active hostility and hatred towards God is an "implicit invitation," a "door that is wide open to Satan." This state results in a totally deplorable state in which the soul that was meant to be the temple of the Trinity ends up as a "dwelling-place of the devil," the devil "enters" according to Balducci to make the person "another self," a satanic caricature of a human being that is an active servant of the devil. Balducci states this state is so deplorable that the person can be thought of as a "child of Satan," a "bearer of evil," a "devil incarnate." It is interesting to note also that Balducci writes all of this in a section of the book that is totally separate from his section on the more traditional form of diabolic possession, therefore like all the other

30   Balducci, *The Devil: Alive and Active in Our World*

authors I have noted, he separates and distinguishes this type of posses-sion from the more traditional cases and clearly says this type is much more serious and deplorable.

There is another line in the above quote by Balducci that is also very similar to a quote that was highlighted in the introduction. Balducci states that when Satan enters a human being in this deplorable state, he is en-tering to make the person "another self" or a "devil incarnate." I quoted Winklehofer in the introduction who said something very similar. Win-klehofer noted that perfectly possessed persons which he does not explic-itly name as such, undergo a "dissolution" of their established personality structure, and in even more clearer terms to confirm this concept, serial killer David Berkowitz, the Son of Sam also said something very similar in regards to his diabolic possession. Berkowitz stated,

> "You get into a state that is so far gone **your own personality is dissolved**, and you take on these demonic entities."[31]

This concept from Winklehofer, Balducci and Berkowitz is very im-portant towards an understanding of what perfect possession consists of and it will be detailed in full in chapter 4. However it is important to note at the outset that it would seem based on what these authors have stated that perfectly possessed people are so utterly taken over by evil that their own personality has been completely "dissolved" and that it is essential-ly the personality of the diabolical spirit that is at work in the everyday life of the person. The possessed person's personality has been totally and completely replaced by a diabolic one[32] so that the person is now "another self"[33], a diabolic self.

Some of the things that the above authors have written leads to an interesting and important theological question, which is the following: Does the state of moral enslavement to the devil, the state of grave moral disorder, the state of the "external"[34] possession or imprisonment of the soul, which is an implicit invitation to *perfect possession*, constitute a real diabolical possession of the will and soul in and of itself? To answer this question, we must first answer an even more simple question which is can the soul or will be possessed at all and if so, what exactly does this state entail, what is the nature of it? This is an important question to answer

---

31   Steve Fishman, "The Devil in David Berkowitz," *New York Magazine*

32   Instead of replaced, it would probably be more accurate to say they have merged

33   Balducci, *The Devil: Alive and Active in Our World*

34   Bamonte, *Diabolical Possession and the Ministry of Exorcism*. Bamonte notes that the state of enslavement of the soul to the devil is essentially an "external" possession of the human soul by the devil.

in the context of this chapter because many of the above quoted authors seem to answer in the affirmative.

Bamonte of course states that yes, the soul can be diabolically possessed, externally that is, when a person has made the intentional although implicit decision to give themselves over to Satan in the form of lifelong, unrepented moral perversity. This is in addition to Father Monden and Father Balducci basically stating the same thing just in different terms.

This is a very complicated question that does not have a simple answer, further complicated by the fact that so many authors contradict each other in this regard. What I mean is that there are many theological authorities that say very clearly that the devil can never possess a soul in any way. That the soul and its faculties of will and intellect remains essentially free up the moment of death. Bamonte however, notes that the state of moral dependence on the devil is a kind of possession in and of itself, albeit external, and also distinct from the diabolical possession of the body.

Malachi Martin is one person who certainly believed that it was possible for a demon to possess the will of a person and he gave the example of Adolf Hitler and his relationship to the German people as an example. Martin writes:

> "In one sense, he possessed the wills and minds of millions of Germans. He never entered their bodies. He caught their wills. You see, if I can control your mind and your will, I possess you. The greater the extent of my possession, the greater is my hold over you."[35]

One of the reasons this is such an important discussion is because diabolical possession has traditionally meant the presence of the devil in the *body* of a person as one element and the action of the devil on that body. Almost all theologians define it this way.[36] A state of grave mortal sin and diabolic possession were looked at as two separate and distinct states. But one ponders if they are really all that different.[37] Theologians have been

---

35   Malachi Martin, *The Kingdom of Darkness*

36   I say almost all theologians, because there seems to be some disagreement among the authorities as to how diabolic possession should be actually defined. For example, Father M, at the Mundelein Conference of 2013 defined possession as a relationship between a human and demon in which the human will has given some form of consent at some time.

37   When someone intentionally lives a life of mortal sin and obstinately chooses to remain in that state, it could be argued this is on the same level as devil worship. Both types of sinners intentionally choose to sever their relationship with God, both choose to have commerce with Satan, albeit in totally different ways, both choose to not repent and in fact reject graces offered to them, both choose to intentionally withhold due reverence and worship due to God. The only real difference between the two is that one is implicit and one explicit. But does the implicit form somehow lessen the sin? I would say no because both a devil worshipper and someone in a totally hardened state of grave sin can both commit the sin against the Holy Ghost and die in a state of

clear that one of the effects of mortal sin is that man becomes a slave of Satan, and I will quote some theological authorities below to demonstrate this. Is this not a kind of possession that is separate and distinct from what bodily possession is?[38] Could we also say that if possession is going to be defined in terms of relationality between human and demon, that could not a human have a relationship with a demon in the form of some type of seriously grave mortal sin like abortion or murder, or some depraved sexual sin. And when a human has a relationship with a demon through the commission of these sins, is this not possession?

However, if we are going to claim that a state of moral enslavement to the devil is an actual form of possession albeit different from bodily possession, we must define the terms of what this means. I said above that diabolical possession of the body has traditionally had two very well-defined terms; that is the presence of the devil in the body and his action on that body. We would not be able to define a moral enslavement or possession in the terms of the devil *controlling* the will and intellect, this is a concept nearly universally believed to be not possible. Basically, all theologians say that the devil cannot control the will in the same way that he controls the body in a bodily possession.

Rather I would define it as a willing collaboration and relationship between the human will and the Devil that is brought about by very grave mortal sin that is habitually committed and never repented that results in an external diabolic possession or slavery of the soul due to a man intentionally willing to stay in this state forever. Another aspect of this will be discussed in the final chapter having to do with the affects sin has on the will, conditioning it further and further into darkness and evil.

Everything I said above is in the context of Bamonte's description of the "*external*" imprisonment of the soul, however, we also have the theologians who even go a step further than Bamonte does, who claim that by mortal sin not only is a person a slave or child of Satan but that the devil actually enters the soul itself. This is what Balducci seemed to say in his quote above when he stated:

> "Then the soul that was meant to be the temple of the Trinity ends up as the **dwelling-place of the devil**. After that, the individual can eventually become a child of Satan, **a bearer of evil, a devil incarnate**."[39]

totally hardened pride and unrepented grave moral depravity.

38   It should also be noted that a person can be bodily possessed but also be in a state of sanctifying grace.

39   Balducci, *The Devil: Alive and Active in our World*

In very similar fashion to Balducci, the Rev Francis Spirago, professor of theology in Austria, gives similar terminology as to the relationship between the human soul in seriously grave sin and the Devil. Spirago writes:

> "When God abandons the soul, **the devil enters into it**. By mortal sin the temple of the Holy Ghost is transformed into a den of robbers, the sister of the angels into the companion of fallen spirits. As a ship that has lost her rudder is driven about at the mercy of the current, so the soul that has lost divine grace is **driven by Satan** into perdition. **Sin gives the devil power over the soul**, for through sin man places himself under the **servitude to obey the devil**"[40]

When Spirago and Balducci state that the devil *enters* the soul, it sounds strikingly similar to what the demon Multus says in the exorcism of Jamsie Z. In *Hostage to the Devil* in the chapter entitled "Uncle Ponto and the Mushroom Souper" the exorcist Father Mark is questioning the demon about a funning looking face that Jamsie has been seeing his whole life. Jamsie had seen this face on a multitude of people including his own father Ara when he was involved in prostitution and drugs and on the faces of other people who were involved in some type of sinful activity, including on the face of Jay Beedem whom Martin identifies as one of the *perfectly possessed*. About the funny looking face and why some people have it, the demon says the following:

> "Obedience to the kingdom, **they give their will, we fill the soul**. What's inside peers out willy nilly"[41]

Additionally, Father Adolf Rodewyk, during his discussion on the specific spiritual state of Judas Iscariot quotes both St Thomas Aquinas and Johannes Smit who both said that Judas's possession was not a bodily possession but rather a form of moral possession where through grave mortal sin the devil "enters" the human heart. Rodewyk notes:

> "St Thomas refers to this passage when he says: "The Devil **enters the heart** when a human being **devotes himself to him unequivocally** in order to give way to his emotional drives, without resisting him at any point." Johannes Smit, writing in *De Daemoniacis in Historia Evangelica* (1913) states specifically "These words do not suggest that Judas had become possessed; it only implies an **ethi-**

40   Francis Spirago, *The Catechism Explained: An Exhaustive Exposition of the Christian Religion*
41   Malachi Martin, *Hostage to the Devil*

cal form of possession, to the degree that the Devil tempted Judas in several ways, so that he might complete the crime he had long planned. Judas did not resist these temptations but **surrendered his heart to the influence of diabolical power**. One may therefore state that **the Devil inhabited him morally.**""[42]

Thus, Rodewyk while commenting on these words from Aquinas and Smit states himself that:

"When a person morally capitulates before the Devil, **then the Devil moves into his soul and establishes his rule**. The greater the degree of moral disintegration he can thus achieve, the easier will he find the execution of his plans."[43]

What are we to say about these passages?

We can say that these passages simply confirm what Francesco Bamonte has said in his work, simply that it is possible for the human soul to be possessed by Satan in an external way, Smit calls these cases an "ethical form of possession" which like Bamonte, Smit states are separate and distinct from bodily cases of possession. This is all important to note because it is important to see what authors have said about this implicit invitation. It seems many different authors have all spoken of the same exact thing just in different terminology.

On the one hand these last few authors seemed to say clearly that the devil enters the soul when it definitively departs from God. On the other hand, very many authors and speakers have clearly said the devil can in no way enter the soul. On that point I must agree. But more on that below. The important thing we learn from what is contained in Bamonte and Rodewyk and which answers the above question is, according to Johannes Smit, the state of moral enslavement to the devil is in and of itself a form of possession. He calls it an "ethical form of possession" and then later states that the Devil inhabited Judas "morally."[44] It can also be stated with the utmost certainty that this ethical form of possession that Smit speaks of is almost certainly identical to what Bamonte calls the "external imprisonment of the human soul," this ethical form of possession is a kind of possession of the will, but not the body, which is an implicit call

---

42   Thomas Aquinas and Johannes Smit, quoted in Rodewyk, *Possessed by Satan*
43   Rodewyk, *Possessed by Satan*
44   In addition to Smit noting the existence of an ethical form of possession, Bamonte was also clear that a state of moral enslavement to the devil constituted an external possession of the soul. I will also quote an additional 11 authors who all link a state of grave mortal sin with some type of "slavery," "subjection," or "bondage" to Satan.

to Satan that can eventually lead to the deplorable state known as perfect possession.

One more speculation in this regard is that the person who is enslaved to the devil via mortal sin, which is in itself a form of possession, may not be bodily possessed, but rather they may be a perpetual open door for bodily possession because of the state of their soul and their state in life. Meaning a person who is completely enslaved to the devil through mortal sin is possessed in an ethical or moral way, but may not be bodily possessed. However, the state of moral enslavement may be a perpetual open door for bodily possession, meaning because the persons will is so enslaved to the devil through sin, he is free to enter that persons body at any time to further his goals according to his plan and kingdom. It would be on these terms that it would be well to remember that people who are in a state of moral enslavement are probably just as dangerous and destructive to society than someone *perfectly possessed*.

In addition to the above passages there are very many other authors who link a life of mortal sin with some type of slavery to the devil. Even the scriptures clearly state that those who commit sin belong to the devil "He who commits sin is of the devil; for the devil has sinned from the beginning."[45] As Bamonte noted above, Jesus Christ had no qualms about labeling certain people children of Satan. In order to further establish this link and further investigate the implicit form of *perfect possession*, it will be worth quoting a few of them.

Father Stang, in his very good and very old little book on the devil states:

> Through mortal sin, man **surrenders himself willingly to the slavery of the devil**. The nature of this slavery consists in paying the penalty due to sin and in an exposure to **the direct influence of Satan who pushes his subject to new sins and tortures him with various afflictions of soul and body**."[46]

A.C. O'Neil in the article "Sin" in the Catholic Encyclopedia states:

> "Sin is an offense against Christ who has redeemed man, against the Holy Ghost who sanctifies us, an injury to man himself, causing the spiritual death of the soul, and making man the **servant of the devil**."[47]

---

45   1 John 3:8 NAB
46   Stang, *The Devil: Who He is and What He Does*
47   A.C. O'Neil, Sin, *Catholic Encyclopedia*

And Arthur Pruess in his work on moral theology based off Father Antony Koch's work, states:

> "Every transgression of the divine law, i.e., every actual mortal sin, deserves temporal and eternal death and delivers the sinner into the **bondage of Satan.**"[48]

Also, from the world of moral theology, Henry Davis S.J. in *Moral and Pastoral Theology Vol 1* states:

> "By sinning grievously man commits spiritual suicide, robbing his own soul of sanctifying grace, and becoming the **slave of the evil one.**"[49]

Also, Gerard Zerbolt in *The Spiritual Ascent* writes:

> "By mortal sin he doth **subject himself to the devil** and in all things indulgeth the impulses of his desires and lusts."[50]

Two quotes from St. Teresa of Avila are also informative. While speaking about the state of a soul in mortal sin she said:

> "No thicker darkness exists, and there is nothing dark and black which is not much less so than this"[51]

And also:

> "A person who commits a mortal sin is not to please him (Christ) but to give pleasure to the devil; and as the devil is darkness itself, the **poor soul becomes darkness itself likewise**"[52]

Even our Blessed Mother Mary while visiting with St. Bridget revealed to her that if sinners would invoke her most powerful name, the devils would flee, our Blessed Mother stated:

> "Even from **the most abandoned sinners** and who consequently are **the farthest from God** and **fully possessed by the devil,** if only they invoke her most powerful name with a true purpose of repentance"[53]

---

48   Preuss, *A handbook of Moral Theology*
49   Davis, S.J., *Moral Theology*
50   Zerbolt, *The Spiritual Ascent*
51   Teresa of Avila, *Interior Castle*
52   Ibid
53   Cruz, *Angels and Devils*, P.259

This is a very revealing statement from the Mother of God and very pertinent to our discussion about the link between serious mortal sin and *perfect possession*. Not only does it show the sheer power she has over the diabolic spirits, but according to her "the most abandoned sinners" who "are the farthest from God" are consequently "fully possessed by the Devil." St Catherine of Bologna also stated:

> "The person who is in mortal sin is not a member of Christ but **of the devil**"[54]

Lastly, Michael Scanlan, an original leader of the charismatic renewal and healing ministries. In his book *Deliverance from Evil Spirits* says:

> "The devil **rules over** lovers of temporal goods belonging to this visible world, those who neglect God, who is eternal, and love what is fleeting and changing are **made subject to him**. By this covetousness the devil **rules within** man and **takes possession of his heart**."[55]

The forgoing passages from these eminent authors and writers, from various backgrounds in moral theology, spiritual theology, and saints will suffice to show clearly that there is indeed a strong link between living a life of seriously grave sin (which I am calling an implicit invitation to perfect possession) and possession or enslavement to the devil. There are many more quotes exactly like this in many more books, for the sake of space and to risk being repetitive I chose these because I thought they showed a great variety in who the authors were who were speaking.

To answer the questions then that I asked above we could state that yes, very serious and grave habitual mortal sin that ends in a person being a total slave of the devil, is in and of itself a kind of possession, a moral form of possession that only concerns the will or soul and not the body; an "ethical" form of possession as Smit notes and a "slavery of the human soul to the devil" as Bamonte notes and also an external possession of the soul as Bamonte also notes. This form of possession is a grasp of the human will, an "external imprisonment of the soul"[56] but *not* a despotic control of the human will. This possession is brought about purely voluntarily by a person engaging in seriously depraved sins continually and furthermore committing those sins not from indifference but from malice,

---

54   Ibid
55   Scanlan-Cerner, *Deliverance from Evil Spirits*
56   Bamonte, *Diabolical Possession and the Ministry of Exorcism*

obstinacy and hardness of heart and never repenting of them but instead continually falling into deeper and darker levels of evil and depravity.

We need to understand that mortal sin gives the human soul some of the same characteristics as that of the fallen diabolical spirit; dark, loathsome, dead, perverse, twisted, without grace or supernatural light, and doomed to perish eternally. That is why Balducci states that people who are children of Satan are "transformed into something like him"[57]. In this case like attracts like and they identify with each other. In closing we will highlight two saints who had the distinct displeasure of seeing, through a vision of the diabolic, the true condition of those in the state of mortal sin. St. John Bosco, who was an exorcist and who endured many assaults from the devils was one such saint. In the very hard to find book *Don Bosco's Experience of the Devil*, Father Adolf Faroni writes:

> "As an exorcist, this young priest could sometimes see demons on the backs of those in mortal sin"[58]

Much more disturbing is St. Teresa of Avila and her vision regarding a priest who was in mortal sin:

> "Once while approaching to receive communion, I saw with my souls' eyes more clearly than with my bodily eyes two devils whose appearance was abominable. It seems to me their horns were wrapped around the poor priest's throat, and in the host that was going to be given to me I was my Lord with the majesty I mentioned placed in the priest's hands, which were clearly seen to be his offenders and I understood that that soul was in mortal sin."[59]

There was one question that I asked above that I left unanswered and I stated I would explore it below. That question is regarding whether the Devil can actually enter the heart or soul of a human being when they commit seriously depraved sins and enter into a state of moral enslavement to the devil. Balducci, Spirago, and Rodewyk seemed to say that this is in fact the case. And these authorities are not slouches in the theological world whatsoever. Both Balducci and Rodewyk were very well-known demonologists and exorcists who wrote voluminously about this subject, Spirago was a professor of theology at a college in Austria and penned a huge theological manual titled *The Catechism Explained*. What they wrote seems to leave no doubt that they believed the devil actually entered the

57   Balducci, *The Devil*
58   Adolf Faroni, *Don Bosco's Experience of the Devil*
59   Alison Peers, *Complete Works of Teresa of Jesus*

soul, it does not seem they were speaking figuratively. This position however directly contradicts many other authors who say under absolutely no circumstances can the devil enter the soul. I quoted Bamonte above who said this very explicitly, who himself is a very experienced exorcist.

It seems that Balducci, Rodewyk, and Spirago hold the minority position because it seems the church and a majority of theologians believe that only the most Holy Trinity can actually enter into and penetrate and live in the very substance of the soul. It has been the constant teaching of most Theologians and demonologists that this area is off limits to the diabolic spirit. For example, Father Royo Marin states:

> "The presence of the devil is restricted exclusively to the body. The soul remains free, and even if the exercise of conscious life is suspended, **the soul itself is never invaded. Only God has the privilege of penetrating into the essence of the soul**, by his creative power and by establishing his dwelling there through the special union of grace"[60]

It should be noted this is a view still held to very tightly by some modern exorcists. I noted Bamonte above. A very recent article in The National Catholic Register gave the opinion of an exorcist who is very well known and has 40 plus years of experience in this field. Giving the opinion of Father John Esseff, the publication states:

> "The devil can tempt us to sin, but he cannot control a person's soul," Msgr. Esseff said."[61]

A very clear church teaching has always been that our Holy God is able to penetrate and live in our soul because he created it and made it for this purpose. God's grace actually enters into the soul and forms a special relationship with it, that it seems no creature (demons) could reproduce.

> "If a man love me, he will keep my words, and my Father will love him, and we will come unto him, and make our abode with him."[62]

That is why those in the state of grace seem peaceful, joyful, happy, serene, and beautiful. The soul takes on Godly characteristics. The soul was not made for an angelic nature to dwell within it in the same way that God is able to. I bring this up because when we read things like Francis Spirago saying "When God abandons the soul, the devil enters into it"

60   Royo Marin, *The Theology of Christian Perfection*
61   Patti Armstrong, www.ncregister.com, Was This Noted *Time* Magazine Author Possessed by Satan, Jan 3, 2019
62   John 14:23 New American Standard Version

in addition to the above quotes from Balducci and Rodewyk, we seem to have a theological contradiction. I really believe that Father Francesco Bamonte's descriptive words of "external imprisonment of the soul," "enslavement of the soul to the devil," and "moral dependence of the soul on the devil" are the best descriptions that strike the best balance regarding whether a diabolical spirit can penetrate the human soul during the state of moral enslavement to the devil.

Suffice it to say for now that it has indeed been the constant teaching and tradition of the church and most theologians that only God can dwell within the substance of the soul, not a diabolical spirit. Therefore, even in the case of a perfectly possessed person who freely gave their body and soul to the devil, the devil cannot actually penetrate to the very substance of the soul and dwell there metaphysically in the same manner as God. The only spiritual substance that can unite with the substance of the human soul in a substantial way is God and specifically his sanctifying grace. Because Satan is not God, and only a creature, he does not possess any natural quality or capability that would enable him to unite to the soul in the special way God does.

As a follow up to all the passages I have quoted regarding the implicit invitation to perfect possession through a life of grave moral disorder and total neglect of God, it could be asked which specific sins can lead to this deplorable condition. Father Bamonte says those that "gravely go against the divine order"[63] and Father Royo Marin gives the specific sin of blasphemy.[64] Peter Thyraeus S.J., a 17th century author, who according to Tanquerey, Royo Marin, Rodewyk, and Father Jeffrey Grob[65] is an authority on possession, gives these sins as ones leading to possession: infidelity and apostasy, the abuse of the blessed sacrament, blasphemy, pride, excesses of lust, envy and avarice, persecution of Christians, hatred of children towards parents, violent anger, contempt of God and other sacred things, and curses and pacts whereby one gives oneself to the devil"[66]

I would add to those, serious sins against the first commandment such as chronic occult involvement, being involved in false religions or cults. Sacrilege, heresy or schism that intentionally deceives the faithful and leads them away from God and the sacraments. Mass killing, serial killing, contract killing or performing abortions. Seriously grave sexual sins such

63   Bamonte, *Diabolical Possession and the Ministry of Exorcism*
64   Royo Marin, *The Theology of Christian Perfection*
65   Father Grob spoke quite extensively about Thyraeus at the Mundelein Conference in 2007
66   Peter Thyraeus, S.J., Hoc Est Daemoniaci quoted in Royo Marin, *The Theology of Christian Perfection*

as pedophilia, necrophilia, bestiality, sodomy, rape, and forms of bondage and masochism. As well as the selling of dangerous narcotics like heroin and methamphetamine to people for the motivation of greed and the complete disregard for the well-being, body and soul, of the addict.

Notice most of the sins I listed involve the destruction, body and soul, of other people. Whenever a human being willfully participates in the destruction of another human being's body and soul, it is not only a direct participation in the work and mission of the diabolical kingdom, but also an invitation, although implicit, to those diabolical spirits who populate the dark kingdom and who do the same work of ruining the bodies and souls of people. In chapters 7, 8, and 9 when we discuss people from history who may have been perfectly possessed, you will find a common theme among them of murder, their own suicide or the suicide of people close to them, cult involvement, occult involvement, the promotion of false and destructive teachings, drug addiction, gross sexual perversion, unabashed avarice and more.

Before I end this section, I need to make one final clarification to avoid confusion. It should be clearly noted, that despite all I have said regarding living a life of serious mortal sin and complete neglect of God being an *implicit* invitation to *perfect possession*, which Auguste Saudreau has so clearly taught, that not all people who make this implicit invitation become *perfectly possessed*, not all people who live a life of mortal sin become *perfectly possessed* or even partially possessed for that matter.[67] One aspect of the nature of perfect possession is the presence of the diabolical spirit in the actual body of the possessed. So even though people who make this implicit invitation may be enslaved to the devil through sin, that does not mean all of them are actually bodily possessed as well.

I do not want to give the impression that I am stating that all people in the state of mortal sin are *perfectly possessed* or even partially possessed, I am not, and that of course is not the case. This chapter mostly applies to people who live their entire lives steeped in serious mortal sin that often destroys other people and who never repent, and in fact harbor an appalling hatred towards Jesus Christ; not people who slip up from time to time and then confess and attempt to amend their lives, there is a big difference.

Furthermore, even if living a life of grave mortal sin results in a possession, some of these people, on realizing their truly deplorable state,

67   In fact, most probably, the vast majority of people who commit a mortal sin are never possessed in any way. Everything that was written in this chapter mostly regards persons who commit serious and grave evil and furthermore commit it perpetually, without ever repenting.

wish to repent and start fighting back against the devil and the possession, which in turn causes all kinds of extraordinary phenomena, which in its turn sometimes leads to church intervention and successful exorcism. Truly perfectly possessed people do not fight back against the devil and do not wish to change. They instead accept the possession, fall even deeper into sin and evil, fully give up the fight against it, and fully cooperate with the possessing demon.

The reason I have spoken at such length about the implicit form of *perfect possession* is because most modern authors who devote any time to this subject generally write that the only way a *perfect possession* can happen is by an explicit invitation. Saudreau and Cristiani and all the other authors I quoted all seem to speak of some kind of implicit invitation in the form of serious and grave mortal sin committed habitually and over a lifetime as leading to some type of serious diabolical slavery or possession that is more serious than the traditional definition of possession. Saudreau being the most explicit in his teaching on this matter.

Saudreau gives the example of Judas, who we know was possessed by Satan, but also who did not display any of the normal signs of possession as shown in previous gospel accounts. When it is said that Satan possessed him at the last supper, Christ made no move to exorcise him, like he did all the other possessed people he came across. Christ was very quick to exorcise and liberate complete strangers who were in bondage to Satan, involuntary bondage that is, people who wanted to be free, people who suffered the attacks of Satan and his demons. How much quicker would Christ exorcise one of his own called upon 12 who fell under this terrible bondage. The difference is, Judas wanted to be under this bondage, he chose it intentionally, but implicitly. Judas also did not display the furious rage of demons as the man possessed at Gerasa did or the man possessed at Capernaum did.

Instead Judas, after the Gospel says he was possessed by Satan, went to the high priests, cruelly and heartlessly betrayed the Son of God for 30 pieces of silver and then killed himself. We see Judas, while under the state of Satanic possession, take an action to organizationally oppose the action of Christ. There were signs of possession, but not the normal signs as in classical diabolic possession (extreme strength, occult knowledge, paranormal phenomena), the signs instead were moral and psychological, the betrayal of Christ and his suicide. Nowhere in the gospel does it say Judas **explicitly** invited Satan in, rather Judas is spoken of as living a life of sin, stealing from the money bag, greed, and plotting to definitively betray Christ, despite knowing Christ personally, seeing the love and Godly warmth in his eyes and seeing all the miracles wrought by him (total obstinacy, malice and hardness of heart)! Perfect possession does not display the usual signs of diabolical possession, but it does display some signs and symptoms of its own which we will speak of in a later chapter. I quoted above the opinion of both Johannes Smit and St Thomas Aquinas that the possession of Judas was not a possession in the traditional sense, that it was only a form of ethical or moral possession. Saudreau however disagrees and specifically cites Judas as the most severe form of diabolic possession, what he called *latent possession*, which is *perfect possession*. In this regard he quotes St. Augustine who states:

"He entered him to possess more fully one who was already his"[68]

I would hold to the position of Saudreau and I do this because it seems the scripture is plainly clear when it says, "Satan entered him."[69]

DEFINITION:

We will conclude this section on the implicit form of perfect possession by saying that the implicit form of perfect possession is when a human being lives a life fully committed to grave mortal sin and never repents. Not because of weakness, but because of malice, obstinacy, hardness of heart and hatred of God. This life of sin may have started with small offenses, but soon escalated into very serious, grave mortal sins which gravely oppose and mock the divine order. These sins are always mortal and very often involve the destruction, body and soul, of other people. When this state is reached the person finds it extremely difficult if not impossible to stop sinning. Very often the person committing these sins finds great satisfaction in the commission of them and commits them with an almost total glee and excitement. These sins create a moral dependence or enslavement of the soul to the devil, which in itself is a form of possession as Bamonte and Smit note and which is also an implicit invitation to become perfectly possessed.

The commission of these grave sins acts as both the invitation to perfect possession and the consent of the will needed for perfect possession. Once the bodily possession has occurred in tandem with the enslavement of the soul, the person does not fight back against it, rather he cooperates with mind and will in the diabolic kingdoms desire to destroy souls and in

---

68   Augustine, quoted in Saudreau, *L Etat Mystique, Les Faits Extraordinaires de la Spirtuale*
69   John 13:27 NAB

fact falls even deeper and deeper into further levels of evil and sin. These people are comfortable and happy with their state and comfortable and happy with the devils possessing and controlling them and because of this and the collaboration they have implicitly entered into with Satan, there is no sign of traditional possession, but rather the presence of moral signs like gross sexual perversion, murder or suicide.

They often eventually wind up in a cult, secret society, or non-Catholic sect and actively and enthusiastically lead others astray from the truth. Like Judas, they oftentimes take actions that organizationally opposes the work of the church and the preaching of the gospel. They actively influence other people to commit various forms of evil. These people have no intention of changing or repenting and even if they wanted to it would be extremely difficult and would only happen by direct miracle of God. These individuals may or may not know they are perfectly possessed. They often end up committing horrific acts of violence on their fellow man or suicide or both. I agree with Nicholas Corte in his book *Who Is the Devil* when he says this type of possession is the most "common," one look at world news and current events in which people all over the world commit horrific acts of diabolic brutality and depravity confirms this.

CHAPTER 2

THE EXPLICIT FORM OF PERFECT POSSESSION

We will now speak about the *explicit form* of *perfect possession* which by definition is a direct and explicit invitation of a human being to a devil, to possess his body and soul. This is done with full knowledge and full consent of the will, to the extent that their nature and state in life allows. This is very often, but not always, done in the context of some type of devil worship, diabolic pact, consecration to Satan, witchcraft or some other type of black magic or dark art. Sometimes it is done in exchange for worldly goods or services, such as money, power, fame, success, unlimited sex, unlimited health or a multitude of other things people ask the devil for. Sometimes the invitation is made from pure hatred of God and his grace and love of the Devil. Some readers may question whether this is even possible or whether or not this type of human depravity exists. I can assure you it does exist, it can happen, and it does happen, often.

> "The human *will* can in the depths of man's spiritual freedom of choice, **give itself over to Satan**."[1]
>
> "A witch is a person supposed to have supernatural power by **compact with the devil. Man may renounce God and Christ and surrender himself completely to the service and control of Satan**. It has been done, it is an open and formal adoration, a fearful crime, the climax of all heresy."[2]
>
> "I submit myself to you both in body and soul, forever into eternity"[3]

As I stated earlier, many modern authors speak of *perfect possession* only through the context of an explicit invitation. As I did in the previous section, I would like to quote these sources at length so that the readers get an idea of what authors have said about this form of perfect possession.

1   Monden, S.J., *Signs and Wonders*
2   Stang, *The Devil: Who He Is and What He Does*
3   Robbins, *Encyclopedia of Witchcraft and Demonology, from a 16th century diabolic pact*

I will start with what I think is the best description from a Catholic perspective. In *A Handbook of Moral Theology,* Father Arthur Preuss states:

> "Sometimes the sin against the Holy Ghost culminates in **a deliberate and complete surrender of the soul to the evil one**, resulting in actual devil worship. The leading characteristic of this terrible sin is hatred of God, which manifests itself in deadly antagonism to all that is good, joy in evil things, a burning desire to seduce others and to commit sin for its own sake. Devil worship is the climax of human malice and embraces all the capitol vices, the sins that cry to heaven for vengeance, and especially those by which a man becomes accessory to the sins of others. Sometimes the soul sinks so low as to enter into a **formal union with the powers of darkness**. This relation is, as a rule, purely moral, but it may develop into a **mystic marriage of the human mind with Satan.**"[4]

The reason I believe this to be the best description of perfect possession is because Preuss describes it as a "mystic marriage of the human mind with Satan." In order to fully investigate what this means, what a "mystic marriage" is, we must learn what a mystic marriage is from the perspective of the human person with the divine, from there we can apply the definition to a mystic marriage with the human to the diabolic. For the purposes of this study, the best description can be found in Pierre Pourrat's, *Christian Spirituality, Vol 2.* Speaking of mystic marriage of the human with the divine, he writes,

> "St Bernard makes use of most forceful images from the Canticle of Canticles in order to describe this extraordinary union of the holy soul with God. Like all spiritual writers, he teaches that this union is brought about by love which has reached such a degree that **the will of the Christian is fully identified with the divine will**: "**such conformity with the divine will marries (maritat) the soul to the Word, to whom it is like by its spiritual nature,** and to whom it is not less like by its will, loving him as it is by him. Then, if it love perfectly, it is a bride. What is there sweeter than this conformity of wills? What more desirable than that love which makes thee O soul discontented, with the teachings of men, to go with confidence to the Word? **Thou remainest united with him, thou dwellest familiarly with him,** thou consultest him on all things, daringly desirous of knowing as much as thy intelligence is able to understand. **This contract of marriage is always spiritu-**

al, always holy. To say contract is not enough, it is an embrace (complexus), a veritable embrace, in which the identification of the two wills makes of the two minds one only same thing." This identification, brought about through love, renders everything common between the Word and the soul, as between bride and bridegroom, " who have nothing belonging to them singly, but who have one and the same table, one and the same bed, and also one and the same flesh."[5]

To apply this definition in reverse to a mystic marriage of the human mind with Satan, leaves us with an excellent description and definition of what *perfect possession* is. It cuts right to the core of what this phenomenon consists of; which is the human mind and will *fully identifying* with the mind and will of the diabolic kingdom, or to simplify the mind and will of Lucifer, which then leads to a kind of marriage of the two. To read this description from Pourrat and then apply it to Preuss's definition of mystic marriage of the human mind with Satan, should be very disturbing to all my readers. It should make it very clear the truly deplorable state of people who are *perfectly possessed*.

The *perfectly possessed* are essentially married to Satan, their wills and minds are in complete and perfect conformity with the will and mind of the devil, they are united to him and dwell familiarly with him. They are engaged in a hateful embrace with him, a mockery of the marital embrace turned into complete diabolic slavery. The two wills, human and diabolic, "makes of the two minds one only same thing"[6]. This identification brought about by hate, renders everything common between the devil and the soul, who have "nothing belonging to them singly," but "who have one and the same table, one and the same bed, and also one and the **same flesh**."[7]

Moving on to an Italian context, this is what some Italian authors have said about *perfect possession* or what they term as *diabolical subjugation*. Father Francesco Bamonte has an equally good description than that of Preuss:

"Demonic possession, though not willed, is suffered; demonic subjugation, on the other hand, is the **voluntary offering of one's body and soul to Satan**. This would establish a powerful moral dependence on the devil since it is sought. As someone who belongs

5   Pourrat, *Christian Spirituality in the Middle Ages, Vol 2*
6   Ibid
7   Ibid

to the devil and has become his direct collaborator, the consecrated Satanist undergoes neither the crisis nor manifests the symptoms of those who suffer the extraordinary action of the devil."[8]

Sticking with Italian authors, Father Gabriel Amorth states:

"Diabolical subjugation, or dependence. People fall into this form of evil when **they voluntarily submit to Satan.** The two most common forms of dependence are the blood pact with the devil and the consecration to Satan."[9]

"Diabolical Subjugation. The Term indicates a voluntary pact-implicit or explicit-with Satan, by which we submit to the lordship of the demon."[10]

"The sixth form of disorder is demonic dependence, which one has when a person concludes a blood compact with Satan; he puts himself voluntarily in dependence of Satan and makes himself a slave of Satan, if only to obtain in exchange human favors or successes."[11]

Also, from an Italian perspective Tracy Wilkinson in *The Vatican's Exorcists* states:

"Willful subjugation to the devil: This is really in a category by itself because the **person has sought out the devil through satanic worship**, black masses, which are rituals that mock and blaspheme Christian beliefs, or other overt activities. Such people almost never undergo exorcisms. Massimo Introvigne, Italy's leading expert on alternative religions and satanic cults, says that in twenty years of study, he has come across only one case of a Satanist who 'converted' and sought deliverance from the devil through an exorcist."[12]

This next passage is from the book *The Rite*, written by American author Matt Baglio. The passage however is also from an Italian source as the person saying it is an unidentified Italian exorcist. According to this exorcist,

"The only exception would be when **a person invites a possession to take place**, such as during a satanic ritual. In this case, says an Italian exorcist, **the presence in the soul is completed, which means that the will of the person completely identifies with the**

---

8   Bamonte, *Diabolical Possession and the Ministry of Exorcism*
9   Amorth, *An Exorcist Tells His Story*
10   Amorth, *An Exorcist More Stories*
11   Amorth, *Get Out Satan*
12   Wilkinson, *The Vatican's Exorcists*

demon, having given himself completely to him. In that case the person becomes **constantly possessed** and is like a demon walking on the earth."[13]

When this anonymous Italian exorcist states "that the will of the person completely identifies with the will of the demon, having given himself completely to him," it sounds almost identical to Porratt's description of a mystic marriage. I would also like to quote Father Bolobanic, who is a Croatian exorcist. In his book *An Exorcist Speaks,* he states,

"Subjugation to the Devil: This term denotes a **voluntary personal act** by which **a person signs a contract with the Devil**. It is also known that a person can sign a blood covenant with Satan. Horrible and abominable scenes occur at so-called black masses. This phenomenon is spreading more and more today and is very much present in our cities."[14]

I will now move on to an American context. Father Thomas Eutenauer in his book *Exorcism and the Church Militant* stated:

"Perfect possession describes a state in which a person not only **freely invites a demon to possess him,** but also **cooperates**, with **full consent of the mind and will**, in the demon's malicious desire to destroy Gods kingdom and children."[15]

And from the same author:

"In essence, the term describes a person who has made the **intentional decision to subjugate his will to the devil** and who lives in **a state of total possession by a controlling spirit or spirits**. Furthermore, he is a person who is perfectly aware of the eternal consequences of his decision and perseveres in that state with full knowledge and consent of the will."[16]

Father M, who is one of the most senior and respected figures in the exorcism ministry in the U.S., and who is a professor at a major university on the East Coast, spoke about *perfect possession* at the *Mundelein Conference on Healing, Deliverance, and Exorcism* in 2008, 2009, and 2010. I will quote from what he talked about at the 2009 and 2010 conferences and will quote what he had to say at the 2008 conference when we investigate

13   Baglio, *The Rite*
14   Bolobanic, *An Exorcist Speaks*
15   Euteneuer, *Exorcism and the Church Militant*
16   Ibid

whether or not *perfect possession* is a reversible state. At the 2009 *Mundelein Conference* Father M. said the following:

"In the end game, if this goes on long enough, either the host personality is worn down and finally submits altogether **or submits willingly to make a kind of new bond or covenant with the demonic** presence, and then the two become integral, there's a sort of seamlessness here. I refer to it as integral possession. Where there is no longer any manifestation of struggle or resistance because that's stopped. And instead what you have at the far end of this is a **completely consensual human host** to at least one if not a small colony of demons."[17]

At the 2010 *Mundelein Conference* the same speaker stated:

"Because as theologians divide up stages of possession, there is this final thing called **perfect possession**, it is when the **individual wills, fully and completely some kind of contract with a demonic being**, and they do not resist it, they consent to it."[18]

Father Chad Ripperger, in his voluminous work, *Introduction to the Science of Mental Health* writes:

"Diabolical Subjugation or Dependence
    This occurs when people voluntarily submit to or place themselves under Satan, e.g. by a blood pact with the devil or by a consecration to the devil."[19]

Lastly, we have Father Royo Marin from the perspective of spiritual theology who states:

"At other times the petition has been directed to the devil himself, **in order to establish a kind of pact or agreement with him in exchange for some temporal advantage.** The unfortunate ones who dare to do this **voluntarily give themselves to the devil**, and as a just punishment from God it will be most difficult to liberate them. Such persons place themselves in great danger of eternal damnation."[20]

I would also like to quote two authors who are not speaking from a Catholic perspective. I think it will very much help us to understand the true nature of what we are speaking about. In *An Encyclopedia of Occultism* Lewis Spence states:

---

17   Father M, Mundelein *Conference on Healing, Deliverance, and Exorcism*, 2009
18   Father M, Mundelein *Conference on Healing, Deliverance, and Exorcism*, 2010
19   Ripperger, *Introduction to the Science of Mental Health*
20   Royo Marin, *The Theology of Christian Perfection*

"The rites of black magic, in all ages and places **deliberately evoke this possession by the devil** and his demons for the communication and benefit of the infallible knowledge it was believed they conferred and its consequent power and control of man and his destinies."[21]

The next quote is from Aleister Crowley, a black magician, and who incidentally I will be profiling in a later chapter. In his *Book of The Law*, which was dictated to him by an ancient Egyptian deity (a devil) it is stated:

"Perfect magic is the **complete and total alignment of the will with universal will, or cosmic forces**. When one **surrenders** to that alignment, one becomes a **perfect channel** for the flow of cosmic forces."[22]

This statement from Crowley is extremely profound and very relevant in the context of the topic of this book. This seems to be a perfect description of the explicit form of *perfect possession* from the perspective of a person who very likely was indeed *perfectly possessed*. Since this book was dictated by a diabolical spirit, we could also say that this is a description of *perfect possession* from the point of view of the diabolic kingdom.[23]

All the passages I quoted have one thing in common. They all speak of the explicit form of *perfect possession*. They all speak of someone voluntarily submitting themselves to the power of the devil. As I stated in the introduction it was necessary for me to quote these authors and really all authors, I could locate who have spoken about *perfect possession* in order to put this subject together into one source material.[24]

I would also like to state that the primary way an explicit invitation to perfect possession is done is through some form of the black arts. That does not mean however, that the black arts are the only way. It is entirely possible for someone to be an explicit servant of devil without also being a bona fide Satanist or black magician. Father Amorth writes:

"I wish to conclude with an important observation. It is not necessary to become a Satanist in order to serve the devil and become one of his followers. There are many, alas, who do not officially

21   Spence, *An Encyclopedia of Occultism*
22   Guilly, *Encyclopedia of Demons and Demonology*
23   It could also be said then that the perspective of the diabolical kingdom is that those magicians who rise high enough in the practice of black magic will almost certainly become possessed in this way. In fact it is probably the goal of the devil to perfectly possess all those people who rise to this level of depravity in the occult world, including magicians, Satanists, witches, ect.
24   Throughout this book I have either made a footnote or directly quoted every single author I was able to locate that treated of this topic, even cursorily.

consecrate themselves to Satan but choose to follow his basic prin-
ciples, and as a result they place their souls at great risk."[25]

However, the primary way is through some form of devil worship or
blood pact. I would like to delve at least cursorily into what a blood pact is.

WHAT A BLOOD PACT IS:

The first mention of a sort of pact with diabolical forces appeared in
the writings of St. Augustine and Origen who spoke of the subject in
the context of any practice of illicit magic or divination being essentially
a pact with evil forces. It seems this same teaching was also taken up by
St. Thomas Aquinas. The first mention of a formal pact with demons can
be found in the writings of St. Jerome which also involve St. Basil. The
basic story is that a young man desired to seduce a woman and goes to
an occult practitioner for help in doing so. The young man is asked to
renounce Christ formally in writing, which he does. The man then writes
out a piece of paper of his desire to Lucifer, goes out at night and holds
the document up into the air at which point he is somehow transported
into the presence of Lucifer who baptizes him in the name of the devil and
sets in stone the renunciation of Christ. Lucifer also demands the document be signed by the man. The young girl falls in love with the man and
eventually, despite resistance from her father, agrees to marry him. It is at
this point St. Basil finds out about the matter and helps the man repent
and saves the young woman. Another early story of a pact with the devil
regards Theophilus who allegedly sold his soul with a contract written in
blood to the devil in order to become a bishop. There are many different
variations of this story, but it can be said this account was the inspiration
for the account of Faust.[26]

The diabolical pact took on a whole new dimension in the middle ages
during the inquisition and the persecutions against witchcraft. It was believed, starting in the 14th century that the basis of witchcraft was a pact
with the devil. This idea gained ground and was codified by the publication of the *Malleus Maleficarum*, the most infamous witch hunting manual.
Probably the most detailed idea of the witches' pact with the devil however can be found in Guazzo's *Compendium Maleficarum*. Francesco-Maria
Guazzo was a leading 17th century Catholic demonologist, he stated that
witches who enter into pacts with the devil share these 11 characteristics:

25   Amorth, *An Exorcist Explains the Demonic*
26   Guilly, *An Encyclopedia of Demons and Demonology*

1. Denial of the Christian faith. Meaning denial of Christ, the Catholic Church, the Virgin Mary and all the saints and angels, as well as an adherence to the devil. Often a trampling of a crucifix was part of this ritual.

2. Rebaptism by the Devil with a new name given.

3. Symbolic removal of the baptismal chrism oil.

4. The denial of Godparents and the assignment of new ones.

5. Surrender of a piece of clothing to the devil.

6. Swearing allegiance to the devil whilst standing within a magic circle on the ground.

7. Request for the Devil to write their name in the book of death.

8. Promise to sacrifice children to the Devil.

9. A promise to pay an annual black colored gift or tribute to the assigned demon (familiar).

10.	Marking with the devil's mark on various parts of the body

11.	Vows of service to the Devil, meaning a promise to smash relics, never adore the blessed sacrament, never use holy water or candles, and to especially keep silent at all costs about their illicit traffic with the Devil.[27]

These pacts were distinguished between an implicit pact, which was usually done indirectly through a different witch or an explicit pact or solemn public pact. The explicit pact was thought to be done formally in a document, signed with the blood of the witch or could be done at a witches sabbat. Witches sabbat's were thought to be meetings of witches, which took place at certain times of the year in which all manner of debauched behavior took place. Eucharistic hosts were profaned, crucifixes and other holy things were smashed or trampled underfoot, blood and urine were drunk, animals and even humans sacrificed, orgies, and the actual appearance in physical form of the Devil, Beelzebub or some other devil, which were given worship and homage.[28]

An example of a pact from the middle ages comes to us from the famous possession case at Loudun of a whole convent of nuns. A certain Father Urban Grandier was blamed for the possessions, because he had supposedly put a curse or spell on the nuns and caused their possession.

27	Guazzo, *Compendium Maleficarum*
28	Robbins, *The Encyclopedia of Witchcraft and Demonology*

The formal pact between Grandier and the devils was introduced at his trial and reads as follows:

> "My Lord and master Lucifer, I acknowledge thee as my God and prince and promise to serve and obey thee as long as I shall live. And I renounce the other God, as well as Jesus Christ, all the saints, the apostolic and Roman church, all the sacraments, and all the prayers and petitions by which the faithful might intercede for me. **And I promise thee that I will do as much evil as I can, and that I will draw everyone else to evil.**[29] I renounce chrism, baptism, all the merits of Jesus Christ and his saints. And if I fail to serve and adore thee, and if I do not pay thee homage thrice every day, I give you my life as thine own. Made this year and day. Urbain Grandier. Extracted from hell."[30]
>
> "We, the all-powerful Lucifer, seconded by Satan, Beelzebub, Leviathan, Elimi, Astaroth, and others, have today accepted the pact of alliance with Urban Grandier, who is on our side. And we promise him the love of women, the flower of virgins, the chastity of nuns, worldly honors, pleasures, and riches. He will fornicate every three days; intoxication will be dear to him. He will offer to us once a year a tribute marked with his blood; he will trample underfoot the sacraments of the church, and he will say his prayers to us. By virtue of this pact, he will live happily for twenty years on earth among men, and finally will come among us to curse God. Done in hell, in the council of the devils. Signatures of the devils: Satan, Beelzebub, Lucifer, Elimi, Leviathan, Astaroth. Notarized the signature and mark of the chief devil, and my lords the princes of hell. Countersigned, Baalberith, recorder."[31]

Clearly there was the presence of hysteria and excesses taken by the judges and witch hunters of the middle ages. Many people, some innocent, were burned alive at the stake during this period of history. That however does not mean all witchcraft was a myth, as some modern writers think. There is very likely a lot of truth to what went on in the practice of witchcraft and satanism in the middle ages. We know this because the same things still go on to this very day all around the world. There is a mountain of evidence that real witchcraft and devil worship exists in today's society and has in fact existed for centuries. When I say real witch-

29   This is an essential element of perfect possession. Perfectly possessed people are always involved in the commission of some type of evil and also spend their lives leading other people into evil as well.
30   Robbins, *The Encyclopedia of Witchcraft and Demonology*
31   Ibid

craft and devil worship, I am **not** referring to modern day wicca, or the Church of Satan, the Church of Satan, or wicca does not practice any kind or form of pacts, in fact Anton LaVay believed the idea of a pact was made up by the Catholic Church. Involvement in wicca and groups like the Church of Satan (atheistic satanism, or public, religious satanism) open doors and lead people to great evil and relationships with demons and they are spiritually dangerous to be involved in. However, there exists in the world a much darker, much more dangerous form of witchcraft and devil worship, which is sometimes multi-generational, and always very secretive and in the shadows. Sometimes this form involves very powerful and wealthy people in our societies. It is this type of witchcraft and devil worship where the pact with the devil is still alive and well and practiced very often.

Modern day pacts with the devil can also be practiced by what I would call self-styled Satanists or witches or dabblers in the black arts. Often people who do this do not know what they are getting themselves into. Very often these people eventually seek the help of an exorcist to get out from under the oppressive force that is wreaking havoc in their lives.

A modern-day example of a blood pact was showcased on the program Paranormal Witness, Season 5, "The Contract." In this case, a teenager by the name of Eric Breakfield was an avid gamer on his computer. One day he gets a message in a chat room from a personage that calls himself "magus." Magus invites Eric to play a game called "The Contract." When Eric opens the link for the game, he is rerouted to a dark web chat room that is actually a web site that claims it is "the contract." According to Eric, on this web page chat room there were all kinds of doctors, lawyers and police officers who engaged in the contract and had now become successful. The personage known as Magus then tells Eric that The Contract is a blood pact, that must be signed in his own blood, and that great success will follow Eric if he signs this.

The next day Eric runs into a mysterious man on the street who is very tall, wears an impeccably neat black suit, and drives an expensive black sports car. The most extraordinary thing about the man however was his eyes. According to Eric,

> "His eyes were like a baby blue. It's like he captured my brain and I couldn't take my eyes off him."[32]

The mysterious tall man goes on to tell Eric that he made his first million before age 23. This was the same quote written out at the bottom of the website of the contract and attributed to the CEO of the contract web site. The man goes on to tell Eric that he knows it's not the money he is after, but rather power that he craves. As the man drives away, Eric notices his license plate says Magus 1. That night Eric contacts Magus in the chat room and tells him he is ready to sign the contract. Eric prints out the contract, signs it in his blood and then burns it. Following the ritual and the signing of the contract, Eric's life does change. He becomes suddenly popular and is able to date the most popular girl in school. Soon though things start to go amiss, Eric starts hearing voices and seeing visions of the tall man with baby blue eyes. The voices tell him to randomly kill people. There is also continuing harassment from Magus who is urging Eric to get recruits and more people to join The Contract. Soon Eric can take no more, he feels he is going insane and will hurt someone. He admits to his family what he has done and is exorcised by his pastor in a dramatic exorcism in the presence of his family.[33]

This story is very disturbing to me because it presents a modern-day version of a blood pact, one done via the internet. With the diffusion of the internet and all the millions upon millions of young people who are on it, I just wonder how common this sort of thing is. How many young people, like Eric have been sucked in by the promises of money and power. And how many have not been able to get out of it, like Eric, but are rather very deep in it. I wonder deeply to just what extent is Satan and his hierarchy at work on the net sucking people into their world. I suspect that the diabolical works on the internet for the destruction of souls at a deeply profound and disturbing level. And what do we make of the tall man with baby blue eyes? Was this a physical manifestation of a diabolical spirit? It is entirely possible that it was, such things are completely within the power of the higher diabolical spirits.[34] Or was this simply a man deeply involved in the practice of devil worship and perfectly possessed. Malachi Martin tells of a similar character in his book named Paul. According to Martin, Paul was a tall, good looking man with piercing eyes from the greater Chicago area who was a very successful broker and mil-

---

33   *Paranormal Witness*, Season 5, The Contract
34   There are other accounts of this sort of thing happening. Often the physical manifestation is dressed in black and is usually tall and often good looking or seductive looking or even looks strangely non-human or androgynistic. See Medjugorje visionary Mirjana's encounter in 1982.

lionaire. Paul was also deeply involved with a high-end satanic cult and is the man who introduced Richard/Rita to the cult.[35]

We can summarize this discussion by saying a blood pact is a formal agreement a person makes with Satan, Lucifer, or another prince of hell. This agreement can be done in the context of multi-generational witchcraft or satanism, dabblers or self-styled satanism, or ceremonial magic (there are instructions for making pacts in some of the old magical grimoires). This agreement can be done in writing, with a formal document and signed with the persons blood or done in public, or in the presence of a satanic or witchcraft coven or satanic cult. Essentially what it entails is the person agrees to sell their soul to the Devil in exchange for something, usually money, power, fame, power to hurt people, power to make someone fall in love, a familiar demon, or magical powers. This pact entails a complete renunciation and repudiation of all aspects of the Christian faith. The person furthermore agrees to actively serve the Devil and lead others to hell as well. Sometimes extremely wealthy, powerful, or famous people engage in these pacts. It is this blood pact that can lead to subjugation or perfect possession.

Father Amorth also lists "Consecration to Satan" as also leading to diabolic subjugation. Consecration to Satan entails some of the same things a blood pact does. Essentially the person is consecrated for service in the diabolical kingdom. There is also a complete renunciation of the Christian faith. Usually it is formal, organized, underground or multi-generational Satanists who undergo this ritual. Just as a priest can be consecrated for service in Gods kingdom, so also can a Satanist be consecrated for service in the diabolic kingdom. In his book *An Exorcist Explains the Demonic*, Father Amorth explains what Consecration to Satan means, he writes:

> "Through a rite of consecration to Satan, the person hands himself over to Satan in body and soul, asks to be received among his hosts, and thus enters into a sect. It normally involves an agreement written in blood, which sounds more or less like this: "Satan, from now on I belong to you, in life, in death, and after death. Accept me as your acolyte. **I give you my body and my soul**, and I shall do what you wish and command, but give me pleasures, success, sex, and riches." Usually the consecration happens during a collective rite, often with a black mass, in which one is initiated into the sect and into the satanic practices... All these cases concern a true and proper selling of the soul to the devil, who maintains his tragic

---

35   Martin, *Hostage to the Devil*

promises, but without ever giving any happiness but only innumerable sufferings. In a word, being consecrated to the devil guarantees a life of pure hell on earth and an eternal hell in the afterlife."[36]

DEFINITION:

I will close this section on the explicit form of perfect possession by saying that the explicit form is an explicit invitation from a human being to Satan, Lucifer, or another prince of hell, in the form of a blood pact, consecration to Satan, or some other form of devil worship, witchcraft, devilry or dark art. As Malachi Martin said many times when being interviewed by Art Bell, the perfectly possessed have made a deal, a pact, and they are happy and comfortable with their deal. The explicit invitation is for the diabolic entity to fully and totally possess, control, and be the master of the person, body and soul for all eternity. This is usually done in exchange for some temporal pleasure like money, power, fame, sex, or special powers, but is sometimes done out of pure hatred for God and love of and desire to serve the diabolic kingdom. The person makes this decision with the full force of their intellect and will, to the extent that their human nature and state in life allows. Furthermore, the person cooperates fully with the diabolic kingdoms mission of opposing the Catholic Church and the preaching of the gospel and destroying the bodies and souls of men, woman, and children. The person also renounces any connection to God, Jesus, the sacraments, The Blessed Virgin, the saints and angels, and the church, and has absolutely no desire to change. They fully intend to remain in this state for the rest of their lives and are totally aware that they will go to hell and are comfortable with that and with the devils possessing them. This form is rarer than the implicit form of invitation but is still fairly common as there are hundreds of thousands if not millions of people in the world who are deeply engaged in some form of practice of the black arts. Lastly, these people can sometimes hold very prominent positions in our society and sometimes be found to commit unspeakable acts against their fellow man and against children especially in the context of generational or familial devil worship and witchcraft.

As a last comment I would like to say that despite what all the authors I have quoted stated regarding people who "sell their souls" to the devil and their subsequent subjugation there is one exorcist, (there may be more) who believes and has stated that some people who intentionally sell their souls and work in direct league with the devil are not necessarily

---

36   Amorth, *An Exorcist Explains the Demonic*

possessed. I guess I would have to agree with this to a point. As I stated in the last chapter, God's permission is always needed for an actual bodily possession to occur. There very well may be cases where a person explicitly gives themselves to Satan, body and soul, and which does not result in a bodily possession but only a subjugation of the soul. In this regard the exorcist I am speaking of is Father Amorth who in his book, Memoirs of an exorcist stated:

> "Just think of how many cases we have of people who consecrate themselves to Satan. They are many. I'm always burning more and more of those notes that say, Satan you are my God, I want Satan, I want to be with you always, I honor you, I adore you. And, give me, give me, give me. Give me riches, give me pleasures, give me success. The Devil gives them these things, but **he takes their soul in exchange.** There is **no possession** in these cases because the Devil already owns their soul, since they have chosen to give it to him. We must keep in mind that the Devil, on his own, cannot reach into the soul: he can cause physical distress, but not reach the soul. He can only reach the soul if a man gives it freely and allows him to take control"[37]

And in another part of this book Father Amorth states:

> Returning to the subject of mages, you told me that 98 percent of them are charlatans. What can you say of the remaining two percent?
> **They are possessed, or in league with the devil.** When one is in league with the devil, possession isn't necessary. They already belong to him.[38]

On this point I only agree with Father Amorth to a certain degree[39]. Clearly, many of the other esteemed authors I have quoted stated very clearly that people who are in league with the devil and have explicitly sold their souls or invited possession are sometimes *perfectly possessed.* Where the distinction can come along is to not go to extremes and absolutes and say everyone who sells their soul and is in league with the devil

---

37   Amorth, *Memoirs of an Exorcist*
38   Ibid
39   People who intentionally give themselves over to the devil are always necessarily in a state of grave mortal sin and their souls are very likely in diabolical slavery. This does not automatically mean however that they are bodily possessed. As I explained in the last chapter there is a difference between a subjugation or slavery of the soul and bodily possession. Human beings are made of both body and soul that makes up the one human nature.

is *perfectly possessed* or on the other hand, saying there is never possession in these cases.

The cases of people who either implicitly or explicitly yoke themselves to the diabolic need to be looked at individually. Sure, some of these cases surely do not result in genuine diabolic possession, the person works on behalf of the demonic without being possessed, but on the other hand, some surely do as has been said many times by many different people working in the exorcism and deliverance ministry as well as theologians of the church. The question could be asked how many of these cases do result in possession, how many people who intentionally give themselves over to the devil and are in a state of slavery of the soul, actually become authentically perfectly possessed as well. Father Dominic Szymanski O.F.M., Conv. a very experienced exorcist thinks many. In his classic book, *Truth About the Devil* he states:

> "Direct Invocation. Should it ever happen, quod Deus Avertat, that a person would **directly give himself to the evil one, possession by the devil would almost certainly follow**. God is just, even in his dealings with the devils and as he would recognize the free choice of the creature who would choose him as a master, **so also will he permit the evil spirits to take possession of those who deliver themselves to the enemy.**"[40]

---

40   Szymanski, Truth About the Devil

CHAPTER 3

THE DIABOLIC PROPOSITION FORM OF PERFECT POSSESSION

T he third way in which a person can become *perfectly possessed* is when a diabolical entity explicitly requests or propositions a person to accept possession and they give their full and unequivocal consent. Adam Blai speaks of this when he writes,

> "a person makes a clear choice to say yes, verbally or in their mind, to the demon's explicit request to fully possess them, knowing full well what they are giving themselves over to"[1]

This can happen in a multitude of different ways. One of the only authors that speaks of this form is Father Cristiani. In his classic book *Actualite de Satan*, which tragically has never been translated into English, he states the following regarding *perfect possession*,

> "Possession in the sense we have studied above is extremely rare, and it is always **marked by a resistance from the victim.**[2] But there exists or there may be a large quantity of possessions in which the subject, far from resisting, far from saying no to the demon, **said yes**, either that it had preceded his intervention, **or that he freely accepted his suggestions.** Most modern novels, which claim to literally describe slices of life, offer us examples of true diabolical possession: cold perversities, calculating and reasoning hatreds, systematic corruptions, and cynical immoralism."[3]

In the above quote Father Cristiani clearly is writing about perfect possession. He notes that the more traditional cases of possession, par-

---

1   Blai, www.religiousdemonology.com
2   I quoted Malachi Martin and noted the Gerasene demoniac in the introduction to highlight this concept. Namely that traditional or partial diabolic possession can be thought of more as a diabolic attack, an involuntary possession where the will of the victim is in conflict with the demon, where the victim is resisting as Cristiani notes above. This is qualitatively different than perfect possession, where the will of the person and the will of the demon perfectly identify with each other and they become willing collaborators in the work and practice of evil. "In this case, says an Italian exorcist, the presence in the soul is completed, which means that the will of the person completely identifies with the demon, having given himself completely to him." Quoted from *The Rite* by Matt Baglio, P.51
3   Cristiani, *Actualite de Satan*, Authors own translation.

tial possession, are extremely rare and are always marked by a "resistance from the victim." He then goes on to note that there exists another type of possession, that is more serious than the previously mentioned partial cases in which a person, instead of resisting, instead of saying no to the demon, says yes and fully accepts the influence and possession of the devil in their lives. Father Cristiani then goes on to give us examples of what he is speaking of and states that people possessed in this way are guilty of "cold perversities," "calculating and reasoning hatreds," "systematic corruptions," and "cynical immoralism."

According to this quote from Father Cristiani and also what Malachi Martin has stated[4], a *perfect possession* can be affected not only through the person inviting the demon either implicitly or explicitly, which Cristiani states occurs prior to the diabolic intervention, but that it can also occur when a human being "freely accepts his suggestion" meaning a human being is propositioned or it is suggested to the person by a demon to fully accept possession. Malachi Martin calls this "familiarization." This is in addition to the implicit invitation and the explicit invitation which we have already discussed. There are three cases from the literature that I would like to highlight to show clear examples of how this can take place.

The first case is from Malachi Martin's *Hostage to the Devil* and can be found in the chapter titled "Uncle Ponto and the Mushroom Souper." This case involves a man named Jamsie Z. Jamsie grew up in New York City with his parents Ara and Lydia. Soon after moving to New York the stock market crash of 1929 occurred and this family fell on hard times. Jamsie's father decided to start work for a cab company, which led to among other things, involvement in prostitution, illegal gambling and drug dealing. After several years in this trade Ara died of tuberculosis. Right before Ara's death, his wife Lydia decided to become a prostitute in New York City to support herself. After Jamsie's father died, Lydia declared that Jamsie was on his own. Essentially Jamsie was abandoned by both parents at an early age, which is one of the major contributing factors to his attempted possession by a familiar spirit.

Jamsie eventually got a job at NBC as a page boy and then moved into a career in radio. Throughout his childhood and young adult years Jamsie experienced two very odd occurrences. The first was that he would see a funny looking face from time to time on people that he knew and sometimes complete strangers. He even saw this funny looking face on both his father and mother after both had gotten involved in illegal and sinful activities. The

---

4   Martin was very clear in Hostage to the Devil, chapter "Uncle Ponto and the Mushroom Souper" that familiarization or a formal proposal from a devil to a human being to accept possession can lead to the most serious form of possession, perfect possession.

second occurrence is that from time to time Jamsie would feel a presence around himself that he could not identify, it was during these moments that he knew he was not alone. Jamsie finally moved to Los Angeles for a radio job and that is where he first encountered the spirit that called itself "Uncle Ponto." It occurred one day as Jamsie was driving home from work when he noticed a weird looking face in his rearview mirror. Jamsie knew the face was not human as it was missing something vital. Additionally, the face and head of the entity were completely misshapen and deformed. Jamsie ignored this initial encounter, however the entity spoke to Jamsie and told him,

> "Oh, for petes sake Jamsie, stop acting the fool. We've been together for years; don't tell me you don't know me."[5]

After this initial encounter Uncle Ponto started to appear regularly to Jamsie. The entities presence would always be accompanied by a very pungent smell that Jamsie described as what red would smell like. Additionally, this smell made Jamsie feel threatened because he associated with it the presence of something gargantuan and overwhelming that made Jamsie feel completely insignificant. Jamsie also always felt that when Ponto appeared, he was the mirror image of something massive lurking in the shadows. This in reality was Uncle Ponto's superior, who in the eventual exorcism of Jamsie called itself "Multus." After a while his curiosity got the better of him and he asked Uncle Ponto what he wanted, Ponto replied,

> "Oh, just to be with you Jamsie. I thought you'd never ask. Actually, I want to be your friend"[6]

This progressed into one day Ponto telling Jamsie

> "let's get married, Jamsie, I'm serious, **let's get married**"[7]

And,

> "you and I, Jamsie, **are one**, real flesh and blood"[8]

And on another occasion,

> "Jamsie, would you mind if some of my associates and family joined us? After all, we **are getting married**, aren't we? And soon eh?"[9]

---

5   Martin, *Hostage to the Devil*
6   Ibid
7   Ibid, I would direct my readers to chapter 2 in which theologian Arthur Preuss describes perfect possession as "mystic marriage of the human mind with Satan."
8   Ibid
9   Ibid

Jamsie described what Ponto was doing as,

> "Ponto wanted to move in completely and **permanently** and immediately, **to take him over, him, and his entire life.**"[10]

The harassment from Uncle Ponto intensified over time as the spirit constantly harassed Jamsie to accept possession. On one occasion when Jamsie was on the verge of suicide Uncle Ponto said,

> "It's no use Jamsie, you and I have **much to do**[11] before your life ends. Why do you think I am to be your familiar?." All I'm asking for, all I've ever asked for, is that you let me **come and live with you**. I won't be in the way. You need a friend like me."[12]

As extended control proceeded, there were times when Jamsie tried to resist Ponto, during these occasions Jamsie would feel a tremendous amount of pain that was described like this,

> "Then without warning, pain blocked his memories and dulled all thought. He felt the pressure inside his chest. He had experienced it before when trying to resist Ponto. It began at his ribcage just beneath his skin; and, as it had during the last few weeks, it started to contract inward toward the center of his body. It seemed to be pulling at his brain trying to force it down his spinal column."[13]

By divine providence Jamsie ended up meeting a priest by the name of Father Mark. Father Mark was an exorcist and told Jamsie that he could help him if he wanted help. When Jamsie asked what could happen to him if he didn't accept help Father Mark stated

> "**you can be worn down; you can be taken.** Like any of us. You're up against a force more powerful than you can ever hope to be."[14]

The harassment from Uncle Ponto became so severe that Jamsie almost killed himself by throwing himself off a cliff, instead he decided to call Father Mark and accept the help of an exorcism that had been offered to him earlier. In the end Jamsie was successfully exorcised and was totally freed of the influence of the spirit.

---

10   Martin, *Hostage to the Devil*
11   This is one of the most important concepts of this study, which is that perfect possession does not occur for elementary or trivial reasons. Almost always the perfectly possessed are people who work collaboratively with the diabolic kingdom to oppose the economy of salvation and introduce various forms of evil into the world.
12   Ibid
13   Ibid
14   Ibid

73

Malachi Martin calls this case an open and shut case of familiarization, which he describes as follows,

> "Familiarization is a type of possession in which the possessed is **not normally subject to the conditions of physical violence, repugnant smells and behavior, social aberrations, and personal degeneracy that characterizes other forms of possession.** The possessing spirit in familiarization is seeking to come and live with the subject. **If accepted, the spirit becomes the constant and continuously present companion of the possessed.** The two persons, the familiar and the possessed, remain separate and distinct. The person is aware of his familiar. In fact, no movement of body, no pain or pleasure, and no thought or memory occur that is not shared with the familiar. All privacy of the subject is gone; his very thoughts are known; and he knows continually that they are known by his familiar. The subject himself can even benefit from whatever prescience and insight his familiar enjoys."[15]

Martin was also very clear that when and if the subject fully consents to the possession that the state known as *perfect possession* then occurs. Father Mark, Jamsie's exorcist, was indeed worried this would be the outcome of this case. Luckily, Jamsie resisted for just long enough to get help and be free of the spirit. It is interesting to note that it was only when Jamsie started to resist that his coworker noticed something was wrong with him and so introduced him to Father Mark. If Jamsie had been fully consensual from the very beginning, there would not have been any such struggle or outward manifestation at all. This case presents a frightening example of what could happen in the case of an attempted familiarization.

Here we have a man, who was abandoned in childhood, who became the object of attack of multiple evil spirits. The goal of this attack of course was full and *perfect possession*, that is why Uncle Ponto said

> "we have much to do before your life ends"[16]

Clearly, Jamsie was going to be used, as all *perfectly possessed* people are, to somehow further the diabolical kingdom and destroy souls. The case of Jamsie Z is a perfect example of what it means to be propositioned by an evil spirit to accept possession. The outcome of these cases is three-fold. The person can fully accept the offer of friendship and totally accept the possession from the very beginning, which will of course lead to *perfect possession.* The person resists and then is worn down over time via infestation, oppression, obsession and various other forms of harassment and eventually succumbs to this and fully accepts the possession, accepts full control of the spirit, and completely gives up fighting, which also can lead to *perfect possession*[17] or can lead to suicide, which is what almost occurred to Jamsie ("you can be worn down, you can be taken," Father Mark said). Or the person resists, a struggle ensues, all kinds of strange and disturbing phenomena occur in and around the life of the individual, and they eventually get help from the church and are freed of this oppression.

The second case I would like to highlight is from the book *The Dark Sacrament* by David Kiely and Christina McKenna. It can be found in the chapter entitled "The Boy Who Communes with Demons." In this chapter we are told the story of a boy named Gary Lyttle from County Donegal, Ireland. Gary is a ten-year-old normal boy, who grew up with his sister and mother and without a father. This is the one thing that this case and the case of Jamsie Z has in common, they both were essentially without a father figure for a good portion of their lives and especially during their formative childhood years.

One day while Gary was walking home from school along a trail by a river something told him to deviate from the trail and check out an old abandoned dump site. Coming upon the dump site Gary noticed a board sticking halfway out of the ground. Gary grabs the board and dislodges it from the dirt, at which point an object flies up in the air, stays suspended in the air for a moment and then slowly lowers itself before coming to rest on the board. Gary proceeded to clean off the board and take it home with him when something extraordinary happened,

> "Then without warning, as Gary sat innocently gazing at the board, something incredible occurred. He experienced what can only be called a vision. In the earth beneath his feet he felt a violent tremor. When it ceased, he heard voices: men and woman's voices moaning and shrieking under the ground. Some were crying out. They were all shouting something like "bim eye ah," Gary says. Or it could have been 'bam eye ah. I didn't know what it meant'. The boy was terrified and attempted to get up but instead was thrown back into a sitting position. He was being held captive for a reason. Slowly, the ground in front of him began to open up, and Gary found

---

17   The reason this can lead to perfect possession is because if and when the victim fully gives up the fight against the evil spirit and accepts the possession, any manifestation of struggle or resistance will then stop. The person will then not appear possessed, but will function normally, despite being totally possessed.

himself on the rim of an enormous cavernlike space. Down in its depths he saw a throne. There was a figure seated upon the throne, but Gary insists that it wasn't the devil, that it was an entity that would make itself known to him by and by. But his attention at that moment was not on the enthroned figure, for from all parts of that great cavern, beings with wings began to rise. He identifies them as demons. They were flying up towards him, hundreds of them. Even at that great distance, the boy could make out their eyes; all seemed to be focused on him, as though a signal had been given and all were launching themselves simultaneously into the attack."[18]

Shortly after this incident Gary ran home afraid out of his wits. Later that day though as he was climbing his stairs he stopped dead in his tracks and screamed. He saw another vision of the entity that he saw on the throne, this time at the top of his stairs. When his mother inquired as to what had happened, Gary told her that he had a new imaginary friend named Tyrannus[19], and that he first met this person down by the river when he first discovered the Ouija board, Gary states that it was Tyrannus who was sitting on the throne in the hellish cavern. Gary described Tyrannus as a very large man, almost a giant, ten times bigger than himself,

> "So this Tyrannus was in our house Gary? Yeah. He scared me. **He was huge. A big man, dressed in black**[20], and he was covered in stuff. Rotten stuff. All dirt, like he'd come out of the ground, and he had wounds and big cuts all over him, and he was laughing"[21]

Soon after these incidents, Gary started having mysterious seizures, in which his body would go completely rigid and his eyes would be locked wide open in terror. A doctor was called, and tests were run but no medical explanation could be found for these occurrences. On one occasion Gary went into a trance and started writing frantically with his left hand. Even though Gary is right-handed, he proceeded to write out a bunch of filthy words and phrases and all types of symbols and pictographs. Gary's mother described the writing as definitely not coming from her son, she said the words were too *elegant* as if from the hand of an artist. It is inter-

---

18   Kiely-McKenna, *The Dark Sacrament*
19   Tyrannus in Latin means "sole ruler." It should also be noted that Tyrannus was the name of an entity worshipped by the ancient druids in Ireland. Being that this case occurred in Ireland I think is very significant. There is no way that Gary could have known this as a child. Based on the druidic and pagan history of this deity, the fact that it appeared as a very large, tall man dressed in black and was also sitting on a throne, it is almost certain this is a devil, a higher level evil spirit, likely a prince of hell."
20   Very similar to the entity or person Eric Breakfield encountered on the street.
21   Kiely-McKenna, *The Dark Sacrament*

esting to note that in the book *The Demonologist,* Ed Warren talks about filthy writing that will appear on the walls of houses that are demonically infested. He distinguishes between writing that is crude and basic and writing that looks very sophisticated and elegant. He states that the sophisticated writing comes from the devils, who he describes as "fallen angels from a higher order."[22]

Things got bad enough that Gary's mother took the advice of a neighbor friend and brought her son Gary to see a Catholic monk in Ireland known for his healing abilities. At this meeting Gary relayed to the priest all that had happened. When the priest asked Gary to tell him about Tyrannus, Gary stated:

> "He shows me stuff. He showed me what I'll be like when I'm grown up, when I'm twenty-eight or twenty-nine. **I'm in an office with a big desk. Tyrannus says that if I come over to him I'll be very rich.** 'Come over', the priest repeated quietly. **He says I'll have great power in the future. And loads of money. But I must do what he wants.**"[23]

What Gary says here to Father Dominic is extremely profound and disturbing. The authors of the book note that it would be extremely unusual for a ten-year-old boy to fantasize about sitting behind a big desk. Usually, ten-year old's imagine themselves to be astronauts or police officers or even sports stars. The fact that this diabolic entity is telling Gary he will be rich and powerful and occupy an important position somewhere while sitting behind a big desk in an office is very profound and very important in understanding *perfect possession.* I would point back to the introduction of this book and the quote from C.S. Lewis in which he says evil is being carried out today by men who wear suits and who operate in clean offices and boardrooms.

Father Dominic goes on to tell Gary's mother that he does not like what he sees in the boy. He says that Gary is intentionally entertaining this demon and choosing evil. Father Dominic then goes on to give a copy of a prayer to the Virgin Mary to Gary's mother and makes her promise that she will have Gary say the prayer twice daily. She agrees and Gary proceeds to say the prayer twice daily, all the while during this period the attacks and phenomena completely stop. Then Gary's mother thinking all is well, lets the prayer fall into abeyance at which time the strange seizure like attacks continue. During this time Gary also starts to display a radical

---

22   Warren, *The Demonologist*
23   Kiely-McKenna, *The Dark Sacrament*

change in personality. He now beats up his sister and swears at his mother, as well as shows gross disrespect to his teachers at school. Gary's mother becomes frightened of her son and seeks help from an Anglican Vicar. The Vicar refers Gary and his mother to Canon William Lendrum, an exorcist who lives in Belfast, Ireland.

Canon Lendrum proceeds to question the boy and asks him if he wants to free from this evil. Gary says he does want to be free from it, but that Tyrannus does not want that, Tyrannus wants Gary to serve him. According to Gary, Tyrannus says that if Gary doesn't do what he wants he will make him feel so bad that he will want to kill himself. Canon Lendrum reminds Gary he has free will and he can choose good, he then leads the boy in a prayer to Jesus. At this meeting Canon Lendrum says that he saw something very disturbing in Gary's eyes:

> "He is unable to portray in full what it was he saw that day when he met Gary's gaze. The closest he can come to an adequate description is that the boy's look was 'old beyond his years-older than mine even, and I'm eighty-two'. He is convinced that, for a moment at least, it was not fully the boy who gazed back at him but a part of another personality entirely. For want of a better name he calls it Tyrannus, and he believes it was the demon that was seeking to **dominate** the boy."[24]

The meeting with Canon Lendrum apparently had no effect because soon after Gary stayed at his grandmother's house for a few days, at which time her house became completely infested with demonic activity. Gary's grandmother became so frightened she submitted herself to the rite of exorcism with Canon Lendrum. After this the book states:

> "At this point in time, in 2007, Gary's mother seems powerless to effect any change in her son's behavior. It would appear that she has relinquished control of her son... At the time of The Dark Sacrament going to press, Gary appears to have his demons still. He fears them **and appears to be in thrall to them**... There are very disturbing signs that point to a problem of a spiritual nature. Gary has now developed a full-blown hatred for anything sacred. Nothing will induce him to enter a church; he has stopped praying. He suffers from depression and has suicidal thoughts. He attacks those closest to him. He seems content to be in the company of his demon, or demons. 'Gary must desire to be delivered of his controllers, Father Dominic stresses. If he chooses to hold on to them,

there is little point in prayers said by me or anybody else. **As long as Tyrannus holds the reins, he concludes, no other power can intervene.**"[25]

This is a disturbing case to me because it does not involve an adult like Jamsie Z, but a child, a ten-year old boy. A child that seemingly has been propositioned by a powerful diabolical force, possibly Satan himself, to accept perfect possession and control in exchange for being successful and wealthy. It appears, most disturbingly, that Gary has to a large degree consented to this possession, although maybe not fully and completely yet. It seems however that the case has progressed far enough to *perfect possession* so much so that one of the exorcists involved in the case, Fr. Dominic, is not even willing to consider doing an exorcism and even states it would have no effect. In the case of a 10-year-old boy, this is extremely disturbing.

Neither of the two cases present a victim that very willingly says yes after being propositioned to accept possession by the diabolic. In both cases the victims were worn down, over time and by various means. Gary was clearly worn down by pure fright and dread. From his statements it appears clear that he fears Tyrannus, so much so that he is unwilling to reject the entity. This case shows clearly that not even children, just over the age of reason, are exempt from being targeted by the diabolical. How many cases like this are out there, that we have heard nothing about, in which consent was given fully and completely right away, where no struggle of any kind occurred. Clearly if the diabolic kingdom identifies someone that could further their work, or a person that may in the future be a massive threat to them and their kingdom, they are going to target that person, Padre Pio was targeted by diabolical forces from a very young age. I think and agree with Father Euteneuer in this respect that there are many more possessed people out there that we know nothing about, that are totally controlled by evil and active servants of the Devil.

There is one very important principle at work in these two cases and many other cases as well for that matter. Jamsie Z as well as Gary Lyttle both had something in common in not having a father figure around for very long. This was something glaringly lacking in both of their lives. The lack of family or especially a father is a major factor in cases of possession. Jamsie's father died when he was very young after being involved in all kinds of illegal activities. Jamsie's mom left him as well as soon as his father died. Furthermore, those who read *Hostage to the Devil* know that

---

when Uncle Ponto did enter into Jamsie's life formally, that the spirit constantly sought to alienate him from any kind of relationships, especially those with woman. In Gary Lyttle's case his father was abusive towards his mother, and so his parents were divorced at a very young age. It is no coincidence that both of these people, Jamsie and Gary, were targeted for *perfect possession.*

The evil spirits that roam about the world seeking the ruin of souls are very skilled at filling gaping holes or wounds in peoples lives. There is no greater hole or wound than a lack of family and meaningful loving relationships. Uncle Ponto, the spirit that oppressed Jamsie Z, was very clear to Jamsie that he was going to fill Jamsie's lack of family with his own "family and associates"[26], as Ponto called them. I strongly suspect that a lack of family and meaningful loving relationships in a person's life is a major predisposing factor for diabolic possession, but especially *perfect possession.* A person without family or meaningful relationships is much more likely to fully embrace and accept the presence of evil spirits in their lives that now act as a replacement to family. Father M., who I spoke of previously, spoke about this topic very extensively at the 2007 Mundelein deliverance and exorcism conference. He cited the example of the episode in the gospels in which the possessed man at Gerasa is told to go back to his family instead of going to follow Jesus. Father M noted that Jesus telling the man to go back to his family after being delivered from a serious possession is a very important and often overlooked fact.

Malachi Martin, on page 425 of *Hostage to the Devil* questions why some people are chosen for possession and others are not. He said,

> "Ponto said to Jamsie as they drove along a highway near San Francisco, 'all those homes up there... there's no welcome for me up there in spite of their boozing and bitching and despair."[27]

It seems clear that the reason Ponto and his like had no welcome up there was because those houses probably had the presence of meaningful, loving relationships and family units, even if they were dysfunctional. Where these things exist, there is really no room for the presence of a diabolic relationship in someone's life.

Is it any great mystery that in the very inner-city neighborhoods in which absent parents, but especially absent fathers is an epidemic that there is also the presence of powerful, criminal, street gangs, which take

---

26   Martin, *Hostage to the Devil*
27   Ibid

the place of the family as well? That then result in an appalling amount of bloody violence and murder. Whether it is a street gang, the mafia, a sub-culture like goth, or a satanic cult, they all act in place of the family, and lead people to relationships with diabolic forces.

I often wonder how many young boys and girls in the ghettoes and other places of America that are without fathers or family units, have been targeted for possession, just like Gary Lyttle was. How many rappers that hail from totally broken families, who came from nothing, and rose to great fame, wealth, and power, can we attribute to the action of the diabol-ic. Their filthy music is certainly evil, and clearly does not lead people to a closer relationship with Christ, but to sin, gangs, drugs, sex, demeaning of woman, gross materialism and the like. How many of them have made ex-plicit pacts with the devil or have accepted the invitation of the diabolic, that in exchange for fame, wealth, and power, that they will lead masses of people astray and into error and sin through the promotion of their mu-sic. We know through multiple source that some of these musicians have curses put on their music, so that it will have a negative effect on people.[28]

It is absolutely no coincidence that at the very time we see a major breakdown in the family in American society, that the need for exorcists has also skyrocketed. I would argue that the systematic undermining and subsequent breakdown of the family in western societies is a coordinat-ed diabolic attack meant to destroy souls and society in general, and also make people more pliable and receptive to diabolic possession.

The last instance that I would like to examine is a brief one and comes from one of the Medjugorje visionaries who was propositioned by a devil to accept possession. In the book *Queen of the Cosmos*, visionary Mirjana relays a frightening experience she had in which she not only witnessed a diabolic apparition but also had the spirit explicitly request that she ac-cept him and reject the Blessed Mother. She states:

> "I knelt down and had not yet made the sign of the cross, when suddenly a bright light flashed, and a devil appeared… terrifying, dreadful, and I did not know what he wanted. I realized I was grow-ing weak, and then I fainted. When I revived, he was still stand-ing there, laughing. **It seemed that he gave me a strange kind of strength so that I could almost accept him. He told me that I**

---

28   Much more than the musicians themselves I suspect some of the powerful music in-dustry producers and executives to be diabolic servants, utterly devoted to leading people astray into sin, utterly devoted to glorifying and glamorizing violence, drug use, materialism, fornication and the like. I deeply suspect that there are many music and movie industry power brokers who are perfectly possessed and carrying out the will of the devil.

would be very beautiful and very happy and so on. However, I would have no need of the blessed mother, he said, and no need for faith. 'she has brought you nothing but suffering and difficulties, he said'. But he would give me everything beautiful, whatever I want. Then something in me-I don't know what, if it was something conscious or something in my soul-told me, no, no, no! Then I began to shake and feel just awful. Then he disappeared, and the Blessed Mother appeared. When she appeared, my strength returned as if she restored it to me. I felt normal again. The Blessed Mother told me, 'that was a trial, but it will not happen to you again.'"[29]

DEFINITION:

In this section we have looked at the third way in which a *perfect possession* can happen, through the explicit and direct suggestion, invitation or proposition of a diabolic entity to a human person. I would define it as follows: *perfect possession* which is caused by an explicit diabolical suggestion or invitation occurs when a diabolical entity, sometimes a low level familiar spirit, like Uncle Ponto, or sometimes by a very powerful devil, like the entity that named itself Tyrannus, or even Satan himself, explicitly invites or propositions a person to accept possession and full control, sometimes in exchange for worldly goods or pleasures. There is no greater example of a diabolical proposition than what was related in the Gospels of Matthew and Luke regarding Satan offering Jesus worldly power if he would just bow down and worship Satan.

For the *perfect possession* to be successful the human person must give full consent of their will; a real definitive decision must be made in the affirmative for possession. If it is not made, like in the case of Jamsie Z, the possession remains partial and opens the door to church intervention and exorcism. Sometimes this consent is slow and occurs over time, all the while the victim being submitted to oppression, obsession, or another form of harassment. The devil slowly breaks down the victims will to resist, until the person, so beaten, dominated and exhausted fully gives in and gives full consent and ceases to resist in any way. Sometimes the devil very craftily leads the person into a minefield where they make decision after decision for the possession, without even possibly realizing it, and all the while the devil is applying tremendous pressure on the will to make these decisions. This is also what happened to Jamsie when Ponto did things like demand Jamsie stay away from woman and alcohol and also ask Jamsie if him and his associates could move into Jamsie's apartment, which Martin says the significance of escaped Jamsie. When Jamsie tried to resist, tremendous pressure was applied to him to make a decision in the affirmative for possession.

Sometimes, however, the person being invited or propositioned by the diabolic responds to the invitation with an immediate yes, gives full consent of their will, and never looks back. Whether the process is slow and methodical and is caused by the constant prodding of the evil spirit or is fast because the person gives full consent right away, does not matter, the result is the same. Once a person makes a definitive decision to accept possession and completely stops fighting or resisting, the condition is deplorable, it is a *perfect possession*.

A Last Comment

Even though there are three ways in which the literature teaches a *perfect possession* can happen; namely through implicit invitation, explicit invitation, or an invitation of the diabolic, all three need to be looked at in the same light. Namely, that of a relationship between a human being and a diabolic spirit. These relationships start in a multitude of ways, they are not confined to the three ways I've detailed in this book.[30] These relationships also progress in a multitude of different ways. There are billions, if not trillions of different evil spirits, each one being their own species, and each one having a distinct personality, intellect, will, and way of approaching and dealing with human beings. No matter the way in which the relationship started or progressed, they all lead to the same thing if the victim consents fully or completely gives in to the evil spirt and stops resisting. That of *perfect possession*, a mystic marriage of the human mind with Satan as Preuss explained, the nature of which we will now discuss.

---

30   See *Hostage to the Devil* and *The Demonologist* for case studies on different ways demons approach souls and progress the process towards possession. In Hostage to the Devil many of these cases were very subtle, almost like a kind of diabolical temptation, to seek further degrees of consent towards the ultimate goal of possession, whereas in Warren's book the process is much more violent, the people being subjected to oppression and violent assaults so as to wear them down with fright and dread all in a process also leading to possession. The point being diabolical relationships can take a plethora of different forms and progress in different ways, and all of them can theoretically lead to perfect possession if the human will gives enough consent and does not resist in any way.

CHAPTER 4

THE NATURE AND ELEMENTS PRESENT IN CASES OF PERFECT POSSESSION

1. THE HUMAN WILL

The first and most important element regards the human will. The human *will* is absolutely essential for any case of *perfect possession* to be a reality. This may not be the case in traditional diabolic possession, or partial possession, which can also be viewed as cases of demonic attack, where some people can end up possessed through a curse put on them from someone else. There have also been cases of traditional possession that have occurred purely due to the will of God, some saints have fallen into this category. Exorcists have given various lists and reasons why people can become possessed. Some of these lists include reasons that would seem to not involve the will of a person or a decision they made.[1]

Even on this point however exorcists disagree. Malachi Martin being a prime example in giving his opinion that no one can become possessed except through a direct act of their will and an invitation. On the other hand, many other exorcists, among them Father Ripperger, have said in the clearest terms that people can indeed become possessed through no fault of their own, including children. The major case of possession that occurred in 1928 in Earling, Iowa would tend be a perfect example. In this case the young woman was possessed by higher level entities after being

---

1   For example, one very old exorcism manual from about 1720 entitled *Tratado de exorcismos* or *A Manual of Exorcism* cites "Although sometimes our Lord may permit it, for his greater honor and glory and to make the human being more worthy, sins are usually the cause of such hardship. Other times the cause is too much concern and despair over losing one's worldly possessions or too much familiarity with the Devil or with persons who have a covenant with him. Other times it may be the sins of fathers or of not knowing the remedies to take against the temptations of the Devil" See A Manual of Exorcism very useful for priests and ministers of the church. Likewise, contemporary exorcists give very similar lists. Even this list from 1720 gives two reasons people may become possessed that do not have to do directly with the human will or that occur without the consent of the human will. The Lord permitting it for his greater glory and sins of the father would be causes of possession that do not directly involve the consenting of the will of the victim of possession.

cursed by her father. There is nothing written in the 2 booklets[2] on this case that would lend to the belief that the woman made any decision of her will to accept possession or invite the demonic into her life.

Perfect possession on the other hand absolutely requires a definitive decision of the human will to give full consent, to the degree that human nature allows. If it is an explicit invitation as described in chapter 2, the person decides with their will to invite the diabolic to possess them fully and control them[3] completely, usually in exchange for something like wealth or power. They give full consent of their will and not only completely identify with the diabolic force, but also completely cooperate in the will of the diabolic to destroy the church and souls. They actively will to deny their maker, accept their enemy, and will to stay in that state for all eternity.

If it is an implicit invitation, the person decides with their will to completely reject God and accept Satan and *perfect possession* through a life lived in total debauchery and mortal sin. The constant and repeated commission of these serious mortal sins acts as the will's invitation, although implicit, and the full consent needed for *perfect possession*. Father Saudreau is clear on this point when he says:

> "do not certain faults of an exceptional gravity give Satan the right
> to enter a miserable man who sinks into the last abysses of vice and
> hardens himself stubbornly? Is there not, in this desired hardening,
> an implicit call to Satan, who's obstinate sinner wants to remain at
> all costs the obedient slave?"[4]

I suspect that the implicit invitation to perfect possession also constitutes a giving of full consent of the will, just not in the same way as an explicit invitation.

If it is an invitation of the diabolic spirit for acceptance of possession and the person immediately consents with the full force of their will, for whatever reason, then it is the same as the explicit and implicit versions of

---

2   Vogl, Begone Satan; F.J. Bunse and Riesinger, *The Earling Possession Case: An Exposition of the Exorcism of Mary a Demoniac and Certain Marvelous Revelations Foretelling the Near Advent of the Antichrist and the Coming Persecution of the Church in the Years 1952-1955"*

3   The concept of the Devil being in full control of perfectly possessed persons may remain a controversial idea throughout this study for some readers. Many of the authors I have already quoted however were very clear on this point. Jesuit Father Devivier in speaking about persons who immerse themselves in the black arts stated that they are "finally surrendered to the control of invisible agencies"; likewise Malachi Martin the author who wrote the most about perfect possession stated that the perfectly possessed have "came under the total control of an evil spirit"; Lastly Father Stang stated "Man may renounce God and Christ and surrender himself completely to the service and control of Satan."

4   *Saudreau, L Etat Mystique*, authors own translation

invitation. All three give full consent of their will for the devil to perfectly possess them body and soul, and completely be the slave of the evil one. As was stated before, these people identify with the diabolic spirit, are comfortable with the diabolic spirit, hate God, fully cooperate in the diabolic spirits mission to destroy the church and souls, and have absolutely no intention of ever changing their mind or repenting. The core part of this element necessary for perfect possession is that the human mind and will fully and completely identifies with the mind and will of the devil and accepts the controlling presence of the devil in their lives.

The only lesser version, which in reality is not the kind of perfect possession as described above, that does not have the degree of depravity present as in the previous three instances is when a person involved in a diabolic relationship is completely and totally broken down by the entity. Father M. noted this as a possibility in the context of perfect possession when he stated:

> "In the end game, if this goes on long enough, either the host personality is **worn down and finally submits altogether** or submits willingly to make a kind of new bond or covenant with the demonic presence"[5]

These people are infested, oppressed, obsessed, harassed, and deceived in a multitude of different ways; physically, psychologically, spiritually, socially, financially, and even familially. There is usually a middle ground to this affair when the person is resisting these attacks and fighting back against them, and sometimes in this stage is when an exorcist is called in. However, sadly, some of these people never get help, for whatever reason no one notices, or it looks like something else, maybe mental illness, or they are even turned away by the church as happened frequently back in the 1970's. Often these people are not religious or have no faith and so they have no protection and no means to cry out for help. They may not even fully understand what is happening to them. These people go on struggling until a point is reached when they are totally beaten in every respect. Their will has been so worn down and pummeled that they finally give in to the constant coaxing, coercing, and cajoling of the diabolic spirit, and they accept the possession with their will and cease to fight against it. There is now no longer any manifestation of a struggle or resistance, "because that's stopped"[6] and the human personality can now no longer be distinguished from that of the diabolic.

---

5   Father M, *Mundelein Conference on Healing, Deliverance, and Exorcism*, 2009
6   Father M; *Mundelein Conference on Healing, Deliverance, and Exorcism*, 2009

Father Ripperger talked about these types of cases at the Mundelein Conference in 2013 when he said that in some cases of possession the demon is so deeply ingrained in the personality and psychology of the victim that the two personalities (human and diabolic) cannot be told apart any longer. Father Ripperger went on to say that the only thing that can be done for such people is to offer masses and pray for them that a degree of separation may occur. Father Ripperger stated,

> "There is a kind of case, I see them once in a very great while where the demon has gotten himself hooked so deep into the person psychologically that there's nothing you can do for them as far as an exorcist other than just pray that they'll receive the grace to somehow get some degree of separation… They get to the point where the demon is so much in control of them that anything you try and do, even if you're trying to liberate them, the demon is working with them or inclines them to do things just to counteract your work."[7]

Now it is possible that some people in this position originally made the decision to explicitly invite possession but then tried going back on that decision and were subsequently worn down by the possessing entity. However it is also possible that many of these people were deceived into entering into some type of relationship with a demon and were subsequently beaten down and worn down over time so badly to the point where they finally gave in altogether and ceased in any way to resist the action of the demonic force.

It seems there are a few different outcomes that can occur with people like this. The reason I bring this up in a book about perfect possession is because a case like this may display some of the same traits as a case of perfect possession in which the person intentionally invited the demon in and never went back on that decision in any way. As I will note later in this chapter and which I already noted above, such people in this state do not display the normal signs of possession and may actually seem to be completely normal people, albeit totally controlled by evil. It seems that one of the outcomes of the people who have been totally broken down by a diabolic entity and have submitted to the lordship of the demon **unwillingly**, could be that they also display none of the traditional signs of possession and function normally in society and introduce evil into society because they are being totally controlled by an evil spirit. Despite the fact that a case like this displays the same traits as perfect possession I really would not classify it as such because

---

7   Father Ripperger; *Mundelein Conference on Healing, Deliverance, and Exorcism*, 2013

despite the fact that the person submitted to the demon, they submitted **unwillingly** after a diabolic campaign to force them into submission, therefore it would seem there would be a chance for liberation if the case were to be uncovered for what it really is.

In addition to the person basically functioning normally despite being totally possessed it would seem there are a few additional outcomes that occur in such cases. It might be that the person who has submitted fully but unwillingly to the demon could also be totally paralyzed by what seems to be an incurable mental illness and so they are confined to a mental asylum for the rest of their lives. I am convinced that this outcome occurs far more often than anyone wants to admit. I believe that there are many people who have been committed in mental institutions for years who have not responded to traditional psychiatric treatment who very well may be totally possessed.

Lastly and most tragically an additional outcome could be that these people not being able to endure any more torture from the possessing entity decide to commit suicide before the demon takes full and total control of them. This was almost the case with the aforementioned Jamsie Z who at the height of his harassment from uncle Ponto, almost threw himself off a cliff to end his misery. I am also convinced that this is an outcome that occurs far too frequently in todays day and age. Sadly because of the fact that faith in God has been steadily declining in modern society, a person who has gotten themselves into trouble with a demonic entity, may not know where to turn for help and so they tragically decide to end it to cease their suffering. In some cases the demon may even propel the person to suicide if there is a reasonable chance the person will be damned for it upon their death. We should not make the mistake though of believing that the demons are responsible for a suicide in every case. There very well may be cases that the demonic kingdom does not want to end in suicide because they wish to use the person on this earth to further their ends in some way and introduce evil into the world.

In conclusion, the core element necessary for a case of perfect possession to be a reality is that the person decides with the full force of their will, to the degree human nature allows, to implicitly or explicitly fully accept the lordship of one or more diabolic entities in their lives to fully control and possess them for all eternity.

2. The Will of the Diabolic Kingdom

The second element that must be present for a case of perfect possession to be a reality is the will or the desire of the diabolic kingdom to bodily possess and fully control the person. Not all people who make an implicit or explicit invitation to be possessed actually are. Jesuit Father Sylvester Joseph Hunter in writing of Satan notes that,

> "He varies his mode of dealing with those who are **willing** to become his votaries, according to their dispositions."[8]

As an extension to my last comment, I can say that not all obstinate sinners are possessed, not all thoroughly evil people are possessed, and even people who make explicit invitations to the demonic to possess them actually end up so possessed. It would seem at the end of the day that diabolic possession in all its forms is still an overall rare phenomenon. It is extremely likely we have God to thank for this.

Despite the fact that demons take obvious pleasure in destruction and possessing people, there may be reasons why the devil would not wish to actually bodily possess a certain person at some particular time and place.

The diabolic kingdom may see fit to simply leave the person in a state of mortal sin and moral dependence on the devil, knowing that there is no need to bodily possess and fully control the person because they are already doing the work of the Devil without being perfectly possessed, and because the person being in a state of total enslavement to sin, will most likely be damned upon their death, which really is the Devil's ultimate goal. This was of course the opinion of Father Amorth who I quoted earlier regarding this topic.

It also could be that they do not wish to bodily possess the person because they foresee the unlikely event that a miracle may occur, the person may have a change of heart, maybe because they have someone praying and sacrificing unceasingly for them, and so the person may eventually be brought to an exorcist and the Devil does not wish a direct confrontation with the church at this time and place.

As an extension of this element, it would seem that Gods permission is also needed for a bodily possession to occur, even if the person directly invited it. God is still the master and lord of the entire universe and is completely in control of everything and sees everything that happens. He keeps the diabolic on a tight leash and certainly does not allow them free reign in doing anything they want. They operate via a specific set of rules that God has laid down. Therefore, for any diabolic possession to occur whether partial or perfect, God must allow it. It also might not be out of the question that God al-

---

8   Hunter S.J., *Outlines of Dogmatic Theology*

lowed a perfect possession to occur[9] to make an example of someone and satisfy his justice, who has repeatedly mocked him, taken advantage of his grace, and trampled upon his sacred body. God, in the end, will not be mocked.

This element is different from more traditional cases of possession because it can occur that God himself forces the demons to harass someone for punishment to get them to open their eyes and come back to the Lord. What this means is that sometimes in more traditional cases of possession God uses the demons, *against their will,* to affect the conversion of some person. God however does not wish anyone to become perfectly possessed and there is no way he would will this and use the demon to do this. A case of perfect possession is really the human will and the demonic will identifying with each other and both consenting to a permanent relationship or "mystic marriage" as Preuss called it. This always occurs to the great sadness of God who wishes us to love him.

This is qualitatively different than God using a demon against their will, possibly through a partial possession or even oppression to affect the conversion of a person. Because of this, and because the fact that God would not use a demon against their will to complete a perfect possession[10], it remains that the will or desire of the devil must be present in the affirmative for any case of perfect possession to have occurred. The diabolic kingdom must have a desire to perfectly possess someone, if they do not, then this phenomenon will not occur. In chapter 5 we will explore the reasons why the devil would want to perfectly possess someone.

3. EXTERNAL DIABOLICAL POSSESSION OR "ENSLAVEMENT" OF THE HUMAN SOUL

The third element is the diabolic possession of the human soul or what Father Bamonte calls "moral dependence of the soul on the devil. Fa-

---

9   This statement may be controversial, but we must remember we all have free will and if we really want to we can give ourselves over to the devil; "The human will can in the depths of man's spiritual freedom of choice, give itself over to Satan" Monden S.J.. In the end it is important to understand that despite the fact that Gods permission is needed for a case of perfect possession to be a reality, God will respect our freedom of will and allow this if it is what we want. This also does not preclude the fact though that like a loving father God may continue calling after us to come home until the day we die despite our intractableness.

10   Because perfect possession would not be used or could not be used to convert someone back to the Lord, it is just a different type of possession with different factors. A person who wishes to be with the demons for all eternity and explicitly invited them to possess his body and soul probably will not be converted because they are so possessed. However, someone who maybe dabbled with the demonic and got in a little too deep and gotten themselves possessed could be converted back to the Lord after being terrified of the ordeal and this may be the reason God allowed the possession in the first place because in his wisdom he knew it eventually would lead the person back to the Lord.

ther Bamonte also calls it "external imprisonment of the soul" or "enslavement of the soul to the devil." In addition, we also examined in Chapter
1 how this can be thought of as a kind of possession in and of itself, separate and distinct from the diabolic possession of the body. Johannes Smit
calls this an "ethical" form of possession. This was discussed extensively
in Chapter 1.

Essentially, what this means is that by their actions and choices the
perfectly possessed person is always necessarily in a state of gravely serious moral desolation and deadly sin. They have often spent whole lives
committing crime on top of crime and moral perversion that goes gravely
against the divine order. This sometimes includes explicitly selling one's
soul to the devil in some type of black magic or satanic ritual but can also
be brought about due to a man living a whole life of very serious mortal
sin that is committed intentionally, habitually, through malice and hatred
of God and is never repented of.

What this comes down to is the "possession of the soul," albeit externally, as Father Bamonte so eloquently explains. Through this possession
of the soul, the Devil maintains a measure of control over the faculties of
the soul, the intellect and will. Father Amorth stated this was possible,
that a demon can control a soul when he said:

> "He can only reach the soul if a man gives it freely and **allows him
> to take control**."[11]

In addition to the above statement by Father Amorth there are many
other authors who have explicitly stated that it is possible for the devil to
in some way possess or control a soul due to the intentional decision of a
man's will to give himself over to the devil. It is important to quote these
authors because as I stated in Chapter 1 there are many other theological
authorities that say under no circumstances can the devil possess or control the human soul.

In this regard, I will again quote Father Amorth, who in another one of
his books stated,

> "It is necessary to clarify that the devil is not able **to take posses-
> sion of the soul** of a man, **unless the person expressly consents
> to it**."[12]

---

11   Amorth, *Memoirs of an Exorcist*
12   Amorth, *An Exorcist Explains the Demonic*

Also, Scaramelli S.J., whose theological opinion in spiritual matters is very highly regarded, states in his *Il Direttorio Mistico*:

> "My opinion is that the devil never succeeds in acquiring such an ascendancy over a person as to enable him to **take possession of** his body and **his soul…unless such a person concurs by some consent and some co-operation.**"[13]

And also, Bishop Ullathorne in *Christian Patience* states:

> "they cannot **act in the substance of the soul** without **its consent**"[14]

Father Delaport in his classic book *The Devil* says:

> "except the **will**, which never **belongs to Satan** unless **with its own consent.**"[15]

Father Pascal Parente S.T.D. PH. D, who was considered at one time the foremost authority on mystical theology in the United States in his book *The Mystical Life* states:

> "In diabolical possession the devil is within man; the stronghold has been captured and occupied. He is within the body but not necessarily **within the soul**, except by **free consent of the will** itself."[16]

And, one of the most eminent authorities of all St. Francis de Sales in his classic *Introduction to the Devout Life* stated:

> "Let Satan rage at the door he may knock and stamp and clamor and howl and but do his worst but rest assured that he can never **enter our souls** but through the **door of our consent.**"[17]

Lastly, Father Louis Monden S.J., in his excellent work, *Signs and Wonders* writes:

> "he is not able to make himself **master of the human soul** at choice unless it be **surrendered to him** in one way or another by a **free act of man's will.**"[18]

13   Scaramelli, *Il Direttorio Mistico*
14   Bishop Ullathorne, *Christian Patience*
15   Delaport, *The Devil*
16   Parente, *The Mystical Life*
17   St. Francis de Sales, *Introduction to the Devout Life*
18   Monden S.J., *Signs and Wonders*

All of the authors that I quoted above have two things in common. They all say that it is indeed possible for the devil to take control of the soul and possess it, and they also all state that this state comes about only when a man makes the intentional decision to give his own soul over to Satan. As was stated above these comments that I have quoted are in direct contradiction to many other authors who have said clearly that they do not feel the devil can possess or control the human soul in any way whatsoever.

It is extremely important to clarify a few points regarding this. First, we must remember that whatever control of the faculties of the soul the Devil maintains it is only because the human person has fully consented to this. Secondly, it is also probable that even if the devil does maintain some measure of control over the faculties of the soul, he probably does not control it completely and despotically as he would control the body in a traditional case of diabolical possession.[19] As I stated in chapter 1 it is probable that it is a control of the soul but a control that is such that the human person still maintains some of his own control over his own faculties, albeit totally and completely turning those faculties to the service of the devil. It is a "collaborative control" as I stated in Chapter 1. It is also important to reiterate as I did in Chapter 1 that despite the fact that it is possible for the devil to possess and even control the soul in some way, the devil is never able to penetrate to the substance of the soul and dwell there in the same manner as God.

It is easy to see how the Devil could externally possess a soul without internally penetrating its substance, which he cannot do. Will Satan not externally possess and dominate our souls in hell, if we are so unfortunate to end up there? The person who lives a life full of grave moral disorder or explicitly invites the diabolic to possess their soul is giving themselves freely to the Devil. And if we so hate God and despise his grace and his offer of love and salvation as to completely give our will to this powerful evil force, then we have given our souls, our very self, over to the enemy of God, the Devil, for him to possess accordingly.

We must also remember that the relationship between a perfectly possessed person and Satan is very similar to the relationships between Satan and his lesser demons. The only difference being demons do not have a body. It is widely believed by many theologians that the more powerful

---

19   Because if this was the case the human person would bear no personal responsibility for moral depravities committed while under the state of despotic soul control and this is likely contrary to the diabolic will which desires our souls, our will, to make decisions for evil which will ultimately result in the final damnation of the soul in hell.

demons in hell completely subjugate and dominate the lesser demons. If even demons, who have will and intellect and are purely spiritual beings are able to be enslaved and dominated by more powerful entities, it is absolutely plausible that the human soul, a spiritual substance would also likewise be able to be enslaved and dominated by the far superior nature of fallen angelic beings. The key in this is that the reason the lesser demons are subject to Lucifer is because they chose to follow him into rebellion and condemnation. Thus, they are now subject to him. Likewise, a human being that makes the intentional choice to follow Satan will also likewise be made subject to him, body and soul.

I am aware that the church teaches every human is free to choose good and evil up to the moment of their death, however, these people do not want to be saved, and have no desire to change their mind, they are already comfortable with their choice. Their will has also been greatly weakened because of constant mortal sin on top of mortal sin. With every mortal sin committed the will is conditioned for further sin and weakened in its resolve to resist temptation and not commit sin. The diabolic spirit also brings tremendous pressure to bear on the will, through painful torture in the body, and other means, that these people are now in a state of complete slavery and usually completely unable to muster the will to change, unless by a direct miracle of God. Furthermore, they have often willed to give up their right to choose, as much as can be done in the human state. It would be like someone signing away their right to freedom by agreeing to be committed in a mental institution. Even if they wanted to leave, they would be unable to, they are now completely at the mercy of the doctors, who control their daily activity, medication, and freedom. The human soul is the very essence of a person and the perfectly possessed fully desire to give themselves fully to the devil, giving themselves fully means intentionally handing over their being, their souls to the control of the evil one.

4. TOTAL AND COMPLETE DIABOLICAL POSSESSION OF THE BODY

The fourth element, and in addition to the possession of the soul, is the diabolical possession of the body, the presence of one or many diabolical spirits in the actual body of the person. Through this presence of the diabolic spirit in the body it exercises complete control of all the bodily faculties, the senses, the memory, the imagination, motor function, etc. If the devil has complete control of all these faculties during the state of crisis in partially possessed people, it would just stand to reason his control would be greater in cases that have progressed to perfect possession. I will quote two highly respected authors who have defined possession of the body. Monsignor Balducci in his excellent and voluminous work *Gli Indemoniati* states:

> "Diabolical possession is characterized by a very real domination that Satan exerts directly on the body of a person... It is undoubtedly the most serious and terrible of extraordinary demonic activity, transforming an individual into a docile instrument to be fatally used by the despotic and perverse power of the Devil."[20]

And also, Augustin Poulain S.J., in his *Graces of Interior Prayer* states:

> "We shall say, in the strict sense of the word, that a person is possessed by the Devil when at particular moments the Devil makes him lose consciousness and seems to take the place of the soul in his body; making use, apparently at least of his eyes in order to see, of his ears to hear, of his mouth to speak, whether to those who are looking on or to his own companions... In a word, the Devil seems to be incarnate in the man."[21]

I quoted these authors who have far more wisdom than I do and do a much better job of explaining what diabolic possession of the body entails, so we can get an idea of what this element consists. These authors clearly say that diabolical possession of the body is when the Devil completely takes over the body of a person and controls the mental, affective, and volitive faculties as Father Syquia has stated.[22] The evil spirit acts in the limbs, eyes, mouth, brain, etc.

In a partial possession the diabolic spirit does not have full and total control, the evil spirit only has full control during the moments of crisis and during these times the victim usually recalls nothing, during the rest of the time the person is usually able to at least function in life, albeit with some restrictions and sometimes with the presence of other maladies, physical and psychological, present in the possessed. In a perfect possession, the diabolic spirit has full and complete control of all the bodies faculties and furthermore is in control of those faculties always because the demon is present always. It should be clearly noted however that this is the result of the human person allowing this, the devil can never take full

---

20   Balducci , *Gli Indemoniati*, authors own translation
21   Poulain S.J., *Graces of Interior Prayer*
22   Syquia, *Exorcist A Spiritual Journey*

and total control and remain in control, always without the decision of the human will to allow such control.

The question could be asked, whether the victim of perfect possession has any situational self-awareness or are they totally unconscious and remember nothing like victims of partial possession. My opinion is that they are self-aware and are aware of their surroundings, but they are also aware that they are enslaved by another force that they have no control over. There is historical precedent for this in the case of a Jesuit exorcist named Jean-Joseph Surin. Although this is not a case of perfect possession, it does show that it is entirely possible for a person to be possessed and also be totally self-aware. Malachi Martin does a great job of describing what this would be like when he defines "familiarization." He essentially says, the person is aware of themselves, but any privacy is completely gone as the human victim shares all thoughts, actions, pleasures, etc., with the evil spirit. In *Hostage to the Devil*, Martin states:

> What was a "familiar"? Jamsie wanted to know. Mark explained that the key to the "familiarity" which such a spirit sought to obtain lay in this: **the person in question consented to a total sharing of his or her consciousness and personal life with the spirit.** Mark gave an example. Normally, when you are walking around, eating, working, washing yourself, talking, you are conscious of yourself as distinct from others. Now supposing you were conscious of yourself and of another self all the time, like Siamese twins but inside your own head and in your consciousness. And supposing that the two, so to speak, shared your consciousness. It's your self-consciousness, **your awareness of yourself, and at the same time, it's the consciousness, the awareness of that other self. Both at the same time. No getting away from one another. "Its" thoughts use your mind, but they are not your thoughts, and you know that. "Its" imagination likewise. And "its" will also.** And you are aware of all this constantly, for as long as you are conscious of yourself. That was the familiarity Mark was talking about.[23]

This is qualitatively different than most cases of partial possession where the victim is engaged in a struggle with the demonic will. In the vast majority of these cases that end up at the doorstep of an exorcist, in the state of crisis the demon completely takes over the person and acts through them, the person then usually has absolutely no recollection of what took place during the crisis manifestation. Because of this, it is often opined by theologians that these people are not morally responsible for their actions when under the actual state of possession.

This is one of the problems with the concept of perfect possession and it is the one problem that is brought up by Monsignor Balducci when in his book *The Devil,* he says he doubts demons take possession of people who are "obstinate sinners"[24]. Balducci states that if the devil were to possess an obstinate sinner that person would then no longer be liable for any sins committed because they would be under possession and this would be contrary to the diabolic will. Despite the fact that Balducci is one of the most learned and scholarly demonologists in the history of the church, that wrote one of the best books on possession ever written (Gli Indemoniati or The Possessed) on this point I believe he is mistaken. I will again quote Augustus Saudreau who very clearly wrote:

> "do not certain faults of exceptional gravity give Satan the right to enter a miserable man who sinks into the last abysses of vice and hardens himself stubbornly? Is there not is this desired hardening, an implicit call to Satan, who's obstinate sinner wants to remain at all costs the obedient slave? The example of Judas would lead us to believe it."[25]

Furthermore, Saudreau was joined in this opinion by Monsignor Cristiani, a foremost authority on diabolic phenomena. Balducci, like others, never considered the fact that some people intentionally invite the devil and wish to be possessed. They do not fight against the diabolic will, they are totally at peace with this arrangement and happy with the state of their soul and state in life. Balducci does not elaborate on the fact that in traditional or partial possession the person is engaged in a battle with the demonic will which struggle is responsible for the extraordinary phenomena surrounding diabolic possession. He does not consider that there may be people who do not struggle against the demonic, that want to be possessed, that make a formal agreement or covenant with the devil to work with him for the destruction of souls.

When I said this is the one potential problem with the concept of perfect possession what I meant is that an argument could be made that the devil would never perfectly possess someone because then the person would be without fault for any terrible acts committed in that state. I have two arguments to make regarding this. First, the person who is perfectly possessed is not unconscious like a victim of partial possession, if they

---

24   Balducci, *The Devil*
25   Saudreau, *L Etat Mystique*

were completely unconscious and the devil moved them and controlled them totally without any knowledge of the human person, then an argument could be made that they are not at fault for any sins committed in that state. In perfect possession however, the person is self-aware, they have knowledge of what is going on, what the demon is doing, and they continually consent to it. Like Father Surin they see what is going on around them and through them, including horrific acts they commit. At any time, the person could be disgusted by these acts, like Father Surin was,[26] and decide to start fighting for their own liberation, which would make the possession a partial one. This is the primary thing that differentiates partial from perfect possession, it is the will of the human person to either fully accept the will of the devil or reject it, those that accept it are at peace, they do not appear to be possessed because there is no struggle, if they reject it they do look and act possessed because there is massive struggle of wills going on. What occurs in the perfectly possessed is that the person fully accepts the will of the devil and when a person in the perfectly possessed state commits some horrific or sinful act they take pleasure in it, they like it, they are comfortable with it, they want to do it again and they definitely do not desire to change.[27] This makes them fully liable for the crimes committed even though they are possessed.

Secondly, the person is liable for any acts committed under the state of perfect possession because they were the ones who through their own will power, decided that they wanted to be servants of the devil and work in collaboration with him. When making this choice they knew full well that they would be used to carry out the will of Lucifer, which includes committing all kinds of horrific crimes and sins against men, women, children, God and the church. They furthermore continuously choose with their will and intellect to remain a direct servant and collaborator of the devil. This also makes them fully liable. Based on these arguments we can see that a perfectly possessed person is not a person who is under the total control of the devil having no say in the matter, these people are direct and willing servants and collaborators of Lucifer. If they are perfectly possessed, it is only because they wanted to be and if any horrific crimes which often include murder and sexual abuse of children occur it is because they have consented to this and in fact enjoy the commission of these crimes. This will become very clear and will even become sickening to some readers who continue on with this book and read chapter 8 in

---

26   Huxley, *The Devils of Loudon*

27   There are very many quotes by not a few serial killers demonstrating this concept, I have quoted some of them in a later chapter.

which I profile some serial killers who very clearly took great pleasure in collaboration with the devil, in committing some of the most heinous acts against their fellow human beings known to man.

5. Unending and Perfect Collaboration with Satan

Active collaboration with Satan in the practice of evil and complete diabolic control

> "By making such a pact, the man or women denies himself God's grace and support, **opens himself to the devil's whim**, and may experience the most severe form of possession… **He can do just about everything with such a person.**[28]

The fifth element of the nature of perfect possession is the immediate and unquestioned authority the diabolic spirit exorcises over the possessed and hence the victim follows any suggestions of the diabolic spirit with "such readiness and promptitude"[29]. The total control the evil spirit has over the person then translates into evil machinations being carried out by perfectly possessed people. It needs to be clearly noted however, as was written above that despite the fact that perfectly possessed people are totally enslaved to Satan, they still retain an element of freedom to do evil and collaborate in evil acts with the action of the demon. This is the element that makes perfectly possessed people extremely dangerous and destructive in society.

Father Euteneuer is absolutely correct when he states that rather than praying for them, what is needed more is to pray for protection from them. Father M. and Malachi Martin both state that perfectly possessed people are truly frightening to them.[30] The danger lies in the fact that it is a diabolical spirit controlling the reins of a human being, controlling and possessing them completely. These infernal spirits are murderers and liars and are filled with an implacable hatred towards man. They seek to do whatever they can to ruin the bodies and souls of men. Perfectly possessed people can often be found to commit mass murder, serial murder, or contract killings, which is the destruction of men's bodies. Father Frederick Houck noted:

---

28   Rodewyk, *Possessed by Satan*, 1975, P.113
29   Saudreau, *Degrees of the Spiritual Life, Vol 1*
30   Both Father M and Malachi Martin actually said that the perfectly possessed were the most frightening people they ever encountered and that coming from two very experienced exorcists with many years of experience.

"When a father kills his wife and children, or when a boy buries a hatchet in his mother's skull because she refuses to give him more spending money, we have a reason to suspect that such monsters are possessed by a devil."[31]

This is partly why we have things occur like the Sandy Hook school shooting, or the Virginia Tech shooting or the Las Vegas shooting, Columbine shooting, or Orlando nightclub massacre or any number of wholesale slaughters of people that go on around the globe on any given day. This is why we have monsters like Henry Lee Lucas and John Wayne Gacy that exist or people like Richard Kuklinski, the ice man, who admitted killing over a hundred people for the mafia in the New York area. Perfectly possessed people are **extremely** dangerous and should be avoided at all costs.

They can also be found to engage in mass deception through lies, half-truths, heresy, false doctrines or false religions and teaching people that good is evil and evil is good, making sin look normal, natural, fun, and glamorous. The film industry, the music industry, the pornography industry, the abortion industry, the business and finance industries, wall street, the judiciary, the political world, the media, and also, sadly, the church are all populated by perfectly possessed people in positions of power, placed there strategically, at the behest of their master, Satan. These people through their maliciousness and desire to serve their master, the Devil, destroy souls by leading people into sin and error via a myriad of deceptions.

It is going to be a very controversial idea indeed for me to speculate that the church has been infiltrated by servants of the Devil. I can say for certain that the Catholic Church is the number one enemy of the diabolical kingdom, and so of course they are going to try and infiltrate so as to destroy it from the inside:

"One of the sad things we see in scripture is continual warnings about false preaching and teaching coming from within the church by those trusted to preach and teach, and the sad story is we have lived through that. We have lived through false preaching and teaching that has turned many people away from the right path. It is just a very very sad fact of our situation in the last 40 or 50 years.[32]

31   Houck, *Our Friends and Foes*, 1948
32   R.M., *Mundelein Conference on Healing, Deliverance, and Exorcism*, 2011

"Earlier, Don Gabriele, you told me that some cults are less serious, while some are much more terrible…

Certainly, some are terribly serious. And unfortunately, they're everywhere. I would say even in the Vatican.

Even in the Vatican?

Yes, even in the Vatican there are members of Satanic cults.

Who is involved? Are you talking about priests, or simply laymen?

There are priests, monsignors, and even Cardinals!

Pardon me, Don Gabriele, but…how do you know?

I know from people who have been able to relate it to me because they've had firsthand encounters. And it's one of the most commonly confessed things by the devil himself during exorcisms."[33]

Who can deny that the sexual abuse scandal in the church is nothing short of a very sophisticated, coordinated diabolical attack, meant to undermine the church, make it look evil, and cause people to separate themselves from it and the sacraments, and hence Jesus Christ, their savior. Bishop Robert Barron talked about this very thing in an article he wrote about the Cardinal McCarrick sexual abuse scandal. His excellency wrote:

"What shook my agnosticism in regard to the evil one was the clerical sex abuse scandal of the nineties and the early aughts. I say this because that awful crisis just seemed too thought-through, too well-coordinated, to be simply the result of chance or wicked human choice. The devil is characterized as "the enemy of the human race" and particularly the enemy of the Church. I challenge anyone to come up with a more devastatingly effective strategy for attacking the mystical body of Christ than the abuse of children and young people by priests. This sin had countless direct victims of course, but it also crippled the Church financially, undercut vocations, caused people to lose confidence in Christianity, dramatically compromised attempts at evangelization, etc., etc. It was a diabolical masterpiece."[34]

33   Amorth, *Memoirs of an Exorcist*
34   Bishop Robert Barron, *The McCarrick Mess*, www.wordonfire.org

That is not to say the priests who committed these heinous acts are not at fault, they are. They cooperated with their will and intellect in the devil's plan to destroy souls, the souls of young boys and young girls who were molested and cooperated in the devils plan to destroy the church. It is very important to understand that the only reason why Satan and his kingdom would want to infiltrate and destroy the church is because the Catholic Church is the true church founded by Christ and the apostles. She is the bride of Christ, the kingdom of God on this earth that the gates of hell will not prevail against. This church is a target of the diabolical precisely because its ministers, the priests, preach the gospel, change bread and wine into the body and blood of Jesus Christ and forgive sins in the sacrament of confession.[35]

6. COMPLETE LACK OF ANY CRISIS STATE

"It is quite possible to have a **perfect case of diabolical possession** without any of the above-mentioned signs."[36]

"Evil sometimes comes in handsome packages"[37]

The sixth element of the nature of perfect possession is a complete lack of any "crisis state" in the possessed person. In traditional cases of possession or what I would call partial possession, the person switches between states of calm and normalcy, to states of crisis, in which all the classical phenomena surrounding diabolic possession occur. I wrote extensively about these phenomena in the introduction so there is no need to delve into them here. Pretty much all the theologians who define possession differentiate between the crisis state and the state of calm. Master theologian and writer on the spiritual life Father Garrigou Lagrange O.P. states:

"Two states are distinguished in possessed persons: a state of crisis, with contortions, outbursts of rage, blasphemous words; and a state of calm. During the crisis, the patient generally loses, it seems, the feeling of what is taking place in him, for afterwards he has no memory of what the devil has, they say, done through him."[38]

---

35   The reason I have such deep respect for Ed and Lorraine Warren is because they understood this concept perfectly, which is in direct contradistinction to the vast majority of modern day "ghost hunters" who don't really understand these concepts at all.
36   Szymanski, *Truth About the Devil*
37   Ann Rule, *The Stranger Besides Me*
38   Garrigou Lagrange O.P., *The Three Ages of the Interior Life*

In cases of perfect possession there is no switching back and forth between crisis and calm. What this comes down to is these people do not look possessed, they don't fit the stereotypical, possessed person, like the man Jesus met at the tombs of Gerasa who was very violent, had outbursts, broke chains asunder, etc. At the 2007 Mundelein Conference on Healing, Deliverance, and Exorcism, Father Fortea was asked a question about a topic like this, and what he ended up saying was that if we were to pray for or attempt to exorcise people like "Hitler, Himmler, or Hannibal Lector," that there would be no reaction, no crisis state[39]. The reason is because these people have accepted the diabolical spirit voluntarily, their will identifies with that of the diabolic, they live in harmony with the presence of the diabolic, and there is no struggle or resistance of any kind. The reason there is a crisis state in partial possession is because there is a struggle going on between the person and the possessing demon, that manifests itself in a crisis state. The demon is forced to fight for his possession and comes to the surface, at which points there is a very clear difference between the human personality and the diabolic personality. In cases of perfect possession, it is impossible to differentiate between the two personalities, diabolic and human. It is if the two have become one, that is why I think Father Preuss' descriptive definition of "mystic marriage of the human mind with the diabolical"[40] is such a good one. Father M describes it as "seamlessness":

> "either the host personality is worn down and finally submits altogether or submits willingly to make a kind of new bond or covenant with the demonic presence, and then the two become **integral,** there is a sort of **seamlessness** here. I refer to it as integral possession. **Where there is no longer any manifestation of struggle or resistance because that's stopped.**"[41]

Father Bamonte describes this in the following way:

> "As someone who belongs to the Devil and has become his direct collaborator, the consecrated Satanist **undergoes neither the crisis state nor manifests the symptoms of those who suffer the extraordinary action of the Devil.**"[42]

And also, Father Euteneuer:

39   Father Fortea, *Mundelein Conference on Healing, Deliverance, and Exorcism,* 2007
40   Preuss, *A Handbook of Moral Theology*
41   Father M, *Mundelein Conference on Healing, Deliverance, and Exorcism,* 2009
42   Francesco Bamonte, *Diabolical Possession and the Ministry of Exorcism*

"Perfectly possessed people look like normal human beings and may often be well respected members of the community."[43]

Father Euteneuer also states,

"Such people do not exhibit satanic behaviors, appearances, or tendencies in public, and no one would ever know they are possessed. They offer no resistance to the devil because they freely consent to his being in them."[44]

Malachi Martin also has something to say in this regard:

"As the term implies, a victim of perfect possession is absolutely controlled by evil and **gives no outward indication, no hint whatsoever, of the demonic residing within."**[45]

Father M., at the Mundelein Conference in 2008, when speaking about perfect possession stated:

"When someone reaches that spot, where the demonic no longer shows itself independently so we can distinguish, or we can see struggle, or there are indications of freedom, one against the other. **When that happens it's very hard to see if there is anything wrong at all**."[46]

Father Syquia in speaking about the same topic states:

"These people do not exhibit the patterns of the crisis state of the possessed"[47]

Father Adolf Rodewyk also speaks of this concept in his book, both in his own words and while quoting Winklhofer. In speculating that many criminals on the worldwide political scene very well may be possessed, Winklhofer notes:

There are more of them than can be observed from the outside … **all characteristic symptoms of *obsessio* were absent.**[48]

Father Rodewyk himself while commenting on Winklhofer and pondering these same possessed criminals on the worldwide political scene

---

43 Euteneuer, *Exorcism and the Church Militant*
44 Euteneuer, *Exorcism and the Church Militant*
45 Martin, *Hostage to the Devil*
46 Father M, *Mundelein Conference on Healing, Deliverance, and Exorcism*, 2008
47 Syquia, *Exorcist: A Spiritual Journey*
48 Rodewyk, *Possessed by Satan*, It should be noted that Father Rodewyk is German Jesuit and in this passage is very likely speaking about Adolf Hitler.

speculates that the crisis state in these individuals may still be present but just very well camouflaged. Father writes:

> In reviewing Winklhofer's ideas, it is necessary to point out that a "criminal on the worldwide political scene" might very well be possessed. This need not show in his daily work, except that he would display an unusually great capacity for work, unusual energy, and a virtually uncanny feeling for interrelations and dangers in his daily activities… **In such a person, the unique excitement of the possession crisis might very well be camouflaged** by strong emotions and much shouting.[49]

Earlier in this study I also quoted Father Rodewyk in another passage in which he states the same concept, basically that it is a common misconception that possessed people are forever ranting and raving and so out of control that their condition is easily recognized. Father Rodewyk notes that there is a certain type of possessed person who may not display the common signs of possession,

> When Satan wants to unleash his powers, he must seek to use a possessed rather than an obsessed person. The Antichrist and his predecessors would have to be possessed human beings. One tends to resist this concept, because of the common misconception that a possessed person is forever ranting and raving, completely out of control, and so violent that his condition can be easily recognized; thus, it is falsely assumed, he could not have any effect on the world around him.[50]

Lastly father Rodewyk notes:

> "a demonic or Satan **controlled** man who may be able to go about his life under excellent camouflage, while doing an enormous amount of damage."[51]

Lastly Father Stang, in his classic work writes about the same people,

> "And though his outward appearance be clean and respectable, --he may be dressed in latest fashion and in costly garb and move only in refined and cultured society,--in reality he is a cesspool of iniquity, a bag of worms, a grave of corruption."[52]

---

49   Rodewyk, *Possessed by Satan*
50   Ibid
51   Ibid
52   Stang, *The Devil: Who He Is and What He Does*

In a later chapter I will also have the occasion to quote Father Jeffery Steffon who wrote a book about satanism titled, *Satanism: Is It Real*. While speaking about the Illuminati Father Steffon states that these people are diabolically possessed, but they are also professionals and they can appear to be "totally normal"[53] because they "have given their total will and personality over to Satan."[54]

In one of the above quotes Father Euteneuer notes that perfectly possessed people "look like normal human beings" and do not exhibit satanic behaviors in public. There are many examples of this that will be cited later in this study however for the purposes of this chapter I would like to quote Ann Rule, who knew Ted Bundy personally. Rule notes that Ted was the epitome of normalcy. She writes about Bundy that,

> Ted has been described as the perfect son, the perfect student, the Boy Scout grown to adulthood, a genius, as handsome as a movie idol, a bright light in the future of the Republican Party, a sensitive psychiatric social worker, a budding lawyer, a trusted friend, and a young man for whom the future could surely hold only success.[55]

Knowing what we know now about Ted Bundy and his crimes leaves one speechless as to how he could present such an air of respectability and normalcy on the outside yet be a diabolic monster on the inside.

I will again give the example of Judas, whom the scriptures tell us was possessed by Satan himself, yet he displayed no crisis state. Also, the Pharisees who kept trying to betray and kill Christ, who Christ said their father was the devil, who Christ said about them,

> "for you are like whitewashed tombs, which outwardly appear beautiful, but within they are full of dead men's bones and **all uncleanness**."[56]

Neither did they display a crisis state. Nor did Christ attempt to exorcise them. Neither did Peter attempt to exorcise Ananias and Sapphira, nor did Paul attempt to exorcise Elymas who he called "a son of the devil." Neither did St. Peter exorcise Simon Magus, whom he said was "in the bond of iniquity" and neither did any of these people labeled as being in league with Satan display any crisis state or traditional signs of possession whatsoever.

---

53   Steffen, *Satanism: Is It Real*
54   Ibid
55   Rule, Ann; Rule, Ann. *The Stranger Beside Me*. Estate of Ann Rule in conjunction with Renaissance Literary & Talent. Kindle Edition.
56   Matthew 23:27 NAB

7. Lack of An Aversion to the Sacred

The last element of the nature of a case of perfect possession regards a lack of an aversion to the sacred. An aversion to the sacred is one of the hallmarks of any case of classical or partial possession. Father John Gmeiner, in his *The Spirits of Darkness and Their Manifestations on Earth*, while speaking about the signs by which a demoniacal possession can be distinguished from a fraudulent case states:

> "to show an instinctive horror when blessed objects, as, holy water, etc., are applied, and to indicate no such feeling when not blessed objects of the same kind, as common water, etc., are used."[57]

In a case of perfect possession there is no aversion to the sacred in the traditional sense.

Malachi Martin states:

> "He or she will not cringe, as others who are possessed will, at the sight of such religious symbols as a crucifix or a rosary. The perfectly possessed will not bridle at the touch of holy water or hesitate to discuss religious topics with equanimity."[58]

To answer the question of why there is no aversion to the sacred is a little more difficult. I would speculate that one of the reasons is because of the strength, power, and place in the hierarchy of the devils who are in control of the perfectly possessed. I do not think it is the work of lower level demonic spirits to permanently and perfectly possess someone. Even Uncle Ponto, who was a low-level spirit, had a very powerful superior, that he had to answer to. If Jamsie Z would have totally consented to full possession, it probably would have been this superior, who would have done the actual possessing and controlling. I believe firmly that it is very often an entity from the Satanic hierarchy[59] that is responsible for a perfect possession. We also see this in the case of Jay Beedem[60]. Whenever Jamsie would get close to Beedem, Uncle Ponto, Jamsie's familiar spirit, would act afraid and completely disappear. In the book Jamsie thought the sudden disappearance of Ponto meant the approach of someone he feared. From what we know of demons, we know that the diabolic hierarchy is ruled through fear

---

57   Gmeiner, *The Spirits of Darkness and Their Manifestations on Earth*
58   Martin, *Hostage to the Devil*
59   Diabolic entities that rule over other legions of demons and that are in direct league with the devil. The names of some of these entities have been given in the scriptures and can be found in ancient grimoires. Many of these entities were worshiped as Gods in ancient civilizations. These entities very likely all fell from the supreme hierarchy, the Thrones, Cherubim, and Seraphim.
60   Martin, *Hostage to the Devil*; see Chapter "Uncle Ponto and the Mushroom Souper"

and subjugation of the lower spirits to the higher ones. Additionally, before Jamsie met Jay Beedem for the first time, Ponto told him that he would not be able to appear as often as normal because "I have my betters."[61] We also see this in the case of Gary Lyttle, who became the object of an evil spirit that called itself Tyrannus (sole ruler). The first time Gary had a vision of this entity it was sitting on a throne in a cavernous pit. Furthermore, Gary described the entity as extremely tall and huge.[62]

Theologically a lower level demon probably does not have the strength of will and intellect to completely and permanently take over and enslave a human being like the higher devils do. The lower demons do not have the power to completely subjugate a human being's will and body and control that person in all aspects of their life. We also see perfectly possessed people engaged in evil on a much greater scale, a much more universal scale. This would also make sense considering what we know of the intellectual power of these higher diabolic entities whose co-natural infused intelligible species or forms are much more universal in their scope and nature.[63] Devils and demons act and work according to their natural abilities. That is why lower level demons will work on a much more individual scale, whereas the devils are working evil on a much more grand and universal scale. The reason this translates into a lack of aversion to the sacred is because these higher diabolical spirits have a much greater ability to resist things of a sacred nature, which I will speak more in depth about in a later chapter.

The second reason I believe there to be a lack of aversion to the sacred in perfectly possessed people is because "the sacred," churches, priests, sacraments, sacramentals are all means of or vehicles of grace to human beings. In a case of partial possession where there is still some freedom of will and where the victim has not yet made a definitive choice for evil, these sacred things could be a means of grace for that person, eventually resulting in their being freed from possession. That is why the demonic will react so violently to them. They do not want the victim to be given any kind of grace or have any chance of being freed. Therefore, they will seek to destroy and deface these sacred items or act violently when they encounter them. In a case of perfect possession on the other hand, the victim has already pretty much rejected grace and wants nothing to do

---

61   The implication given by Malachi Martin is that Jay Beedem, whom Martin notes was perfectly possessed, was possessed by some type of higher-level diabolical spirit.
62   The appearance of an extremely tall or huge apparition of a diabolical spirit has been thought by some to indicate that the spirit is a higher-level diabolical spirit.
63   Collins, *The Thomistic Philosophy of the Angels*; Blackmore, *The Angel World*; Farrell, *A Companion to the Summa, Vol 1*

with it in the future. Therefore, there is no danger to the Devil if his host encounters the sacred, because grace cannot be given if the person does not want it and actually despises it. That is why Father Royo Marin says the following:

> "It is useless to try and win these people over by persuasion or advice. It will make no impression on them and may even produce contrary effects."[64]

And why Father Euteneuer says:

> "The exorcist should not have any illusion that he can save them but should leave these servants of the Devil in the hands of Almighty God and pray to the Holy Spirit for their conversion."[65]

The third reason I believe there is no aversion to the sacred in the classical sense and no crisis state is because in a case of perfect possession, anonymity and secrecy is paramount. This is how the Devil can use these people effectively to further his kingdom. If a perfectly possessed person had an outburst of fury and rage every time he encountered the sacred, the possession would be uncovered for what it is and the devil's work through that person would not be as effective or effective at all. As I've said previously, sometimes perfectly possessed people are respected members of the community and leaders. How are they going to work and plan evil in secret and make it look righteous if people think they are possessed or that it is the work of Satan. They would not be able to at all. Evil relies heavily on being disguised as something else to work effectively for the destruction of souls. While speaking about perfect possession at the Mundelein Conference, Father M stated:

> "When that happens it's very hard to see if there's anything wrong at all. Because all of it goes into hiding. It's very subtle. **It perfects itself as a force in the world disguised as something else**."[66]

Likewise, Pope Benedict, in his classic series of books on Jesus of Nazareth writes:

> "all the wiles and cruelty of the evil that **masks itself as life** yet constantly serves to destroy, debase, and crush life."[67]

---

64   Royo Marin, *The Theology of Christian Perfection*
65   Euteneuer, *Exorcism and the Church Militant*
66   Father M., *Mundelein Conference on Healing, Deliverance, and Exorcism*, 2008
67   Joseph Ratzinger, *Jesus of Nazareth*, Holy Week

If people knew the real nature of the evil spirits behind the major structures of sin in our culture, many of them would be totally terrified, disgusted, and probably moved to repentance. The greatest trick, in my opinion, of the evil one, is not to make people believe he doesn't exist, but to make people believe that good is evil and evil is good. One of the clearest examples of this diabolical philosophy can be found in the writings of Friedrich Nietzsche, who I believe to have been possessed. His writings and philosophy have infected a great many people over many years and have been the source of untold evil and destruction on this planet.

Even though an aversion to the sacred in the traditional sense is not present in cases of perfect possession, there is still an aversion to the sacred, it just takes a different form. At the end of the day, these spirits perfectly possessing people are fallen angels and they absolutely hate God and the things of God with a burning passion we humans cannot comprehend, and if we could comprehend it and knew the true nature of it in all its horror, we would be scarred for life. Therefore, this aversion to the sacred in cases of perfect possession takes the form of organized and deliberate blasphemy and sacrilege in different forms of devil worship like the black mass, where eucharistic hosts are often profaned in the most hideous, ghastly, and unspeakable ways. It could take the form of trying to undermine and corrupt church teaching to make it look outdated, archaic, stupid, ridiculous, discriminatory, and not with the times. It could take the form of murdering and desecrating people's bodies, which are temples of the Holy Spirit and used for the creation of new life. It takes the form of actively leading other people into sin and error, so that their souls become blackened; their souls that are made in the image and likeness of God and meant to live with God in heaven forever.

CONCLUSION:

This 7-prong nature of perfect possession has never been defined before. But if one studies these phenomena and intensely looks at these cases and all the literature on it, they all have these 7 things in common. This is completely and radically different than a case of partial possession which only contains 1 of the elements I just spoke about, the diabolic presence in the actual body. Traditional or partial possession absolutely displays a crisis state and an intense aversion to the sacred. Furthermore, in partial possession the will may not always be needed for possession, we have exorcist's testimony of small children being possessed due to generational curses for example. Yet in a case of perfect possession, full consent of the will is always needed. Furthermore, partially possessed people can sometimes be in the state of grace, yet perfectly possessed people are always in absolute moral depravity, their souls are completely the possession of Satan and their home will be hell for eternity. Lastly, partially possessed people can sometimes resist the moving's and suggestions of the devil, whereas in perfectly possessed people they are in complete slavery to diabolic forces and as Father Saudreau stated carry out his wishes "with such readiness and promptitude" which makes them deadly and destructive in society. I reiterate these things in this conclusion because it is extremely important to understand what exactly separates a case of partial possession from a case of perfect possession, how exactly they differ between themselves. Based on what I have written it should be very clear to the reader that they differ greatly.

I have very often pondered what is the most important difference between partial and perfect possession, what is the one thing that differentiates these cases the most. The answer must be found in the consent given to the demonic force. As I stated in the introduction cases of partial possession almost always start when some kind of door is opened to the demonic world, sometimes this door does constitute a giving of a kind of consent to allow the demonic in ones life. The reason these cases are partial however is because at some point along the line of the demonic/human relationship that has developed, the human person has decided for whatever reason that they want to be free of the infestation. This desire to want to be free, however small, then forces the evil spirit to fight more openly for the human person which causes all kinds of reactions, some paranormal, psychological, medical, etc...

In a case of perfect possession, while the human/demonic relationship is developing, the human person either step by step, or at some point in this relationship starts giving more and more consent to the evil spirit. In genuine cases of perfect possession, the human being in the end has given full and total consent to an evil spirit to totally, completely, and perfectly take over someone's life, to total and unquestioned diabolic possession. Because the human person is completely consensual, there are no bizarre phenomena normally associated with cases of possession. The evil spirit does not have to fight for its "home," it is now free to act through that person and begins to put in place well laid plans that come from superior evil spirits and that will result in some kind of evil being introduced to mankind.

CHAPTER 5

WHY DOES PERFECT POSSESSION OCCUR?

Now that we have looked at the three ways in which a perfect possession can be invited and have also defined the seven-prong nature of this state, we can endeavor to examine the reasons why perfect possession exists. To do this effectively we must examine the issue from the point of view of the human, the diabolical, and the divine. Examining why this terrible evil exists will not be an easy task. In Father Thomas Euteneuer's book, *Exorcism and the Church Militant*, he states:

> "We may never know why people so perfectly surrender themselves to the source of all evil"[1]

In the case of men, there are multiple reasons why they could become perfectly possessed. In some cases, and these are the most disturbing, the person purely hates God with a sickening passion, and wishes with the full force of their will to become a servant of the Devil. These people do not want to go to heaven, they desire to go to hell and spend eternity with the diabolic realm. They furthermore usually hate their fellow man as well, and are often very cruel to people, especially children, the elderly, and the disabled. They may even make it their mission in life to allow for the legal killing of these people. We know for a fact there are people in the world who advocate for the killing of the unborn, the elderly, and the disabled, they appear on the news often, and they disguise their vile work as being from a place of compassion. True Christians know better and can see through the deception. These people can become perfectly possessed in several ways, sometimes through formal Satanism and devil worship, but sometimes not. Sometimes they just make it their life mission to oppose all things holy, good, and beautiful and intentionally enter relationships with demons. They can develop these relationships with demons in a multitude of different ways and take these relationships to their absolute extreme. Father Vince Lampert spoke about one such person in an interview with the UK Telegraph:

There was a gentleman, his family contacted me. They were concerned about him and I went to visit him. He told me that throughout his life he had cultivated relationships with demons and with Satan and that when he died it was his desire to spend eternity with these demons. He said, 'I know my family is concerned about me, but this is the free choice that I make' So, in that case you really can't force an exorcism on someone against their will. We all have free will. We can pray that someone might have a change of heart. But this is someone who was heavily involved in the worship of demons. This man was perfectly possessed; he had established a harmonious relationship with the evil in his life. And he was not willing to have an extended conversation with me about it."[2]

The truth is we will never know why some people make this decision. Why some people, after seeing the truth, beauty, love, and mercy of God, decide to reject him completely and choose to hate him and embrace Satan. It is the mystery of our free will, it can be dangerous but also beautiful; on the one hand we can choose to feed the hungry, cloth the naked, comfort the afflicted, and preach the love and sacrifice of Jesus Christ or we can kill the helpless, persecute the needy, desecrate the holy, worship devils, and actively lead others into perdition.

Another reason, people choose to invite the diabolical explicitly is because they want something in exchange. Whether it is money, power, fame, or a host of other things. These people are fully aware that by committing this treason against God they will be damned upon their death. It does not matter to them, they would rather eat, drink, and be merry in this life than have eternal life in the next. Michael Patella writes,

"There are people who prefer the vain promises of the devil"[3]

And so, they sell their souls to the Devil in exchange for something and they agree to become an explicit servant of the Devil and to lead other people into sin. It seems so arbitrary to us, yet for some people money and power and the adoration of fame is everything, and they are totally willing to give everything to get it. It doesn't matter the cost, even if it is to the tune of their eternal soul, they still go through with it. Satan offered Jesus all the kingdoms of the world in all their glory and splendor, if he would just fall down and worship him. Jesus of course rejected him, but there are many others who are proffered the same deal and they readily accept.

---

2   Rachael Ray, Leading US exorcists explain huge increase in demand for the Rite – and priests to carry them out, www.telegraph.co.uk, Sept 26, 2016
3   Patella, *Angels and Demons: A Christian Primer of the Spiritual World*

It frightens me to think of these people on their death bed. Will they regret their decision and curse themselves for loving the pleasures of the world, which are so fleeting? Or will they curse the Devil for deceiving them into accepting this deal, or will they curse God and embrace the unspeakable horrors which await them on the other side of the veil. We don't know. I think many of these people do regret their decision right before the end, when they see the truly nightmarish consequences of their decision about to come upon them, and they fall into complete despair and do not repent. I think there is also a good portion who fully embrace their decision all the way to the end and go out with their nose upturned to heaven in a look of hardened pride and obstinacy. I think there is only a very small portion, and it only happens by miracle, that truly regret their decision and attempt to repent somehow before they die. The problem with this, is the Devil is not going to give up easily one who has been his, his whole life[4]. But in the end God's mercy is all powerful, and he promises us we can truly repent and display true contrition all the way up until the last breath leaves our body and our heart beats for the last time.

There are also people who do not make any explicit agreement with the Devil and who simply live their whole lives ignoring God completely and committing grave sin upon grave sin. This is the implicit form of perfect possession. These people choose to reject the gospel because they are comfortable in their sins, they are in a state of hardness of heart and will not be brought out of their stupor except, again, by direct miracle of God. Why people choose to reject the gospel and live their lives in mortal sin can happen for a plethora of reasons. It could be they just simply do not believe in the gospel, they believe it is hogwash, and choose to live their lives the way they want, exploring every pleasure imaginable. It could be they have some deep wound from their childhood or adult life which has caused them to hate the world and hate other people and hate God, who they blame for their state. I can't even tell you how many people that are out there who directly blame God for everything bad that happens in their lives. Some go so far as to curse him and completely reject him and then live lives full of sin just to spite him.

It might be that the person has no family, is extremely lonely, and so predisposed to getting into destructive relationships. People without any

---

4   In this case a major spiritual battle for the soul of such a person may ensue. Praying for such people on their death bed is so utterly important I can not stress it enough. Especially saying the divine mercy chaplet at the bedside of the person and entrusting their soul to the immaculate heart of Mary. Even having masses said for their soul after they die would be beneficial as all time is present to God at once.

kind of family at all are much more likely to readily accept the diabolic in their lives, which can take the form of cults, gangs, false religions, and particular grave sins. It also could be they have been completely deceived by false doctrines and doctrines of the world. The doctrines of materialism, moral relativism, sexual liberation, and the like. This is very common in today's culture, millions of people have been deceived into thinking sin does not exist, hell does exist, and there are no consequences to living a morally bad life. The thing that makes this so insidious is these false doctrines disguise themselves as doctrines of compassion, equality, and free choice. So, people think they are doing the right thing by fighting for abortion rights because everyone deserves the right to "choose," yet what they are really doing is advocating for the killing of the unborn, the most helpless among us and a practice that is unimaginably diabolical in nature. It would take a whole book to analyze all the reasons people choose the diabolic and choose to live their lives in complete debauchery and frankly I am not a psychologist and not really equipped to analyze in depth all the reasons people choose evil.

As a general principle however, when the implicit invitation to perfect possession has occurred it is usually because of hardness of heart and obstinacy, the free choice to disbelieve the gospel and become hostile to it, the love of pleasure above all else, pride, which is simply refusing to worship and bow down to God and obey his laws even though he very clearly deserves this worship, and deception, where someone has been completely deceived that evil is good and good is evil and that God is not a father but a cruel judgmental entity who doesn't want gay people to be happy, and doesn't want woman to have the free choice for abortion, and wants old people to suffer until natural death finally takes place, and who allows untold evils to overcome people, and who doesn't care about us or love us at all.[5]

From the point of view of the diabolic kingdom, there are a few reasons why they would perfectly possess someone. The first and most obvious reason is because they hate people and are jealous of people and wish to totally enslave them and then drag their souls to hell upon their death. It is clear that devils love to enslave human beings, this is an aspect of the warped diabolic nature. We see instances of this in the Old Testament.

5   This may seem ridiculous to a Christian to read this; however, these are things that people actually believe about God. One of the first lies that comes out of the mouth of Satan in the scriptures is a lie about who God is "You will not die." For God knows that when you eat of it your eyes will be opened, and you will be like God, knowing good and evil.." Our modern society is full of satanic lies about who God is, many of these lies are introduced into the world by people who are servants of the devil.

The Israelites being enslaved by the Egyptians who worshipped devils in the form of pagan gods. Anytime the Israelites strayed from the true God and partook of the illicit practices of their pagan neighbors God usually punished them by allowing them to be enslaved to the pagan nations and their pagan Gods, who are devils. In a later chapter when I speak about signs and symptoms present in perfectly possessed people, one of the signs is when a human being is able to totally enslave another human being or multiple human beings through a variety of means.

The second reason, and this one is clear from the literature and the records of exorcisms, that the demons experience some type of relief from hell when they have a human host. This is one of the reasons they fight so hard to keep their home. This was the case with the demon legion in the gospels and was also the case throughout Malachi Martin's book *Hostage to the Devil when the possessing entities scream out that they have lost their home.* It seems demonologist, Ed Warren holds this same view, that they somehow escape temporarily from the full effects of hell when they reside within the body of a human being. Father Chad Ripperger at the Mundelein Conference on Exorcism, Deliverance, and Healing also noted this same concept, that when the demons are in possession of someone, they somehow temporarily experience some type of relief from the misery of hell.

The third and most important reason a diabolic spirit would perfectly possess someone has to do with the cosmic battle between good and evil. Those who end up perfectly possessed are in some way important to the diabolic kingdom. This dark kingdom has its own plan for the destruction of the human race and the Catholic Church, and they strategically place their servants in specific spots all over the globe and in our societies where they will be able to do the most damage, body and soul, to their fellow man, and also further the interests of the diabolic kingdom. The true hard-core evils in the world that are truthfully satanic are not happening in traditional cases of infestation, oppression, and possession.

They are happening on Wall Street and financial districts all over the world, business districts, plush boardrooms in big cities in every country, and political capitols all over the world. Adolf Rodewyk writes,

> "it is necessary to point out that a "criminal on the worldwide political scene" might very well be possessed.[6]

---

6 Rodewyk, *Possessed by Satan*,

Likewise, in an excellent passage packed full of truth Father Thomas Euteneuer notes,

> "Satan is normally hidden in the "dark sea of human sin and error," like Leviathan of the Old Testament, but nowadays he is walking tall in powerful structures of sin like abortion, pornography, sex slavery, rapacious greed and terrorism. He flexes his muscles in the massive diffusion of errors and sinful practices like the doctrines of myriad false religions, pernicious ideologies like radical feminism and "pro-choice" extremism, the militant homosexual movement and the aggressive mass media which is the ministry of propaganda for Satan and all his works and all his empty promises."[7]

True hard-core evils are happening in medical clinics, filming studios, palatial estates on Long Island, Malibu and the Hollywood Hills, music recording studios, publishing houses, and fancy apartments in the Vatican[8]. They are happening in courtrooms, secret government facilities, and illegal drug manufacturing centers in places like Mexico, Columbia, and Afghanistan; they can even happen in legal drug manufacturing labs in places like Stamford, CT, where a company that resides there is basically responsible for the entire opioid crisis and the destruction of millions of lives in exchange for billions of dollars[9]. True evils are happening at radio stations, mainstream media newsrooms, universities, scientific laboratories, and video game design studios. They are happening in places like Davos, Switzerland where the elite of the elite in business and finance meet yearly, they are happening in places like the Bilderberg Hotel, the original meeting place for the Bilderberg group and also happening in whatever places the council on foreign relations, trilateral commission and the club of Rome meet, all of which are organizations made up of powerful people meeting in secret, plotting who knows what kind of evil. They are happening from Palo Alto, L.A., and Paris to the deserts of Syria, Iraq, and the ghettos of Chicago. These evils are perpetrated by evil men and women, some of whom are explicit servants of the devil and indeed perfectly

---

7   Euteneuer, *Exorcism and the Church Militant*
8   I am referring to the fact that there were a number of priests and others involved in a drug fueled homosexual orgy in the Vatican apartments in the same building as the Congregation for the Doctrine of the Faith. This type of depravity in the direct vicinity of the CDF and taking place in the Vatican is a clear indication of diabolic activity. I always remember what Ed Warren once said that "the devil can be found in the shadow of the church"
9   Purdue Pharma, a massive multibillion-dollar corporation and the maker of addictive painkiller OxyContin© has been attributed by many as being the original source of the opioid crisis in this country. It is known that Richard Sackler aggressively pushed for the sale of OxyContin and also mislead doctors as to its potential for abuse. The actions of Purdue and Sackler in particular have contributed to the destruction of millions of lives.

possessed. The people running this world system[10] who are servants of Lucifer have set up this system of "the world" with their masters help to make sin look fun, glamorous, normal, natural, fulfilling, and necessary. Juan Carroll Cruz notes,

> "Having studied here the operations of the devils, we can well surmise that it is **they who inspire the many violent and sexually explicit movies that have prompted many of the crimes we so often hear about in the news. Likewise, we may justly consider that the devils inspire the many tv programs, soap operas, and bestselling novels which depict explicit sexual encounters and the seeming glamour and romance of sexually loose living.** All such immoral activity plays straight into the plan of the devil for the damnation of souls. In addition to the productions of the movie industry, **the books emerging from secular publishing companies depicting violence and explicit sexual immorality surely also have their inspiration ultimately from the devil.** Many of these immoral books get onto the fiction shelves of our public and school libraries, even though they should have no place next to the classics."[11]

In an also excellent passage that clearly teaches this concept, Father David McAstocker writes,

> "Human beings are tricked in devious ways. They prefer the temporal and ephemeral to the eternal, the flashy and colorful to the solidly real, the subjective to the objective. And who are the deceivers? Thousands upon thousands of teachers who, under a **false cloak of culture and science spread abroad all kinds of false philosophy. Journalists and magazine writers who use the printed page to spread false ideas among their readers. Dramatists and script writers who use the stage and the screen for the propagation of scurrilous and lascivious notions. Men and women of various ages and positions in life- all marching, either consciously or unconsciously, under the aegis and impulse of that archdeceiver, Satan."[12]

Lastly Zsolt Aradi notes that,

---

10 The scriptures constantly condemn something called "the world" which is really the kingdom of Satan, made up of devils and servants of the devil, institutions and people who are all marching under the flag of Anti-Christ.

11 Cruz, *Angels and Devils*

12 McAstocker, *Speaking of Angels*

118

"The devil infiltrates everywhere, the church as well as philanthropic institutions. Assuming many forms he can become the man of the world, the busy businessmen."[13]

This is the supreme goal of the kingdom of evil really. That through diabolical dupes set in high places, a world system has been set up with powerful structures of sin, all to lead men and women over the precipice and into the eternal pit of hellish torment. The devil has no greater goal than to lead people into hell. The way he does it is not by appearing personally, like he did with Christ, but to use human beings to lead other human beings into evil. Some of his human servants are not explicit servants of the devil, some are implicit servants, convinced they are doing the right thing in the name of equality, choice, compassion, science, and progress; implicit or not, they are still servants of the devil, even though they do not believe so. And though probably in the minority (hopefully) there are also present explicit servants of the devil, who are in these high places doing the devil's bidding intentionally. Intentionally corrupting souls and leading them by the hand into eternal damnation. Intentionally seeking to carry out the will of Lucifer on a daily basis.

In the book *Hostage to the Devil*, Malachi Martin wrote about a perfectly possessed man named Jay Beedem. One overlooked fact about Beedem is that he was the manager of a radio station. The significance of this is easily overlooked, however ask yourself how many people a radio station influences on a daily basis, how many people listen every single day. A perfectly possessed man in charge of a radio station is now able to influence these people on a daily basis by introducing things on the radio that on the surface may not look harmful or destructive, but actually slowly lead people away from God. This is a major part of why people are perfectly possessed and what they then do once they are. The reader will also recall chapter 4 in which I related the case of Gary Lyttle from the book the Dark Sacrament. The devil who propositioned this boy to fully accept possession showed the boy that he would be a wealthy businessman, working in a large office, with a big desk in a big city, this again is a detail easily overlooked, nevertheless it is extremely significant to understanding why people are perfectly possessed.

I also just recently read an article penned by the National Catholic Register in which famed movie director Frank Capra felt that towards the end of his career Hollywood turned on him and did not want him to make movies any longer that contained moral and Godly themes, movies such

---

13   Aradi, *The Book of Miracles*

as "You Cant Take it With You" and "It's a Wonderful Life." In addition to feeling Hollywood had turned on him, Capra believed that the devil himself had tempted him one evening to start making immoral movies.[14] This story on the surface may seem insignificant or just a story, but for me it is very significant. I am convinced that two industries that may contain the most perfectly possessed people are the film industry (Hollywood) and the music industry. These two industries form the larger (entertainment industry) which in today's world of 2019 is thoroughly diabolic. These industries are used by Satan and his servants to totally corrupt young minds and adult minds for that matter. These industries blatantly glorify serious sin, depravity and occultism and make Catholic morals and belief seem stupid, outdated and not hip. In the next chapter I will quote a few entertainers from this diabolical industry who openly admit that they are either possessed, in league with the devil or have sold their souls to him.

This subject is going to be a bit of a mystery from the point of view of God. Some might ask why he would allow for such an evil as perfect possession. Right from the start we can answer with free-will. God created us as totally free beings, with a right to choose good and evil. Our free-will is a very powerful and very dangerous thing, but it can also be very beautiful, because it can be used to love God and our fellow man, which is the reason God created us as free beings. God, over and above all desires that we love him as he loves us, the only way that love is legitimate is if it is done through a free choice of our will. God does not want people who are robots and who are forced to love him. He wants us to come to know him, and through knowing him, love him. There is risk involved in this though, there is risk involved in creating free beings, the angels and man. We can on the one hand choose to love him, as our father, our creator, and our savior or on the other hand we can choose to totally, irrevocably reject him, hate him and serve Lucifer. There are people in the world who, knowing God, knowing his beauty, his power, his mercy, his care for us, still choose to hate him and reject his offer of love and salvation. There are other people, who's sin may be less serious who despise God in some way because they feel they have been wronged by him in some way, or they are deceived as to who God is. The point is that we can choose to reject God, if we want, and this is the reason there must be a hell. There must be a place for those people to spend eternity who want nothing at all to do with God, which is what hell is. God is beauty, love, mercy, light, joy,

14   Matthew Archbold, Frank Capra vs. The Devil, *National Catholic Register*, Nov 28, 2018

120

and peace; hell, the place where God is not, is ugliness, hate, ruthlessness, darkness, and misery.[15]

As an extension to our being free beings, if we want we can reject God completely and at the same time choose to embrace the enemy of all things holy, Lucifer. We can choose, implicitly, or explicitly to become a votary of the devil, to be possessed by him and enslaved to him. When a human being wants this, either through a direct invitation or an indirect invitation and through their actions, God will respect our free will. He may not like it, he may even delay it to send the last graces of repentance, but in the end, he will let us have what we truly want. And if we truly want to become fully possessed and controlled by a devil and cooperate in the devils work of destroying souls, then God will allow it.

The other reason God may allow a perfect possession to happen is based on his justice. While it is true that God is a loving father and is extremely patient with us, he will only allow himself to be mocked for so long. If he is acting as a loving father and continually sending someone graces to repent and reconsider yet these attempts are constantly thrown right back in his face and spat upon, he will eventually stop sending the graces. He will allow, based on his justice, what we asked for by our actions.

The other side to this coin is are there cases in which God does not allow a perfect possession for some reason? I would speculate that, yes, there are cases in which he will not allow this evil to occur, cases where he puts a stop to it for various reasons. The factors that come into play here are three. The first is that it could be God is just so merciful with some people that he may not allow a perfect possession to happen even if someone explicitly asked for it or invited it. It could be that these people are meant to play a major part in the economy of salvation, they are just too important for God to give up on and he will do whatever it takes to save them. The second is that the victim may have someone in their life, maybe a patron saint, their guardian angel or a parent or relative who has made untold sacrifices for that person. They have spent day in and day out shedding tears for their conversion and salvation. They have had masses said, they have fasted, they have prayed rosary after rosary in front of the blessed sacrament. At some point this person's sacrifices can outweigh the evil done by the person and God will touch their heart in some unknown way, like only he can, to affect their conversion.

---

15   Martin von Cochem, *The Four Last Things: Death, Judgement, Hell, and Heaven*

The third reason he may not allow a perfect possession is because the person was deceived into entering a relationship with a demon and then were subsequently beat down, pummeled, enslaved and subjugated by the evil spirit totally. They have been so dominated by the superior angelic nature of the evil spirit that they have stopped struggling completely and have accepted their situation. God may choose to either stop these cases before they get that far and get the person help or deliver them in some miraculous way after the possession has reached its final stage. Again, God's justice is pure and righteous, and he knows these people who are perfectly possessed in this way are less at fault for their condition than the people who make explicit and implicit direct invitations.

As a last comment, I would like to say that we will never be able to discover all the reasons why this terrible evil occurs. That is why evil is called the mysterium iniquitatis. The mystery of iniquity, it is just that, a mystery that we cannot by design know everything about. God has revealed to us pretty much all of the information we need to know about it. He has revealed to us in the scriptures and through the church that there is an incorporeal entity at work in the world whose name was Lucifer, whose name is now Satan or the devil. He has revealed to us that this entity and his angels hate us, are jealous of us, and wish to deceive us and destroy us. He has revealed to us that there are human beings, acting via their free will who choose to fully give themselves to this evil entity and become his servants. He has also revealed to us that these people are enemies of God and the Christian faith and are sometimes located in positions of authority in our world.[16]

---

[16] There are various examples of this that are clearly enumerated in the scriptures.

CHAPTER 6

WHO CAN BECOME
PERFECTLY POSSESSED?

Let me start off by saying that people from every race, nation, creed, political leaning, economic status, educated status, and profession can and are perfectly possessed and have been throughout history. It would be impossible to examine this from every aspect. But if the person has willed it, the devil has desired it, and God has given permission, anyone can become perfectly possessed, it does not matter who they are, where they are from, what they do, etc.

It could be that regular middle to lower class people become perfectly possessed. Regular family men, who nothing appeared to be wrong with until they kill their whole family and then themselves.

> "When a father kills his wife and children, or when a boy buries a hatchet in his mother's skull because she refuses to give him more spending money, we have a reason to suspect that such monsters are possessed by a devil."[1]

Lower to middle class drug dealers who spend their whole lives destroying others via the poison they are selling. Middle class families who are deeply involved in satanism or witchcraft, sometimes multi-generational.

> "Today the ranks of black magicians are filled with ordinary people, clerks, factory hands, white collar workers, and professional men, all bonded together in a **devotion to evil**, sadism and the defiance of society's standards of behavior."[2]
>
> "We read now of businessmen, clerks, secretaries, and factory workers joining the ranks of the Satanists."[3]

---

1   Houck, *Our Friends and Foes or the Angels Good and Bad*
2   Haining, *The Anatomy of Witchcraft*
3   Haining, *The Anatomy of Witchcraft*

Serial killers like Henry Lee Lucas, who admitted to Bob Larson that he was a servant of the devil, a member of a satanic cult, and fully possessed by the devil. Larson notes,

'But the one thing I do believe is **that Satan controlled Henry Lee Lucas's life**. **He said so unequivocally**, and his life of crime bears testimony to some out of control malevolent force within him."[4]

Serial killers like John Wayne Gacy, Richard Ramirez, Ted Bundy, Jeffrey Dahmer, Gary Ridgeway, and David Berkowitz, the Son of Sam; who the evidence suggests, was not a lone gunman, but part of an organized satanic cult in the tri-state area[5]. It is interesting to note that David Berkowitz asked Malachi Martin to visit him in prison, which Martin did. Apparently, Berkowitz wanted Martin to write his autobiography, which Martin declined. Martin later claimed that Berkowitz was a perfect example of a case of perfect possession and it should be noted that Berkowitz is the only person (except Jay Beedem) that Malachi Martin ever positively identified as being perfectly possessed[6]. Martin was asked by Art Bell (Coast to Coast AM) on numerous occasions if certain specific people (President Bill Clinton) were perfectly possessed and Martin always refused to answer. The profound thing is that Berkowitz actually confirmed what Martin said about him. In an interview with New York Magazine, Berkowitz said something very revealing that is quite pertinent to our discussion:

"There is no doubt in my mind that a demon has been living in me since birth. As a child, I was fascinated with suicide. The demons are real. I saw them, felt their presence, and I heard them. You get into a state that is **so far gone your own personality is dissolved, and you take on these demonic entities**. It was like another person was in me. **Doing a lot of directing**. I struggled, but things became overwhelming. I lost my sense of myself. **I was taken over by something else, another personality**."[7]

---

4   Larson, *Larson's Book of Spiritual Warfare*
5   The great book *The Ultimate Evil* by Maury Terry goes into this case in depth. The facts of this case point to the fact that David Berkowitz was not a lone gunman but rather part of a very dark satanic cult in the greater New York and Connecticut areas that was responsible for the killings and the killing, skinning and sacrifice of untold German Shepperd's.
6   http://www.tribulation-now.org/2009/08/06/perfect-possession-father-malachi-martin/
7   Steve Fishman, The Devil in David Berkowitz, *New York Magazine*

Mass shooters like James Holmes[8] Stephen Paddock, Adam Lanza, Seung-Hui Cho, and Nikolas Cruz all of who never displayed any indications of being possessed. Although all four men did display various signs of some type of disturbance or mental illness. Lanza slaughtered 20 first grade children, seven adults, and himself on December 12, 2012. There are some very disturbing details in the life of Adam Lanza, that point to a problem of a spiritual nature, rather than just to mental illness. The main symptom present in Lanza's life is moral in nature, specifically the slaughter of young children and adults as well as his own suicide. There were also psychological symptoms that have been well documented since the shooting. I listened to a somewhat disturbing recording of Adam Lanza when he called in to a radio station about a year before the shooting, his voice is very robot like and metallic, it just sounds odd. Looking at his pictures after the shooting also gives one a sense that this person was evil, a confirmation that was also given by Lanza's father.

> Adam Lanza's dad says the boy would have killed him "in a heartbeat" and wishes his psycho mass murderer son had never been born. In a shocking new interview, Peter Lanza dubbed his gun-crazy boy "evil" for killing his mom, 20 kids, six staff and then himself at Sandy Hook Elementary School, Connecticut, on Dec. 14, 2012 You can't get any more evil," he told The New Yorker.[9]

Seung-Hui Cho committed the worst mass school shooting in American history, gunning down 49 people 32 of whom died at Virginia Tech University on April 16, 2007. Cho, like Lanza and Paddock also committed suicide. From everything I have read about Cho it seems he was a disturbed individual his whole life. He worried and disturbed his parents so much in high school that they went to their pastor for help, a very significant fact. Cho also had a particular effect on the people around him, he disturbed people and made people feel very uncomfortable. Several of his professors recalled very disturbing behavior from Cho and recommended he get counseling. According to news reports there were 6 teachers in the English department at Virginia Tech that were particularly disturbed

---

8   James Holmes in an interview with a court appointed psychiatrist claimed that before and after the shooting he would see shadows moving around him, additionally this same psychiatrist makes a comment to Holmes about how his pupils are extremely dilated giving him the look that his eyes are black and dead like. Additionally, Father Dwight Longenecker clearly has said that he believes James Holmes was taken over by an evil spirit.

9   Lee Moran, Adam Lanza was Evil and Would Have Killed Me in a Heartbeat says his Dad, *New York Daily News*, www.nydailynews.com, March 10, 2014

by Cho's behavior. Extremely significant is that one professor got the feeling from Cho that he was evil.

> Nikki Giovanni, a feminist poet and veteran teacher there, had been so unnerved by Cho that she confided to colleagues that she thought he was "evil," The Sunday Telegraph has learnt. The young Korean so disturbed Ms. Giovanni that in late 2005 she issued an ultimatum: either Cho was taken out of her class or she would quit. It then fell to Lucinda Roy, a Briton who was the departmental head, to try to teach the young man one-to-one, as other students refused to sit in the same room as him. She, too, was so worried by the threatening manner of the student, who insisted on wearing sunglasses and pulling his baseball cap low on his forehead, that she and her assistant worked out a warning system in case she felt in danger. [10]

According to survivors of the shooting Cho had a blank look on his face while he was shooting people, like he was in a trance. Stephen Paddock also never displayed any classical signs of possession although he did hold something in common with Adolf Hitler in that both men experienced night terrors. Paddock's girlfriend told a news outlet that Paddock would wake up screaming and sweating, screaming "Oh my God" over and over.

> "Marilou Danley, 62, said Paddock, 64, 'would lie in bed, just moaning and screaming, "Oh my God,"' according to an ex-FBI official briefed on the situation. Investigators - who interviewed Danley after she arrived back in the US from the Philippines on Tuesday night - believe that he may have been in 'mental or physical anguish,'"[11]

As we all know Paddock committed the deadliest mass shooting in American history in Las Vegas, NV in which 58 people were killed and hundreds injured. Beyond that, as of the date of this writing, the FBI still has no clear motive for this act of atrocity.

Just like Adam Lanza, Nikolas Cruz, and Seung-Hui Cho there are some disturbing signs in the life of Stephen Paddock that point to a problem of a spiritual nature. I read every news article I could find on Paddock and there are some very peculiar relatively unknown things in his life

10   Philip Sherwell and Tim Shipman, He Never Spoke but he frightened everyone, The Telegraph, April 22, 2007
11   James Wilkinson, Las Vegas shooter's girlfriend says he would 'SCREAM in bed at night' and investigators say he may have been in 'mental anguish' - but they STILL don't know why he murdered 58 people, dailymail.co.uk, Oct 5, 2017

that would not normally catch someone's eye or that would just appear as weird or peculiar. One example is related by a neighbor of Paddock who lived in Reno. When Paddock walked past his neighbor who was hanging Christmas lights the neighbor yelled out Merry Christmas to Paddock who ignored him said absolutely nothing in reply. This same neighbor said that Paddock would get up very early in the morning to go for walks but would always be very careful to not walk in front of their house. The assumption here is that this house may have had religious icons or statues in it that Paddock wished to avoid. Also significant is the fact that Paddocks father was a diagnosed psychopath who robbed a bank and then escaped from Federal prison. Paddock has also been described as a very powerful and convincing personality who could get people to bend to his will. This last thing is significant because it is present in all the people who I will be profiling in later chapters.

Mary Lou Danley in addition to relating that Paddock would wake up screaming and moaning also related to investigators that in the months before the attack Paddock would constantly complain that he was sick somehow. Danley told FBI officials that Paddock said he had a "chemical imbalance" and that doctors could not cure him. Even more disturbing is the fact that Danley who is a Catholic and attended mass several times weekly said that Paddock would very often tell her that "your God doesn't love me"[12]

In addition to Mary Lou Danley one of Paddock's brothers apparently told investigators that he thought his brother had some type of mental illness and was "paranoid and delusional."[13] Also significant is that multiple people relayed that in the months before the shooting Paddock seemingly became "obsessed"[14] with guns and mass shootings and also searched the internet repeatedly for information he could use to be a more effective killer. There was also a housekeeper who had a disturbing encounter with Paddock 4 days before the shooting. She was cleaning Paddock's suite at the Mandalay bay and while there Paddock sat, eating soup and staring at her the whole time. The encounter apparently disturbed the housekeeper and left her with a feeling of uneasiness.[15]

12   Ken Ritter and Michael Balsamo, FBI Finds no specific motive in Vegas attack that killed 58, Associated Press, Jan 29, 2019
13   Ken Ritter and Michelle Price, Las Vegas gunman became unstable but didn't raise suspicions, Associated Press, Aug 3, 2018
14   Ibid
15   Ken Ritter and Michelle Price, Vegas shooting papers hint some may have encountered gunman, Associated Press, May 16, 2018

There was also an FBI Behavioral Analysis Unit report compiled on the personality of Paddock which sought to try and find some type of motive for the massacre. Disturbingly the report notes,

> "The LVRP assesses that Paddock displayed **minimal empathy** throughout his life and primarily viewed others through a transactional lens of costs and benefits. Paddock's decision to murder people while they were being entertained was consistent with his personality. He had a history of **exploiting others through manipulation and duplicity**, sometimes resulting in a **cruel deprivation** of their expectations without warning."[16]

Beyond noting that Paddock may have wanted to gain the same infamy as his bank robbing psychopathic father, the report, the FBI, and the Las Vegas Metropolitan Police Department have found no solid motive for the massacre that killed 58 people and injured over 500. There are videos that have been released that show Paddock in the 5 days leading up the shooting in which he is seen arriving at the Mandalay Bay Hotel and Casino with multiple bags that we now know were stuffed with guns and ammunition. The videos show Paddock eating in the sushi bar, gambling at a video poker machine all night and taking the elevator many times up the 23rd floor bearing multiple suitcases. Commentators have noted that the videos are disturbing only because we know now what the gunman was planning and what was in his suitcases. Beyond that the videos are relatively unremarkable. They show a normal looking older man walking around the casino, talking to casino workers, that did not look or act differently than any other normal person walking around the casino. Paddock didn't have black eyes or a forked tongue or horns sprouting out of his head. He acted completely normal in the days leading up to the attack even laughing with hotel employees all the while planning to mow down with a hail of automatic weapon fire a crowd of thousands of people enjoying themselves at a music festival.

This is the nature of true evil, of perfect possession, it disguises itself very well, blending in with modern society so no one is the wiser. You could be standing next to a man of unfathomable evil in an elevator and never know it.[17]

---

16   Federal Bureau of Investigation, FBI Behavioral Analysis Unit's Key Findings in Oct 2017 Las Vegas Mass Shooting, Jan 30, 2019

17   The videos of Paddock show him sharing an elevator multiple times with many different people. Paddock can be seen talking with people and carrying his bags which were full of guns and ammunition. He can also be seen talking and laughing with the hotel employees, smiling at them and even tipping them.

We all know that this massacre committed by Paddock left many dead, injured, maimed and probably scarred for life. This man left a path of destruction that is extremely disturbing and profound. After the massacre and after the FBI returned the 23rd floor back over to the hotel, hotel workers were still extremely hesitant and many refused to go onto the 23rd floor, sensing some kind of evil there. The problem became so pronounced that the hotel brought in a Catholic Priest to perform a blessing in the room and on the 23rd floor. According to the priest who performed this blessing, he felt like he was "pushed back- as if to keep me from entering"[18] when he attempted to enter the hotel room. Pressing on, the Priest completed the blessing, hopefully casting out whatever evil dwelt in that room.

> 'The Rev. Clete Kiley told the Chicago Sun Times he felt surrounded by "the mystery of evil" when he conducted a Roman Catholic ritual in the room.'[19]

Because of the fact that Paddock, Lanza, and Cho all killed themselves immediately after slaughtering dozens of people, we do not know what their explanation is of why they did what they did. One mass shooter who did not kill himself however did live to tell authorities why he gunned down 17 students in cold blood at a Florida High School. And the disturbing answer from Nikolas Cruz, the Parkland school shooter, the devil told him to do it. This from the Washington Post:

> "He confessed to carrying out the massacre, police said. But he went on to say more than that, saying during a lengthy interview that for years he had heard a "demon" in his head giving him directions. When asked what the voice told him to do, the suspected gunman said: "Burn. Kill. Destroy" … He recalled never telling anyone about the voices but later acknowledged that he told his brother and, possibly, a girl he had dated. He asked the police to bring him a psychologist… He described hearing the male voice — one that told him "to hurt people" — every day, adding that it got worse after his mother died a few months before the massacre… In the portions made public, he is captured saying the voice ordered him to kill animals, told him to buy the AR-15 used in the

---

18   Associated Press, Chicago priest blessed hotel floor after Las Vegas Massacre, Oct 25, 2017
19   Associated Press, Chicago priest blessed hotel floor after Las Vegas Massacre, Oct 25, 2017

attack and directed him to take an Uber to the school. He also said the voice spoke to him the morning of the attack"[20]

The public defender for Nikolas Cruz has also stated that there is something particularly disturbing about Mr. Cruz, something in his 40 years of being a defense attorney he has never seen before. In the same article in the Washington Post, Howard Finkelstein, Cruz's public defender stated:

"He is the most damaged and broken human being I have encountered in 40 years of doing this type of work."[21]

That is not to say that I am making a pronouncement that Adam Lanza, Seung-Hui Cho, Stephen Paddock, and Nikolas Cruz were perfectly possessed, I am not. We must be careful with definitively labeling someone perfectly possessed. Because of the nature of perfect possession and the lack of crisis state, lack of aversion to the sacred, and really lack of any sign of classical possession as well as the fact that they can blend in well with modern society makes it very difficult to make this determination. All we can do is come to a reasonable assumption about a particular person based upon their life, actions, and fruits. Sometimes nothing can be known until after the person has already died or after the person has committed some act of unfathomable brutality, at which point we can go back and examine their life and find things, indications that there was a spiritual dimension to the problem.

The Columbine school shooters are also an example of mass shooters who may have had a negative spiritual problem that caused them to act out an act of murder. It has been documented that both kids were heavily involved in the occult, hated Christians, and even actively targeted Christians during their act of mass violence. Moreover, both shooters killed themselves after committing the depraved act of violence. Whenever a person commits some terrible act of depravity like ruthlessly murdering multiple people and then take their own lives as the final act of hostility towards God, we have very good reason to believe people like this may have been perfectly possessed or at least severely diabolically obsessed in some way. I hearken back to the passage I quoted in an earlier chapter from Alois Winklehofer in which he states,

"We must recall that Satan entered Judas (John 13:27); but the same applies to people who suddenly, without evident prehisto-

---

20   Mark Berman, Parkland shooting suspect told police he heard a demon voice in his head telling him: Burn. Kill. Destroy, *Washington Post*, Aug 6, 2017
21   Ibid

ry, **turn into criminals, attack children, and later kill them and who, when arrested, commit suicide.** When something as horrible as all that suddenly emerges from previously peaceful and apparently levelheaded personalities, there can hardly be any explanation but the impact of alien forces which in some uncanny manner have brought about the **dissolution** of an established personality structure."[22]

In addition to the people I have already highlighted, one more type of person that can and has become perfectly possessed are drug traffickers, drug lords and mob bosses. First, mob bosses and drug kingpins are almost always involved in some type of occultism. It is a well-known fact that drug lords in Mexico worship the devil in the form of Santa Muerte, an unholy and evil diabolic mockery of Our Lady of Guadalupe. Moreover, it is proven that these drug lords and drug traffickers worship this entity of death with human sacrifices. According to an FBI report this violence and ritualistic murder has risk of spilling over the border into the United States,

> "The latest variant of the Cult of Santa Muerte promotes extreme, corrupt, and criminal—**even evil**—behaviors. Law enforcement agencies need to provide a balanced, yet vigilant, response. The rise of a fully criminalized and dark variant of Santa Muerte worship holds many negative implications. Of greatest concern, the inspired and ritualistic killings associated with this cult could emerge across the border and manifest domestically in the United States."[23]

Moreover, we have to look at the general and overwhelming amount of evil these drug cartels are involved in. Not only are they involved in cult worship of the devil with human sacrifice, they also promote, partake in and order an appalling amount of bloody violence all over North America. Rival cartels kill other cartel members and this violence is everywhere, including in the United States. In 2017 alone over 25,000 people were murdered in Mexico. When one adds up the murders in Mexico due to drug violence over the last decade the numbers become appallingly staggering. Not only are the numbers of murders truly staggering but the epic brutality of these murders is also extremely disturbing. It has been said by many sources that rival cartels often drink the blood and eat various

---

22   Adolf Rodewyk, *Possessed by Satan*

23   Robert Bunker PH. D, Santa Muerte: Inspired and Ritualistic Killings, FBI Report. For a secular FBI agent with a Ph.D. to call any behavior "evil," an inherently religious term, I think is significant.

body parts of their rival cartel members whom they murder. Bodies are completed mutilated, headless corpses are strewn all over Mexican roads and bodies dismembered and hanging from bridges are a common sight.

> "in a particularly twisted initiation ritual, young members of the Jalisco New Generation cartel were forced to eat the hearts of murder victims. Local prosecutors claimed two teenagers, aged 16 and 17, remained unrepentant after they were drugged with crack then forced to eat human flesh **by senior cartel bosses.** A similar event took place in 2015 when hopefuls of La Familia Michoacana were forced to eat their rivals after torturing them and cutting them up while alive… Los Zetas cocaine kingpin Heriberto Lazcano, who was killed in a shootout with Mexican Marines in 2012, was notorious for feeding victims to the lions and tigers he kept on his ranch. But it was his practice of eating human flesh that thrust him into international headlines two years ago. A reporter who spent time with him told El Blog del Narco, "After sentencing him (the victim) to death, he orders him to bathe, and even to shave his whole body and let him de-stress for two or three hours, even better sometimes he gave them a bottle of whisky to relax, then he ordered a very quick death so there is no adrenaline in the meat to prevent it getting bitter or hard." He would then devour the man's buttock flesh in tamales after it had been cooked in lemon and served on toast."[24]

If that were not convincing enough for the reader, the cartels have also kidnapped and brutally murdered a great number of Catholic priests. These cartels also import thousands of tons of dangerous and soul draining narcotics into various countries in the form of heroin, cocaine, and methamphetamine. These drugs destroy countless lives. The people who are in the upper tiers of these drug trafficking organizations and are responsible for this unfathomable and pervasive evil are almost certainly perfectly possessed. The amount of pure evil that is originating in Mexico from the murders and also the narcotics sales is just too big to not be diabolically inspired. And there are specific people at the heads of these cartels that are directly responsible for this darkness.

The mafia is no different than the cartels, these also practice the occult and various ceremonies for initiation into the mafia. It is no different than a satanic cult, once you are initiated into the mafia and take that blood oath, you are in it for life, there is no getting out, except by death. To become a made-man in the mafia one must take a blood oath while burning a

24   Corey Charlton, Inside Mexico's drug gangs who force members to eat the hearts of their victims, news.com.au, Jan 20, 2019

prayer card of the Virgin Mary or another saint, a total and sick blasphemy and evil practice. These blasphemies have gone so far that Sicilian Mafia members have often been found to meet at Catholic shrines and perform their satanic rituals right under statues of the Blessed Mother. When one understands demonology, one also understands what a total blasphemy and mockery of the faith this is. Dripping one's blood on a blessed holy card and then burning it while uttering a blood oath of loyalty to the mafia, a murderous organization, is stunningly and utterly diabolic in nature.

How many crimes do the mafia engage in that corrupt our society, how many brutal murders can be attributed to these people? The answer is very many. These people are also very likely perfectly possessed, they are willing participants in the direct work of Satan; corruption of society, bribes to officials, occultism, blasphemy, mockery of the faith by claiming to be Catholic, all manner of crime, and murder are just some of the things they are involved in on a scale around the world that is monumental. Pope Francis summed it up very well on the spiritual state of mafia members when he declared:

> "They have nothing at all in them that is Christian. They call themselves Christians, but **they carry death in their souls and inflict it on others,**"[25]

One person who stands out in this regard and who was a very powerful and extremely ruthless and murderous gangster in the city of Boston was a man named Whitey Bulgar or James Bulgar. Bulgar was widely feared by many people, and he took pleasure in murdering people. He was believed by many to be totally evil. Tom Duffy, a retired State Police major who investigated Bulgar, said of Bulgar after he was arrested in 2011:

> "You could go back in the annals of criminal history and you'd be hard-pressed to find anyone as diabolical as Bulger... "Killing people was his first option. They don't get any colder than him,"[26]

This same thing has been said about many other brutal and murderous mafia figures as well. People like Carmine Galante who started his criminal career at age 10 and was diagnosed as being a psychopath as early as 1931. People like Al Capone, George Clarence (Bugsy), Lucky Luciano,

25   Rachael Cruz, Pope Francis says the Italian Mafia is not Christian, 'They carry death in their souls', www.christiandaily.com, March 28, 2018
26   Denise Lavoie and Alanna Durkin Richer, Whitey Bulger, Boston gangster, found slain in prison at 89, Associated Press, Oct 30, 2018

Meyer Lansky, Albert Anastasia, Anthony Accardo, Carlo Gambino, John Gotti, and many many more too numerous to list here.

There are also many historical personages that very well may have been perfectly possessed. People who started wars, heresies, attacked the church, brutal dictators, etc...

> "By the wise council of God, the devil is permitted to have a hand in the making of history. We cannot reckon without him, nor could we explain without him the superhuman perverseness of some historical personages, such as Cain, Pharaoh, Antiochus, Judas, Nero, Domitian, Arius, Mahomet, Luther, Voltaire, Robespierre, the Antichrist that is to come; nor the super human perverseness of associations such as continental freemasonry.... the reformation.... the French revolution and the present world war with its atrocities, sacrileges and immoralities."[27]

I could add many people to that list, and it is obvious that there have been people throughout history who have chosen to align themselves with and serve the Kingdom of Hell. The whole history of the world is a battle between good and evil. The people named by Dom Louismet are all known for attacking God by attacking his followers and murdering people or directly attacking the church in some way. The scriptures are clear that people like this who attack God and become his enemy and become a subsequent servant of the devil, become possessed by him. Judas is the best example we can provide.

Even though it is clear from history that people of every class can be perfectly possessed, I think the people that disturb me the most and cause the most destruction and ruin in our societies are the people who occupy high positions in our society. I am speaking of very powerful people on the world stage that are in politics, business, finance, education, science, law enforcement, entertainment, media, law, and most unfortunately religion. Some readers may think that this is too terrible to be true, that is sounds like a nightmare. It is a nightmare, but it is true. There are some very respected and highly educated Catholic priests as well as government agencies who believe this to be true. There is also a ton of evidence for this assertion, some of which we will be analyzing. Jesuit Father Joseph Husslein in one of the best books ever written on the spiritual world stated:

> "It is not excluded that the men whom **Satan rules** may enjoy the **utmost worldly distinction and respect**. More than that, such

---

27   Dom Louismet O.S.B., *Mysticism: True and False*

men may often profess the noblest motives, or assume an air of sanctity, that might deceive the elect."[28]

This should not be surprising to anyone who knows the bible and understands the true nature of the battle between good and evil, between the Kingdom of God and the Kingdom of Satan. The bible consistently condemns something called "the World," which can be defined as the collective society or kingdom of Satan made up of people, places, and institutions that are anti-Christ, that conflict with Jesus Christ and his kingdom, that work for darkness and oppose the light, and work to destroy the bodies and souls of men. This world or as it is better called "kingdom" intertwines throughout our material world and our societies. It is made up of many different people and institutions all held together by the power of the devil, his servants in high places, and the power of sin. There are businesses that are part of it, colleges and universities, medical facilities, banks, political capitols, countries, armies, charitable foundations, think tanks, production studios, courts, etc. Some of these people are explicit servants of the diabolical kingdom and are perfectly possessed. It is these people that are the true enemies of Jesus Christ. In an interview with Bernard Janzen Malachi Martin noted,

> "From the testimony of demons and the situations with which we exorcists are involved, as well as from what the church tells us, it is quite clear that what Lucifer is concentrating on today is groups. He concentrates on group organizations. Let's take my own country, the United States. Running right through its society, especially in government offices at the local, state, and federal level, including in Washington, Lucifer has acquired a phalanx of servants who do his bidding and do his bidding automatically. I have met some of them and they are completely possessed. They simply do his will morning and night. They are successful and have a very good time in life. They have a very good life as far as material things go. There are groups that carry out the devil's will."[29]

Like I stated previously this kingdom is held together and coordinated by the power of the devils, Lucifer who is its leader and finally the innumerable armies of demons marauding across the planet. There is some debate on whether the people that are a part of this kingdom are knowingly coordinating for this kingdom with other people or are they all being directed by the higher diabolical intelligence, it is an open question.

28   Joseph Husslein S.J., *The Spirit World About Us*
29   Malachi Martin, *The Kingdom of Darkness*

But the answer is probably both. The kingdom itself is directed by the supreme diabolical intelligence, however there is also some evidence that the human members coordinate amongst themselves as well, especially those human members who belong to the same coven, cult, or secret society. We know that there is in existence many different secret societies and cults in the world, but whether all these are connected and coordinate amongst themselves also is up for debate. Another way this Kingdom has been referred to historically by some of the saints was "The Mystical Body of Satan" in which all these people, institutions, and really all sinners were thought to be a part of.

> "Gregory the Great said, as you will remember, that all those who sinned, so long as they were under the influence of this sin, were members of the mystical body of Satan."[30]

One of the best-known secret societies, that is actually a high-end cult made up of very powerful people all around the world is the Illuminati. The Illuminati may very well be the top and most powerful cult in the world. The Illuminati was started in 1776 by a man named Adam Weishaupt. From the very beginning its members included very wealthy and powerful people including members of the infamous Rothschild family.

> "Over the following years, Weishaupt's secret order grew considerably in size and diversity, possibly numbering 600 members by 1782. They included important people in Bavarian public life, such as Baron Adolph von Knigge and the banker Mayer Amschel Rothschild, who provided funding. Although, at first, the Illuminati were limited to Weishaupt's students, the membership expanded to included noblemen, politicians, doctors, lawyers, and jurists, as well as intellectuals and some leading writers, including Johann Wolfgang von Goethe."[31]

In more modern times there have been a plethora of researchers, victims, exorcists, and therapists who have all confirmed the same thing; namely, that there exists in the world a very high level satanic cult that pulls strings behind the scenes, that is called the Illuminati. Father Jeffrey Steffon writes that,

> "The top-level Satanists are sometimes called the illuminati, pure worshipers of Satan. **These people are possessed, but they are**

also professionals. Because the illuminati have given their total will and personality over to Satan, they can appear to be totally normal. They appear as angels of light, but in reality, are dedicated to darkness. Hard-core Satanists wish to remain unknown.[32]

I noted the above quote in an earlier chapter, when I was discussing the fact that people who are perfectly possessed display absolutely no crisis state or aversion to the sacred in the traditional sense. This is exactly what Father Steffon notes. He notes that the Illuminati who are "professionals" are indeed possessed but can appear to be "totally normal" because they have "given their total will and personality over to Satan." The above quote by Father Steffon is a very important passage that helps us to understand perfect possession and it also simply confirms all the other quotes from various authors I listed above. In similar fashion to Father Steffon, Daniel Ryder notes of the illuminati that,

> "Many cult survivors, and others in diverse research areas around the world have independently stated that the international leadership of the cult is called the "Illuminati."[33]

In a very important and relevant passage to our discussion Father Malachi Martin also stated,

> "There is an international organization which is formally dedicated to Satan. We know that its members include some very important people. It includes people whose names you see in the international news. Many of them are very prominent, whether they are financial people, politicians, academicians, or diplomats. They always seem to bunch together and support each other. They are engaged in arranging treaties and international trade agreements. They are involved in the United Nations. We are certain that this organization exists, but we have no name for it. It is a shadowy organization which reaches its black hand and changes everything. We do not know much about it, but we do know that it is very powerful. The men who comprise this organization are not sitting around in a cellar with heavy hats and kneaded brows, looking sharp and evil. They are often respected individuals who want to do away with religion."[34]

---

32 Jeffrey Steffon, *Satanism: Is It Real?*
33 Daniel Ryder, *Cover up of the Century: Satanic Ritual Crime and World Conspiracy*
34 Malachi Martin, *The Kingdom of Darkness*

In this passage by Malachi Martin he simply confirms what other authors and speakers have stated, that there exists in the world a dark shadowy organization, which is really a cult that is made up of very powerful and wealthy people who are utterly devoted to the service of Satan. Martin does not explicitly state that this organizations name is the illuminati, but it is the illuminati that he is essentially referring to. Lastly Author Laurie Matthew notes that,

> "There are some groups that seem to recruit individuals by invitation only and the higher up the group, the more selective and secretive it becomes. Somewhere at the top of it all, many survivors believe, there are groups such as the Illuminati."[35]

The above statement from Father Steffon in which he notes that true hard-core Satanists wish to remain unknown is very true. The secrecy that is involved in this type of satanic activity is essential to its existence and success. Because of this there is a lot we do not know about this organization of evil. A lot of what we do know comes from cult survivors who have worked with Catholic exorcists and therapists. What we know for sure is that it exists, operates in the modern world of 2019, has been operating for possibly hundreds of years and is extremely powerful and influential and includes some of the most prominent people in the world.

In addition to the Illuminati we also know that there are satanic cults all over the world that are made up of very powerful people that also hold positions of authority in our society.[36] Places like New York City, Los Angeles, Washington D.C., London, Paris, Sydney, and Brussels are some of the places where these high-end covens or cults operate. It would seem that the very high-end coven or cult structure in the world is usually not multi-generational (except in the case of very prominent and powerful familial lines) but made up of people who hold powerful positions or are wealthy and influential. It is not completely known how these people are approached to enter the cult, but we do have evidence to suggest it may involve in some instances, blackmail.[37] It has also been suggested that entrance into these powerful covens only occurs by invitation and

---

35   Laurie Matthew, *Where Angels Fear: Ritual Abuse in Scotland*
36   It should be noted however that not all satanic cults are comprised of wealthy and powerful people. Some cults or covens, which are mostly trans-generational are made up of regular middle to lower class families, sometimes occurring in extremely rural areas as well. The phenomena of multi-generational satanism will be delved into in Appendix A.
37   In the case of Jeffrey Epstein evidence has been uncovered to suggest he was heavily involved in the blackmailing of wealthy and powerful individuals. More will be said about the Epstein case in a later chapter.

that after a very long period of consideration and possible intel gathering to blackmail the person into staying in the cult once they are in. A good example of this was shown in the movie The Firm, with Tom Cruise. In this movie Cruise is a lawyer for a big law firm but later finds out the firm is controlled by the mafia and is involved in some extremely illegal activities. When Cruise's character tries to leave the firm, he is blackmailed into silence and staying in the firm and being complicit in the illegal activities. The blackmail tool being photos of him and a prostitute engaging in sexual activity on a beach which was of course a set up to get damaging information against his character. I think that entrance into these cults operates in the same fashion. Once in the cult there is no getting out, and if an attempt is made the person or their family will either be killed or completely and totally ruined in some way.

I would now like to examine some statements from churchmen, authors and governments regarding the existence of these people. I would like to start with Father M. who I would describe as one of the senior most figures behind the scenes in the exorcism ministry in the United States. He is a professor at a major East Coast University, works in the Vatican on a commission and gives advice to Bishops all over the U.S. on exorcism and is involved with teaching and training priests in this ministry. This priest is highly educated, highly respected, greatly revered and his word carries great weight. At the 2010 Mundelein Conference on Exorcism, Deliverance, and Healing he stated the following:

> "And then I would say this, there is another class of person who becomes possessed and gets themselves involved in very formal covens, very high-end social covens. They do not enter these covens because of psychological or personal distress, they enter them as a form of social self-promotion. They enter them because they hold public office, because they are ordained ministers, they are professors, medical doctors, teachers and pillars of society. They enter them because of other motives and reasons, not to say that once in them they don't experience damage or warping or difficulties. But their kinds of possessions and what they are interested in, the power and the network and the gain they get from these things, they are of a different class of person. They are the most frightening people that I have ever met. Because as theologians divide up stages of possession, there is this final thing called **perfect possession**. It is when the individual wills fully and completely some kind of contract with a demonic being, and they do not resist it, they con-

sent to it. It is rare, but there you have it, and they become highly destructive in society, almost a kind of insidious hard to put your finger on, but whatever that guy does, somethings up there. **These people have high positions in our society.** Father J did you tell them about the priest from Ohio? Priests find themselves involved in covens, priests find themselves murderers, priests find themselves sacrificing live human beings and so forth. Businessmen, pillars of society, attorneys, law enforcement. There is a high-end coven structure in the United States that does this, and something to be very careful about."[38]

This statement from Father M is very profound indeed and scary. I know a lot of readers of this book will refuse to believe that this could possibly be true, that there are people who occupy high and important positions in our society that are completely and totally taken over by the devil and spend day in and day out in faithful service and loyalty to the prince of this world. I understand that line of thinking, you don't want it to be true, it's too terrible a reality to consider. I myself would like to be able to say that he is wrong, that all the authors I am quoting are wrong. Unfortunately, through years of research, and a veritable mountain of evidence, this author has concluded that this is indeed true. That this high level of evil does in fact exist in our modern society and most frighteningly that it is increasingly being practiced out in the open. This is qualitatively different than even just 50 years ago when all this stuff was really underground and secret.

Although very secretive, you can sometimes get an inkling or have a suspicion about a particular powerful person by watching and reading about their actions and life. What are they working for? Are they secretly providing funding to build Christian missions in Africa, feed the hungry, cloth the naked, and comfort the afflicted or persecuted, or are they secretly pouring money into causes like abortion, gay marriage, movies and tv that directly undermine the faith or make sexual sin appear to be natural, normal, and ok? Are they funding entities like the Freedom from Religion Foundation, are they promoting anti-Christian or anti-family laws? Are they the founders and organizers of foundations and global initiatives that work in secret to undermine the faith and breed corruption and pay to play scandals? Are they secretly funding nonprofit organizations like "Media Matters" who consistently attacks traditional and Christian values? Are they the organizers of conferences that talk about the coming

---

38   Father M, *Mundelein Conference on Healing, Deliverance, and Exorcism*, 2010

"great reset"?[39] Are they entertainers whose music videos contain a phalanx of blatant occult imagery? Are they politicians and other prominent figures who through and through display blatant deception on a daily basis, does it appear that there is "no truth in them"? The old saying from Jesus Christ is always applicable in these instances, "you shall know them by their fruits."

Additionally, occasionally, this level of evil is brought out into the open and we catch a glimpse of it. Every once in a while, these people themselves, entertainers are a prime example, admit that they are possessed or in league with the devil and have sold their souls to him. Beyoncé, Nicky Minaj, Kesha, Ozzy Osbourne, Jimmy Page and many more too numerous to list here have all admitted to in some way being possessed or influenced by evil forces.[40] I want to give some concrete examples of this, so I will quote a few of them. However, the reader should know that I could cite page after page of quotes from musicians, actors and entertainers either admitting they are possessed or that they have made pacts with the devil. Here are some examples:

> "I swear I wanted to be the Amy Grant of music, but it didn't work out and so I sold my soul to the devil." Katy Perry

> "All you people out there, Satan is my master. He has always been." Justin Timberlake

> "I don't know if I'm a medium for some outside source. Whatever it is, frankly, I hope it is not what I think ... Satan." Ozzy Osbourne

> "I am definitely drawn to the occult" Kesha

> "We do worship the devil" Nine Inch Nails

> "I sold my soul to the devil; I'll never get it back" Eminem

> "I sold my soul to the devil; I know it was a crappy deal" Kanye West

> " I grew up in a very Christian environment — a very healthy environment and a loving a family — but there were parameters that

39 Michael Bloomberg recently hosted a conference with the World Economic Forum that included the likes of George Soros and other globalists, in which the primary topic was the so called "great reset," which these globalists are using, along with the COVID-19 19 pandemic to attempt and remake our world into something other than it is now. It is entirely possible they are working toward a one world government and new world order which will probably be the kingdom of Anti-Christ.
40 Another example is the extremely popular entertainer Eminem, who has an alter ego he calls Slim Shady and has been said to put curses on his music. Another example is the bluesman Robert Johnson who is said to have sold his soul to the devil, after which he became a guitar virtuoso. Another prominent example is John Lennon who admitted in the open that he sold his soul to the devil and that this was the reason for the Beatles success.

I didn't understand, that I questioned it, and it took me until my adult years until I could really try new things... That was satanism, it works really well, I made a pact - Brad Pitt

"If you sell your soul to the devil, you get more grain." – Drake

"I sold my soul to the devil." – DMX

"I don't give a damn if I go to hell." – Madonna

"In the music industry it's still very much this exploitative thing, it's still very much people signing their lives away, ya know the old deal with the devil stuff. That is still going on, it's unbelievable in this day and age that's it's still going on" - Billy Corgan, The Smashing Pumpkins

"Interviewer: Why do you still do it, why are you still out here.

Bob Dylan: Well it goes back to that destiny thing and I made a bargain with it you know a long time ago and I'm holding up my end.

Interviewer: What was your bargain?

Bob Dylan: To get where I am now

Interviewer: Should I ask who you made the bargain with?

Bob Dylan: (laughs) with with with with ya know with the chief, ah the chief commander.

Interviewer: (incredulously) on this earth?

Bob Dylan: (laughs) On this earth and in a world we can't see.

Sometimes victims come forward, multiple victims all alleging the same depraved acts by rich and powerful people. Sometimes news stories appear detailing just the surface of these terrible acts. Sometimes police and investigators who have kept their integrity get a little bit too close to the truth, some of these have been killed, violently.[41] In multiple instances massive cover ups have ensued, people have been silenced, threatened, killed, and even victims charged with perjury for spotlighting the activities of some rich and famous personages. I will be analyzing some examples of this from recent memory in the next chapter. When I say this evil is increasingly being brought out into the open what I am referring to are events like the opening of the longest tunnel in Europe in which European leaders presided over a blatantly satanic presentation,

European leaders, including German Chancellor Angela Merkel, French President Francois Hollande, Italian Prime Minister Matteo

---

41   See the next chapter and the case of Gary Caradori and the Franklin Scandal.

Renzi, Liechtenstein Prime Minister Adrian Hasler, and Austrian Chancellor Christian Kern took part in the opening of the world's longest tunnel, running 57 km under the Swiss Alps. The historic event was overshadowed by the opening ceremonies which contained blatantly satanic and graphically sexual overtones.[42]

I am referring to Super Bowl halftime shows that are blatantly satanic, Madonna's and Katy Perry's are prime examples. The opening ceremonies of the Olympics or the world cup. I am referring to music videos and performances by various artists at the Grammy's and Music Video Awards.[43] I am referring to blatant satanic imagery in advertising, and for that matter blatant occult and luciferian symbolism all over the world including in places like the Israeli supreme court building[44], the bank of America building[45] in New York city, Rockefeller plaza and the Denver international airport. and I could go on and on.

In addition to Father M there is also another priest, Father Joseph Brennen who talks about the fact that cult members who are explicit devil worshipers can be very prominent members of the community. Father Brennen is an expert on the subjects of satanic cults and satanic ritual abuse. He has been working as a counselor and therapist helping people and healing people who have been damaged by involvement in satanism for many years. He has been recognized by his bishop and bishops from surrounding areas regrading his expertise on this subject. In his book, The Kingdom of Darkness, Father Brennen writes:

"Cults also vary in the make up of their membership. Some are composed of teenagers and adults; others are for adults only. Some members may be incorrigible, anti-social teenagers, **while others are pillar of the community types who may be the president of a bank, a leader in a church, or the otherwise respectable businessperson who's been active in community betterment projects for many years.** You just never know."[46]

---

42   Life Site News, Europe's top leaders watch bizarre satanic ceremony opening world's longest tunnel, June 6, 2016

43   There have performances by certain artists that have been blatantly satanic and outrageously blasphemous. Nicky Minaj's performance at the 2012 Grammys in which she came dressed as a nun with a mock pope as a stand in and in which she conducted a mock exorcism ritual and also mocked numerous different Catholic sacraments is a prime example of what I am speaking about. Not only should Minaj be condemned for this blasphemy but the powerful producers of the Grammys who allowed this blasphemy to be on national television are also gravely at fault.

44   This building was bought and paid for by the Rothschild family and contains a stunning amount of occult imagery and symbolism.

45   Contains giant paintings with blatant masonic and occult imagery

46   Brennen, The Kingdom of Darkness

I would like to quote next two passages from studies conducted by government agencies. The first is the well-known report by FBI Agent Kenneth Lanning that investigated the existence of satanic ritual abuse. When this report is read it becomes clear Agent Lanning does not believe in the existence of these high-end satanic cults. He lists a whole bunch of other mumbo jumbo of what these reports could be, but he still concludes in the report that no large-scale satanic cult conspiracy exists that is ritually abusing children and committing human sacrifice. Agent Lanning does however admit of the existence of something he calls "Multidimensional Child Sex Rings." When he goes on to describe these child sex rings, they have all the same characteristics of what a satanic cult would have. Knowing this information, and knowing that these things exist, I was a bit flabbergasted that this FBI agent still concluded that large scale satanic cult activity does not exist. When I investigated it further it seems there is very substantial evidence out there that points to the fact that the FBI has in the past and continues to cover up high end satanic cult activity. The speeches and works of Ted Gunderson, the former head of the FBI office in Los Angeles documents this issue very well.

There is an absolute mountain of evidence that these cults do exist in our society if you know where to look. I will be sharing some of that evidence as this book proceeds and will also highlight some of it in Appendix A. While Agent Lanning is describing these multidimensional child sex rings, he states the following:

> "The multiple offenders are often described as members of a cult or satanic group. Parents, family members, **clergy, civic leaders, police officers, and other prominent members of society** are frequently described as present at and participating in the exploitation."[47]

The next passage, which is very similar to the previous quotes comes from a report done by the government of South Africa regarding human trafficking. In the section entitled "Human Trafficking for Satanic Cults" it is stated:

> "**Members of satanic cults are usually white and are often affluent members of society, including doctors, lawyers and businessmen (including women).** One police officer said he had heard of the practice of human sacrifice by satanic cults as well as snuff films allegedly perpetrated by such cults. The respondents

said if these cults are unable to acquire victims from local criminal syndicates they resort to kidnapping-often from rural areas.
Respondents said satanic cults often operate with the assistance of
corrupt SAPS officials. The respondent in question even provided researchers with an opportunity to view a recording of a satanic
ritual that involved the sacrifice of a human being."[48]

This report was commissioned and approved by the National Prosecuting Authority of South Africa. Some readers may say, well this is half-
way around the world in Africa. I would reply that yes, this report is from
South Africa, however South Africa is a westernized country. All areas
of the globe have their own occult inculturation, where human diabolic activity takes a specific form. In Mexico it's worship of Santa Muerte
and Brujeria (Mexican Witchcraft), in Haiti it is Voodoo, In Cuba it is
Santeria, in the Congo it's Palo Mayombe, in Brazil, Macumba. It just so
happens that in western countries like the U.S., Canada, Britain, Australia, and most of Europe, that the form of inculturation diabolic activity
takes comes in the form of organized, underground and sometimes very
high level satanic cults that practice satanic ritual abuse of children, human and animal sacrifice, black masses, and orgies. You will notice that
the passages from the U.S. report and the South African report are almost
identical, both stating that prominent and affluent members of society
engage in this type of activity and that from official government reports!
These two reports simply confirm what Father M, Father Brennen, Father
Steffon and many other Catholic exorcists and those working in this ministry have said regarding higher end satanic cults that count as members
affluent, wealthy and powerful members of society.

I would next like to quote all the things Malachi Martin has to say on
this subject. I know that Malachi Martin was a very controversial figure
that had a lot of rumors swirling about his life. Here is what I know about
Malachi Martin. I know that he was an extremely intelligent, brilliant and
highly educated Catholic priest and Jesuit. Martin completed his initial
schooling in Dublin and then went on to study at the Catholic University of Louvain in Belgium. It was here that he earned a doctorate in ar-
chaeology, oriental history and Semitic languages. After this he started
postgraduate studies at both the Hebrew University of Jerusalem and at
Oxford University in the UK where he studied intertestamentary studies
and knowledge of Jesus Christ and of Hebrew and Aramaic manuscripts.

---

48   Republic of South Africa, National Prosecuting Authority, Tsireledzani; *Understanding
the Dimensions of Human Trafficking in South Africa*, Research Report, March 2010

He also undertook additional study in rational psychology, experimental psychology, physics and anthropology. Malachi Martin was also one of the very first persons to study the Dead Sea Scrolls. The fruit of this research produced a book *The Scribal Character of the Dead Sea Scrolls,* published by the University of Louvain in 1958. He also published 24 articles on Semitic paleography in various journals and did extensive archaeological work in Egypt. It was in Cairo, Egypt that Martin first encountered exorcism. He also was the private secretary to Cardinal Bea SJ during the second Vatican council. Additionally, he was a professor at the Pontifical Biblical Institute in Rome where he taught Aramaic, paleography, Hebrew and Sacred Scripture.

In the year 1965 Martin requested a release from the Jesuit order. Martin claimed that he was granted a release from the Jesuits as well as a release from his vows of poverty and obedience, keeping the vow of chastity. Martin claimed he fulfilled and kept his vow of chastity till the day he died. Author Michael Cuneo believed that Martins claim in this regard was correct and called it "qualified exclaustration"[49]. In 1966 Martin, still an ordained Catholic priest (he was never laicized, just released from certain vows) moved to New York City. Martin claimed that upon his arrival he received written permission from Cardinal Terrence Cook to exorcise his secular priestly ministry. Unfortunately, there is no proof of this, however, I see no reason why the Cardinal would not allow Martin to exercise his priestly ministry especially if it was under obedience to the Cardinal. Martin was an extremely highly educated Jesuit priest with direct contacts and ties to the Vatican and the Cardinal probably counted Martin as a great asset to have in his Archdiocese. Martin claimed till the day he died that he was a priest, that he said mass every morning.

The part of Martin's life that gets a bit dubious is his involvement in the exorcism ministry. It is known for sure that he practiced major exorcisms, what is not known is if he had permission from the ordinary to do so. I can tell you that Martin claimed he had permission from some authority located in the Vatican, and this may not be totally unbelievable. Keep in mind Martin was a highly educated and brilliant Catholic priest with many connections to the Vatican, he taught there and worked there for years. What I know is that Malachi operated in the late 60's, 70's, 80's and early nineties. This was a time when there was barely a handful of full time authorized Catholic exorcists in the United States and the whole topic of the devil and possession was treated with scorn in most chanceries. He

49   Cuneo, *American Exorcism: Expelling Demons in the Land of Plenty*

worked extensively with people like Ed and Lorraine Warren, John Zaffis, David Considine, and Ralph Sarchie. All these people have spent their lives helping people diabolically afflicted. I know for a fact that Ed Warren, whenever possible would go to the Catholic Church with proof papers and attempt to get sanctioned exorcisms for people in need. If he was denied, and he was often, this is when he would go to people like Bishop Robert Mckenna and Malachi Martin for help. The Warrens overall goal was to help people afflicted in this way, and if that meant an unsanctioned exorcism, then that is what they did. I believe this is what Martin was doing. I think he saw an unbelievable need for exorcism and tried to help in any way that he could. There can definitely be a debate on whether this was the right course of action or not. On the one hand I know the church canon law explicitly states a solemn exorcism cannot be performed without the permission of the local ordinary. On the other hand, what moral responsibility did Martin and people like the Warrens have to help people who were diabolically afflicted when the church hierarchy would not. It is a tough question indeed and will be left open.

Overall, I think Martin was a highly educated, brilliant Catholic priest until the day he died. I think he tried in the best way he knew how to help people. I think he was human and was not perfect and was a sinner like the rest of us. I see no reason to denigrate his name with some of the rumors that are out there about him. I know that he had a very profound effect on the people closest to him, and that these people loved him and cherished his friendship very much. I also know that Martin because of his extensive work in the Vatican in his early years, remained in contact with and maintained many different Vatican sources and contacts. Martin died in 1999 of a brain hemorrhage after falling from a ladder in his apartment. He stated before he died that he did not fall but was indeed pushed off the ladder by a demonic entity. Retaliation in the case of Martin from the diabolic is not surprising considering all the information Martin knew and had in his possession regarding various topics like satanic cults, exorcism and possession and priest pedophilia.

Keeping all this in mind about the life of Malachi Martin I can state unequivocally that he spent a good portion of his later life talking about high level satanic cults. He gave multiple interviews on Coast to Coast AM in which he talked about this frequently. He also detailed a high-level satanic cult in his book *Hostage to the Devil*. In the book he writes about a man named Paul who was a successful businessman and millionaire who introduces Richard/Rita to a satanic cult that subsequently partakes of a black mass at a very large estate somewhere on the outskirts of Chicago. Martin also spoke about these things quite extensively in interviews he gave with Bernard Janzen. This is what he had to say on the matter of high-level satanic cults and prominent people who are perfectly possessed.

"The peculiar thing is that these people are usually highly sophisticated, and the last thing you would suspect is that they were in league with the devil."[50]

"The perfectly possessed are often completely urbane. They are calm, clean, and efficient. They are good doctors, good lawyers, good architects, and good bankers. They are good painters, artists, and dancers. They are beautiful people. Except they are not beautiful. They are not beautiful at all. They are perfectly possessed."[51]

"As I said before, there are thousands of covens in America. These are worshipping covens and they are not composed of ignorant men and women. These people are not lacking intelligence. They are not jobless or homeless, no! They are doctors, lawyers, architects, and brokers. They are painters and dancers. They are even cardinals, bishops, priests, and nuns."[52]

"My dear man, you should have seen the last coven we had to deal with. I mean it was a galaxy of names if you wanted anything done in medicine or finance in New York City or Albany, the state capitol. In this coven there were topflight people, perfectly well behaved in normal life. There were family men, family women, and high society members. And, oh! They were known to people. Some of them were very well-known names in New York and probably in Washington too. It is really only the perfectly possessed that frighten me. I met some of them in Washington and elsewhere in this country. They frightened me because they were so completely dedicated."[53]

"Every day, on the major international stock markets in places like Tokyo, Singapore, Frankfurt, Paris, London, and New York, billions of dollars are sloshed around in stock deals. There are millions of small investors all over the world. Yet, there are only a handful of financial people who dominate all those markets. They know what is going on. They govern money. They govern the daily flow of capital and capital goods to and from each country. And without this daily flow of capitol a country dies. They not only govern money, but they decide who lives and who dies. They decide! And we are

50   Malachi Martin, *The Kingdom of Darkness*
51   Ibid
52   Ibid
53   Ibid

convinced that they are firmly in the camp of Lucifer. They serve his aim, which is to create a world without God, and which is inhuman, in our sense of the word. They have a lot of power."[54]

Let us for a quick moment examine some of these statements from Malachi Martin. The first thing that is clear regarding the existence of very topflight and powerful people involved in devil worship and who are perfectly possessed is that Martin's statements are substantially similar to all the quotes I have already listed regarding this issue. It is not like Martin was the only one saying these things. There are multiple different people and even government agencies all saying the same thing, namely that there is in existence in the U.S. and the world very high-level satanic cults made up of very prominent, wealthy, and powerful people. Also, when Martin talks about bankers, lawyers, high society members and politicians in Washington being involved in cults and covens and being perfectly possessed, he is probably referring to the Illuminati. He references this topic in the below quote but does not explicitly name it the Illuminati. Martin writes,

> "There is an international organization which is formally dedicated to Satan. We know that its members include some very important people. It includes people whose names you see in the international news. Many of them are very prominent, whether they are financial people, politicians, academicians, or diplomats.[55]

There have been many people and many sources who all confirm the same thing, that the most powerful cult or satanic organization in the world is the illuminati that is doing a lot of the directing and work of the kingdom of Satan. As far as the rest of his statements, they will be borne out with the proceeding information. Considering Martin's education, intelligence, and extensive work in the exorcism ministry, I think his statements are profound, and should give all of us great pause.

Rev. George Mather, director of the New England Institute for Religious Research has also spoke about the fact that very prominent and sophisticated people can be involved in satanism. During an interview about some of the dangers of Halloween, Mather stated:

---

54   Malachi Martin, *The Kingdom of Darkness*
55   Ibid

"The serious-minded Satanists tend to be upper-class, well-educated sophisticated types. They look at the world and say `evil's winning. I want to be on the winning side."[56]

Lastly, I would like to examine the case of an ex Satanist who is now a very prominent Catholic and member of the deliverance and charismatic renewal communities. Her name is Betty Brennan and at one time in her life she was deeply involved in what she calls "upper echelon satanism." After the death of her daughter, Brennan, who played the cello, decided to join an orchestra in the greater New York area. She quickly befriended the head cello player in the orchestra who she describes as an older man who was also a practicing psychologist. She was eventually led to a party with this man where she was introduced to the practice of devil worship. She goes on to say that she became very deeply involved and was involved with everything short of human sacrifice. At a talk in which she relayed her conversion story, Betty Brennen states:

> "I played the whole game, and it didn't really show because basically an upper echelon, that's the deceit, it really doesn't show. It's only the people that are in lower echelon that are on the drugs and the alcohol and have all the other problems that people look at. But it's the guys that are really behind the scenes that are calling the shots that nobody really seems to go after in the 4th, 5th, and 6th echelon which are basically the prominent people of society, your doctors, your lawyers, your physicians, your psychologists. These are the people that are shooting and calling the shots."[57]

At another talk on spiritual warfare Betty stated:

> "And I got really, really involved. These were not basically your average people. They were educated people, they were fine musicians, some of them were wonderful teachers, some of them were professors."[58]

While Betty had a conversion and left the coven, she still had problems for years afterward. She has relayed stories about attacks on her and various harassments. At one of her talks she relayed the story of being sideswiped by a vehicle after leaving a prayer meeting, the people who hit her cried out to her "where is your God now." She also states that she

---

56   Donald Blount, Lutheran Minister Will Share His Views of Occult, *The Morning Call*, Oct 19, 1992
57   Betty Brennan, *Trappings of the Occult*
58   Ibid

received many threatening phone calls from cult members beckoning her to come back to the coven. She finally got free of all of this and now works extensively with Father Richard Maclear doing deliverance and exorcism all around the world.

Betty Brennan, a woman who has personal experience with this type of satanism has confirmed what all the other authors I have quoted stated. Betty identifies "prominent people of society"[59], doctors, lawyers, physicians, psychologists, musicians, teachers and professors that are involved in upper echelon satanism and perfectly possessed. Despite the fact that Betty does not explicitly use the term perfect possession this is essentially what she is referring to when she says that the people involved in this type of satanism don't appear to have problems or be possessed, that the people involved in this are behind the scenes and calling the shots. Betty Brennan has also referenced the illuminati in some of her talks, so she is another reliable person who confirms the existence of this powerful cult.

Some readers may be absolutely shocked that three of the authors I quoted above have stated that it is possible that ministers, Catholic Priests and even Bishops may be involved in the practice of Satanism and indeed be perfectly possessed. Father Brennan, Father M, Malachi Martin, and Agent Kenneth Lanning all referenced Catholic Priests or clergy being involved in devil worship in the context of perfect possession. This is the one area I do not like to talk about much, because it is frightening and disturbing. Although frightening and disturbing it certainly is not surprising. If we really believe that the Catholic Church is the one true church founded by Jesus Christ and his apostles, that has the true bread of life and the other sacraments, then we can be certain this church and its ministers will be the primary target of attack of the Kingdom of Hell. Ed Warren was once asked as a general rule where can the devil be found to be at work, Ed replied that primarily the devil can be found to be lurking in the shadow of the church, the Catholic Church, as he and Lorraine were practicing Catholics. This simple statement from Ed Warren is so true on many levels and presents a deep understanding of demonology. Father Brennan, Malachi Martin and Father M are not the only priests who have talked about this either. There have been other priests who have said similar things and there is also direct evidence out there of some priests, very few, being involved in ritualistic satanism. Father Dwight Longenecker is one such priest who spoke briefly about this; in doing a review about Malachi Martins book *Hostage to the Devil* and the topic of perfect possession, Father Longenecker stated regarding the perfectly possessed that,

> What is most disturbing, however, is something I suspected for some time. Malachi Martin talks about those who are "perfectly possessed." In other words the demonic possession is complete. These people no longer exhibit the preternatural signs and beastly manifestations and revulsion at the crucifix, a priest or the Eucharist. They are able to outwardly practice their Catholic religion, but inwardly they have given themselves completely to Satan. These individuals may be functioning (on the outward level) perfectly adequately as Catholics–**even priests, bishops and religious– but they are Sons of Satan. These are the ones who subvert the faith and turn the faithful to the darkness while appearing, on the outside, as angels of light.** The writers of the New Testament were well aware of these false teachers. St Paul warns about them. St John calls them beasts and the anti-Christ.[60]

We have to remember also that even though these men are ordained minsters of God, they still have free will and most regrettably some of them choose to turn away from the path of God and choose to give themselves over to Satan. Another very well-known Catholic Priest who has mentioned this is Father Gabriel Amorth. In an interview with The Telegraph Father Amorth stated:

> "The evil influence of Satan was evident in the highest ranks of the Catholic hierarchy, with "cardinals who do not believe in Jesus and bishops who are linked to the demon," Father Amorth said."[61]

It is very important to understand that the Catholic Church and specifically her priests are priority number one for destruction and corruption by the dark forces of evil at work in the world. The devil does everything he possibly can to destroy, undermine and corrupt our church. This is partly why the Blessed Mother has been so insistent in some of her apparitions to pray for our priests. This is why the church asks us to pray for priests. This is why praying for priests is so important and crucial. Catholic priests bring the real presence of Jesus Christ out into the world for the salvation of mankind, they consecrate bread and wine into the body and blood of Christ, they preach the gospel and forgive sins; for this they at-

---

60   Father Dwight Longenecker, *Hostage to the Devil*, www.dwightlongenecker.com
61   Nick Squires, Chief Exorcist Says Devil is in Vatican, *The Telegraph*, March 11, 2010

tract the particular scorn of the devil and his angels. An American exorcist who operated in the late 1800's and early 1900's stated,

"The forces of hell also try to corrupt priests. The demon who brags about ruining Judas and who parades under that name is planning with his associates to bring about deception, corruption, and destruction of priests. Their one aim against priests is to make them traitors. There always have been such, and there will be such in the future. This demon admitted that he is in charge of all the sacrileges and is the cause of every type of betrayal. It is his aim to seduce priests to carry out his plan. He takes the future into consideration: "There will be many apostates," he said, "and I will use your priests to erect my own church."[62]

"Satan has attacked priests, and the priesthood of the church like no other group, knowing that in this way he is attacking the source of power in the church. Priests make present the sacrificial body and blood of Jesus on altars around the world, and as long as priests are holy and continue their priestly worship, Satan and his forces are bound. So, the most concentrated attack of Satan has been on priests."[63]

A pressing question in this matter must be; how in the world could a priest be perfectly possessed considering their everyday life of performing the sacraments and encountering the presence of Christ? I think one of the answers lies in the strength and hierarchy of the devils possessing them. I said in the last chapter that I did not believe it was the work of lower level entities to perfectly possess people, that this is probably strictly the domain of the higher level diabolical spirits. When we read the scriptures, we find that some demons are absolutely terror stricken upon coming in to contact with Christ, not so for Satan himself. Satan boldly approached Christ and dared to tempt him. Not only dared to tempt him but dared to exorcise his power over him by moving his body to the parapet of the temple and the top of the high mountain and further dared to proffer Christ the kingdoms of the world if he would bow down and worship him. This is a far cry from the panicked demon of Garasa who begged Christ not to send them to the abyss. We also can remember the episode of the boy possessed who even the apostles could not liberate, the apostles who were to be ordained by Christ himself, this after these same apostles had already been successful in many exorcisms. It took Christ himself to come

---

62   Ed. Theodore Geiger, Trans. Celestine Kapsner, *Mary Crushes the Serpent: 30 Years' Experience of An Exorcist Told in His Own Words*

63   Father George Kosicki C.S.B., *Spiritual Warfare: The Attack Against the Woman*

and liberate the boy. I could also site the case of St. Paul and the girl with the oracular spirit. Even though Paul was successful in liberating this girl, he was immediately and violently retaliated against by the spirit. Being hauled before the judges by the girl's masters and the crowd chanting to have them beaten and whipped, which they were and then subsequently chained with a stake in a prison. The violence of the retaliation and the coordination between the girl's masters, the judges, the crowd and the prison guards are an indication of the strength of the spirit Paul exorcised from the girl.

Theologically speaking, Satan or Lucifer, and some of the other princes and rulers of hell fell from the highest choirs of angels, the Cherubim and Seraphim. These angels were created in the highest choirs, in the highest hierarchy to serve directly at the throne of God and ceaselessly contemplate his awesome majesty. They were (and the holy ones still are) the closest to God, both in what their functions are and also in their nature and faculties. Simply speaking, it was infused into their very nature to be close to God. Not only that but the Seraphim's overarching characteristic is love, they are on fire with love for God. Love is accomplished in the will primarily. Therefore, the seraphic angels must have wills of such power and brilliance that we can only begin to comprehend. What all this translates to is the fact that these fallen Cherubs and Seraphs, now being devils, whose nature were closest to God, are now uniquely able to tolerate the presence of God, even though they hate him. They are able to come into contact with the sacred and holy and deal with it, so to speak, much more effectively and for much longer than can their inferior associates. This is precisely the reason why in major cases of diabolic possession, when one of these entities actually shows up, present for so difficult a challenge to the exorcist. These exorcisms are usually the longest, most challenging, violent, and dangerous. These entities really will not vacate the body of the possessed until they are forced to by Our Lady, St. Michael, or Christ himself. At the Mundelein Conference in 2014 Father M. stated that he and a bunch of the other priests had just completed a very long and arduous exorcism where Satan himself was present in the possessed person. Father M then stated that when Satan himself shows up in an exorcism he will not move or leave until Our Lady shows up to force him to yield. We see this in the Earling possession case of 1928 and the St. Louis possession case of 1949. In both cases the victims had visions of St. Michael the Archangel coming and forcing the devils to cease their activity via a flaming sword he was wielding. And as mentioned earlier the episode in the gospel where not even the apostles could liberate the boy but Christ himself. This same concept can also be seen in the case of Annaliese Michel, a German woman who was, according to Ed Warren, possessed by the high devil, Beelzebub.[64] Annaliese towards the middle of the exorcism had a vision of the Blessed Virgin Mary, who asked her if she wanted to be delivered or suffer for priests and the youth of Germany. Michel chose the ladder and died after the 66th reading of the Ritual Romanum, only being delivered from the devil in death.

This same concept can also be seen in infestation cases in which religious objects in a house are violently attacked in some way. There have been cases where crucifixes have exploded, were bent in half, and spontaneously combusted into flames. There have been cases where holy water from Lourdes, France has frozen, where rosaries have exploded into hundreds of pieces, and statues of the Virgin Mary have had their arms removed or been melted and burnt.[65] Ed Warren once said that when Marian sacramentals are attacked and desecrated in some way, that it is usually a sign of a higher diabolical intelligence[66], because only the most powerful and blasphemous of devils would dare desecrate something portraying our Blessed Mother.[67] It is significant to note that some cases of infestation are taken care of with relative ease, a blessing or a mass said in the house or simple deliverance prayers. There are other cases however that go on for a very long period of time and sometimes are never taken care of. A case in Pittsburg for example took over a year and weekly masses and deliverance sessions offered before that case was concluded. There are even some cases of infestation that never get resolved, even after years of masses and exorcisms on a specific premise.

Based on these facts it should not surprise us that a priest could be perfectly possessed and function quite normally in everyday priestly life as Father Longenecker stated. If a priest has indeed chosen to give himself voluntarily over to Satan and over to the worship of the devil, then it is entirely possible. There are examples from history I could cite. Examples

---

64   Warren, *The Demonologist*

65   The reason this displays the same concept is because most of the time all of these sacramentals are adequate enough to banish evil spirits from a premises, just the presence of these sacramentals terrifies and causes pain to most demonic entities, However, the higher entities will often violently attack these in some blasphemous way.

66   Even this statement from Ed Warren presents a deep understanding of Mariology and demonology and the specific theological relationship between Lucifer and the Blessed Mother.

67   Whichever diabolic entity is responsible for the mockery of Santa Muerte and all the related devilry in Mexico, must be one of the highest if not the highest devil in hell. To directly mock our Lady of Guadalupe and even cause people to commit murder, cannibalism and human sacrifice at the behest of this entity is truly satanic in nature.

in which priests were burned at the stake for making pacts with the devil. Examples of priests presiding at black masses.

Unfortunately, there are some modern-day examples of this as well. I hesitate to give concrete examples, but if someone wishes to do further research they can certainly investigate the case of Father Gerald Robinson of Toledo, Ohio, who was convicted of ritually murdering a nun. The woman who originally pointed the finger at Father Robinson told police he was part of a coven made up of several priests in the Toledo area who were practicing devil worship and ritually abusing people.

There is also the case of the so-called Chicago boys club in which it is believed a small group of priests were involved in devil worship and even murder. There is also a very prominent Cardinal who had connections to this case and was also accused of being involved in satanism by a woman, which story appeared in one of Malachi Martins books.[68] I will not name the Cardinal, however if one were to even cursorily investigate this subject you will find out who it is. You will also discover that this cardinal was a very influential advocate for liberal policies in the church.[69] And he was definitely the one responsible for introducing communion in the hand in the United States through a very shady process of gathering votes. He was also a known homosexual who even had a gay choir perform at his funeral. There is also the case of Immaculate Heart of Mary Seminary in Winona, Minn, who this Cardinal was also associated with and which also had allegations of Satanic Ritual Abuse.

One can also look into the case of Father John Feit who brutally killed a woman on Holy Saturday night (the highest Satanist holiday) just after he heard her confession, which is an intentional sacrilege. There is also the case of a priest in Australia that was involved in SRA. One can also read the book *The Dark Sacrament*, the last chapter, *Devilry on the Dingle Peninsula* in which the priest, Father Lyons, was very likely perfectly possessed. The book *Lucifer's Lodge*, by William H. Kennedy also provides some disturbing examples for anyone who wants to delve into this subject.[70] Then

68   The book in question by Malachi Martin is titled *Windswept House*, which in the prologue details a satanic ritual performed in South Carolina by Bishop Russel and a young Father Bernardin in which Bernardin supposedly raped a 9-year-old girl and desecrated the Eucharist. The ritual in South Carolina was held in tandem with another satanic ritual at the Vatican in St. Paul's chapel in which several Vatican prelates took part in a ritual to enthrone Lucifer himself in the Vatican.
69   This priest was also good friends with another priest during his South Carolina days who was accused of satanic ritual abuse, Monsignor Hopwood.
70   Additional books would be *The Smoke of Satan* by Philip Lawler, *Infiltration* by Taylor Marshall, *Am Church Comes Out* by Paul Likoudis, *Rite of Sodomy* by Randy Engel, *Goodbye Good Men* by Michael Rose, *In the Closet of the Vatican* by Frederick Martel, *The Bad Shepherds* by Rod Bennett, the Pennsylvania Grand Jury report on priest abuse and the Netflix documentary *The Keepers*. For anyone brave enough and with strong enough faith to delve into this subject you will find very

there is the very recent case of a priest in Idaho who was arrested and sentenced to 25 years in prison for possessing thousands of images of extremely violent, disturbing, and graphic child pornography. During the investigation it was also discovered that this priest was actively seeking out satanic interests online and seeking murder victims. This priest admitted to urinating in the communion wine at least once[71]. The detectives involved in this case never hesitated to state that this was the most disturbing and evil case of child porn they had ever come across. The house that this priest lived in needed to be exorcised by the diocese before it was sold. Lastly, we have the very recent case of a priest in Louisiana being caught having sex and filming pornography on the altar of his church with two satanic priestesses, a direct mocking and blasphemy of Christ who resides in the tabernacle right behind the altar.

Readers must remember that the reason apostate Cardinals, Bishops, and priests exist who have been targeted and attacked by the devil and who have chosen to follow Satan instead of Christ is because the Roman Catholic Church is the one true church founded by Jesus Christ and the apostles. This is the only church that can trace its bishops and its priests back to the original 12 apostles and back to Jesus Christ himself. It is the only church that holds the keys to the kingdom of heaven, the only church that can forgive sins, validly ordain priests, and change bread and wine into the body and blood of Christ. It is the only church that has the power and authority of the papacy, the only man in the world who can claim to speak authoritatively and dogmatically regarding doctrine and morals. It is precisely these reasons why Lucifer makes this church and its priests his priority for destruction and infiltration. Satan targets these priests and bishops and entices them over time to abandon themselves to the practice of evil. This, or they were already involved in satanism upon entering the priesthood and sought to infiltrate the church somehow.[72]

Scripture speaks quite extensively about false prophets and false teachers in the midst of the true church who are in league with Satan. And yes, there is a reason the principle ceremony and ritual of satanic cultists is the black mass. A take-off and mockery of the Catholic Mass, not a prot-

---

disturbing and clear examples of Catholic priests, bishops and Cardinals that very likely were not servants of Christ but of Satan, that were ravenous wolves in sheep's clothing portraying themselves as angels of light corrupting the church from within and steering people away from the true faith, and who by extension may be or have been perfectly possessed. See Cardinals McCarrick and Bernardin. See also the cases of priests being murdered in Madison, WI and Buffalo, NY.

71   An explicitly satanic practice from the black mass.

72   I have left out many other facts known to me regarding priests being involved in satanic activity, whole books have been written about this subject.

estant service, not a Jewish service, not an Islamic service, but a Catholic Mass. The fact that consecrated hosts are profaned and desecrated at these diabolical gatherings is direct proof of the real presence of Christ in the sacred species. Betty Brennen once said that a bona fide witch would be able to tell the difference between a consecrated host amid hundreds of unconsecrated hosts. This is because bona fide witches are perfectly possessed and the spirits controlling them can tell the difference. The Satanists know the Eucharist is the true body of Christ and in their perfectly possessed state, they wish to denigrate and desecrate the real body of Christ, not just a piece of unleavened bread. That is also why if possible, it is an actual Catholic Priest or defrocked priest who performs the black mass, it is the ultimate blasphemy and mockery of Christ and his church.

So instead of leaving the church and vilifying the church because of the existence of pedophile priests and apostate bishops, it is precisely the reason you should stay in the bosom of the church and cling to its orthodoxy and teachings and fight for her with all your might. When you see the church besmirched and mocked in the news or on the television, that is all the more reason to never leave her protective abode. When you see politicians, world leaders, and prominent actors slandering the church and telling lies about her, it is all the more reason to try and convert others to her truth. When you hear people talking about priests and how they are all child molesters or liars it is all the more reason to invite your priest over for dinner and make him feel loved and at home. I know for a fact many priests live a very lonely existence and some of them get depressed. So be kind and loving towards your priests, pray for them and realize that they are tempted and harassed to a degree normal men are not.

Ask yourself why the Catholic Church is the one attacked and mocked in the news and in entertainment. Why are protestant churches not mocked, why are Jewish synagogues not mocked, why are Islamic mosques not mocked? It is because the Catholic church is the pillar and foundation of truth and the evil forces in this world are intent on doing whatever they can to destroy the church and separate as many people as they can from the salvation she offers. There is no reason to lose hope however, Jesus did say explicitly the gates of hell will never overcome the church. So, take hope and faith and be good faithful Catholics, knowing you are at home in the one family of believers that has a proven divine origin, not only proven by the truth of scripture, tradition, apostolic succession and history, but proven from 20 centuries worth of documented, authentic miracles, starting with Christ, in the form of miraculous healings, conversions, the shroud of Turin, eucharistic miracles, incorrupt saints, and many many more too numerous to list here. Suffice it to say there have been many volumes written on the history of miracles that have taken place within the confines of the Catholic Church.[73]

CONCLUSION

We have examined the fact that people from all races, creeds, economic status, and geographical locations can and have been perfectly possessed. I have also highlighted specific classes of people that can become perfectly possessed like serial killers, mass murderers, drug traffickers, mob bosses, cultists, entertainers and rich and prominent members of society. The message I am trying to get across to the reader is that there is a reason many different people from many different walks of life can throw in their lot with Lucifer. The devil is the ruler of this world, he rules the people who are his servants. He is a very shrewd angelic person, he strategically places these people where he wants them so that they can do the most damage in society. It is people that he wages his war through. He usually does not appear personally in his fallen angelic form to corrupt people. He uses other people, his servants, to accomplish his goals and further his kingdom. There have always been and always will be evil people in the world that are servants of Satan and totally taken over by him.

I would now like to give the reader some concrete examples from history of people who may have been perfectly possessed. I do this, so we can have a further understanding of the type of people who this evil befalls and the types of activities they are involved in. These are topics that should be talked about. The people in the world that are servants of the darkness do not want to be discovered as such. They wish to operate in secret and under false premises. That is why it is always beneficial to expose them for what they are and expose their machinations to the light.

---

73   Juan Carroll Cruz has written several books about these subjects

CHAPTER 7

VIP's Involved in Nefarious Activities and the International Occult Elite

"Listen Bill, I don't think you realize what kind of trouble you were in last night. Who do you think those people were? Those were not just ordinary people there. If I told you their names... I'm not going to tell you their names, but if I did, I don't think you'd sleep so well"
– Victor Ziegler to Dr Bill Hartford, pool room scene from *Eyes Wide Shut*

Wherever we encounter criminals on the worldwide political scene, it is well to assume the existence of possession. In such cases, the driven human being, the 'possessed', displays the distorted logic of self-made ideology, cold hatred, and unscrupulous disregard for mankind. All those restless schemers, surrounded by murder, characterized by restlessness, involved in anonymously inspired crime, all such people are most probably possessed by Satan.[1]

In recent months we have been witnessing the formation of two opposing sides that I would call Biblical: the children of light and the children of darkness... who often hold strategic positions in government, in politics, in the economy and in the media... They are subservient to the deep state, to globalism, to aligned thought, to the New World Order[2] which they invoke ever more frequently in the name of a universal brotherhood which has nothing Christian about it, but which evokes the Masonic ideals of those who want to dominate the world by driving God out of the courts, out of schools, out of families, and perhaps even out of churches.[3] A global plan called the Great Reset is underway. Its architect is a

---

1   Alois Winklhofer, Traktat uber den Teufel, (Frankfurt, DE: Knecht, 1961), quoted in Adolf Rodewyk, *Possessed by Satan*, (Garden City, NY: Doubleday & Company, 1975)

2   After much careful thought and study, I now believe I know how they will bring this about. President Reagan gave us a hint. I think it will have something to do with ufo's and et's and the supposed threat they pose to humanity. This of course will all be a deception. The question on ufo's and et's, the phenomena surrounding them, and their origin and purpose will be covered in a separate book I will be starting soon.

3   Archbishop Carlo Maria Vigano, June 2020 open letter to President Donald Trump

global élite that wants to subdue all of humanity, imposing coercive measures with which to drastically limit individual freedoms and those of entire populations. In several nations this plan has already been approved and financed; in others it is still in an early stage. Behind the world leaders who are the accomplices and executors of this infernal project, there are unscrupulous characters who finance the World Economic Forum and Event 201, promoting their agenda.[4]

In the last chapter I examined many statements from priests and others that have explicitly stated that it is indeed common for very prominent, powerful, and wealthy individuals to be involved in devil worship and be perfectly possessed. Now that we have examined the relevant statements from authorities on this subject, I would like to provide some real-life examples of exactly what those experts were referring to. Namely real-life examples where very prominent, wealthy, and powerful individuals all over the world have been implicated in devil worship, human sacrifice, orgies with children, VIP sex trafficking rings involving minors, and rampant pedophilia and sexual abuse of both children and adults. As I stated above the nefarious activity of some of the world's elite is necessarily very secretive. They do everything in their power to keep what they do unknown. However, I think by the grace of God who wishes to show us these things, sometimes we catch glimpses of what these people are involved in.

The following chapter is made up of real stories that are the best glimpses I know of into a very dark world indeed. They feature some of the world's most powerful, wealthy, and prominent people, people at the pinnacle of elite high society, engaged in very nefarious, evil, and downright diabolical activities. The activities I am about to highlight are what all the authors I quoted in the previous chapter were referring to regarding the rich and powerful being involved in devil worship and being perfectly possessed. And because these authors referenced these things in the context of perfect possession, these things deserve a chapter in a book about perfect possession. Father M, Malachi Martin, Father Brennan, Father Steffon, Betty Brennen, Agent Lanning, and the government of South Africa all wrote or made statements to the effect that wealthy, powerful, and prominent members of society are sometimes involved in satanic cult activity; which when an individual is involved in such cults they voluntarily give their body and soul over to the devil for him to use as he wishes. Furthermore, Father M, Malachi Martin, and Father Steffon

---

4   Archbishop Carlo Maria Vigano, October 2020 open letter to President Donald Trump

detailed the activities of some of the worlds elite in the specific context of perfect possession, Father M and Father Martin using that term explicitly and Father Steffon noting that the illuminati are possessed but also professionals, showing no sign of possession due to the fact that they have given their total will and personality over to Satan. What Father Steffon speaks about is perfect possession.

Before reading this chapter, I will warn the reader that these stories are very disturbing and sick, and after reading this chapter you may be totally disgusted and tempted to lose hope in some of our institutions of government tasked to protect children and enforce laws. But the truth is the truth, and darkness must be exposed to the light.

THE FRANKLIN SCANDAL AND COVER UP

Starting with evidence that is present in the United States, I think it would be worthwhile to examine a few different scandals, one from the 1980's and numerous from the present day. These scandals or conspiracies highlight exactly what we are talking about in this section, namely the involvement of very powerful people in pedophilia and satanism who are also perfectly possessed. The first one and the best documented one with the most evidence is known as the Franklin Scandal. The Franklin Scandal refers to an investigation that was started when the Franklin Community Credit Union in Omaha, NE was shut down by the FBI and IRS. The man running this credit union was Lawrence King Jr. a rising star and prominent political figure in the republican party that was a major political player with significant connections to Washington D.C. The investigation into the credit union started as a fraud and embezzlement investigation, but soon ballooned into a massive conspiracy and scandal that reached all the way to Washington D.C. and the White House. In a good overview of the scandal John DeCamp states,

> "It's a web of intrigue that starts at our holy of holies, Boys town Nebraska. One of the most respected institutions in the United States. And spreads out like a spider web to Washington D.C. Right up to the steps of the nation's capital, up to the steps of the White House. It involves some of the most respected, some of the most powerful and richest businessman in this United States of America. And the centerpiece of the entire web is the use of children for sex and drug dealing and drug couriers. The compromising of politicians, the compromising of businessmen, and worst of all the cor-

ruption of key institutions of government that have the duty and responsibility to make sure these things never happen."[5]

There were investigations done by the Omaha Police Department, Nebraska State Patrol, FBI, and the Nebraska Legislature. Pretty much all of what we know about this affair comes to us from the Nebraska legislative committee tasked to investigate this scandal and its chief investigator Gary Caradori, as well as from the two books published on this, but especially the definitive work done by Nick Bryant, *The Franklin Scandal*. It appears based on the evidence gathered by John De Camp and Nick Bryant that the OPD, NSP, and the FBI were involved in a massive cover up of this scandal. Therefore, most of the information, like victim statements that have been corroborated by other victims comes to us from the work done by Gary Caradori, John De Camp, and Nick Bryant.

The story starts when the Franklin Community Credit Union is raided and shut down by the feds on November 4, 1988. From this point on the allegations of nefarious activity exploded.

> "The financial scandal turned into something more when it became known that children from Omaha and its surroundings said they had been flown from city to city to be abused at parties held by Franklin's officers and well-known Nebraskans, including nationally prominent Republican party activists."[6]

The Conspiracy of Silence documentary about this case also noted that,

> "Those perpetrators named by the children formed a ring of rich and powerful pedophiles in Omaha. Men from industry, politics, the media, even the police. Besides Larry King, ringleaders were department store billionaire Alan Baer, and the celebrity columnist of the Omaha Herald newspaper Peter Citron."[7]

Rumors in the Omaha area were already rampant well before the credit union was shut down. The rumors were essentially that Larry King and several other prominent people in the Omaha area were involved in the trafficking and molestation of young children. The first people to make allegations before Franklin Credit Union was shut down were foster chil-

---

5   John DeCamp, *Conspiracy of Silence* documentary, Unaired, accessed from youtube.
com
6   John De Camp, *The Franklin Cover Up*
7   *Conspiracy of Silence*, Unaired documentary

dren that were in the care of a sadistic family that was related to Larry King.

The Webb family had several foster children that they mercilessly abused day and night meting out whippings with a piece of rubber hose and withholding food on a regular basis. Eventually the authorities and DSS became involved and removed several of the children from the home. After some of the children were placed in new foster homes they started to make bizarre allegations regarding not only their foster father molesting them but also a cousin (Larry King) of the foster family that would molest them as well and have them flown to places like Chicago, New York, and Washington D.C. for sex parties and orgies. The more the children felt comfortable in their new surroundings the more they opened up. Nick Bryant notes that,

> "As Eulice grew more and more comfortable with Sorenson, she tentatively asserted that the Webb's powerful cousin, Larry King, had flown her and other children, via a charter plane, to Chicago in the fall of 1984 and to New York in the spring of 1985. Eulice said that King forced her to wear negligees and attend orgies. She told Sorenson that Boys Town students were on the flights, and **she recognized a nationally prominent politician, who procured a kid at the orgy in Chicago and quickly slipped out.**"[8]

Additional allegations came from three different young girls who had been in a residential psychiatric facility for young girls named Uta Halee. Out of the three girls, only one eventually completely opened up about what had happened to her. Allegations made by the girl were that Larry King and several other very prominent people in the Omaha community were involved in devil worship and the photography, molestation, trafficking, and murder of children. This child relayed a story that she had been involved in the North Omaha Girls Club and it was from there that she met a man named Ray who introduced her and several other girls to these sex parties. This young girl also claimed that prominent people were involved in child pornography and the photographing of children. John De Camp states that,

> "She stated that a number of adults, whom she referred to as leaders from the North Omaha Girls Club, both male and female, were engaged in the photography of nude children. She also indicated

that a number of prominent individuals were also involved, including doctors and lawyers."[9]

Writing about the same minor female and the same allegations, Nick Bryant notes,

> "Moore told Carmean that at the age of nine she and a handful of other girls had been transported from the girl's club to a studio and photographed in the nude. Moore said that the adults who participated in photographing the children were the leaders of the girl's club. She also indicated that other prominent individuals were involved, including doctors and lawyers."[10]

As disturbing as these revelations are, the young girl would go on to detail far more evil deeds than just the photographing of young naked children. This young girl told hospital staff that after getting involved with this crowd of prominent individuals she was soon brought to parties where grown men would have sex with young girls.

> "The men at the party were in their mid-thirties—they initially sat around and talked to the girls about their "problems." They then started to drink and take drugs with the girls, and, after the girls were "wasted," the men started having sex with them. The girls didn't have a choice of who would have sex with them.[11]

The young girl then went on to detail how after she was taken to these parties for six months, she eventually was brought to what was described to her as a "power meeting." These so-called "power meetings" consisted of very dark and depraved satanic rituals in which multiple children were ritualistically sacrificed and ritually abused. Nick Bryant writes,

> Moore said she attended parties for approximately six months before she was taken to her first "power meeting" in the summer of 1982. The meeting was held in an abandoned shack, and Moore told hospital personnel that "candles and other weird stuff" were at the power meetings. Moore identified the men by pseudonyms— Ace, King's Horses, Jerry Lucifer, and Mike. The men were dressed in robes adorned with upside-down crosses, and the leader wore a long black cape and gold skull head rings on his fingers. Moore and the other girls were told that the room would start spinning; and after the room started to whirl around Moore, she realized she'd

---

9   De Camp, *The Franklin Cover Up*

10   Bryant, *The Franklin Scandal*

11   Bryant, *The Franklin Scandal*

been drugged. At approximately 7:00 P.M. Moore was locked in a small room with a Caucasian baby girl—Moore and the infant were alone in the room for about five hours. At around midnight, she said, the men opened the door to find Moore holding the little girl. They took the infant from Moore and told her that she would achieve "power" by killing someone she really loved. Moore then detailed a series of inconceivably gory and horrific events that entailed the men ritualistically murdering the infant. Though the events that Moore described are incomprehensible, she provided hospital staff with the unflinching, meticulous specifics of the events as she said they unfolded. After the infant was murdered, Moore divulged to hospital personnel that she became hysterical and one of the men had to hold her down. Moore then disclosed that she was forced to remain locked in the small room for approximately twenty-four hours. While Moore sat in the dark, locked room, she said she heard the men whipping and beating one of the girls.[12]

This young girl named Moore, a pseudonym, also went on to detail other sacrifices that she had been a witness to.

Moore also told Richard Young staff about four additional "sacrifices." She said that a little boy was ritualistically murdered because he threatened to notify authorities of the sacrifices. She also named one of the girls who had been slaughtered. As Moore continued to describe the various sacrifices, Richard Young's "Nurses' Notes" detail that Moore started to have dreams about the cult murdering Richard Young staff, she wrote a suicide letter, and also conveyed to staff that she could not "forgive herself." In September, Moore told the staff that she harbored no more secrets, but she was convinced that she was "going to hell." In October, a nurse walked into Moore's darkened room and found her curled into a fetal position.[13]

It should also be noted that this young girl implicated Larry King, a prominent school superintendent and others in this satanic activity. John De Camp in his book uses a different pseudonym for the young girl and calls her Loretta, De Camp notes,

"Loretta... provided additional information of her previous involvement in cult activity which included the witnessing of homi-

---

12   Bryant, *The Franklin Scandal*
13   Bryant, *The Franklin Scandal*

cides of several young children and which also included references to Larry King and others involved in the cult activities."[14]

Right around the same time that this young girl (Moore) was making these extremely disturbing disclosures to hospital staff the initial Omaha Police Department investigation into Larry King was started. This occurred when a photographer named Rusty Nelson invited a young adult girl and her mother to his apartment for a photography session. As the mother was looking around Nelsons apartment, she noticed multiple pictures of young girls and boys in the nude. She subsequently filed a police report with the OPD. The department deputed an officer Carmean to investigate these allegations at which point Carmean quickly discovered that the apartment Nelson was living in was leased by Larry King who also leased an additional luxury apartment at the Twin Towers Luxury apartments. The Twin Towers apartment of Larry King would later be named by multiple victims as the location of multiple instances of sex parties, and orgies involving children as young as 10 years old.

It was at this time that hospital staff, contacted the OPD regarding the allegations Moore was making. Since officer Carmean was already investigating Larry King, he met with Moore to conduct an interview. Moore related to Carmean all the same things she had related to hospital staff including the involvement of King and others in devil worship and cult activities as well as parties involving sex with minors.

> "During the course of their conversation, Moore divulged to Carmean that she believed Larry King to be a "supporter and participant" of both the child pornography and the devil worship. She also talked about a "sex and drug" party at one of King's residences, where she witnessed three or four teenage boys performing oral sex on each other"[15]

It should be noted that Moore correctly pointed out the location of these sex parties, which officer Carmean corroborated by his investigation. Unfortunately, like many of the investigations into Larry King, the investigation conducted by Officer Carmean hit a brick wall and went nowhere. According to Nick Bryant, he was told by Rusty Nelson that the OPD intentionally put a stop to the investigation after a high rankling Omaha Police Department official was paid off to ensure the investigation went nowhere.

---

14   De Camp, *The Franklin Cover Up*
15   Bryant, *The Franklin Scandal*

At the same time the OPD was investigating Larry King, Nebraska's Foster Care Review Board also started to receive allegations about Larry King and his involvement with children. The board received the allegations of the foster children who had been placed with the Webb's and they started to investigate for themselves. After they commenced their investigation, they began to receive other reports of young people being abused at the hands of Larry King and others. These new allegations came from children who were not affiliated with the Webb's or Moore, the young girl who made the disturbing allegations of child murder and satanic cult activity.

The Foster Care Review Board became extremely disturbed with the information they had been gathering and decided to contact the OPD and officer Carmean. They also contacted the Nebraska Attorney General's office and made it clear they felt an intensive investigation had to be undertaken. It soon became clear to the review board however that these allegations were not being investigated properly. They realized this when some of the original victims were not re-interviewed, that despite the original victims relating horrible instances of child pornography, pedophilia, devil worship, and ritualistic homicides. When the board started looking into why the allegations were not being investigated, they found out both officer Carmean and Officer Hoch who had been investigating Larry King for the OPD had been pulled off the case. They were also told that the FBI was taking over the investigation. According to Nick Bryant, the OPD was told to "back off" the investigation and the Nebraska Attorney General's Office was also told the FBI was taking over the investigation. Despite the FBI taking control of the investigation they completely failed to interview any of the potential witnesses to the crimes that had been detailed.

It was shortly after this that the Franklin Community Credit Union was shut down by the Feds. After this happened the Nebraska state legislature got wind of the activities at Franklin and decided to start a committee to investigate what happened at the credit union. Senator Loran Schmit was the head of the Legislatures banking committee and so he introduced Resolution 5 which other senators quickly jumped on board and eventually formed the Franklin Committee. This action by Senator Schmit would almost lead to his eventual ruin. In his book Nick Bryant states that after the Franklin Committee was formed Senator Schmit received an anonymous call urging him not to pursue the investigation because it would lead to the highest levels of the Republican party in Washington D.C.. Bryant also notes that Schmit was almost completely ruined financially as a result of his involvement in the Franklin Committee.

I will note that Senator Schmit was not the only one almost ruined by this investigation. There were multiple people involved with this investigation who were either followed, harassed by random people, had their phones tapped and homes broken into, experienced harassment by the feds, and some even killed. John De Camp in his book The Franklin Cover Up states that during the investigation of the Franklin Scandal more than 15 people associated with the Franklin scandal died, many of them mysteriously and violently. To get a full scope of just how big this cover up was and just how bad the people trying to do the right thing were besmirched and harassed and ruined you must read the two books on this scandal. People being mysteriously killed during investigations into powerful people is nothing new, this same thing happen during Maury Terry's investigation into the satanic cult behind the Son of Sam killings. A cult that led to some very wealthy and prominent people on Long island and Manhattan.[16] While Terry was investigating, people related to the investigation, especially some of the possible perpetrators started turning up dead, many dying very violent deaths.[17]

Despite the threat Senator Schmit received on the day the Franklin Committee was formed they plowed ahead with the investigation. Because this committee was formed and the fact that the committee had serious questions about the response of local, state, and federal law enforcement to the investigation thus far, the agencies in question, namely the Nebraska State Patrol and FBI were basically forced into conducting an investigation that made it appear as though it was on the up and up. It soon became clear again however that the FBI would not conduct an investigation, but rather a cover up. After doing research into this case, I myself concluded that the FBI investigation into these allegations was an absolute joke. Victims were subjected to intimidation tactics by agents and agents routinely threatened investigators, one from DSS, who was told to back off her investigation. After reading Nick Bryant's book it is difficult to keep a positive outlook on some of our institutions of government tasked to protect children.

---

16   The Son of Sam case is another example where an investigation by Maury Terry led to some very high profile and powerful names in the New York and Los Angeles area being implicated in devil worship. One high profile individual named Roy Radin was a wealthy man who lived on Long Island. Radin was thought to be one of the leaders of the Son of Sam cult and was eventually murdered himself in a ritualistic killing outside of Los Angeles.

17   Maury Terry, The Ultimate Evil

"A February 5, 1989 World-Herald article, by James Allen Flanery, discussed federal and state investigations into Franklin-related child abuse. The article quoted the FBI's Nick O'Hara, who said that the FBI had maybe "one or two follow-up interviews to conduct," but after "dozens of interviews" he concluded that there was no "substance to the initial allegations," even though the FBI had yet to interview the initial victims to come forward—Eulice Washington and Shawneta Moore!"[18]

The Franklin Committee undeterred moved forward with their own independent investigation of all the allegations. The Committees original investigator, a man named Jerry Lowe, upon initially reviewing all the relevant documents and allegations was absolutely shocked no enforcement action was taken thus far by the proper authorities.

"What appears to be documented cases of child abuse and sexual abuse dating back several years with no enforcement action taken by the appropriate agencies is ... mind boggling," he wrote.[19]

Lowe then went about interviewing all the principle witnesses, including Moore and Eulice Washington. Moore related the same things to Lowe that she had related to hospital staff, officer Carmean, and the FBI. Namely that she was a victim of child pornography, pedophilia, and devil worship perpetrated by Larry King and other prominent individuals. Upon interviewing Eulice Washington, Washington told the same story of being flown to Chicago for a sex party by Larry King in which she witnessed a nationally prominent politician, recognizable through his political campaigns, procure a young boy named Brant, and leave the party with him. Eulice said that Brant had come from Boys town and that he flew with Eulice to Chicago but did not fly back to Nebraska with Eulice.

She also related a story of an additional sex party that Larry King hosted in New York City at a hotel.

"As in Chicago, she stayed in a hotel room by herself. Lowe asked her where the little girls lodged, and she replied she didn't know. Once more she was forced to wear a negligee without underpants and sit on a pedestal poised like a mannequin—she pointed out that it was a different negligee than the one she wore in Chicago. She recounted that the party in New York had considerably more

18   Nick Bryant, *The Franklin Scandal*
19   Ibid

sexual activity than the party in Chicago. At one point, she was surrounded by men who were masturbating in front of her."[20]

As the investigation went on investigator Lowe started filing his progress reports with the committee, the committee being totally shocked with the information he was providing. The committee then decided to subpoena a number of witnesses and investigators including people from the foster care review board who had compiled a report on the allegations against Larry King and the officers from OPD who had initially investigated King. The board also called members from the attorney general's office and demanded to know why they had not adequately investigated all of the allegations. As a result of the hearing Senator Schmit, the chairman decided the committee needed a new direction to find out the facts and obtain prosecutable evidence. This new direction caused investigator Lowe and 2 other people to resign from the committee.

It was at this point in the investigation that the committee hired Gary Caradori to be the new chief investigator for the Franklin Committee. Caradori was a former Nebraska State Police investigator who owned his own private investigative firm. By all accounts he was a tireless, upstanding, and elite investigator. Gary Caradori began in earnest by reviewing all the relevant documents in the case. He quickly became privy to the potential magnitude of the case. Undaunted however, he proceeded with his investigation. He discovered very quickly the kind of opposition he would be against. According to Nick Bryant, Caradori received a call from a friend of his who was a Lieutenant in the Omaha Police Department. This Lieutenant told Caradori to tread lightly and be careful because the sexual abuse aspect to the Franklin case had been covered up from the start. Caradori and his co-investigator Karen Ormiston also discovered that their phones had been tapped. Caradori confirmed this with the telephone service. In addition, Caradori and Ormiston also felt they were being followed and Caradori even had his house broken into. These multiple harassments would be just a prelude to what would come later in the investigation.

Gary Caradori started combing the streets of Omaha looking for potential victims of the child sex trafficking ring. Nick Bryant says in his book that Caradori would commonly put in 100-hour work weeks. Caradori's wife stated that Gary started taking long hot showers to try and cleanse the evil that he was being exposed to. Because Caradori knew some of the allegations included potential flights with minors to places like Washing-

---

20   Ibid

ton D.C., Caradori started investigating the charter companies that Larry King had been using. At one of these charter companies Caradori hit the mother lode when he found flight receipts for Larry King proving that he had minors accompanying him on these flights. Right before Caradori left with the copies of these documents the CEO of the company burst in and demanded Caradori leave the documentation there. Later after Caradori had subpoenaed these records they came back with all incriminating information deleted. Shortly after this Caradori was hit with an FBI subpoena that demanded he turn over all relevant Franklin documents to the FBI.

After intensively investigating for the committee Gary Caradori compiled a list of potential victims. One name on this list was Alisha Owen. Caradori went about interviewing Owen and discovered that she indeed had been a part of this pedophilia ring. Owen maintained that she was introduced to the sex parties at Larry Kings residence by some other boys who were from Boys town. Owen told a story substantially similar to some of the previous witnesses, namely that she had attended parties at the residence of Larry King in the Twin Towers luxury apartments where a number of prominent Omaha citizens would use drugs and have sex with children. Owen specifically implicated Omaha's chief of police who Owen said forced her to have sex with him. Owen has named another Omaha citizen who was a prominent businessman who owned multiple department stores. Alisha Owen went on to testify to Caradori, under oath mind you, that she had gotten in over her head very quickly and could not see a way out. She started partaking in regular sexual encounters with the chief of police, group orgies and sex parties, and started to be flown around by Larry King to be used for sex in various cities. Nick Bryant notes,

> Owen said she began to meet Wadman on sporadic Wednesday afternoons, engage in group sexual encounters, and also flew with King to Los Angeles and Kansas City to be pandered as an underage prostitute—Owen described extremely sadistic abuse on the out-of-town trips.[21]

From Alisha Owen, Gary Caradori discovered the existence of further victims, namely Troy Boner and Danny King. Caradori subsequently tracked down both Boner and King and they both agreed to testify as well. At the end of Alisha Owen's, Troy Boner's, and Danny King's testimony Caradori had amassed about 21 hours of sworn statements from

---

21   Nick Bryant, *The Franklin Scandal*

all three victims. All three victims basically corroborated each other and corroborated the statements of the initial victims Eulice Washington and Shawnita Moore. Alisha Owen, Troy Boner and Danny King all relayed to Caradori under oath that they had been a part of a nationwide sex trafficking ring that pandered to elite, wealthy, and powerful people all over the nation. Very prominent Omaha citizens were implicated and corroborated by all three, specifically Larry King, the chief of police, a department store billionaire, a celebrity newspaper columnist, a newspaper publisher, a judge, a prominent attorney, the former mayor, a former parks game commissioner, and a school superintendent.[22]

Furthermore all 3 corroborated the fact that they were flown around the country with Larry King to engage in demented sex parties and orgies where other prominent people would molest them, rape them, subject them to sadistic abuse, threaten them and their lives and force them to engage in depraved acts with adults. All three victims also testified to the fact that there were many other victims of this sex trafficking network, some victims had come from Boys town Nebraska and some victims had been abducted. All three victims believed that some of these children were sold or murdered.

With evidence mounting Caradori turned the videos over to the committee who debated what to do with them. It was eventually decided that the committee should turn the videos over to the FBI. Gary Caradori vigorously disagreed with this course of action as he thought the FBI had been actively working to implement a cover up. Caradori was also concerned the FBI would leak the videos to the media thereby thwarting his investigation and his ability to have further victims trust him and give testimony to him. Caradori's concerns were proven right when excerpts from the victims sworn statements started showing up on the local news. Furthermore, the victims became the target of FBI harassment, Alisha Owen was even jumped and beaten up in the prison where she had been incarcerated for writing bad checks.

This is where John De Camp enters the story. John De Camp was Senator Loran Schmit's personal attorney. De Camp had accompanied Schmit, who was the chairman of the committee investigating Franklin to the Omaha offices of the FBI to talk about the Franklin Investigation. When Senator Schmit told the special agent in charge that the Omaha Chief of Police was one of the targets of the investigation, the agent in charge pro-

---

22   Nick Bryant, *The Franklin Scandal*, John DeCamp, *The Franklin Cover Up, Conspiracy of Silence,* unaired documentary.

claimed that he was a good friend of the chief of police in Omaha and that they better tread lightly.

> "he said, O'Hara discharged a grave warning to both Schmit and DeCamp: He contended that anyone who cast aspersions on Wadman's character would be subjected to the wrath of the FBI.[23]

Because of this experience and also the general belief by De Camp that local, state, and federal officials had not responded to or investigated the allegations relating to Franklin pedophilia properly and may have even initiated a cover up, De Camp decided to write what is now known as the De Camp memo. In the memo De Camp highlights what the allegations are and who the perpetrators are accused of being. De Camp wrote:

> "The allegations are that the most powerful and rich public personalities of the state are central figures in the investigation."[24]

Because De Camp named some of the perps who were very well known and highly respected figures in Omaha, the memo caused a media firestorm, which Gary Caradori frowned upon to say the least. Caradori found it frustrating that once again his investigation would be undermined by the media.

Meanwhile Gary Caradori continued his investigation and discovered the names of further potential witnesses. At this point in the investigation Caradori was subjected to an attack from multiple different fronts. The Omaha World Herald started running news stories discrediting Gary Caradori's investigation and the victim witnesses.[25] Caradori was also continuously subjected to threatening phone calls, being followed and having his phones tapped. Another line of attack on Caradori came at his personal business, Caracorp, which was a private investigative agency. Caracorp was hit with a federal subpoena demanding it turn over all relevant documents relating to the possible perpetrators. Caradori's billing practices were called into question and he forced to have to defend himself.

> "After Caradori politely explained Caracorp's charges, he turned his attention to the "unnamed sources" provoking the Secretary of State's inquiry: "This infatuation with my billing and their scrutiny of my abilities and integrity can only be construed as something similar to a 'witch hunt.' Why? Am I too close to something they do

23   John DeCamp, *The Franklin Cover Up*
24   Ibid
25   It should be noted one of the perpetrators of all this abuse was a man named Peter Citron who worked for the *Omaha World Herald*

not want to become public?" Caradori also touched on the peril he and his employees had faced throughout the investigation: "I must reiterate that we—my employees and myself—have been followed and questionable situations have arisen during this investigation. Threatening situations have resulted numerous times."[26]

Caradori's investigative techniques and his interview techniques also came into question. There were daily news stories run in Omaha World Herald besmirching Gary Caradori and ruining the credibility of his witnesses. As far as the Omaha World Herald goes it should be noted that the previous CEO of the paper who was now its editor, was named as a perpetrator of pedophilia and being part of the network that molested and trafficked children by multiple victims. Caradori started to take major heat by the feds and the media after the FBI finally decided to interview the same witnesses that Caradori had taped. The FBI, using multiple different intimidation tactics and threats of perjury was successful in getting Troy Boner and Danny King to recant their original testimony to Gary Caradori. Alisha Owen on the other hand refused to recant and ended up being sentenced to a four-year prison term for perjury.

Caradori was accused of partaking in shoddy investigation techniques and witness leading, this despite his partner, Karen Ormiston passing a polygraph test denying these allegations. Gary Caradori, since becoming the lead investigator for the Franklin committee was subjected to an amount of harassment, threats, and assaults on his character that border on the unbelievable and would make one think he was investigating the Nazi's in 1930's Germany or the Soviet Government in 1950's Russia.

> "By June 1990, Caradori had been immersed in the nightmare of Franklin for nearly a year. The nightmare included uncovering organized child abuse of a horrific nature, persistent media assaults, harassment and intimidation, and a seemingly concerted effort by state and federal law enforcement to sabotage his investigation. But Caradori realized that the nightmare also had a trap door: Federal and state authorities were possibly in the process of framing him to take the fall for scripting the child-abuse allegations."[27]

Caradori became convinced that the feds were going to try and frame him at which point he hired a prominent attorney to defend him. In a letter to that attorney Caradori wrote:

---

26   Nick Bryant, *The Franklin Scandal*
27   Nick Bryant, *The Franklin Scandal*

"In short what we have discovered is only a small part of a **nation-wide child exploitation network**. It is obvious that the people behind this organization are **powerful and ruthless** and are going to great lengths to keep this matter contained." He further stated that the network "**extended to the highest levels of the United States.**"[28]

Lead on by his impeccable moral standard and his desire to protect further children from being molested and exploited by powerful men, Caradori continued his investigation despite all the dangers lurking in the darkness. It was at this time that Caradori compiled a list of possible victims that he still wanted to interview which exceeded 60 persons. One of these persons was Paul Bonacci who also agreed to talk to Caradori. Bonacci related and corroborated all the same things that all of the previous victims had testified to. Specifically, that he had been part of sex trafficking ring that involved child pornography, pedophilia, pandering, drug trafficking, child abduction, murder, and devil worship all perpetrated by wealthy and powerful people not only in Omaha but all around the country. Bonacci had been so abused and traumatized by this group of evil men that he developed multiple personality disorder. Bonacci corroborated and named the same victims, perpetrators, activities, and places that Owen, Boner, and Danny King had testified to. Bonacci also revealed information to Caradori that never appeared in the news, that the only way he could have known this information would have been if he was actually present during the occurrences. This information regarded one of the perpetrators alleged victims that had never been named a victim except in sealed court testimony. It also included information revealed by Troy Boner regarding one of Larry King's sick sexual predilections.

Nick Bryant writes,

> "Bonacci also spoke of the same sadistic abuse that had been described by Owen, Boner, and Danny King. He discussed being repeatedly tied up, whipped, cut by knives, and burned by cigarettes. Bonacci showed Caradori a scar that was left by a knife wound and also cigarette burns on his arms—he claimed to have cigarette burns on his genitals, too. He recalled a party at the Twin Towers, in Baer's[29] apartment, where he was forced to perform oral sex in rapid succession on five adult males."[30]

28   Ibid
29   Department store billionaire, Alan Baer
30   Nick Bryant, *The Franklin Scandal*

Out of the four victims that Caradori had taped interviews with the revelations made by Paul Bonacci were by far the most disturbing. Unlike Boner, Owen, and King, Bonacci testified to witnessing acts of devil worship and the ritualistic sacrifice of children. Bonacci related one incident in which he was used and forced to participate in the making of a snuff film. According to Bonacci this snuff film took place somewhere north of Sacramento, California where there were giant redwood trees. Bonacci related a story that Larry King and Bonacci had picked up another child by the name of Nicholas in Colorado and then met a camera crew and a producer along with a kidnapped child named Jeremy in the redwood forest. Nick Bryant writes of the incident,

> "The producer subsequently drove Bonacci, Nicholas, King and the pilot of the plane to a remote wooded area, where they met a few additional men, who comprised the "camera crew," and also a young boy named "Jeremy"—the producer said that Jeremy had been kidnapped. Jeremy was jostled into a small cage, and after he was let loose from the cage, Bonacci and Nicholas were ordered to run him down and drag him back to the older men. Bonacci stated that Jeremy divulged to him that he was from Idaho—he described Jeremy as roughly twelve years old, having braces on his teeth, with blond hair and brown eyes. Bonacci sobbed when he told Caradori and Ormiston that he and Nicholas were forced to have sex with Jeremy while members of the camera crew kicked and beat the three of them—an adult male then kicked Jeremy in the face, molested him, and, as Jeremy screamed, shot him in the head with a handgun."[31]

Paul Bonacci further claimed, like the other victims that Larry King flew him to Washington D.C. to have sex with prominent politicians and other powerful people in the capitol.

> "Bonacci implicated King in a DC blackmail operation and said that he made numerous trips to DC with King to be used as a boy-toy for politicians and other powerbrokers who in turn were then "compromised." Caradori asked Bonacci to name the compromised politicians, but Bonacci could only identify one by name — he was in the US Congress."[32]

Regarding his involvement in satanism, Bonacci mentioned that Larry King, a school superintendent, and the department store mogul that oth-

---

31   Ibid
32   Nick Bryant, *The Franklin Scandal*

er victims had implicated in pedophilia and child pornography were all involved with satanism and ritual murder as well. John DeCamp writes,

> "According to testimony from Paul Bonacci, Larry King had been recruited to a satanic cult by December 1980 at the latest. In his written history, Bonacci described how King picked him up after school one day in December, "and took me to the Triangle which is in a wooded area in Sarpy County. I witnessed a sacrifice of a human baby boy. Everyone was chanting, and it was a yearly ritual around the time of Christ's birth to pervert the blood of Christ. They used daggers and cut the boy and filled a cup with his blood and mixed urine in it and forced all of us to drink from the cup and chant 'Satan is Lord Lucifer our King. Realm of darkness come now empower us your slaves.' Then they all began to chant some weird sounds and I got scared and was threatened I'd become the next sacrifice if I told anyone about it. "Bonacci said he witnessed the participation of another Franklin-related figure: "I did see [Alan] Baer take part in satanic activity on several occasions."[33]

Because of the fact that the victims in this case and even the investigators were being subjected to endless harassment and threats, and the suspicion that state and federal authorities were involved in a cover up, Gary Caradori decided that he quickly needed to produce evidence in this case that could not be questioned, that could not be intimidated, a smoking gun. Caradori had already heard from several people the name Rusty Nelson, who worked as a photographer for Larry King. Caradori ended up finding Nelson and setting up a meeting with him in Chicago to obtain incriminating pictures of some of the powerful perpetrators engaged in compromising sexual acts with children. After learning he would be able to obtain these pictures Caradori mentioned to Senator Schmit that he was going to be able to obtain substantial evidence that would corroborate the testimony of all the victims. Caradori also told Alisha Owen's mother that she would be the happiest mother in the world after he returned from his Chicago trip, this after Alisha Owen, a victim of the child sex ring, had been subjected to appalling treatment by the police, prison officials, the courts and the FBI.

Gary Caradori left Omaha on July 9, 1990 accompanied by his 8-year-old son who loved baseball. Caradori and his son would attend the all-star game in Chicago. Caradori also met with Nelson in Chicago, received the pictures and conveyed as much to his wife and Senator Schmit, albeit

33   John DeCamp, *The Franklin Cover Up*

cryptically because he knew his phones were tapped. Caradori and his 8-year-old son left Chicago on July 10, 1990 at about 2:00am. By 2:30am Caradori's plane exploded in midair over an Illinois cornfield. The wreckage of the blast would be scattered for up to 1800 ft from where the fuselage was located. Caradori, who was investigating rich and powerful men, who had received numerous threats to his life, who just received smoking gun evidence implicating the perpetrators was now dead. His briefcase which his wife stated he would keep all his important documents was never located.

Caradori's death shocked the committee and frightened everyone involved. The NTSB which investigates plane crashes failed to come up with a cause for the plane exploding in midair. The back seat of the plane was also never recovered, leading to the belief that it was vaporized after the detonation of a bomb. Senator Schmit and Gary Caradori's wife both firmly believed Gary and his son were murdered, that it was a public assassination.

> "Mary Caradori rendered her own verdict on the deaths of Gary and A.J.: "My son and Grandson were murdered." Many Nebraskans echoed her opinion. They have growing grounds for suspicion. From late 1988, when the Franklin case first broke into public view, until mid-1991, at least 15 people associated with the case as investigators, alleged perpetrators, or potential witnesses, died sudden deaths, many of them violent.[34]

The investigation into the Franklin Scandal by the Nebraska legislature seemingly died with Gary Caradori. Shortly after Caradori's death the two grand jury's that had been investigating these allegations in tandem with the FBI came out and said the whole affair was a perfectly planned hoax perpetrated by Troy Boner, Alisha Owen, Danny King, and even Gary Caradori. Shortly after this the legislative committee was shut down and the investigation seemingly went into oblivion. Additionally, the grand jury also recommended perjury charges against Alicia Owen and Paul Bonacci, the two witnesses that would not recant their testimony that they gave to Gary Caradori. Alisha Owen was convicted of perjury and sent to prison for four years. The prosecutor ended up dropping the charges against Paul Bonacci, however. John De Camp, who was Bonacci's attorney stated this was because he was going to expose the whole scandal and cover up at trial. It should also be noted that Troy Boner, who recanted his

---

34   John DeCamp, *The Franklin Cover Up*

testimony under intimidation from the FBI later recanted his recantation to John De Camp and to the investigators who produced the Conspiracy of Silence Documentary; the producers of this documentary even went so far as to subject Troy Boner to a polygraph which he passed.

De Camp was attempting to get a new trial for Alisha Owen who was convicted based on the testimony from Troy Boner who said all the allegations were fabricated and that Owen was lying. Boner then wrote an affidavit in which he detailed that his original testimony to Caradori was indeed truthful. Unfortunately, right before the hearing to grant Alisha Owen a new trial that Boner was going to testify at, Boner was again threatened with prosecution and harsh prison time if he recanted his recantation in open court. Boner folded under pressure again and Alisha Owen did not get a new trial. Troy Boner's affidavit is detailed in John De Camps book in full. Boner says in the affidavit that one of the reasons he was coming totally clean was because of his brother's mysterious death. Both Troy Boner's brother and Alisha Owen's brother would both die mysterious deaths. Troy Boner himself died a mysterious death, like many other Franklin personalities, in 2003 when he stumbled into a hospital claiming people were after him. The next morning, he was found in his hospital room bleeding from the mouth and quite dead.

In 2001 an author by the name of Nick Bryant decided to investigate the Franklin scandal for himself. Nick Bryant took the investigation even further than Gary Caradori and John De Camp were able to. Bryant located new victims who substantially corroborated the previous testimony of all the victims. I will note that Nick Bryant during his investigation was treated to some of the very same harassments, threats, surveillance, and danger that previous investigators into this subject were subjected to. One of the victims that Bryant interviewed relayed identical stories that had been told by previous victims. This new victim that Bryant found had not spoken to anybody previously about the abuse he endured. Bryant notes,

> "Also, unlike Harris, Cayman divulged that he was subjected to extremely sadistic pedophiles—he related stories of pedophilic sadism similar to those conveyed by Alisha Owen, Troy Boner, Danny King, and Paul Bonacci. "A lot of the parties were outrageous—it was like one big orgy, but some of these parties weren't always nice. You'd get tortured, handcuffed, beaten, and videotaped. To this day, I have scars all over my body from flying with King. Doctors have asked me where I got all these scars."[35]

---

35   Nick Bryant, *The Franklin Scandal*

This same victim, like Shawnita Moore and Paul Bonacci also related stories of some of the perpetrators being involved with devil worship and satanism. Nick Bryant writes,

> "I didn't broach the subject of Satanism, but Cayman, like Moore and Bonacci, said that some of the gatherings were satanic: "They would have these weird rituals, but I didn't realize what they were. At first, I thought whatever, but, as I got older, I started to realize that these were satanic rituals. There was cutting, blood drinking, chants, and dancing."[36]

It should be noted that the victims I have written about here were not the only victims in this investigation. Both Gary Caradori and Nick Bryant compiled the names of many additional victims, some of who refused to speak to investigators and many who were living very troubled lives riddled with drug addictions due to the abuse they had endured in childhood.

The last aspect to this case that I would like to highlight is the connection of this case to Washington D.C. Not only were very prominent and wealthy Omaha citizens implicated in being involved in this pedophilia network, but additional powerful and influential personages in Washington D.C. were also implicated. Most of the flight receipts that Gary Caradori and Nick Bryant got their hands on from Larry King's charter flights were to Washington D.C. Larry King was a rising star in the National Republican party in the 1980's when the bulk of this illegal activity was being perpetrated. Larry King also had a house in Washington D.C. that he would host parties at.

There is a reporter for the Washington Times who also delved into the issue of child exploitation in our nation's capital. This reporters name is Paul Rodriguez and he appeared in the *Conspiracy of Silence* documentary and talked extensively with Nick Bryant. After investigating the problem of child pornography and pedophilia regarding very powerful people in Washington D.C., Rodriguez quickly concluded that there is a big problem with this in the nation's capital.

> "As Rodriguez delved deeper and deeper into DC's skin trade, he found that children were prized commodities among some of our nation's powerbrokers."[37]

---

36   Ibid
37   Nick Bryant, *The Franklin Scandal*

One of the very disturbing things that Rodriguez discovered was that there was in existence actual auctions of children right there in our nation's capital and in other places as well. This is also something Paul Bonacci testified to. Nick Bryant notes that

> "Rodriguez had been burrowing into DC's seamy underside for months, enduring a succession of horrors, when he got wind of an actual auction of children. He was never able to corroborate the auction's existence, even though the mere mention of it shocked him. Both Paul Bonacci and Rusty Nelson told me about auctions they attended in Nebraska and Las Vegas, but the very idea of children being auctioned off in America was anathema to me, and I found it almost impossible to believe them. However, I eventually befriended a reputable and top-notch private detective in Nebraska named Dennis Whalen, who told me that he had actually attended such an auction in search of an abducted child.[38]

As Rodriguez delved deeper and deeper into the dark world of VIP pedophilia in Washington D.C. one name kept coming up on his radar, that of Craig Spence. Craig Spence was a very prominent and powerful political operative in D.C. who had connections to some of the most powerful people in the country.[39] Both Rodriguez and Nick Bryant both investigated Craig Spence and found that he had direct ties to Larry King. It was further discovered that both Spence and King were running a pedophilia network in Washington D.C. that catered to powerful politicians and others that was also used for the purpose of blackmailing these politicians. Multiple witnesses that Bryant interviewed corroborated the relationship between Spence and King. Bryant interviewed one witness, who previously ran an escort service that worked with Spence and King, who related something extremely disturbing.

> "As Vinson discussed the sordid exploits of Spence and King, I asked him a few questions specifically about King. He didn't hold King in very high esteem and described him as "cunning." Vinson then recalled a conversation he had with King that was "strange as hell," literally. "King said they had clients who actually liked having sex with kids as they tortured or killed the kid."[40]

---

38   Ibid
39   Craig Spence was found dead in a hotel room in 1989; "Craig J. Spence, 49, a Washington lobbyist, party-giver and shadowy central figure in a District sex scandal last summer, was found dead under unexplained circumstances Friday in a Boston hotel room." *Washington Post*
40   Nick Bryant, *The Franklin Scandal*

This same person, named as Vinson by Nick Bryant went on to tell Bryant that after he rebuffed Spence and King things turned for the worse in his life. Vinson, the man who ran the escort service that worked with Spence and King had told Bryant that Spence and King had both consistently requested that he provide children for sexual services. After Vinson refused, Vinson's house was vandalized, and he was threatened by an associate of Spence as well as being threatened by a very highly placed Justice Department official who was a client of Spence, who Spence provided with underage boys for sex. Furthermore, Vinson's escort service was immediately raided and shut down and Vinson's mother as well as an additional relative of Vinson had their houses raided by the Secret Service. Vinson stated to Bryant that the reason he was being subjected to harassment was because he knew too much information about wealthy and powerful people in D.C. that took part in sex trafficking. Bryant notes,

> "Somebody set us up because they were scared about what we knew about high government officials," said Vinson. "I think it's because they wanted to get our files. We had some very big-name clients in all walks of life—**on Capitol Hill, the military, and even the White House."**[41]

After interviewing Vinson and some other people related to the escort service in D.C. it became clear to Nick Bryant that Vinson did in fact have a multitude of information that could possibly implicate very high-level people in the government. Bryant notes,

> "In my conversations with Vinson and his associates, the names of eminent government officials who patronized the escort service have come up, including a US Congressman. The escort service's documentation salvaged by the Washington Times corroborates their contentions: **"There were high-ranking US government officials, foreign government officials, law enforcement, clergy, and members of the press,"** said Rodriguez about the lists of Vinson's clienteles retrieved by the Washington Times. **"There were members of the United States Congress on those lists** too," he added.[42]

According to Nick Bryant, Craig Spence had connections to some very powerful people in Washington D.C. This is very disturbing considering that Spence was teamed up with Larry King who we know for sure was

41   Ibid
42   Nick Bryant, *The Franklin Scandal*

providing children for sexual encounters with older men and because according to Vinson, the previous owner of the escort service, Spence would constantly ask him to provide children for sexual services for his clients. Nick Bryant also discovered the fact that Spence would have sex parties that included children at his house in Washington D.C. In an interview with A.M. radio station WVOX Nick Bryant stated that,

> 'Craig Spence had connections to everybody, **he had connections to congressmen and senators, to the upper echelon of both the Reagan administration and first Bush administration, and he would have these parties at his house that would include the upper echelon of politics, the upper echelon of media, the upper echelon of academia**. And the would start out as political parties like a cocktail party in Washington D.C. that goes on probably every night. Then later at like 10:30 or 11:00 or 11:30 something very inappropriate would go down." [43]

Necessarily I have only given a brief play by play of the whole Franklin Scandal and all the evidence surrounding it. Nick Bryant's book, the definitive work, spans more than 600 pages. My goal here was to give my readers the bulk of the story and a good summary of the story. Based on the work of the Franklin Committee and its chief investigator Gary Caradori, John De Camp, author of the Franklin Cover Up, and Nick Bryant, author of the Franklin Scandal; there is absolutely overwhelming evidence that Larry King, and many other extremely prominent, respected, and wealthy members of the Omaha community were in fact engaged in a nationwide sex trafficking and pedophilia ring that included elements of devil worship, human sacrifice, kidnapping, drug running, and the use of young children for the sake of horrible sex acts with rich and powerful men. Furthermore, the evidence clearly shows that elements in our nations capitol were also involved including many prominent politicians. And lastly that our institutions of government that are supposed to protect children were in fact rather protecting the powerful men involved and engaging in a massive cover up that very well may have included the assassination of more than 15 people to keep this quiet. Many readers may think there is no way this could be true, I would urge you to read the two books on this subject and watch the documentary (*Conspiracy of Silence*) that never made it to air, it can be found on youtube.com. I would also recommend watching an additional documentary about this case called *Who*

---

43   Interview with Nick Bryant, Author of the *Franklin Scandal*, 1460 on WVOX

Took Johnny Gosch. In this case the evidence, collected by fearless investigators, risking their lives to get this information, really speaks for itself.

The Jeffery Epstein Scandal[44]

"He Was EVIL Personified!"[45]

I spent such considerable space on the Franklin Scandal because that is
the one with the best evidence and the most well-known. Many readers
will have no idea who Jeffrey Epstein is and all the facts and allegations
relating to what he was involved in. I personally was not even aware of
Jeffrey Epstein until I started conducting intensive research into this topic. Jeffrey Epstein is a very secretive and mysterious individual and not a
lot is known about him. It is known that he runs some kind of financial
business that consists of managing money for some of the most powerful
families (one investment banker in New York speculates that he manages
Rockefeller money), and people in the world, however, it is not known
exactly what his investments are, who his clients actually are, how he con-
ducts business, etc. We know that Jeffrey Epstein is very likely a brilliant
man who became a calculus and physics professor at a very young age
and then went to work for Bear Stearns in his early 20's after his brilliance
in mathematics was noticed by Bear Stearns partner Ace Greenberg. He
quickly gained a reputation as a financial genius and an extremely shrewd
investor. He subsequently left Bear Stearns and started his own money
management firm in which he only agrees to accept clients that have 1
billion or more to invest.

We know that Epstein is a billionaire, owns the largest private residence
in Manhattan, owns the largest mansion in New Mexico, has a mansion in
Palm Beach, FL, owns his own island in the Caribbean, Little St. James,
owns a helicopter and yacht, and owns two private jets, one a Boeing 727
named The Lolita Express, which will figure prominently in this case. We
know that Epstein is constantly in the company of young beautiful woman and girls and that he lives a decadent lifestyle; a Vanity Fair magazine
article[46] relayed that Epstein had a book written by the Marquise De Sade

---

44   The bulk of this was originally written in 2018 and early 2019 before Epstein's re-arrest
on federal sex trafficking charges on July 6, 2019.

45   This is a Quote from Melinda Gates who met Epstein only once and literally had nightmares about him after the meeting.

46   During the writing of this Vanity Fair article, Vicky Ward who was writing the article
had come across stories of woman being abused at the hands of Epstein. When Ward confronted
Epstein about this, he told her "If I don't this piece I'm going to have a witch doctor place a curse on
your unborn children." Not only that but the editor of *Vanity Fair*, Graydon Carter found a severed
cats head in his garden and a bullet on his doorstep. After this Carter made the decision to exclude
the sex abuse allegations in the *Vanity Fair* piece because according to him they did not meet the

titled, *the Misfortunes of Virtue*, laying around his house during an interview with the magazine. The Marquis De Sade is who the word sadism or sadist was named after, he was a notorious 18th century French sexual deviant who advocated for and wrote about unbridled sexual depravity and was also accused of blasphemy against the Catholic Church.

> "The notorious Marquis de Sade, a professed atheist and a worshipper of nature, the author of appallingly obscene novels who, after a scandalous life interspersed with richly deserved terms of imprisonment, died in 1814, described in his works satanic orgies in which consecrated hosts were used."[47]

We also know that Epstein has a dark side and can be extremely ruthless. At some of his previous jobs back in the early 80's it was said that people were terrified of him. One account, from Vanity Fair Magazine, has him mercilessly cutting down fellow employees in public so badly that a manager called it "irresponsible." He has been described as a brilliant, ruthless man with cold and steely eyes.

We also know for sure that Jeffrey Epstein is connected to and friends with some of the most powerful people in the world, including former president Clinton, Duke of York, Prince Andrew, Leslie Wexner, owner of Victories Secret,[48] Donald Trump, socialite Ghislaine Maxwell daughter of media titan Robert Maxwell, Kevin Spacey, prominent attorney and professor Alan Dershowitz and many others who are known for their prominence, wealth, and power.

> "A list of people who have associated with Jeffrey Epstein over the years would take in the world of celebrity, science, politics - and royalty."[49]
>
> "But Epstein's contacts book – seen by the Guardian – reads like a directory of the world's global elite. Under the letter B alone are listed Tony Blair, Michael Bloomberg, and Richard Branson. Elsewhere there are multiple contacts – typically at offices, homes, and via aides' mobile phones – for Bill Clinton, Rupert Murdoch, Donald Trump, Dustin Hoffman, Naomi Campbell, and dozens of other A-listers."[50]

---

legal threshold required for publication. See *Filthy Rich*, Netflix Documentary

47   Nicholas Corte, *The Devil*

48   Even Les Wexner said of Epstein that he was "so sick, so cunning, and so depraved"

49   Andrew Buncombe, Jeffrey Epstein: the billionaire pedophile with links to Bill Clinton, Kevin Spacey, Robert Maxwell – and Prince Andrew, *The Independent*, www.theindependant.co.uk, January 2, 2015

50   Paul Lewis, Jeffrey Epstein: inside the decade of scandal entangling Prince Andrew, *The Guardian* www.theguardian.com, Jan 10, 2015

Jeffrey Epstein was arrested in 2005 by the Palm Beach Police Department and was accused of multiple counts of having sex with minors, molesting children, and underage prostitution. He eventually would reach an absolute sweetheart deal to all these charges in which he only ended up serving 13 months of an 18-month sentence. Moreover, he was allowed to leave the jail every day for up to 16 hours for work release privileges. This after signing a non-prosecution agreement with the U.S. Attorney's office and arriving at an agreement with prosecutors in Palm Beach. If the authorities would not have garnered Epstein such a sweet deal, he could have been exposed to and should have been exposed to a far more severe sentence for far more serious crimes such as sex trafficking and rape. Luckily, for Epstein, he is a billionaire and is connected to very influential and powerful people. Epstein had the money to assemble a veritable dream team of attorneys that included famous lawyer Alan Dershowitz and former Clinton prosecutor Ken Starr, and these attorneys did what they were paid to do, namely get Epstein to serve a pathetic, cushy sentence that prosecutors agreed to even though there was massive evidence that Epstein was engaging for years in the trafficking of young girls and was a dangerous and violent pedophile.[51]

Despite Epstein basically skating free and avoiding serious consequences for his actions, the information and evidence of what he was involved in has come into the public light through a number of different sources including news stories, a book by James Patterson, and documents from lawsuits that have been filed against Epstein by some of his former victims. One such document portrays Epstein as running and being a part of an international sex trafficking ring.

> "The motion portrays Epstein as running a "sexual abuse ring," loaning out underage women to **"prominent American politicians, powerful business executives, foreign presidents, a well-known prime minister, and other world leaders"**[52]

The story of Epstein starts with a Palm Beach Police Department investigation into Epstein after a 14-year-old girl had told her mother that

---

51   Ill note that very many sources have said that during the palm beach investigation that the police, investigators, victims, victims attorneys and even prosecutors were subjected to a campaign of terror, threats and harassment from Epstein and his legal team. Many of the victims and the victims attorneys were followed day and night, had their trash rifled through and were even threatened. The principle detective investigating Epstein, Det. Joe Recarty also died under mysterious circumstances during the investigation.

52   Paul Lewis, Jeffrey Epstein: the rise and fall of teacher turned tycoon, Investment banker maintained impressive list of powerful contacts before downfall, *The Guardian*, www.theguardian.com, Jan 4, 2015

she had given Epstein an erotic massage and subsequently had sex with him. After the Palm Beach Police started investigating the FBI quickly became involved as well due to some of the allegations that Epstein was flying young girls aboard his private jet to engage in sex with powerful personages, some of which took place on Epstein's private island. Epstein was also accused by multiple victims of keeping sex slaves, one of his sex slaves was alleged to be model Maria Abromich, whose parents sold her at a young age. The investigation would last over a year and included undercover operations, collection of Epstein's trash, surveillance of Epstein, and a raid on Epstein's home, in which a high school transcript of one of the victims was collected as evidence.

> "When police eventually raided Epstein's mansion, they discovered one of AH's high school transcripts along with a container of peach flavored "Joy Jelly" lubricant and Amazon receipts for explicit books such as Slave Craft: Roadmap For Erotic Servitude Principles."[53]

The FBI eventually identified over 40 victims that may have been exploited in this manner by Epstein and others. Epstein was arrested in 2005, and finally reached his sweetheart deal in 2008 and pleaded guilty to one single count of procuring a minor for prostitution. He then served his 13-month sentence and has since gotten out of jail. Since being released from jail however Epstein has been hit with numerous lawsuits from previous victims alleging all kinds of sadistic abuse at the hands of the rich and powerful.

Based on documents that have been released it seems there were three different classes of victims in the saga of Jeffrey Epstein. The first class of victims were mostly recruited locally from the Palm Beach area by 3 of Epstein's associates; Ghislaine Maxwell, daughter of Media Mogul Robert Maxwell and prominent socialite in New York and London; Haley Robson, an 18-year-old working for Epstein; and Sarah Kellen, another aide of Epstein's. The young girls would almost always be recruited from poor and working-class backgrounds. They would be told by Epstein's co-conspirators that they had a chance to make some good money by giving an older man a massage. Once they agreed to do this they would be driven to Epstein's mansion in Palm Beach, where it is said the walls are decorated with pictures of naked woman, usually given something to eat, and then led upstairs for a meeting with Epstein. Epstein would enter the massage

---

53   Ibid

room wearing only a towel and then would strip naked and would request the young girls to strip down as well. According to court documents sometimes Epstein would masturbate in front of the girls and fondle then with sex toys, some of the girls even claimed they had sex with Epstein on numerous occasions and others have said that Esptein forcefully raped them.

> "Mr. Epstein, through his assistants, would recruit underage fe-males to travel to his home in Palm Beach to engage in lewd con-duct in exchange for money," it said. She added that some of the girls were expected to strip naked and give massages to Epstein while he masturbated, while others had full intercourse with the financier. "Some of those victims went to Mr. Epstein's home only once," Villafaña's letter added. "Some went there as many as 100 times or more"[54]

Apparently, this went on for many years until one of Epstein's victims finally spoke out, initiating a major police investigation. It is said that some of the girls being appalled and scared only had single encounters with Epstein whereas some girls travelled to the Epstein household possi-bly 100 times or more. As I said earlier the FBI established that there were at least 40 victims of Epstein's pedophilia, making his pathetic 13-month county jail sentence even more outrageous considering some of the vic-tims of Epstein were apparently as young as 12 or 13.

> "One victim, in sworn deposition testimony, said Epstein began sexually assaulting her when she was 13 years old and molested her on more than 50 occasions over the next three years. The girls testified they were lured to Epstein's home after being promised hundreds of dollars to be his model or masseuse, but when they arrived, he ordered them to take off their clothes and massage his naked body while he masturbated and used sex toys on them."[55]

The second and third set of victims[56] is where things descend into a far deeper category of depravity. According to court filings from law-

54   Paul Lewis, Jeffrey Epstein: inside the decade of scandal entangling Prince Andrew, *The Guardian*, www.theguardian.com, Jan 10, 2015
55   Malia Zimmerman, Flight logs show Bill Clinton flew on sex offender's jet much more than previously known, Fox News, www.foxnews.com, May 13, 2016
56   The second set of victims were mainly white young females from either the United States, Britain or France that would give Epstein massages, have sex with him, be raped by him, were forced to participate in orgies and were sex trafficked to other rich and powerful people. The third class of victims we know almost nothing about because they were all foreign, spoke absolute-ly no English and have all pretty much disappeared.

suits from victims that are suing Epstein civilly, some of the victims were coaxed and forced into providing sexual favors for more people than just Epstein. Just like the Franklin Scandal, there have been some very prominent names brought up in lawsuits against Epstein alleging Epstein provided young girls for some of his wealthy friends. One lawsuit alleges that Prince Andrew, Alan Dershowitz, Glenn Dubin[57], and Bill Richardson[58] were perpetrators of this abuse.[59] The abuse apparently took place in various places including Epstein's Palm Beach mansion, Ghislaine Maxwell's London home, flights aboard the Lolita express, and orgies involving multiple young victims on Epstein's private island in the U.S. Virgin Islands.

> "He allegedly had a team of traffickers who procured girls as young as 12 to service his friends on "Orgy Island," an estate on Epstein's 72-acre island, called Little St. James, in the U.S. Virgin Islands."[60]

One of the places of the alleged abuse occurred on Epstein's private Boeing 727 jet nicknamed The Lolita Express. The private jet was reportedly used for Epstein and his associates to have sex and orgies with young girls.

> "The tricked-out jet earned its Nabakov-inspired nickname because it was reportedly outfitted with a bed where passengers had group sex with young girls."[61]

Many names of the rich and powerful have showed up on the flight manifests of Epstein's private jet. Some of these included the Duke of York, Prince Andrew, Kevin Spacey who is himself embroiled in a sex scandal, Chris Tucker, Jean Luc Brunel, and former president Bill Clinton who flew on Epstein's Jet 26 times, even ditching his secret service detail 5 times. I'm sure it is just a coincidence that Clinton, a known philanderer, was ditching his secret service detail and privately flying with Epstein, a notorious pedophile, in the company of young girls.

One of the victims who filed a lawsuit against Epstein that was subsequently settled by Epstein, was named as Jane Doe #3, her real name is Virginia Roberts. Roberts alleged that since the age of 15 she was Epstein's sex slave and not only was perpetually abused by Epstein but was

---

57   Billionaire Hedge fund manager
58   Former Governor of New Mexico
59   It is also widely known that Epstein was close friends with Harvey Weinstein, and it has been alleged by multiple victims that Epstein trafficked them to many prominent people, Harvey Weinstein included.
60   Ibid
61   Ibid

also loaned out to other powerful and prominent men. Roberts lawsuit alleges that Jeffrey Epstein and his powerful friends were running an international sex trafficking ring.

> "Epstein … trafficked Jane Doe #3 for sexual purposes to many other powerful men, including numerous prominent American politicians, powerful business executives, foreign presidents, a well-known Prime Minister, and other world leaders."[62]

Roberts lawsuit also alleges that she was witness to many depraved acts between Epstein, his powerful friends and many young girls who were victims. One specific allegation that was made was that Epstein was provided with three 12-year-old French girls for his birthday. The girls were a gift to him for his birthday given to him by a prominent French citizen.

> "During the four years she claimed to have been a fixture in Epstein's hedonistic world, she claimed she saw Epstein and his close associates abuse women from across the world, including three French 12-year-olds who she alleged were sent to him as a birthday present"[63]

Roberts also detailed how she was paid money by Epstein to have sex with Prince Andrew, one occurrence happening on the private island of Epstein in the context of an orgy with multiple young girls besides just Virginia Roberts.

> "The court filing alleged that Epstein forced Roberts "to have sexual relations" on three separate occasions with "a member of the British Royal Family, Prince Andrew (a/k/a Duke of York)." The encounters are alleged to have happened in New York, at Maxwell's London home and in the US, Virgin Islands as part of an "orgy with numerous other under-aged girls"[64]

Virginia Roberts lawsuit also alleges that she was made by Epstein to have sex with famous modeling scout Jean Luc Brunel, who himself was accused of sexual impropriety with young girls by a CBS News 60 minutes documentary. Roberts alleges that Brunel, one of the most famous personages in the modeling business in the world, would use his access to young girls to exploit them for Epstein and others.

---

62   Josh Gerstein, Woman who sued convicted billionaire over sex abuse levels claims at his friends, *Politico*, www.politico.com, December 31, 2014
63   Paul Lewis, Jeffrey Epstein: inside the decade of scandal entangling Prince Andrew, *The Guardian*, www.theguardian.com, Jan 10, 2015
64   Ibid

"It explicitly alleged that Epstein was effectively exploiting Brunel's access to young women for the purposes of sex trafficking. "He would bring young girls (ranging to ages as young as twelve) to the United States for sexual purposes and farm them out to his friends, especially Epstein," the filing states. "Brunel would offer the girls 'modeling' jobs. Many of the girls came from poor countries or impoverished backgrounds, and he lured them in with a promise of making good money." Roberts alleged she was forced to have sex with Brunel, too, and was made to "observe" the French model scout engaging in "sexual acts with dozens of underage girls."[65]

Virginia Roberts is not the only one making these allegations. In similar fashion to the Franklin case, there are multiple victims all making the same allegations, all corroborated by each other. One such victim who also filed a lawsuit against Epstein summed up her involvement with Epstein perfectly.

"I made a pact with the devil in exchange for excitement and glamour,"[66]

Ill also note that despite his 2007-2008 charges and conviction, Epstein continued to operate as if nothing had happened. When one studies this case in depth and examines all of the evidence concerning Epstein and his activities and really his whole life it becomes very clear that he thought he was essentially untouchable and totally above the law. A quote by Father Chad Ripperger will put this into stark context,

"That's what demons try and get people to do, by thinking that the rules don't apply to them or that they can or that the authority structure doesn't apply to them, they don't have to obey authority, because of what they want takes precedence over that."[67]

The case of Jeffrey Epstein is an open and shut case of special treatment under the law for the rich and powerful. With the mountains of evidence that have become available in this case, Epstein and all his co-conspirators should be serving substantial federal prison terms for sex trafficking of minors. The case of Jeffrey Epstein is just one more case of the rich and powerful partaking of extremely deviant and debauched sexual behavior.

65   Paul Lewis, Jeffrey Epstein: inside the decade of scandal entangling Prince Andrew, *The Guardian*, www.theguardian.com, Jan10, 2015
66   Ibid
67   Father Chad Ripperger talk on Authority Structure

Even though none of the victims have made any explicit references to satanism that we know of, it is very curious that Epstein is reading books written by the Marquis de Sade, who is known to have participated in or at least written about orgies in the context of black masses. Orgies involving young, underage girls with rich and powerful men taking place on private islands and in mansions (which is what Epstein was accused and convicted of) sounds like something right out of the movie Eyes Wide Shut. For those who do not know, this movie portrays two characters, Tom Cruise and Nichole Kidman, who slowly get themselves involved in a very high end satanic cult made up of some of the most rich and powerful people in New York City. This cult is shown in the movie to be participating in a ritual done at a very large mansion in which all the participants are wearing black cloaks with hoods and masks. The ritual begins with a high priest, dressed in red, incensing the participants gathered in a circle of 12, then soon degenerates into an all-out orgy. The Cruise character who sneaks into this ritual is found out to be a fraud and subsequently has his life and well-being threatened if he is to tell anybody where he has been or what he has seen.

Some fun facts about the movie: Father M referenced this movie multiple times at the Mundelein Conference as an example of a high-end coven. This was also Stanley Kubrick's last film, he died very suddenly days after turning the final script into the studio. His family had said he was in good health and his death shocked a lot of people. It has of course been speculated that he was killed for revealing too much about the elite and their devilish activities. What is portrayed in the movie is indeed a satanic cult, but the ritual shown is not a black mass as some have said but rather a fertility ritual to the ancient pagan God Ishtar. There are clues all over the movie, including in the beginning scene of symbols for the Deity Ishtar, who was worshipped in ancient times with orgies and fertility rituals. Fertility rituals could be renamed prosperity rituals because these orgies were ritually done so that the cult would become prosperous in all ways, in new life, in more animals, and an abundance of crops. In the modern practice of these rituals they are done for prosperity according to the standards of modern worldliness, meaning wealth, prominence, and power. This is part of a greater point, that not all cults and covens are explicitly dedicated to the worship of Satan or Lucifer, some are dedicated to the worship of some of the other devils and ancient pagan deities (Baal, Moloch, Astaroth) who they have made pacts and covenants with, sometimes for generations. The mansion where the ritual took place is in real life a mansion owned by the Rothschild family. The chair or throne that the high priest is sitting on depicts a symbol at the top that represents the 33rd degree of Freemasonry.[68] This is interesting because Father M was asked about the connection between freemasonry and high-level satanic cults at the Mundelein Conference and he said he did not know of any connection. Yet there have been other people like Father F, who also have spoke at the conference that have explicitly stated that the very highest levels of Freemasonry are a satanic cult and luciferian and that the lower degrees of masonry do not know about the true nature of the highest levels. There is a ton of imagery and symbolism in this movie and a lot that has been speculated about it. What I know for sure is that Stanley Kubrick was one of the most expert and meticulous directors in Hollywood history and he was not known to insert things into his movies for no reason. It has been said about him that if there was something in one of his movies, he meant it to be there and it meant something. Kubrick was also known to have said that the greatest and most gripping movies are those based on real life or truth.

UPDATE

The Jeffrey Epstein case once again exploded into the news headlines in the summer of 2019 when he was arrested by a team of FBI and Homeland Security agents at Teterboro airport in New Jersey on July 6, 2019. He was subsequently charged by the federal government in a multi count indictment with sex trafficking and conspiracy to commit sex trafficking of minors. A week later he had a bail hearing and was denied bail altogether despite the fact that his legal team had offered to put up in excess of $100 million dollars to secure his release.

On July 23, 2019 at approximately 1:30am Jeffrey Epstein was found on the floor of his cell weeping, injured and semi-conscious. Guards at the MCC found marks on his neck. Epstein himself said that he recalled absolutely nothing from the incident but later had said it was his cellmate who attacked him. His cell mate at the time was a former New York City police officer who was being held on 4 counts of murder. This cell mate was also massive, built like a gorilla, and could have easily choked Epstein

---

68   The symbol is of a double headed eagle with a large crown on top, which also incidentally is the symbol used in the Rothschild family red seal. I don't think it is coincidental that the mansion where the ritual takes place is Rothschild owned nor that the double headed eagle symbol on the high priests throne is of Rothschild family origin. It is likely Stanley Kubrick was trying to tell us something and it is also likely this is why he died an early death.

to death. One wonders why this particular person was chosen as a cell mate for Epstein.

After this incident Epstein was given a new cell mate and was placed on suicide watch. Despite all this, and even though Epstein was in one of the most secure jails in the world.[69] And also despite the fact that he was actively appealing his bail order and had filed a motion to dismiss all charges based on the double jeopardy concept, he was found dead in his cell on August 10, 2019 at approximately 6:30am. When guards found him, he had one of his sheets wrapped around his neck and was hanging from the top bunk bed, although with his feet still on the floor. The death of Epstein exploded into the news like a nuclear bomb. Many people, even some of his victims lawyers had speculated earlier that his life was in danger just due to how much incriminating information he had on many powerful people the world over.

The New York City medical examiner conducted an autopsy on Epstein and despite all the evidence to the contrary ruled the death a suicide by hanging. Anyone with a brain however knows darn well that Epstein did not commit suicide, he was almost certainly murdered. The evidence pointing to this is overwhelming. That evidence would include the fact that he was taken off suicide watch just a few days before his death, a fact that shocked many with corrections and law enforcement backgrounds. His new cell mate was also unbelievably moved out of his cell just hours before his death, an extremely unusual occurrence for many reasons.[70] We also know that during the night of his death the two guards that were supposed to be watching him supposedly fell asleep and left him unsupervised for almost 8 hours and then falsified the logbooks at the jail.[71] It has also been reported that screaming was heard coming from Epstein's cell on the night of his death. Then there is the little tidbit that the 2 cameras that were pointing at Epstein's cell on the night of his death were not functioning that night.[72] And the decisive piece of evidence is that during the autopsy it was discovered that Epstein had sustained multiple bone breaks in his neck, among them the hyoid bone which sustained three separate breaks.

---

69   MCC, Metropolitan Correctional Center, housed inmates such as John Gotti and El Chapo, had not had a successful suicide in more than 40 years.
70   Inmates who have had a prior suicide attempt always have a cell mate so they can essentially keep an eye on each other. Epsteins cell mate was also moved out of cell at night, which is extremely unusual as almost all inmate movement of that type is done during the day.
71   The two correctional officers have been prosecuted for conspiracy for falsifying the log books
72   The cameras have since been turned over to the FBI who is investigating Epsteins death.

Jeffrey Epstein's brother Mark Epstein hired famed pathologist Dr. Jeffrey Baden to view the autopsy along with the New York City medical examiner. Dr. Baden[73] has concluded that the breaks in Epstein's neck bones are far more consistent with homicidal strangulation rather than suicidal hanging. Dr. Baden even went on Fox News and proclaimed that based on the evidence it is likely Epstein was murdered. In the days after Epstein's death not a few famous personalities commented on the fact that it was likely he was murdered. U.S. Rep Al Green stated,

> "It's supposed to be impossible for this to happen, impossible. When the impossible occurs, we have to act with immediacy. We need to see the video immediately, and if the video doesn't show us what it should, and there's some technology that failed, Mr. Cavuto, we cannot allow ourselves to believe absurdities. … We have to see what happened, immediately."[74]

Epstein's death was very convenient for all the worlds elite that were involved in the activities that Epstein was involved in. If the Epstein case would have went to trial it is almost certain many of those activities would have come to light, a situation the world elite just could not afford to have happen. Dead men tell no tales as one news commentator put it at the time.

In my original section on Epstein, I noted that he knew, was friends with, and mingled with[75] the elite of the elite in finance, banking, politics, media, entertainment, the law, and even royalty, both British royalty and middle eastern royalty. Jeffrey Epstein's little black book as it has been called contained at least 1000 names of the absolute pinnacle of power in all corners of society and all around the world. While it is definitely true not all of his rich and powerful friends have been accused of being a party to the sex trafficking, many of them have, including Former Governor of New Mexico Bill Richardson, Billionaire hedge fund manager Glenn Dubin, prominent MIT scientist and professor Marvin Minsky, British Prince Andrew, famous modeling agent Jean Luc Brunel, former

---

73   Dr. Baden is not the only one who concluded Epstein was murdered, Dr, Cyril Wecht, also an expert in these matters has said the same thing regarding the absolute rarity of the breaking of the hyoid bone in hanging cases, especially hanging cases like Epstein's where there was no where for him to jump to hang himself. One study has shown that Hyoid bone fractures only occur in %1 of suicidal hanging cases. Hyoid bone breaks however are much more common in cases of homicidal strangulation.

74   Ian Hanchett, Green on Epstein Death: 'We Need to See the Video Immediately', *Breitbard News*

75   Not only that but was a client of and was money manager for some of the powerful people in the world including the Rockefeller and Rothschild families. Epstein was close friends with Evelyn De Rothschild.

U.S. Senator George Mitchell, Famous Harvard law professor and lawyer Alan Dershowitz and according to several other lawsuits against Epstein another unnamed prince; an unnamed foreign president; "a well-known Prime Minister"; and an unnamed hotel chain owner from France. I also failed to note in the first section that Epstein was a participating member in both the Council on foreign relations and the trilateral commission[76], the council on foreign relations being founded by the Rockefeller family. Epstein also sat on the board of Rockefeller University.

Many other very disturbing and dark facts have emerged as well in the months after Epsteins death. One point I did not touch upon above was that Epstein was apparently deeply interested in eugenics and transhumanism, even going as far to donate to causes that worked on this type of science and also organizing parties and events where the elite of these fields would gather and discuss these topics with equanimity. According to other sources it was ultimately Epstein's goal to seed the human race with his own DNA by impregnating multiple women at his ranch in New Mexico and using said ranch as a baby breeding facility. One of Epstein's previous sex slaves even claimed that he and Ghislaine Maxwell had asked her to have "their" baby for them but that the baby would have to be turned over to Epstein and Maxwell immediately and Virginia Roberts would never get to see the infant.[77]

Even more damning are the allegations of activities that occurred on Epsteins private island in the Virgin Islands. I already noted above how multiple women have come forward alleging that Epstein forced them to participate in orgies with multiple other women and other very powerful people including Prince Andrew.[78] However many others, including the personality behind the Q-Anon posts claims that Epstein had tunnels under the island that were used specifically for the purposes of human sacrifice of children. Q also claimed that Epstein spent 29 million dollars filling in those tunnels before arrest.[79]

---

76   Both the Council on foreign relations and the trilateral commission are groups where the elite of business, finance, media, politics, entertainment, the arts, and the law meet yearly to discuss and plan future world events.
77   It is likely the children he planned to have in New Mexico and by Virginia Roberts were to be used for the purpose of human sacrifice in luciferian and satanic rituals.
78   It also needs to be noted that many of Epstein's American or European victims have said that Epstein also had many other underage girls around on his island that spoke no English at all and participated in the orgies as well. It is almost certain these were foreign sex trafficking victims brought in to take part in orgies and sacrifices.
79   It was indeed confirmed by British news source *The Daily Mail* that Epstein had a giant cement truck shipped to the island for some unknown purpose.

I can not definitively say whether or not these underground tunnels actually existed or not.[80] What I do know for sure is that on Epsteins island, far away from any of the other buildings and situated on top of a large hill, which is the highest point on the island, sits a blue and white temple like building with a golden dome on top. The most significant aspect of this building in my opinion is the two golden statues that adorned each corner of the building. These statues have been described differently by different people who saw them. Some have noted that they resemble eagle like birds, one of them looking like an owl. This is significant for many reasons, the first is that I noted above how the symbol of an owl was originally used by the Illuminati which they called the owl of Minerva.[81] Secondly these statues give the top of the building an exact resemblance to the double headed eagle with a crown on top that is used by the Rothschild family and the 33rd degree of freemasonry and was also the symbol used on the top of the high priests throne in the movie Eyes Wide Shut.[82] Needless to say I doubt that this is a coincidence.

Other researchers have noted that the temple building bears an almost identical resemblance to a 15th century Mamluk temple. The Mamluks were people who bought and sold children into sexual slavery. In addition to the temple structure on the island is an extremely curious giant sun dial[83] that is surrounded by stones[84] and benches. When viewed from the air it almost looks like some kind of a magic circle where sacrifices take place.[85] However far more significant is the sun figure itself which is situated at the exact center of the sundial. This sun figure bears an absolute exact resemblance to the "masonic man" figure used in some masonic rituals, literature and art. Not only that but a whole book could be written regarding ancient civilizations and their worship of various sun gods some of which demanded child sacrifice and ritualized sex. In addition to all this one contractor who worked on the island noted the presence of gargoyle like devil statues all over the island, each holding a shield adorned with a

---

80　In 2019 two researchers snuck onto the island and did seemingly uncover the existence of underground passageways on the island.

81　The owl of Minerva is also the symbol used by the Bohemian club, an elite gathering of the rich and powerful where they seemingly decide world events.

82　Others have noted the existence of another statue on the ground next to the temple that looks like the Greek deity Poseidon and yet others have noted at least one of the eagle like bird statues looks like the Egyptian deity Horus.

83　Sun dials were used in ancient pagan religions to track the movement of the solar deities they worshiped and also mark the specific times when these deities required human sacrifice.

84　Many have noted these resemble rune stones, stones used for many occultic and magical practices as well as used by ancient pagan cultures.

85　Some have noted that what look like benches could actually altars.

6-pointed star. Epstein's island also had many other statues of paganistic gods including Hecate and Poseidon.

The evidence that points to Jeffrey Epstein being involved in a world-wide sex trafficking ring that catered to the most powerful in the world and has many elements of occultism is absolutely overwhelming. This story simply confirms what the other stories in this chapter detail, that the ruling elite of the world partake in these activities because they are children of their father, the Devil.

The Sexual Abuse and Pedophilia Scandal in Hollywood

> "I can tell you that the number one problem in Hollywood was, and is, and always will be pedophilia. That's the biggest problem for children in this industry... it's all done under the radar. It's the big secret,"[86]

Superstar child actor Corey Feldman made this claim back in 2011 before anyone really had an inkling of what was going on in Hollywood. Industry executives knew of course, but they were not talking. For this revelation Feldman was ostracized and mocked. Barbara Walters even told him that he was "ruining an entire industry." Feldman also said this on the View:

> "I'm saying that there are people who were the people who did this to both me and Cory that are still working, they're still out there and they're some of the richest most powerful people in this business."[87]

Since then and in the wake of the Harvey Weinstein scandal and many other scandals in Hollywood, Feldman has been vindicated. He has been speaking about this issue since 2011 and has done his best to get the information out there. Feldman has said that he was molested by multiple powerful people in the film industry, he said he also has direct knowledge of his lifelong friend and fellow child actor Corey Haim being raped and sodomized by a very powerful Hollywood personage. Feldman has claimed this is what lead to Haim's lifelong battle with drugs and alcohol and eventually his death at the young age of 38.

---

86   Corey Feldman, *Nightline*, 2011
87   Corey Feldman, *The View*, 2011

Feldman has since gone on to say that the pedophilia in Hollywood is a symptom of something much bigger and much darker going on. In an interview with Newsweek Feldman said:

"I believe that pedophilia in Hollywood is the symptom of a huge network motivated by dark forces... It was almost demonic"[88]

In an interview with Vanity Fair magazine, he relayed the same perspective:

"It's all connected to a bigger, darker power. I don't know how high up the chain that power goes, but I know that it probably is outside of the film industry too. It's probably in government; it's probably throughout the world in different dark aspects."[89]

Feldman even appeared on the Dr. Oz show to highlight some of the allegations he had been making, it was on this show with Dr. Oz that Feldman finally confirmed who one of his molesters had been. In an interview with Good Day LA, Dr. Oz said:

"it's not just a small problem, there was an easily demonstrable ring of individuals who were taking advantage of young people, male and female, and I think this blurs the sexual line, its just wrong. And these offenses were committed because people thought they had immunity, they could get away with it."[90]

What Dr. Oz and Corey Feldman have said seems to be true; namely, that there exists in Hollywood the presence of a ring made up of very prominent and powerful people in the film industry that have been engaging in pedophilia and the sexual exploitation of children for years and possibly decades. Everything that has come out in the wake of the Harvey Weinstein scandal and others has born that assertion out.

In 2012 an article appeared in the Los Angeles Times which highlighted the arrests and conviction for pedophilia, and child pornography, of multiple members of the Hollywood establishment. Some of the personages that appeared in the article were prominent child manager Bob Villard who has worked with major stars such as Leonardo DiCaprio. Villard was arrested in 2005 and accused of committing a lewd act with a child. Villard also has a previous history of investigations and convictions for child pornography. The article also profiled the arrests and convictions of

---

88   Emily Gaudette, Corey Feldman, www.newsweek.com, Nov 17, 2017
89   Yohana Desta, www.vanityfair.com, Nov 10, 2017
90   Dr. Oz, *Good Day LA*

two different members of the Nickelodeon production team for molesting children. The article went on to state:

> "People like this are predators who prey on little kids who want to be the next Justin Bieber — and they're told, 'That's what's done, this is all normal in the industry,' " said Katie Albracht, the Los Angeles County deputy district attorney who prosecuted the 2005 Villard case."[91]

In 2015 a documentary produced and directed by Oscar nominated director Amy Berg was released titled "An Open Secret," the documentary would profile seven very powerful personages in the entertainment industry in Hollywood that had serious and credible accusations of pedophilia leveled against them. One perpetrator shown in the documentary was Mark Collins Rector, a very prominent Hollywood producer and investor who started the internet entertainment channel DEN. Rector was accused by multiple underage boys of molesting them and spiking their drinks and then molesting them while they were passed out. Rector was also accused of throwing extravagant parties at his mansion that would also have the presence of some of DEN's investors, other prominent Hollywood types. Rector would apparently pass the young boys around to his clients and force the boys to perform unwanted sexual acts. Rector was subsequently charged with these offenses but left the country. He has since renounced his U.S. citizenship.

Another very powerful Hollywood director that was profiled in the documentary was Brian Singer. Singer is an extremely prominent director in Hollywood, having such films as X-Men under his belt. Singer has a history of being accused of lewd acts with young boys but has never been charged. It has been alleged in multiple lawsuits over the years that Singer throws large parties at his mansion in which the presence of younger boys is a staple. These parties are said to descend into a drug fueled orgy involving gay sex between Hollywood executives and young men and boys. One of Singers victims alleged in a lawsuit that he was 15 years old when he was raped and sodomized by Singer. There are an additional five powerful Hollywood executives profiled in this documentary, that I would highly recommend watching.

According to an article by redstate.com there is also an extremely powerful Hollywood executive that has been accused of pedophilia for years by many different sources. I won't name the man, but he is a very high up

---

91   Dawn Chmielewski, *Los Angeles Times*, Jan 8, 2012

executive at Nickelodeon and the actual creator of many of its hit shows and directly responsible for the fame of many young stars.

And then we have people like Kevin Spacey, an extremely prominent actor who was working on a hit show "House of Cards" when he was hit by multiple accusations from multiple sources of inappropriate contact with young boys.

> "The first accusation of sexual misconduct against Oscar-winning actor Kevin Spacey landed on Oct. 29, and a little more than a week later more than a dozen men — including five who said they were teens at the time — have come forward to allege he sexually harassed, assaulted or attempted to rape them."[92]

Another very prominent Hollywood executive that has been accused of this activity is Brett Ratner, founder and CEO of RatPac entertainment. The illicit sexual activities of Ratner allegedly go back decades and involved famous music mogul Russell Simmons, who has also been accused of sexual impropriety. Ratner has not been accused of pedophilia, but he has been accused of forcing women to perform oral sex on him and even instances of possible rape among many others.

Harvey Weinstein, the most well-known of those in Hollywood accused of repeated sexual assault has been accused by many victims. The number of extremely prominent Hollywood actresses accusing Weinstein of sexual assault and downright rape is shocking. The more shocking part however is that Weinstein was able to operate so long with impunity. Many of the allegations against Weinstein go back to the early 1990's. Tragically there may be evidence that some other A-list stars like Matt Damon, who is one of the most talented actors in Hollywood, may have been involved in covering for Weinstein.

The people I have mentioned here are just the tip of the iceberg as far as sexual assault and pedophilia in Hollywood goes. All of this has been coming out in a steady stream over the last couple of years. Time magazine even published an article profiling 136 prominent people who have been accused of sexual misconduct since the Harvey Weinstein scandal broke. We need to remember also that people like Woody Allen and Roman Polanski, two confirmed pedophiles who are also extremely prominent members of the Hollywood establishment have been welcomed and defended by Hollywood. Woody Allen still works in Hollywood and there was a campaign started by many Hollywood elites to allow Polanski to come back to Hollywood from his exile.

One other very dark aspect to Hollywood and the Los Angeles area in general is the presence of high-level satanic cults. The Franklin case presented us with documented and corroborated accounts of powerful people engaging in devil worship and human sacrifice. This activity definitely goes on in the greater Los Angeles area, in fact I would say LA is a hotbed of this activity. Father S is a priest that was heavily involved in the new age movement and the occult before having a conversion in Medjugorje and eventually becoming an exorcist. At the Mundelein Conference for Healing, Deliverance and Exorcism in 2010 Father S stated that there are high level satanic cults that meet in the hills above Malibu that include very prominent people such as doctors and lawyers.

"According to one doctor who has written several books, she had a patient who was a Satanist and she was in Los Angeles. And Satanists took her to several Satanist meetings. And she says one of the largest groups of Satanists is in Los Angeles, right above Malibu in the mountains there. And a lot of the Satanists there are people who are professionals. There are lawyers, there are doctors, there are ministers, all kinds of people."[93]

Peter Haining in his book *The Anatomy of Witchcraft*, talks about satanic cults in LA as well. He profiles one specific cult called the Chingons, whose leader is an extremely influential Los Angeles businessman.

"Another cult of animal sacrificers who meet in the Santa Ana Mountains just outside of Los Angeles. Dedicated to "The Worship of Evil" the members steal family pets and ritually disembowel them, eating their hearts as a sign of their obedience. The leader of the group is known simply as The Grand Chingon and current rumors have it that he is a very wealthy Los Angeles businessman."[94]

This same author goes on to say that the Hollywood Hills abound in the presence of cults:

"Innumerable groups abound in the Hollywood Hills and along Benedict, Laurel and Topanga Canyons-most practicing Satanism."[95]

---

93   Father S, *Mundelein Conference on Healing, Deliverance, and Exorcism*, 2010
94   Haining, *The Anatomy of Witchcraft*
95   Ibid

The internet is absolutely saturated with conspiracy theories and possible evidence of satanic cult like activity in Hollywood and the music industry. Whether it is occult imagery in music videos which is very real, or blatantly satanic lyrics, or certain stars having OTO tattoos on themselves, owl tatoos or the plethora of stars and entertainers who cover one of their eyes denoting the all-seeing eye of Lucifer, the evidence is almost overwhelming. Additionally, the number of musicians and actors that have explicitly stated that they have sold their souls to the devil, are possessed by the devil, and know that the devil or some dark power works through them to help them produce their vile content, is legion. I can't delve into every single aspect of this, space just does not allow it. It is a well-documented fact that many musicians and actors have talked about how they are possessed. Because they cooperate with the possession and also cooperate with the devil's work of leading souls astray with their vile content and also display no signs of a crisis state or aversion to the sacred, their cases of possession must be classified as perfect possession.

What is clear is that there is something very dark and insidious going on in the movie industry, music industry and entertainment industry. The allegations of massive organized pedophilia and devil worship notwithstanding, the real evidence of the pervasive darkness in these industries comes from what these industries produce for consumption by the general public. I would argue that most, a great majority of movies, tv shows, and music that comes out of these industries is essentially demonic. As I stated previously these things undermine the faith, make sin look fun, glamorous, normal, and natural. Make the occult look flashy and mysterious. Make the Catholic Church look evil, scandalous, outdated, misogynistic, discriminatory, etc. Make belief in God look outdated, archaic, ancient and stupid, and make atheism look scientific, trendy, and popular. And most disturbingly, suck in and hook children with all these concepts. The concepts of free sex, drug use, rebellion, materialism, hatred, masochism, homosexuality, the glamour of violence and murder and complete lack of respect for authority such as parents are all concepts that weave through modern movies, tv shows, and music like a spider web of demonic evil that pollutes, infects, and contaminates the people who ingest this material.

What is produced in Hollywood and the music industry is the only proof I need that these industries are sullied by something extremely powerful, dark, and evil. The allegations of people involved in these industries of pedophilia, sexual depravity, and satanism is not surprising at all considering the filth that daily comes out of these industries. Based on the filth that comes out of these industries it is pretty clear that there are executives, investors, and performers in these industries attempting to intentionally lead people astray from the true faith and into various forms of deception, bondage, and sin. This leads to the natural conclusion, in my opinion, that these people are explicit servants of the diabolic kingdom and very likely have sold their souls for fame and are possessed and controlled by the prince of this world, and the shocking thing is that many of them have actually said as much. There are a shocking number of actors and musicians who have admitted to being possessed in some way. For more information regarding occult symbolism and the general satanic nature of the entertainment industry I would highly recommend the videos of Pastor Joe Schimmel of Fight the Good Fight Ministries. He did a very long and detailed video series entitled *They Sold Their Souls for Rock n Roll and Hollywood Unmasked that* goes into great detail regarding many of the facets of the evil nature of the movies and music industries.

In conclusion, what is extremely clear based on the available evidence is that there exists in Hollywood, and the entertainment industry as a whole, a network, an organized group of individuals, very powerful and wealthy individuals, who are engaging in rampant and sick pedophilia and possibly satanism and have been doing so for decades under the radar. In the introduction to this book I mentioned "organized pedophilia" as one of the activities perpetrated by perfectly possessed individuals. This mini study on what is going on in Hollywood is a prime example of that concept and should be extremely disturbing to all my readers.

The Dr. Phil Show

> "the story you are about to hear is so shocking, so unbelievable that your mind is going to struggle to allow you to accept that things like this exist. But they do, and they are happening right now all over the world, even in small towns all over the United States."[96]

On March 17, 2017 a show entitled *Private Planes, Black Tie Parties, Elite Sporting Events: The Shocking Story of One Woman's Life in Sex Trafficking* aired on The Dr. Phil Show on national television. Dr. Phil went on to interview a woman named Kendall, who claimed that she was sold to a very powerful and very rich sex trafficker at birth by her natural parents.

---

96   *The Dr. Phil Show*, March 17, 2017

She goes on to allege some of the very same things that have been alleged in the Franklin case and the Jeffrey Epstein case.

> "Kendall: My whole life I traveled all over the world and would go to some of the biggest events to meet clients. Dr. Phil: On the outside her clients were pillars of their community. But behind closed doors, she says they were sinister and evil human beings. Kendall: They were in law enforcement, doctors, psychiatrists, judges, politicians, and even people who owned sports teams. They were all extremely rich and prominent members of society. I attended many parties for people who had just got elected into office."[97]

Kendall went on to relate that the man who bought her was an extremely prominent individual, with connections to the worldwide elite.

> "The man who owns me is smart and rich and he has connections to powerful people all over the world."[98]

Kendall went on to relate on the show some extremely sadistic abuse, some of which I would classify as satanic ritual abuse. Kendall related that not only was she passed around to the rich and powerful all over the world and forced to perform sick sex acts for these people, but that she was just one of many children she knew this was happening to. Kendall alleges that the man who owned her would lock her in cages, viciously beat and physically abuse her if she disobeyed or did not please a client, was told the only way she could get out of her life was to kill herself, was forced to eat feces, was told it was Gods will this was all happening to her because she was born into it, and was also made to be a participant in the murder of children.

Kendall relayed a story in which not only had she seen her captor murder multiple children, but she was also made to take part in one of their murders. Kendall also alleges that she was allowed to get pregnant three times because that is what some of the rich and powerful clients paid for. She says that after having the babies they were immediately taken from her and she has no idea what has happened to them. It should be noted that being locked in cages, being made to eat feces, participating in and witnessing the murder of children, and then being told this is all the will of God, is all a hallmark of overt satanic ritual abuse. Kendall did not say on the show that her captor was a Satanist, however, the activity she is

---

97   Ibid
98   Ibid

describing has been described very often in the context of ritualistic satanism.

Some of the things Kendall alleges are unbelievably shocking and Dr. Phil even addresses that fact on the show. He goes on to tell the audience that his staff spent 4 months researching and corroborating Kendall's story.

> "For nearly 4 months we researched Kendall's story trying to verify its authenticity. And after speaking confidentially to agencies, we were able to confirm that Kendall has in fact been trafficked…
> I can tell you that a very reliable source has confirmed to us that Kendall has in fact been trafficked, raped, molested, and severely abused by a very large, very dangerous organization."[99]

This piece of evidence from Dr. Phil is significant because this did air on national television and Dr. Phil does have a reputation at stake. Moreover Dr. Phil explicitly states that his production team researched Kendall's story and confirmed its authenticity after talking to federal agencies. I believe those facts give this story the air of credibility and believability that maybe our next case does not have.

Pizza gate

Pizza gate refers to a conspiracy theory started on the internet that came about after the release of emails from Hillary Clinton and her campaign chairman John Podesta by Wikileaks. What Pizza gate refers to is the content in the emails of Hillary Clinton but especially John Podesta being linked to pedophilia and satanism. Some of the emails have phrases and words in them that pedophiles do use as code words. This information led to a pizza restaurant in Washington D.C. called Comet Pizza, whose owner is James Alefantis. Alefantis has many connections to the top strata of the democratic party in Washington D.C.[100] Based on all of the available evidence available to internet investigators, many have come to the conclusion that the Podesta brothers, Clintons and this pizza restaurant are involved in a high-level sex trafficking ring that specializes in pedophilia and has elements of satanism. I am not going to spend a lot of time on this one because there is just too much we do not know and there is not a lot of corroborating evidence, unlike the other cases and in-

---

99   *The Dr. Phil Show*, March 17, 2017
100   James Alefantis was named one of the top 50 most powerful people in Washington D.C. by *GQ* magazine, this despite him being a lowly pizza shop owner.

stances I have spoken about thus far. What I would like to do is just briefly highlight what we actually know as fact in this case.

The most important thing I want to say about the Clinton/Podesta emails is that this whole incident is simply confirmation of what we already know. Namely, that the worldwide elite engage in sex trafficking, pedophilia, and various forms of occultism. Pizza gate is the most recent scandal of all the scandals I am detailing. We have already learned what is going on with the elite based on the other scandals I am detailing, the Clinton/Podesta emails are just conformation of everything we already know of what they are engaging in and who they serving.

- Some of the emails that were released from the account of John Podesta, Hilary Clinton, and Tony Podesta by Wikileaks contain some extremely strange wording and phrasing. These words and phrases really make no sense and would lead one to believe that the people engaging in these conversations are speaking in code. Some of the words that these people are using are "pizza" and "handkerchief" and "pasta" which have been confirmed as being code words for pedophiles.

- The pizza restaurant that is part of pizzagate, Comet Ping Pong Pizza, is actually referenced in the Podesta emails more than a dozen times. This despite the mainstream media claiming there is no connection between the pizza restaurant and The Podesta's and Clinton.

- The owner of Comet Ping Pong Pizza is James Alefantis who is in fact a good friend of both John and Tony Podesta and Hillary Clinton. Alefantis was named by GQ Magazine as the 49th most powerful person in Washington D.C. Alefantis is a homosexual and was once in a relationship with David Brock who was at the helm of Media Matters, an anti-Christian organization that is funded by billionaire George Soros.[101]

- Since the whole pizza gate story broke Alefantis has made all of his social media pages private. However, before he was able to do this internet sleuths archived a lot of the images on Alefantis' Instagram pages. The images that were on Alefantis's Instagram pages are extremely disturbing and graphic and have to do with children. For a person that claims to be completely innocent and a victim of a conspiracy theory, Alefantis has failed to explain the sick images on his Instagram pages.[102]

101   Ben Swann, CBS News
102   Ibid

• There is a pizza restaurant right next door to Comet Ping Pong Pizza named Besta Pizza, which according to many sources are both very well connected to the DNC and to each other. The logo of Besta Pizza was a triangle in the form of a pizza. According to a declassified FBI report this symbol is code for pedophiles and denotes "boy love." When one compares the Besta Pizza logo and the symbol from the FBI, they are identical. After the Pizza gate story broke however, Besta Pizza quickly changed its logo.[103]

• Comet Ping Pong Pizza, the restaurant owned by James Alefantis, whose Instagram pages include very disturbing images of children, and that has connections to John and Tony Podesta, whose emails have shown clearly code words normally used as code words for pedophilia, has bands that perform there on a regular basis. The two bands that regularly perform there are called "Sex Stains" and "Heavy Breathing." I have confirmed that the music videos for these two groups joke about pedophilia in their songs and their music videos also contain the same boy-love symbol that was the logo for Besta Pizza. For a restaurant that is supposed to cater to children these two music groups would seem to be highly questionable and inappropriate.[104]

• In the Podesta emails, John Podesta speaks frequently about his very close relationship with and friendship to Dennis Hastert, the former Republican speaker of the house who is currently serving a stiff prison sentence for pedophilia. When sentencing Hastert, the Judge declared him to be a serial child molester. Both Podesta's and Bill and Hillary Clinton also have connections to Billionaire Jeffery Epstein who is also a convicted pedophile and ran a private island, dubbed Orgy Island, in which he kept sex slaves but also forced underage girls to participate in orgies with the rich and powerful.[105]

• According to a Washington Post report, visitors to the home of Tony Podesta saw multiple color pictures adorning his bedroom that were done by an artist named Katy Grannan a photographer well known for her documentary style pictures of naked teenagers.[106]

• At the Comet Ping Pong Pizza restaurant itself there are also paintings done by an artist that is notorious for paintings depicting young children in sexually explicit poses and situations. Many of

---

103   Thomas Horn, *Shadowland*
104   Ben Swann, CBS News
105   Ibid
106   From a 2004 *Washington Post* article about Tony Podesta

the works done by this artist cannot even be shown on television or YouTube based on their explicit content.[107]

• According to some of the emails released from the accounts of John Podesta, both Podesta brothers have connections to a woman named Marina Abramovic who is a well-known Satanist who engages in a demented form of occultism called spirit cooking in which blood, semen, breast milk, and other bodily fluids are mixed together and drenched and splattered on effigies representing children. According to the hacked emails, the Podesta brothers attended at least one of these satanic rituals.[108]

• Despite all this evidence and many other pieces of evidence out there that I have not listed, the FBI nor the Washington D.C. Police force have lifted one finger to investigate this. The mainstream media has labeled it fake news, and pieces from New York Times have attempted to debunk it.

There is a mountain of circumstantial evidence pointing to the validity of the Pizza gate scandal. I have only listed some of the available information and evidence regarding pizza gate. If all these pieces of information that I have just listed were all put together and turned out to be all just a coincidence, it would be the coincidence of the century. Usually where there is smoke, there is fire, especially in the case of very influential and wealthy people engaging in this type of activity. Based on what we know about the Franklin Scandal and Jeffrey Epstein, it should surprise absolutely no one if Pizza gate turns out to be fact rather than fiction. I also would like to mention that some of these scandals intertwine. An example is the fact that the Clintons and the Podesta's are all good friends with Jeffrey Epstein and have frequently flown on his jet and gone to his island in the Bahamas.

THE BOHEMIAN GROVE AND SKULL AND BONES SOCIETY

"The Seat of Satan in America is north of San Francisco"[109]

Bohemian Grove refers to an organization north of San Francisco in the redwood forest called the Bohemian Club. The Bohemian Club was founded in 1872 and was established as a club for men who enjoyed taking part in the arts and literature. Over the years the club grew rapidly,

---

107   Ben Swann, CBS News
108   Marina Abramovic, very curiously was also recently photographed with Lord Jacob Rothschild, while both were admiring a painting by Sir Thomas Lawrence, painted in 1797 titled "Satan Summoning His Legions
109   Taken from a 1990 prophecy of a mystic; revelation1 (spiritdaily.com)

expanding as it did always being home to the rich and elite of this country and the world. In modern society the Bohemian Club is known to be the most recognized club for the world's elite. There are joining fees in excess of $10,000 and one must be invited by current members to join the club. The club is absolutely not open to the public and during the clubs 2-week summer gathering security is extremely tight and absolutely no outsiders are allowed in. In fact, very recently an editor for Vanity Fair magazine was caught and arrested for trying to sneak into the grove. That is not to say nobody has been successful at getting in. Alex Jones, the conspiracy theorist, famously sneaked into the grove back in 90's and videotaped one of their rituals known as the cremation of care ceremony.

Which leads me to my next point about the grove, not only is it an elite club known for having some of the most powerful people in the world as members and attendees, but during the 2-week summer gathering in which these members are present, the members partake in bizarre occult rituals. The primary ritual they partake in is called the cremation of care ceremony. This ritual consists of all the things a traditional satanic ritual would have; men in robes and hoods, a high priest, chanting, an altar, fire, a satanic idol, and a human sacrifice. The members essentially burn in effigy a human figure they call "care" on an altar in front of a giant 40-foot owl during the ritual. The giant owl has been widely believed to be Moloch, an ancient pagan deity that was worshipped with human sacrifice, who is widely believed to be one of the most powerful devils of hell. The other fact about the owl worth mentioning is that at one time the owl was confirmed to be a symbol for the illuminati, this has been confirmed by historical sources. The fact that the owl was a symbol for the illuminati and is now the symbol for the bohemian club is I think extremely significant.

Members of the grove have included some of the most powerful men in the world including previous and current presidents, presidents and prime ministers of foreign nations, CEO's of multinational corporations, movie stars, and artists. President Nixon was caught on tape saying the grove was "the most faggy g d thing you could ever imagine." It has also been reported by multiple people that there are gay orgies and group sex that go on at the grove. There have been former prostitutes and escorts who have come forward with information that some of the powerful people at the grove take part in this type of activity. One might ask, what are the elite of the world doing at an exclusive club closed off from the general public, participating in gay orgies and satanic rituals? Its clear these people serve Lucifer, their master and lord. Christians, who love Jesus Christ, do not partake of this type of activity. I believe world events are to a certain degree formed and planned at places like the Bohemian grove, the Bilderberg group, the Trilateral Commission, and the Council on Foreign Relations.

The Skull and Bones Society is a secret society that counts as its members people like Former Presidents George H.W. Bush, George W. Bush, and William H. Taft, former Senator and Secretary of State John Kerry, John Dulles, founder of the CIA, William F. Buckley, PBS Host, Fred Smith, founder of Fed Ex, Henry John Heinz, heir of Heinz Ketchup, and John S. Pillsbury, heir and former Minnesota governor, just among a few. The Skull and Bones Society also known as The Order of Death was founded at Yale University in 1832. The founding of this elite secret society came as a result of President John Quincy Adams purging freemasons from roles in government. It had been thought at that time that Freemasonry had gained inordinate power in United States politics. A Yale student then went to Germany to acquire a charter from a freemasonic lodge there and used it in founding of the Skull and Bones society. The building in which the society is housed is reportedly extremely eerie and adorned with coffins and skulls on the inside.

According to many sources the rituals employed by this secret society are overtly satanic in nature. They apparently include a mock resurrection ceremony, drinking blood or fake blood from a skull, and members dressed up as the devil. New initiates must drink the blood from the skull and pledge allegiance to figures dressed up as a devil, the pope, a black knight. There are also members who dress up as skeletons, representing death. It has been speculated that the dressed-up figures of the devil, pope, and black knight is a representation of the diabolic trinity; Satan, Lucifer, and the Antichrist. It is also very well known that initiates must take a blood oath never to reveal anything about the group or even admit their membership to the group publicly. There is direct evidence that this is factual because previous president George W. Bush and Senator John Kerry were asked about the Skull and Bones society during the 2004 presidential campaign by late journalist Tim Russert and both absolutely refused to discuss the topic and quickly changed the subject.

The Skull and Bones society have a yearly meeting of its 800 or so members on a secret private island on the St. Lawrence River, not too much is known about what goes on during this meeting. As with the Bohemian grove, the Skull and Bones society is a secret society made up of the elite of the elite in politics and business who partake in dark occult rituals in secret.[110]

High Level Satanic Cult and Pedophilia Activity Worldwide

Everything I have discussed thus far have been events and things that have occurred in the United States. These things however are not just a U.S. phenomenon, there is evidence that similar activities go on internationally as well. I will touch briefly on some of them to give the reader of the overall world picture of what some of the elite have involved themselves in.

Great Britain

This from The Los Angeles Times:

> "The allegations about so-called VIP pedophiles involve prestigious London addresses, some of the highest-ranking members of Britain's establishment and the suspected abuse of young boys in the 1970s and 1980s, including three who were slain. Six members of Parliament have been implicated in the scandal, which threatens to expose a powerful political elite who may have raped and exploited juveniles for more than a decade and put their self-interests ahead of the protection of children. John Mann, a member of Parliament, has presented Scotland Yard with a dossier that he said names 22 high-profile figures, including three serving in the House of Commons and three members of the House of Lords, who are believed to have been involved in a pedophile ring. There are no allegations that the six members of Parliament were involved in incidents in which children died. The dossier includes the names of 14 Conservative politicians, five Labor politicians and three from other parties, Mann told reporters. He also alleges that up to five pedophile rings were operational at the same time during the 1970s and 1980s, and that two whistle-blowers who knew about nefarious activities by members of Parliament met suspicious deaths.[111]

In 2015 60 Minutes Australia ran a special regarding a very high-level pedophile ring centered in the U.K. According to 60 minutes this scandal involved some of the most powerful politicians in all of Britain. The accusations came from multiple victims and they were that the very highest

---

110   Anthony Sutton, *America's Secret Establishment*
111   Christina Boyle, Britain investigates alleged VIP pedophile ring from 70's and 80's, *Los Angeles Times*, Dec 23, 2014

members of British politics were involved in a VIP pedophile ring that included accusations of sick and sadistic sexual abuse, murder of children and elements of satanism. This quote from 60 minutes Australia:

> "Without question the biggest political scandal Britain has ever faced will be exposed tonight. It involves a secret network of the highest office holders in the land. Past and current members of parliament, cabinet ministers, judges, diplomats, even one of the countries top spies. These men are accused of some of the most sadistic child sexual abuse imaginable on hundreds of victims, some as young as 8. More confronting still are claims that children were killed in order to protect this network of predators, including one boy whose father worked at the Australian High Commission in London. For over 40 years the evil child predators acted with complete impunity, hiding behind the façade of respectability."[112]

And also, this quote from the same program:

> "A sex scandal at the very highest levels of the British establishment, child sexual abuse victims come forward to point the finger at very powerful men. Serving members of the British Parliament, cabinet ministers, lords, spies, even senior police; incriminated in a VIP pedophile ring for the privileged and powerful."[113]

In similar fashion to the Franklin Scandal, many of the victims were plundered from homes for troubled boys in the U.K. Also similar to Franklin are the accusations of a monumental cover up by high-ranking British authorities so that this deviant and evil activity among Britain's most respected does not come into the public light. The 60 minutes special includes an interview with a former detective inspector who investigated claims of pedophilia against a member of the British House of Lords. According to the former officer there was substantial evidence that this senior politician had molested at least 9 boys from a boy's home; when the officer was ready to make an arrest of the subject he was prevented from doing so by his superiors. Also present in this case are allegations and evidence that children were murdered to protect the wealthy and powerful people involved in this organized pedophilia. According to 60 minutes,

> "police have reopened the case also acknowledging they have credible evidence of murders committed by the Westminster pedophile ring."[114]

112   CBS Australia, *60 Minutes*, 2015
113   Ibid
114   CBS Australia, *60 Minutes*, 2015

Also present in this case, like in many others are allegations that the pe-dophilia was associated with some sort of ritual context. One of the victims being interviewed for the special describes that the pedophilia took place with multiple offenders and in the context of some type of dark ritual.

One very prominent individual who was named as being part of this massive pedophile ring was Tory MP, Enoch Powell. The UK Independent notes that Powell was,

> "Widely regarded as one of the most powerful orators in modern Brit-ish politics, Mr. Powell's time as a frontline politician came to an abrupt end when he was sacked in 1968 as shadow defense secretary by Edward Heath the morning after the Rivers of Blood speech."[115]

And in similar fashion to some of the other allegations of the rich and powerful in Britain, Powell was also accused of committing satanic ritual abuse by a member of the high clergy of the Church of England.

> "The name of the late MP, one of the most divisive politicians of the late 20th century, was provided to Scotland Yard after a cler-gyman came forward with claims from the 1980s relating to ritual satanic abuse."[116]

One of the highest-level names that has surfaced as being accused of pedophilia and satanism is former Prime Minister (1970-1974) Edward Heath. Heath died in 2005, however, in 2014 multiple victims came for-ward to accuse Heath of brutal pedophilia and satanism and as a result 7 different police agencies in Britain began to investigate Heath. As a re-sult of the investigation the police found that the allegations were serious enough that Heath would have been questioned extensively by police. Some of the more disturbing allegations have to do with devil worship and child murder.

> "The pedophile ring – which they say Sir Edward was part of – stabbed, tortured and maimed youngsters in churches and burnt babies in satanic orgies before men, women and children gorged themselves on blood and body parts, police have been told."[117]
>
> "In August 2015 Heath was under investigation by the Hamp-shire, Jersey, Kent, Wiltshire, Gloucestershire and Thames Valley

115   Cahal Milmo, Tory MP Enoch Powell investigated as alleged member of Westminster paedophile network, UK *Independent*, March 30, 2015
116   Ibid
117   Rebecca Camber, Group of women who say they were abused by Sir Edward Heath also claim their parents ran a satanic sex cult that was involved in SIXTEEN child murders, UK Daily Mail, Feb 19, 2017

police, and London's Metropolitan Police. Operation Midland of the Metropolitan Police in London is investigating alleged offences of an abuse ring around Edward Heath alleged to be responsible for extreme child abuse and three murders."[118]

According to the information available in this case Heath was accused of being involved in devil worship by six different people, all 6 people relaying stories and allegations of a very similar nature. All six victims also relayed a very obscure allegation about Heath, namely that he had very long fingernails that he used to abuse victims, even though all six victims did not know each other. Some of the allegations were made to a very prominent doctor who specializes in child abuse, the allegations were then turned over to police. One of the victims alleged that in addition to Heath many other very prominent individuals in British society were involved in satanic cult activity.

> "14 individuals hold an Aristocratic title and appear to be particularly involved with the provision of venues for 'rituals'. The roles of 16 politicians mentioned included Councilor, Secretary of State for Health, Education and Home Office as well as Chancellor. 6 police officers are mentioned including 3 Chief Constables. 8 Church leaders feature including a Cardinal and a Bishop. 4 law professionals are mentioned including a judge. 8 Journalists, 4 TV Presenters and 7 Entertainers are mentioned. Four individuals each fall into the professions Physician, Psychologist or Psychiatrist.[119]

There is also evidence to suggest that Heath was involved with Peter Jaconelli and Jimmy Saville, who is definitely one of the most notorious pedophiles in the world. Ted Heath, Jaconelli, and Savile are all supposed to have been in a pedophile ring that included taking children to pedophile parties to be abused. According to the UK Daily Mail,

> "North Yorkshire Police detectives started examining Sir Edward Heath's relationship with Jimmy Savile and his pedophile friend Peter Jaconelli, who was known as 'King Cornet'. 'King Cornet' would also crawl the streets with Savile in his pink Rolls Royce looking for boys to abuse and the pair were believed to be at the head of a nine-strong pedophile ring."[120]

118   Dr. Rainer Hermann Kurz, *The Satanist Cult of Ted Heath: Ethical Implications of Authority Compromise*
119   Ibid
120   Martin Robinson, Jimmy Savile's nephew claims his friend was abused at 14 by Ted Heath as picture emerges of the ex prime minister with known paedophile dubbed 'King Cornet', *Daily Mail*, Aug 6, 2015

Peter Jaconelli was another very prominent politician accused of pedophilia and running in the same crowd as Heath and Savile who both have been implicated in downright devil worship. Jaconelli was Mayor of Scarborough and also became very wealthy through an ice cream business. He is accused of operating and molesting children for nearly 40 years.

> "Officers believe that there are 32 abuse cases related to Jaconelli, between 1958 and 1998, and included allegations of indecent assault, inciting a child to engage in sexual activity, gross indecency and rape."[121]

Jimmy Savile, the other piece to this diabolic puzzle was accused of molesting up to 500 children during a period that spans almost 50 years. Jimmy Savile was a very prominent TV personality with the BBC, radio DJ, and celebrity in Britain and was actually knighted by the queen and recognized by Pope John Paul II for his work with charities. Savile had relationships with many of the most prominent, wealthy, and respected people in Britain, yet he is accused of being a diabolical caricature (photographs of him confirm this) of a human being and preying on children without reproach or consequence for year after year.

> "In all, Savile is believed to have abused at least 500 girls and boys, some as young as two, most between 13 and 15, as well as countless adults ranging up to 75 years old. With unfettered access to Leeds General Infirmary, the health service report said, he raped and fondled boys, girls, men and women in offices and corridors. He also allegedly committed sexual acts on dead bodies, and even told several hospital workers that he made jewelry out of one man's glass eyeball."[122]

As if the Savile scandal was not diabolical enough, we can throw in allegations of satanism and devil worship into the bargain. Two of Savile's victims who are from different parts of Britain and do not know each other both alleged that Savile sexually abused then and beat them during black masses held in the basement of the hospital Savile was a volunteer at.

> "She recalled being led into a room that was filled with candles on the lowest level of the hospital, somewhere that was not regularly used by staff. Several adults were there, including Jimmy Savile

121   Ibid
122   Terrence McCoy, How BBC star Jimmy Savile allegedly got away with abusing 500 children and sex with dead bodies, *Washington Post*, June 27, 2014

who, like the others, was wearing a robe and a mask. She was molested, raped and beaten and heard words that sounded like 'Ave
Satanas', a Latinized version of 'Hail Satan', being chanted. There
was no mention of any other child being there and she cannot
remember how long the attack lasted but she was left extremely
frightened and shaken."[123]

The second victim alleged that she was forced to attend a black mass
on a very wealthy London street in which she was sexually abused and
beaten as well.

"Five years after the hospital attack, he abused a second victim
during another black mass ceremony held at a house in a wealthy
London street. The first part of the evening started off with an orgy
but half-way through some of the participants left. "Along with
other young women, the victim was shepherded to wait in another
room before being brought back to find Savile in a master of ceremonies kind of role with a group wearing robes and masks. She too
heard Latin chanting and instantly recognized Satanist regalia."[124]

These scandals and allegations I have touched on from the U.K. barely
scratch the surface. There have been investigations and allegations of elite
satanic and pedophiliac activity in Britain for many years. For the sake of
space, I was not able to highlight various other major scandals in Britain
like the Jersey child abuse allegations that also involve very prominent
members of the community involved in organized pedophilia, sadistic
torture, child murder, and satanism. This from the BBC,

"Jersey Police said Operation Whistle had identified 16 suspects
of public prominence in total, but 11 were dead. Operation Whistle has partly focused on abuse involving Persons of Public Prominence (PPPs), which police define as "well-known people in the
public eye"[125]

The Jersey investigation is an extremely disturbing one for many
reasons, primarily among them being that children were systematically
abused, tortured, and sometimes killed on the island going back decades.
Even more disturbing is the fact that police launched a massive investigation and excavation of the site and found a plethora of human remains,
very many of them being children. Police have also uncovered torture

123   James Fielding, Jimmy Savile was part of satanic ring, UK *Express*, Jan 13, 2013
124   Ibid
125   BBC News, Five public figures investigated over Jersey child abuse, Feb 17, 2016

chambers that featured blood splatter. Police also said some of the children's bodies found had been charred and burned and it also appears as though someone tried to cover up or hide the bodies more adequately in the 1970's. According to the UK Independent,

> "At least four punishment rooms were uncovered alongside a concrete bath where victims described being held in cold water for hours before being repeatedly abused. Also found were flecks of blood, a set of shackles and graffiti above the bath which read: "I've been bad for years and years." Forensic archaeologists have now uncovered more than 100 fragments of bone and 65 milk teeth. Two of the bones have been identified – one from a child's leg, the other coming from a child's inner ear. Police believe the milk teeth, meanwhile, were extracted after death because many still have large parts of the root attached to them. Some of the bones are also charred, while others show signs of trauma including lacerations. There is also archaeological evidence suggesting that efforts were made to conceal them at some point during the late 1960s and early 1970s."[126]

Lastly, I would like to leave my readers with a quote from the late Harry Price, demonologist, psychic researcher, and expert on witchcraft and magic. In 1931 Price came out and said he knew for a fact that black masses were being practiced in London on a regular basis and that they were not being performed in abandoned buildings but in some of the most wealthy and prominent neighborhoods in all of London. Price stated:

> "In all the districts of London, hundreds of men and women of high education and belonging to the best families, worship Satan and pay perpetual homage to him; black magic, witchcraft, the evocation of the devil, these three forms of medieval superstition are practiced nowadays in London on a scale and with a liberty of action unheard of in the Middle Ages."[127]

Belgium and the Marc Dutroux Affair

The case of Marc Dutroux is substantially similar to the cases of high level pedophilia and Satanism in the U.S. and Britain in that it absolutely stinks to high heaven of prominent officials being involved in corruption and cover up so evil and so depraved it makes one want to lose hope in our governmental institutions and laws that are supposed

126   Jerome Taylor, Jersey mystery: police find remains of five children but may abandon murder inquiry, www.independant.co.uk, Aug 1, 2008
127   Corte, The Devil

to protect children. It involves a man, named Marc Dutroux who was arrested for kidnapping and murdering young girls. Two girls were found alive at one of his estates in a specially built dungeon for his victims. The victims describe being kidnapped and held against their wills and used as sex slaves. Dutroux, a co-conspirator, and a victim all go on to allege that they are just small players in a larger organization that trafficked children internationally and that is involved in satanism. Furthermore, the people involved in this organization are some of the most wealthy, respected, and powerful people in all of Belgium.

> "Marc Dutroux, his accomplices, and victims all claimed they were part of a larger international network of pedophiles and that many of the worlds elite participated in orgies. The exploited pre-teen and teenaged girls were supplied for this ring by a vast global network of procurers who kidnapped and sold young attractive girls and boys to this cabal. In essence, Dutroux was claiming to be a low man on a very high totem pole of perverts who sought sex slaves to appease their sick desires. The issue of satanism connections came up early in the police investigation of Dutroux and his crew of child abductors."[128]

The Dutroux scandal almost brought Belgium to its knees, there were massive protests in the streets (the biggest in Belgium since World War 2) by the Belgium public who were furious with the police for what they perceived as police incompetence and even a possible cover up. This story dominated headlines in a large part of Europe for a good portion of the later 1990's and early 2000's. Dutroux and his accomplices were finally brought to justice at trial in 2004 and sentenced to life prison terms. Some of the families of the victims however boycotted the trial because they were furious with police incompetence and a cover up at the highest levels of Belgium's establishment.

The story starts in 1986 when Marc Dutroux is arrested and jailed for the rape and sexual molestation of multiple young girls. For these offenses Dutroux was sentenced to 13 years in the Belgium prison system in 1989. Because Belgium had extremely liberal and lax laws Dutroux only served a fraction of his time and was released after 3 years. This despite the prison warden labeling Dutroux as a definite psychopath and over the objections of Dutroux's own mother who wrote to the parole board stating her son was a monster and would be dangerous to society if he were released.

Nevertheless, Dutroux was released and in subsequent years young girls started disappearing from the areas in which Dutroux owned houses. Dutroux owned 7 houses at this time, this despite being unemployed; it seems kidnapping and selling young girls and purveying child porn is a very lucrative business. Police started an investigation and even questioned Dutroux at his house. During this police contact, police heard cries for help from young girls that were locked in Dutroux's torture dungeon. Stunningly, Dutroux was able to somehow convince police that the noises were coming from outside and the police failed to investigate further. These 2 girls would later go on to die of starvation in Dutroux's dungeon while he was incarcerated for a 100-day stint. This incident is eerily reminiscent of the incident which occurred in Milwaukee, WI in the early 1990's when serial killer and cannibal Jeffrey Dahmer was able to convince police one of his victims was simply a quarrelsome lover, this after the victim escaped from Dahmer's apartment and sought help, while naked and bleeding in the street. Police subsequently turned the underage boy back over to Dahmer and Dahmer killed the man later that night.

During the period that police were investigating there was a level of police incompetence that defies belief and is so breathtaking it borders on the unbelievable. Police ignored several tips from confidential informants that explicitly stated Dutroux was kidnapping young girls to be used in child pornography and sex trafficking. One tip came from someone who had direct knowledge of Dutroux building a sound proof dungeon in his basement, another tip came from a person who said Dutroux offered him money to help kidnap young girls. A tip even came in from Dutroux's own mother who told police she had direct knowledge that Dutroux was keeping hostage young girls at some of his houses. The police failed to adequately investigate these leads despite the fact that Dutroux was already a convicted and dangerous sex offender. As a direct result of this police incompetence and even possible cover up, multiple young girls died and were kidnapped by Dutroux. Thankfully, a measure of justice was finally served when an investigation concluded that police had indeed been complicit in a cover up to protect Dutroux and his pedophile network, this from the Los Angeles Times:

> "Police investigating the kidnapping and murder of children detained 23 people after predawn raids, including nine police officers. The raids were the latest indication that police in the southern city of Charleroi may have helped cover up the alleged crimes of Marc

Dutroux, accused in the murders of at least four girls and the kidnapping and sexual abuse of others."[129]

The police investigation finally changed for the better when a new Magistrate was assigned to the case, Jean-Marc Connerotte. A break came when a witness to one of the kidnapping's remembered a partial license plate number of a van seen in the area of the kidnapping. The plate number and van led the police right to the doorstep of Marc Dutroux. The investigative magistrate, Connerotte, ordered that Dutroux's house be raided and searched. When police did this, they found two young girls alive in the basement of one of Dutroux's houses. Further investigation revealed multiple dead bodies buried on lands Dutroux owned. These would include multiple young girls and even one of Dutroux's accomplices whom he had murdered. The two young girls that had starved to death were only 8 years old, this in addition to 2 more dead girls who had been kidnapped while on a camping trip. The 2 victims that were rescued told a harrowing story of being kidnapped and then subjected to torture, sexual abuse, and being videotaped for purposes of child pornography.

During the follow up investigation after Dutroux's arrest, it became known that Dutroux and his accomplices were consistently claiming that they had not acted alone but were in fact part of a much larger network that kidnapped, sold, trafficked, and killed children for the purpose of sex trafficking, child pornography, and orgies with children that involved rich and prominent members of Belgium society. Furthermore, the defendants revealed the people involved in this ring were very prominent members of Belgium society. One of the defendants, a man named Michel Nihoul declared that his case would never go to trial because he knows enough information about the prominent members of Belgium society that it would bring down the whole government. Nihoul, who has proven connections with very important people in Belgium's society admitted to organizing sex orgies at a Belgium chateau in which politicians, government officials, police, and other prominent members of Belgium's society were present.

> MICHEL NIHOUL: The 63-year-old property surveyor, a fraudster first convicted in 1968, holds the key to the theory that Dutroux was only one part of a pedophile network. Nihoul is reported to have procured girls for drug-fueled sex orgies attended by government, police and judicial officials.[130]

---

129   Times Wire Reports, 9 Police Detained in Child Murder Case, *Los Angeles Times*, Sept 11, 1996
130   News 24, Who's who in Dutroux trial, www.news24.com, June 17, 2004

"Jean Michel Nihoul, a businessman who confessed to organizing an orgy at a Belgium chateau, which several government officials, police officers, and a former European Commissioner attended."[131]

After this information came out the investigating Judge, Connerotte, started investigating leads that a major sex trafficking organization was partly responsible and involved with these crimes. Judge Connerotte, made a public appeal to the public that if anyone had information regarding this VIP pedophile ring that they should come forward to police. And come forward they did, 11 victims in total came forward detailing horrific acts of sexual abuse, torture, murder, orgies, and devil worship all involving very prominent members of Belgium society. One of the victims that came forward was named Regina Louf, and the story she related is absolutely horrific. The activities that some of our prominent members of society take part in are evil beyond any comprehension of someone with a normal conscience. These articles from the BBC and The Guardian:

> In 1996, she named and described in great detail, to a specially assembled police team, the people and places involved in the pedophile ring. Senior judges, one of the country's most powerful politicians - now dead - and a very influential banker were included. One of the regular organizers of these parties, she said, was the man she knew as 'Mich', Jean Michel Nihoul. The sessions not only involved sex, they included sadism, torture and murder; and again, she described in detail, the place, the victims and how they were killed.[132]
>
> "In 1996 she related her experiences to a police team under carefully filmed and supervised conditions. She described certain regular clients including judges, one of the country's most powerful politicians (now dead) and a prominent banker. She gave the police the names by which she knew these men, detailed the houses, apartments and districts where she'd been taken with other children to entertain the guests. This 'entertainment' was not just sex, she told the police. It involved sadism, torture and even murder, and again she described the places, the victims and the ways they were killed. One of the regular organizers of these parties, she claimed, was the man she knew as 'Mich', Jean Michel Nihoul, 'a very cruel man. He abused children in a very sadistic way', she said. Also there, she said, was the young Dutroux."[133]

131 Kennedy, *Satanic Crime: A Threat to the New Millennium*
132 Olenka Frenkiel, Regina Louf's Testimony, BBC News, May 2, 2002
133   Olenka Frenkiel, Belgium's silent heart of darkness Waiting for justice, *The Guardian*, May 5, 2002

I know this may be totally shocking and almost unbelievable to my readers. However, you should know that some of the police investigating Regina Louf's claims absolutely believed that she was telling the truth. She had described places, people, and things she could not have known unless she was actually there. Specifically, one of the murders she described being witness too fit the description perfectly of a murder that was unsolved prior to this. Louf described the victim, and some of the torture she was exposed to, some of which I will not mention because it is too horrific. Louf's descriptions of what she witnessed lined up exactly to what the police had found when they found the victim's body years prior. This article from The Guardian details this:

> "By now the police believed they had verified key elements of Louf's story. At least one of the murders she described matched an unsolved case. One of the police officers in the team, Rudi Hoskens, had been assigned to re-examine that case and was convinced she had witnessed the murder: 'She gave us some details that made us think it's impossible to give without having been there at that place - the way the body was found at that time, and the way she described the person who was killed.'[134]

In addition to Louf's testimony being highly credible and believed to be true by police, an additional 10 victims also came forward describing similar abuse and situations. And this is where the cover up comes into play. Just as Judge Connerotte started gathering very substantial evidence to substantiate the claims of the victims and the claims of Dutroux and his accomplices that they were smalls parts of a much larger organization, he was sacked and taken off the case. It was reported that he was removed from the case because he had attended a fundraiser dinner for some of the victims and their families. Judge Connerotte was replaced by a different magistrate who took the case in a completely new direction. A direction that would ultimately discredit and besmirch the 11 victims that had come forward and completely cover up the existence of a Belgium sex trafficking network that counted the wealthy and powerful as participants and members.

The spectacular incompetence of the police investigation of Dutroux, the possibility of prominent members of Belgium society being involved in unspeakably depraved activities, evidence of a massive cover up, and now the man who was viewed as a hero by Belgium's public for rescuing

---

the two girls from the dungeon, Judge Connerotte, being taken off the case proved to be too much for the general public of Belgium. In 1996 they took to the streets in numbers not seen since World War 2 to protest and demand their government institute changes and reforms. News reports of the protests vary, but they say they contained anywhere from 300,000-400,000 protestors. Whole segments of Belgium society shut down because workers walked off the job.

Even though Dutroux and his accomplices were arrested in 1996, the case did not go to trial and justice was not served until 2004. This was another point of outrage for the victims, their families and the Belgium public. Because of the massive coverup, the only people to ever go to trial were Dutroux, his wife, a co-conspirator, and Michel Nihoul. They were all given lengthy prison terms, including Dutroux being sentenced to life for the rape and murder of young girls. One of the most breathtaking parts of the trial occurred when the former investigative magistrate on the Dutroux case and hero of the Belgium people, Judge Jean-Marc Connerotte testified on the stand and under oath. During questioning Connerotte broke down and started sobbing in open court as he related the death threats he had received and how his life was put in mortal danger after deciding to pursue leads into a sex trafficking organization that counted as members Belgium's elite. This from the London Telegraph:

> "The Belgian judge who saved two young girls from Marc Dutroux's pedophile dungeon broke down in the witness box yesterday, alleging high-level murder plots to stop his investigation into a child-sex mafia. Jean-Marc Connerotte choked in tears on the fourth day of the trial, describing the bullet-proof vehicles and armed guards needed to protect him against shadowy figures determined to stop the full truth coming out. "Never before in Belgium has an investigating judge at the service of the king been subjected to such pressure," he said. "We were told by police that [murder] contracts had been taken out against the magistrates. As the danger mounted, emergency measures were taken."[135]

We have reason to believe that Judge Connerotte is absolutely telling the truth, and for two reasons. The first is that in almost all of the other high-profile investigations into VIP pedophile and satanic activity there have been death threats and even people killed to silence them. The Franklin Scandal is an especially good example of this. The second reason

---

135   Ambrose Evans-Pritchard, Judge tells of murder plots to block Dutroux investigation, www.telegraph.co.uk, March5, 2004

is because just like the Franklin Scandal, well over 20 people died mysteriously and violently that were related to the Dutroux affair. Everyone from victims, perpetrators, and even a prosecutor all committed suicide, and it was confirmed that one man had been poisoned after his body was sent to the U.S. for medical testing, after the man's wife spoke out about this, she was found dead a short time later!

> "Since his arrest, 20 potential witnesses connected with the case have died in mysterious circumstances, fueling suspicions of a cover-up reaching the highest levels."[136]

> "Bruno Tagliaferro was someone who knew, or claimed to know, about the abduction of Julie and Melissa and the car which was used. The Charleroi scrap metal merchant told his wife in 1995 that Dutroux was trying to get him killed. It was something to do with the car in which girls had been taken. When he was found dead, apparently of a heart attack, his wife Fabienne Jaupart, refused to accept the verdict. Samples of his body sent to the US for analysis showed he'd been poisoned. Jaupart told reporters she was determined to find her husband's killer, but soon she too was found dead in her bed, her mattress smoldering. It was declared suicide. Since 1995, there have been 20 unexplained deaths of potential witnesses connected with Dutroux."[137]

In addition to there being substantial evidence of a VIP pedophile ring that trafficked, raped, and murdered children and a massive cover up of it, there is evidence to suggest the elite people involved in this activity were also explicit devil worshippers. Whenever victims talk about orgies involving rich and prominent men in which children are abused, raped, and tortured, and even killed we can be certain this is some type of satanic ritual. This despite there being no allegations of some of the more overt satanic activity like men wearing hoods and masks, occult symbols, etc. Many victims describe orgies involving children, being raped, tortured, and even forced to eat feces and drink blood. These things are all elements of fertility rituals and black masses. Remember, the elite people involved in this activity do not want to be found out as explicit servants of the devil, therefore they may disguise these rituals as something less evil than overt devil worship, disguise it as just a sex orgy and nothing else. Furthermore, even if the police and media have evidence from the testimony of victims regarding the explicitly satanic and ritualistic nature of these

136   Olenka Frenkiel, Belgium's silent Darkness t heart of, *The Guardian*, May 5, 2002
137   Ibid

activities, they will often leave these details out so as not to make the case look fantastical or outlandish.

Despite this, in the Dutroux case there is actual evidence that this VIP pedophile ring was involved in overt satanic activity. This from the Sunday Times as quoted by William H. Kennedy:

> "Brussels Satanic sects involved in bizarre rites including human sacrifice are being linked by Belgium police with this summers string of grisly pedophile murders in which at least four children died. Five witnesses came forward last week and described how black masses were held, at which children were killed in front of audiences said to have included prominent members of Belgium society. One investigator said it was "like going back to the Middle Ages." The tentacles of the sects appear to have stretched beyond the borders of Belgium, to Holland, Germany and even America. The witnesses – several of whom claim to have received death threats – say that young babies were handed over by their parents willingly in return for money. In other cases, the victims were abducted. The witnesses, who are believed to have identified the sites where the masses took place to the police, said organizers had also photographed participants and threatened to hand over the pictures if they went to the police."[138]

And even after all these years, victims of Belgium's VIP pedophile network are still coming forward. The Daily Mail ran a story in 2017 about a woman who detailed her abuse at the hands of an "Aristocratic Pedophile Ring" that conducted orgies with children at prominent estates, and even killed children who they thought would go the police. This from the Daily Mail:

> "A former child sex slave sold into a Belgian aristocratic pedophile ring where boys and girls were raped, tortured and murdered has revealed the horrors of her five years of abuse… It was around her sixth birthday Miss Lucas was taken to an orgy for the first time, in a castle. She was used for an S&M show, chained up with an iron dog collar and made to eat human feces. 'Afterwards, left lying there like a broken object, I felt so humiliated', she said… Children were scared into silence and members of the network killed those who threatened to go to the police. She told Mail Online: ''I had to do it [the rapes] because there was always the threat of being killed. 'Children were killed. Boys were more often tortured but girls were

---

killed… However, she was saved when one of her abusers made a deal with the politician in charge of the pedophile network while she was tortured. They made a deal where he would work for the politician in exchange for her being spared."[139]

The case of Marc Dutroux and the VIP sex trafficking ring in Belgium is one of the more disturbing cases I have highlighted. Necessarily I could not include all the available information on this case, it would require a book in itself. What is clear based on the evidence is that very prominent members of Belgium's society were and maybe still are involved in a sex trafficking network that kidnapped, tortured, sexually abused, and murdered young girls and boys in the context of ritualistic satanism. The evidence also shows a very clear and well-defined cover up by the Belgium authorities. Judge Connerotte summed up the cover up well when he said:

> "You would have thought that the Dutroux dossier was so serious that investigators would do everything in their power to discover the truth," Judge Connerotte said. "But exactly the opposite happened. Rarely has so much energy been spent opposing an inquiry."[140]

AUSTRALIA'S VIP PEDOPHILE NETWORK

In late 2015 a woman named Fiona Barnett came forward with the group SNAP and gave a press conference in which she claimed to be the victim of a VIP pedophile ring operating in Australia and Sydney specifically. Ms. Barnett related that her abusers were some of the most powerful people in all of Australia, including 3 former Prime Ministers. She also went on to claim that victims were exposed to vicious sexual abuse, orgies, torture, murder of children, and ritualistic satanism. This from the Sydney Morning Herald:

> "Speaking outside the Royal Commission into Institutional Responses to Child Sexual Abuse, Fiona Barnett called on the authorities to investigate the alleged ring, which she believes is still operating. Ms. Barnett alleged the ring involved hundreds of perpetrators, including a political elite, such as a former governor-general and a former education minister, but she did not name them.
> "Throughout my childhood I was a victim of Australia's VIP child sex trafficking ring," she said. "The people involved in this elite

139   Thomas Burrows, Former child sex slave sold into Belgian aristocratic paedophile ring where boys and girls were tortured and KILLED reveals the horrors of her five years of abuse, www.dailymail.co.uk, Jan19, 2017
140   Ambrose Evans-Pritchard, Judge tells of murder plots to block Dutroux investigation, www.telegraph.co.uk, March5, 2004

pedophile ring included high-ranking politicians, police and judiciary."[141]

Ms. Barnett, like many other victims all around the world claimed to witness sex parties (orgies) in which rich and powerful people were involved. From the Daily Telegraph:

> THE victim of an alleged child sex trafficking network claims she was prostituted at dozens of pedophile parties, which were attended by political elite at Canberra's Parliament House. Speaking to the media outside the Royal Commission in Sydney today, Fiona Barnett, from northern NSW, also claims she witnessed "hundreds of crimes" — including murder, rape, abduction and torture — at the hands of the so-called elite pedophile ring 40 years ago. The network, which Ms. Barnett maintains still operates today, included high-ranking politicians, and police and judiciary members."[142]

The same article from The Daily Telegraph interviews the leader of SNAP, a man named Nicky Davis. Davis goes on to say that Barnett is certainly not the only one who has made allegations like this in Australia. Davis said in the article that they have hearing stories from victims like this for years:

> "Child sex abuse advocacy group, Survivors Network of those Abused by Priests Australia (SNAP), says it has heard from several other alleged victims who say they have witnessed similar offences of rape, torture and murder perpetrated by the most senior people in Australia. "We're not talking about an isolated incident and an isolated survivor. It's a pattern, it's widespread and it's continuing today," SNAP leader Nicky Davis said."[143]

In similar fashion to most of the other allegations around the world, Barnett also described being witness to and forced to participate in satanic rituals, in which children were murdered, by Australia's elite. According to Barnett she was made to participate in black masses in which some of Australia's elite performed human sacrifice and orgies in worship of the devil Baal and other ancient pagan deities. Since Barnett came forward and went public in 2015, additional victims of Australia's VIP pedophile

---

141   Rachel Browne, Political elite were part of pedophile ring, alleged victim Fiona Barnett claims, *Sydney Morning Herald*, Oct 23, 2015
142   AAP *The Daily Telegraph*, Victim of alleged paedophile ring claims she was abused at parties attended by *political elite*, *The Daily Telegraph*, Oct 23, 2015
143   Ibid.

network have come forward as well. Like many other victims Barnett has been threatened, castigated, besmirched, and called a liar.

VIP PEDOPHILE RING IN PORTUGAL

In 2002 news stories started to appear regarding a VIP pedophile ring operating in Portugal. Police started investigating when former residents of an orphanage started making allegations that they had been sexual abused in horrific ways by rich and powerful men who were pillars of society in Portugal. The Guardian notes,

> "A scandal over a pedophile ring run from a state orphanage gripped Portugal yesterday as it threatened to engulf diplomats, media personalities and senior politicians. Photographs of unnamed senior government officials with young boys from Lisbon's Casa Pia orphanage were among the evidence reportedly available to police after they arrested a former orphanage employee called Carlos Silvino."[144]
>
> "He [Silvino] was just one element in a huge pedophile network that involved important people in our country," Mrs. Costa Macedo explained in a newspaper interview. "It wasn't just him. He was a procurer of children for well-known people who range from diplomats and politicians to people linked to the media."[145]

One of the people instrumental in bringing this elite pedophile ring to the attention of authorities and the media was former Secretary of State for Families, Teresa Costa Macedo. According to Macedo she compiled a dossier of high-level pedophilia over 20 years ago and handed it over to authorities who did nothing about it and in fact lost it. Macedo has been subject to some of the very same threats and intimidations other whistleblowers of elite pedophile and satanism rings have been.

> "Former secretary of state for families, Teresa Costa Macedo, said she had sent a dossier containing photographs and testimonies from children to the police 20 years ago but they had done nothing about it, while she was subjected to a campaign of threats… She said she had been the target of a campaign of intimidation to make her stop investigating the case. "I received anonymous threats, by phone and post. They said they would kill me, flay me and a lot of

144   Giles Tremlett, Portugal's elite linked to pedophile ring, www.theguardian.com, Nov 27, 2002
145   Ibid.

other things," she said. That campaign had started again yesterday, she said, with threatening phone calls made to her home."[146]

Unlike some of the other elite sex trafficking rings I have highlighted in this chapter, some members of the Portugal ring were actually brought to justice and given stiff prison terms. Those convicted included a prominent politician and former ambassador, a very prominent TV personality who was once the most well-known tv personality in all of Portugal, and an a very high-profile doctor. This from the Independent:

> "To most people Portugal's state-run orphanages seemed like a safe haven for thousands of children who had been robbed of their parents. They were called the Casa Pia, or Houses of the Pious. But for an elite pedophile ring, which included a former ambassador and a prominent television celebrity, Casa Pia orphanages were something entirely different. They were supermarkets stocked with children to abuse. Yesterday, at the conclusion of the longest trial in Portugal's history, seven defendants were convicted of using the orphanages to rape and abuse scores of teenage boys in a case that has sent shockwaves through the country's political elite and raised serious concerns over the efficiency of Portugal's judiciary. Six of the seven were given jail terms of between five and 18 years."[147]

FRANCE AND THE DOMINQUE STRAUSS KAHN SCANDAL

In 2011 the very prestigious head of the International Monetary Fund or the IMF, Dominque Strauss Kahn resigned from his post in disgrace after he attempted to rape a hotel maid in a prominent New York City hotel. Soon after this Strauss-Kahn was charged in France with charges related to his procurement of prostitutes for sex orgies involving prominent and elite members of French society and other members of the elite worldwide. Strauss-Kahn even admitted to attending sex orgies in some of the world's most lavish and posh hotels but tried to justify it as being a fetish that he cannot control. This case dominated headlines around the world in 2011, The New York Times writes,

> "The lurid details of the case, which included accounts of exclusive sex parties, nevertheless captivated France and shined an uncomfortable light on the sexual escapades of certain circles of a rich and powerful elite."[148]

146   Ibid
147   Jerome Taylor, Guilty after six-year trial, Portugal's high-society pedophile ring, www.independent.co.uk, Sept 10, 2010
148   Aurelien Breeden, French Court Acquits Dominique Strauss-Kahn in Case That Put His

According to reports these orgies involving rich and prominent members of society, occurred all over the world.

> "Dominique Strauss-Kahn, the former head of the International Monetary Fund, went on trial Monday on accusations that he participated in a prostitution ring that extended from the north of France to Brussels, Washington and New York."[149]

It also became known that the elite attending these orgies were immensely powerful and wealthy businessmen, politicians, lawyers, police, media people, and musicians.

> "Mr. Strauss-Kahn is charged with "aggravated procurement in a group," or pimping, and using his subordinates to obtain prostitutes for lavish sex parties. In addition to shining a spotlight on a clandestine world of Champagne-fueled sex parties that prosecutors say were attended by lawyers, judges, police officials, journalists and musicians… Prosecutors say exclusive orgies were organized in major world cities by businessmen who were seeking favor with Mr. Strauss-Kahn, and that their money was used to finance prostitutes, including for Mr. Strauss-Kahn, who sometimes sought out sex with several partners in one evening."[150]

The case of Dominque Strauss-Kahn is just one more confirmation of what we already know to be true, namely that enormously powerful, wealthy, and prominent members of society's all over the world engage in totally depraved activities in the form of sex orgies sometimes involving children, kidnapping, torture, rape, murder, and devil worship. Depraved activities which are organized and carried out in very tight knit, high-end covens and cults all around the world.

FORMER DUTCH BANKER RONALD BERNARD

In 2017 videos of an interview started appearing on YouTube that featured a man named Ronald Bernard. Bernard was a former international Dutch banker who had left the industry and was now speaking out about the international banking system and some of the things he did, witnessed and experienced while working in this industry. In all his interviews Bernard makes it clear that in his position as an international banker he worked with, worked for, and had clients that were at the pinnacle of wealth and power all over the world. Mr. Bernard states,

Sex Life on View, *New York Times*, June 12, 2015
149   Dan Bilefsky, Strauss-Kahn, Former I.M.F. Chief, Goes on Trial in Sex Case, *New York Times*, Feb 2, 2015
150   Ibid.

I was in the finance world, as a top criminal. I did asset management, currency and deposit trading. And out of this profession at the end of my days, the last 5 years, I was serving the top of the top in this world, the most richest people on earth, to serve them in their program.[151]

One of the first disturbing things Bernard reveals is just the totally morally corrupt nature of the international banking industry. This is a fact that Malachi Martin noted in an interview with Bernard Jansen. Martin noted that there is an international organization, dedicated to Lucifer that controls the wealth, banking systems, and money flows of countries all over the world. Martin noted that this organization, if they wanted to have the power to destroy not only companies but whole countries as well. This is a fact that Bernard confirms in his first interview.[152]

Bernard notes that he was told before getting involved in the banking industry to not do it unless he could put his conscience %100 in the freezer. Bernard notes that while working as a banker he helped both his employer and clients destroy other companies all around the world. Bernard notes that at the time it was all like a big joke, he and his colleges would cheer and celebrate when they would successfully destroy a company, because they would profit from it. Bernard notes that his actions and the actions of his colleagues literally destroyed people's lives.[153] Bernard notes that this type of activity is common in the banking world, he notes it is an industry totally devoid of any moral sense, totally corrupted by evil. He notes,

> In the world I come out of there is no ethics and no morals at all, everything was allowed to fulfill the agenda they have. And the agenda they are running is a from the bible, they are following from the revelations of the bible, the prophecies of the bible[154], and they are quite on track with their agenda.[155]

It is later in the interview however that Bernard notes far more disturbing activities. As I said above Bernard notes multiple times in his in-

---

151   https://www.youtube.com/watch?v=ol5k-mNYpbY
152   Mr. Bernard also notes that the people he worked for had an agenda, a program, that included the starting of wars, conflicts, diseases and economic crises all for the goal of destroying people and enriching themselves.
153   Bernard notes that some of the people who owned these companies that he helped destroy to profit his clients, later committed suicide as a result and that the people he worked for would have a good laugh about all that and the fact that they left children behind.
154   The fact that Bernard says this is extremely significant to those who study and know the theology behind underground satanic and luciferian practices.
155   https://www.youtube.com/watch?v=ol5k-mNYpbY

terviews that the circles, he was running with were the elite of the elite in the world. He notes that he worked for, socialized with, and had as clients some of the most wealthy and powerful people in the world. When the interviewer asks Bernard what the most horrible thing he had ever experienced while working in the banking industry and what caused him to leave this industry, he goes into the fact that some of the people he worked for and worked with, were luciferians and Satanists. What Bernard has to say is quite stunning and is worth quoting at length. In his interview with Irma Schiffers, Bernard notes,

> Schiffers: Can you tell me the worst thing that has happened that caused the tipping point in your situation?
>
> Bernard: Well, that was the beginning of the end you get so deep into these circles and you sign a lifetime contract, not with blood[156] or anything. To never disclose names of companies, organizations or people. I think that is why I am still alive. You have to stick to it. If we are talking about the worst things that I have experienced, I just told you about things that made the freezer glitch[157], my conscience started to show itself. Let's put it this way, I was training to become a psychopath, and I failed. I did not complete the training and didn't become a psychopath.[158] My conscience came back and the most difficult part for me was because I had such a great status there. I was a success. I was trusted with the people playing at this level. To put it carefully, most of these people followed a not so very mainstream religion. So, you have Catholics, Protestants, all sort of religions. These people, most of them, were luciferians. And then you can say religion is a fairy tale, God doesn't exist, none of that is real. Well for these people it is truth and reality and they served something immaterial, what they called Lucifer. And I also was in contact with those circles, only I laughed at it because to me they were just clients. So I went to places called Churches of Satan.
>
> Schiffers: So now we are talking about Satanism?
>
> Bernard: Yes, so I visited these churches, just as a visitor, dropped by, and then they were doing their holy mass with naked women and liquor and stuff, and it just amused me. I didn't believe in any of this stuff. And was far from convinced if any of this was real.
>
> Schiffers: It was just a spectacle to you?

156 He notes in a later interview that signing a contract in blood was the next step, but that he did not make it this far. He states that people who do this are already dead inside.

157 He is referencing the fact that when he first got into international banking, he was told to not go into it unless he could put his conscience %100 in the freezer.

158 Its really training to become perfectly possessed.

Bernard: Yes, in my opinion the darkness and evil is within the people themselves. I didn't make the connection yet. So I was a guest in these circles and it amused me greatly to see all these naked women and the other things. It was the good life. But then at some point I was invited which is why I'm telling you all this to participate in sacrifices… abroad.[159] That was the breaking point, children.

Schiffers: You were asked to do that?

Bernard: Yes and I couldn't do that. That is the world I found myself in… The purpose of the whole thing, eventually in that world is that they have everybody in their pocket. You need to be susceptible to blackmail.[160]

Mr. Bernard goes on to say that after being invited to participate in the sacrifice of children he completely broke down, started refusing assignments in his banking job and essentially became a threat to this group. He also claims that at one point after this he was abducted by this group and tortured so that he would not reveal anything about what he had seen and experienced. This quote is from the first interview Mr. Bernard did about his experiences. Since he has done many others all relating the same exact story. Mr. Bernard even went on to testify about his experiences at the Westminster seating's of London for the International Tribunal for Natural Justice (ITNJ) Judicial Commission of Inquiry into Human Trafficking & Child Sex Abuse where he told the same story about being witness to satanism and luciferianism inside the international banking industry and also being invited to participate in child murder.

Conclusion

The reader will note that many of the news stories I quoted came from secondhand news sources and not the mainstream media. This factor is not a coincidence. Very rarely are these diabolical activities highlighted by the mainstream media. The reason is because some of the executives that control the media in this country are involved in the very same activates.[161] Necessarily because of space and the risk of being repetitive I was not able to include all of the information available to me regarding VIP's involved in these activities. I can tell you that the stories I have highlighted are not the only ones out there. There have been similar VIP pedophile

---

159   It is at this point in the interview that Mr. Bernard starts crying.
160   https://www.bing.com/videos/search?q=ronald+bernard+banker&docid=6080165561
99972773&mid=51B03254168B4410B05651B03254168B4410B056&view=detail&FORM=VIRE
161   See the recent case of CBS president Les Moonves

rings uncovered in Dutch society, Norway, Canada, and Mexico just to name a few.

Earlier in this study I also mentioned the incident that occurred during the opening of the Gotthard Tunnel in Switzerland. The opening ceremony of this tunnel was explicitly satanic including elements of goat worship, or Baphomet worship. There were several European heads of state that attended this ceremony. There was also an additional major pedophilia ring uncovered in the 1970's that was centered right in the heart of our country in Chicago. This ring centered around a man named John Norman who catered to an elite clientele and sold children for the purposes of child porn and sex with adults. The Chicago Tribune ran a whole series of articles on this ring, which incidentally implicated prominent members of society including well known government officials and powerful people in Chicago business and politics. This case also has a very disturbing connection to serial killer John Wayne Gacy who raped and murdered 33 boys and young men in Chicago in the late 1970's. Gacy always claimed that he had accomplices in these murders that worked for his company. It seems the evidence backs up his claims because Gacy was out of town on business when at least 3 of the victims, found in the crawl space underneath his house, originally disappeared. One of Gacy's employees happened to be a man who also worked for John Norman to procure young boys for sex.

There is also the very curious case of the disappearance of Shannon Gilbert from the gated community of Oak Beach, Long Island and the subsequent discovery of 11 sets of human remains and the Long Island serial killer. Gilbert just so happen to disappear in the very early morning hours of May 1st, which just so happens to be one of the most important satanic holidays that is named Walpurgisnacht and is celebrated with a blood sacrifice from a female victim.[162] I don't want to delve deeply into this case, but I will say there is evidence very wealthy and prominent members of Suffolk County, including the former police chief James Burke and a prominent doctor Peter Hackett were involved in a sex and prostitution ring and held orgies with escorts and then killed them. This from a documentary on the case produced by People Magazine Investigates:

> One of the theories in this case is that there was a group of wealthy
> men that were involved in the murders and that it was a sort of eyes

---

162   May 1st, 1776 is also the date Adam Weishaupt founded the Illuminati.

wide shut scenario where these guys were picking up these escorts and then having their way with them and then killing them.[163]

I highly recommend that people who want to further investigate this case watch the two-part series produced by People Magazine and also the episodes of 48 Hours Mystery that produced documentaries on this case. As People Magazine has found there is evidence to suggest that the Long Island serial killer is actually a group of wealthy men on Long Island who are using prostitutes for drug fueled orgies and then killing them and dumping their bodies off of Ocean Parkway near Gilgo Beach.

There are also many other instances of whistleblowers and people who sought to investigate these things that were threatened, harassed and even possibly killed. One example is previous Georgia State Senator Nancy Schaefer, who was killed in a supposed murder suicide with her husband. This occurred after she endeavored to investigate child abuse at day care centers and foster homes in Georgia. Then we have what has been called the "Clinton Body Count," a phenomenon in which upwards of 30 people closely associated with the Clintons or were going to blow the whistle on them, ended up dead, some in very mysterious circumstances.[164] I already noted the Franklin scandal in which more than 20 people met the same fate.[165]

The number of rich, prominent, powerful, and famous people that we have discovered are monsters that have taken on human form is totally shocking, appalling and disgusting. Names like Jeffrey Epstein, Bill Cosby, Matt Lauer, Harvey Weinstein, Kevin Spacey, and many more. So why do the rich and powerful seemingly have such voracious and insatiable sexual appetites for children. It is a good question and one I don't have all the answers to. I do agree with Corey Feldman however that the VIP pedophilia rings are all just a symptom of something far darker beneath the surface, a symptom of something much bigger and much darker as Feldman put it. I do know that this type of thing has been going on for centuries and even thousands of years. The stories about Tiberius Caesar and his raping and killing of children are well known for example. And the ancient fertility cults also operated in an identical way, sacrificing children to ancient pagan Gods and performing orgies for the prosperity of crops, animals, and children.

---

163   *People Magazine* Investigates, The Long Island Serial Killer
164   Vince Foster, James McDougal and Seth Rich are all prime examples.
165   What this means largely is that the elite and powerful will go to any length, any extreme to keep their activities secret. It also confirms that they are evil and servants of the devil. Human life seems to mean nothing to them and they gladly take it at any whim.

I of course am detailing these things in a book written about perfect possession. As I will detail later, sexual deviancy and sexual depravity is a hallmark of the perfectly possessed, and for many reasons. Furthermore, we must understand what pedophilia does to the children who are victims of it. It literally destroys some of them, physically, psychologically and spiritually. Ask any exorcist and he will tell you about cases of possession in which the door that was opened was because of a sexual assault. When someone is sexually abused, they become damaged, they have a wound that the demonic realm exploits for entry into the person's life and eventually their body.

What I think this is about, partially, is the ruination of the souls of the most innocent among us, children. Children who are victims of pedophilia often develop major problems later in life. Many are addled with drug and alcohol addiction, many commit suicide, some even become possessed. Some blame God for their ordeal and reject him. Some are filled with an implacable hatred throughout the rest of their lives and refuse to trust anyone. And most disturbingly, some end up being perpetrators of pedophilia themselves, thus furthering the cycle of sin, abuse, and the sewer of depravity. Pedophilia is a soul sucking act done to a child, it harms them in some deep place in some corner of their soul and few are ever healed of it, they carry their wound for the rest of their lives.

I do not think that this is about the sex however. I don't think that rich and powerful people all over the world engage in the same type of depraved sex acts because they all have the same sick fetishes. I think the pedophilia and the orgies that we know go on have a much deeper meaning to them. They are engaging in this activity for a reason. Similarly, these people group together not because of their common interest in orgies, not because they are all connoisseurs of sex parties. They band together because they are in covens. They are in diabolical organizations dedicated to the devil and the service of evil.

The people I am referring to are explicit servants of the diabolic kingdom. Their sexual deviancy is their way, partially, of worshipping the fallen angel. They think of it in some sick way as a sacrament, as an act of service and worship to their prince. By engaging in pedophilia and the sexual victimization of others they are actively participating and cooperating in the work of the diabolical kingdom to ruin and destroy souls. Additionally, one of the foremost hallmarks of the dark form of devil worship that these elite people practice is the reversal of all things holy, the reversal of the Christian faith. In the Christian faith, children are considered innocent and holy, Christ himself doles out dire warnings to anyone who would hurt or corrupt a child. The reversal of this innocence is the very taking of it in a despicable act of pedophilia. As I said, pedophilia is the violation of a children's innocence, a corruption of its holiness, a direct mocking of Christ who holds these children in his very heart.

What this really comes down to in the end is the cosmic battle between good and evil, between light and darkness, between Jesus Christ and Lucifer. Human beings have been thrust into the midst of this battle. We have free will and we have to choose which side we will serve. Satan offered all the kingdoms of the world and all their riches to whoever would bow down and worship him. The incontrovertible fact is that many wealthy and powerful people choose to take the fallen angel up on his bargain. They know that by worshipping him and serving him and offering sacrifice to him they may be the recipients of material wealth and power for the duration of their lives on earth. What will happen to them eventually however is they will be catapulted into the lake of fire and brimstone to burn for all eternity with those spirits they chose to give their allegiance to.

The exact theology of the high-end coven and cult structure in the world is not exactly known. These things are kept a very tightly held secret by the people who practice them. We do know that they believe by making pact's and covenants with certain devils (Satan, Lucifer, Baal, Moloch, Ishtar, Ashtaroth, etc.) and offering human and animal sacrifice to them they will be given the material wealth and power they desire. We know they throw in their lot with these devils, they choose to serve them fully and totally. They sell their souls and give themselves body and soul to the diabolic kingdom. This is the price they pay for living a life of elegance, power, and debauchery. We know they believe that by serving these devils they will rule with them during the time of the antichrist and before his coming, they think Lucifer will be triumphant in the end and usurp the reign of Jesus Christ. We also know that they believe there is a coming catastrophe about to be brought upon the world and it will be they who will emerge from it to rule the world. We know they commit the most horrible forms of blasphemy you can possibly imagine. The black mass, the reversal of the most holy of all of Catholicism's sacraments. They profane eucharistic hosts in ways I prefer not to mention because they are so sick and demented. They perform human and animal sacrifice to appease and please the devils they serve. We also know the act of having orgies are a part of the black mass and can also be part of a fertility ritual. Fertility rituals in ancient times included these same elements, orgies and human and animal sacrifices. Lastly, based on the activities these people are involved in and their wooden allegiance to the diabolic kingdom, I am confident in making the assumption that the prominent members of society who engage in all the activities I have mentioned and highlighted, are very likely perfectly possessed.

> There's about 150 people that run the world. Anybody who wants to go into politics, they're all fucking puppets, OK. There are 150, and they're all men, that run the world. Period. Full stop. **They control most of the important assets, they control the money flows, and these are not the tech entrepreneurs.** Now, they [tech entrepreneurs] are going to get rolled over in the next 5-10 years by the people who are really underneath pulling the strings. And when you get behind the curtain and see how that world works, what you realize is that it is unfairly set up for them and their progeny.[166]

---

166   Chamath Palihapitiya, former Facebook Vice President speaking to students at Stanford University

Chapter 8

Examples from History: Serial Killers

In this section on serial killers who may have been perfectly possessed I could have picked from a huge field of human evil and depravity. This was by far my least favorite section of the book to research. Studying depraved acts committed by the worst serial killers is draining to say the least. Just as I did in the last chapter I am endeavoring to give the reader the best examples with the clearest evidence I know of. Therefore, some of the serial killers I will be profiling have admitted they were possessed. Some of them have been heavily involved in the occult and devil worship, and they have all committed acts of depravity against their fellow human beings that are unspeakable. Just because I am profiling these people does not mean I am definitively labeling them as perfectly possessed. I am simply going to analyze their lives and highlight to you the reader some things present in their lives that may be an indication of dark spiritual forces at work. This will necessarily be done briefly as an in-depth research into serial killers and the evil surrounding them would require multiple volumes. This chapter is going to contain graphic content and may be disturbing for some readers, reader discretion is advised.

H.H. Holmes: America's First Serial Killer, (1861-1896)

> "To parallel such a career, one must go back to past ages and to the time of the Borgias or Brinvilliers, and even these were not such human monsters as Holmes seems to have been. He is a prodigy of wickedness, **a human demon**, a being so unthinkable that no novelist would dare to invent such a character."[1]

H.H. Holmes, whose real name was Herman Mudgett, is known by the infamous title as America's first serial killer. He mostly operated in Chicago in the late 1800's and confessed to killing 27 victims, although some people estimate that he killed up to 200 people.[2] No one can be sure because he did a bulk of his killing during the World Fair in Chicago when some of his victims found lodgings at his infamous murder castle, many of whom simply disappeared and were never seen or heard from again. When one examines the life of Holmes it is difficult to find any trace of goodness, light, or truth anywhere. It seems his life was wholly devoted to the service of evil.

Holmes was born in New Hampshire in 1861 and had a reputation as a brilliant young man. He excelled in school and people in his town were convinced he would grow up to be a fine young man. According to Author Harold Schechter, Holmes's father was extremely abusive and beat him often.

> "From earliest childhood, he had been subjected to the regular brutalities of his father, a fierce disciplinarian who wielded the rod with an unsparing hand.[3]

From a very young age Holmes displayed a dark side. At age 11 he began collecting live animals and doing secret medical experiments on them. Keeping skulls and other body parts as souvenirs in a metal box that he kept in his parents' cellar.

When Holmes reached adult age, he moved to Philadelphia where he worked as a druggist and doctor. Philadelphia is probably where he killed his first victim. He was working as a druggist at the time and gave a woman a concoction he had made, and she subsequently died. It has also been speculated that Holmes performed illegal abortions in his early days in Philadelphia. After the death of the woman from Holmes's homemade concoction, great suspicion fell on Holmes and he immediately fled to Chicago.

Upon arriving in Chicago, he quickly went to work at a drugstore in the suburb of Englewood. This drugstore was owned by an older couple, of which the husband was dying of prostate cancer. The man's wife, who was totally overworked decided to hire Holmes almost on the spot and did not make inquires as to his past and previous dealings in Philadelphia. All accounts of Holmes portray him as an extremely suave, well-mannered individual. He was apparently always well dressed and portrayed an air of success and sharp intelligence. This is the case with a lot of serial killers and psychopaths in general. They have an outer facade of respectability

---

2   Other accounts state that he himself confessed to killing 200 people in his murder castle
3   Schechter, *Depraved: The Shocking True Story of America's First Serial Killer*

and genuineness, yet beneath the surface lies a monster capable of the most perverted and debased acts known to man.

Holmes, by his winning personality soon convinced the elderly widow to sell the pharmacy to him. This occurred right after her husband's death of prostate cancer. The elderly widow then took living quarters above the pharmacy. Soon her view of Holmes changed however when he began missing payments for the purchase of the drug store. She began to complain and even filed suit against Holmes. Shortly after she completely disappeared never to be seen or heard from again. Holmes explained to customers of the drug store that she had moved away to California. It is extremely likely Holmes murdered the elderly widow.

Like many of that era in American life Holmes possessed a lust for riches that was palpable. He also had much darker desires brewing in his heart. A blood lust that could not be quenched. With these thoughts in mind he commenced work on what would later be known as the "Murder Castle." Not having the actual money to build this grand building it is known he swindled his way through it. Taking out loans on credit and refusing to pay contractors when their work was completed. This would be just one of many brazen swindles and capers Holmes would commit throughout his life.

It is said that the murder castle was 3 floors, the downstairs being for shops that Holmes would run, such as a pharmacy. The top two floors however were for much more sinister purposes. And was the primary place he murdered some of the victims. According to the history channel:

> The castle featured soundproof rooms, secret passageways and a disorienting maze of hallways and staircases. The rooms were also outfitted with trapdoors over chutes that dropped his victims to the buildings basement. The basement was a macabre facility of acid vats, pits of quicklime (used on decaying corpses) and a crematorium, which the killer used to finish off his victims.[4]

The castle was also outfitted with a giant walk in safe in which Holmes killed a number of his mistresses. According to author Harold Schechter, Holmes would lock the women in the safe and when the poor thing would become hysterical with fright, screaming for their life, Holmes would masturbate and listen to them die of asphyxiation.

During the years Holmes lived in and operated the Murder Castle he brutally killed an unknown number of victims. The first people to lose

---

4   History.com Editors, Murder Castle, History, https://www.history.com/topics/crime/murder-castle, Dec 26, 2020

their lives to this monstrosity of a human being were Holmes mistresses who bought his air of respectability and though he was a fine young businessman. One woman in particular was found to be with child by Holmes. When the woman demanded Holmes marry her, Holmes convinced her an abortion was necessary. Holmes performed an intentionally botched abortion on the young lady, killing her. Holmes then dissected and de-fleshed the woman and sold her complete skeleton to a medical clinic for $200. He also murdered her young daughter that she had from a previous marriage. The little girl that he murdered in this instance was only four years old. Her decomposing body was later found by police in a vat of quicklime in the cellar of the murder castle. This would be one of many young children Holmes would murder.

Additional victims came from the Chicago World Fair. During the time of the fair many people found lodging in Holmes castle. Holmes had a gas pipe system set up in the murder castle in which he would flood any number of rooms with toxic gas from controls he operated from his sleeping chamber. Some estimates say during the time of the world fair Holmes killed up to 100 people. How many he killed will never be known because many people simply disappeared. And the fact that Holmes had acid vats, quicklime and a kiln in the cellar that could reach 3000 degrees, to incinerate bodies, makes it likely he was able to expertly conceal the evidence. When police later searched his murder castle they found plenty of evidence of human remains in the kiln and buried in the cellar.

Soon Holmes dirty deeds caught up with him in Chicago and he fled town. Before he fled however, he attempted an insurance swindle by setting the third floor of his murder castle on fire. The fraud was discovered, and Holmes left with one of his stooges, a man he had totally seduced and brought under the control of his will, Benjamin Pitezel.

Pitezel had been seduced and deceived into working for Holmes for many years. Pitezel was an alcoholic and had a wife and 5 young children. They were a very poor and destitute family. It was said Holmes was extremely adept at deceiving people and bending people to his will. This is a common trait of many of the people I will be profiling. According to author Harold Schechter:

> In later years, Holmes cool manipulativeness – his skill at spotting and exploiting the weak points of his victims – would generate a host of wild claims. Countless articles and pamphlets would depict

him as a being of nearly supernatural power, possessed of the ability to mesmerize his victims with a single, piercing stare.[5]

After they fled Chicago Holmes convinced Pitezel to take part in a life insurance fraud in which they would fake Pitezel's death and receive $10,000 from the life insurance company. Unbeknownst to Pitezel, Holmes planned to kill him all along and collect all the money for himself. Holmes murdered Pitezel in Philadelphia for the insurance scam, filling his lungs with chloroform. This despite knowing Pitezel's wife and young daughters and knowing they were a very poor family whose children loved their father and who also depended heavily on their father's financial support.

This is where the case of H.H. Holmes takes an even farther ghastly and diabolic turn. Wishing to defraud the Pitezel family of the $10,000 they had gotten from the insurance company, Holmes started planning the murder of the whole family. What makes this story so tragic is that Holmes acquired three of the young Pitezel children under false pretenses from Benjamin Pitezel's wife, Carrie. Carrie of course being deceived by Holmes and not knowing his true intentions. Holmes then kept all three children in various hotel rooms in various cities while Holmes was committing additional frauds and running from the law. According to hotel workers from the time who were tasked with bringing the children food, the children were usually in a terrible state and would sob all day because they missed their other two siblings and their mother.

> Ackelow – who had no trouble remembering Alice and her siblings – painted a grim picture of the three forlorn children, shut up in their room for days on end. He talked of the times his teenage son had brought the children their meals and found them weeping miserably, overwhelmed by the loneliness and unrelieved tedium…. Geyer was no nearer to finding the children. But each day was bringing new evidence of the misery they had endured under the heartless custodianship of Holmes"[6]

After taking the children hostage and lying to Carrie Pitezel about the whereabouts of her children, Holmes finally acted out his machinations. Holmes ended up murdering the young Pitezel boy, Howard, first. Holmes then went on to murder the two young girls who had been so distraught at not seeing their mother. Holmes was in the process of planning

---

5   Schechter, *Depraved: The Shocking True Story of America's First Serial Killer*
6   Ibid.

the murder of Carrie Pitezel and her two remaining children when he was arrested in Boston. The totally corrupt and depraved nature of Holmes's actions and Holmes himself was noted by the lead officer in charge of finding the missing children:

> He was struck anew by Holmes's monstrous nature – the heartless cunning of a man who had contrived to keep three desperately homesick children apart from their mother while coolly plotting their utter destruction.[7]

Shortly after the bodies of the little children were located in Toronto a man named Winshoff came forward and declared he had proof of Holmes's innocence in this matter. When Winshoff finally revealed his supposed evidence, it was discovered that he was a spiritualist and that he had gotten messages from the spirit world declaring that Holmes was innocent and that he should be released at once.

Despite this and despite the constant lies and deception and pleas of innocence from Holmes the murder of Ben Pitezel and his three children would be the ultimate undoing of Holmes. He was eventually caught for this crime, convicted and was executed by hanging in Philadelphia. All along during this time Carrie Pitezel was under Holmes's spell and believed Holmes that not only were her three children safe and sound but that her husband, Benjamin, was alive and well also. When Carrie discovered her 3 children were found murdered and her husband was murdered she had a massive mental breakdown. The murder of the three Pitezel children is extremely disturbing and heartbreaking to read about. The fact that Holmes kept these two little girls and the little boy hostage for months, during which time they became very homesick and sobbed for the presence of their mother and siblings, is purely diabolic. It takes a special kind of evil to completely and heartlessly ignore the children's tears and pleas for their mother and then go on to ruthlessly murder them.

The life of H.H. Holmes was fully and totally devoted to the service of evil. His biographers can hardly find one iota of light in this man's life. He spent his whole life deceiving, swindling, philandering, and murdering. He was an exceptionally skilled liar and was able to deceive a great many people throughout his life. He deceived building contractors, business owners, the police, insurance companies, investors, and his mistresses and wives. His whole life was essentially one big lie.

---

7   Ibid

"Deception was so deeply ingrained in H.H. Holmes character that he was incapable of telling the truth about the simplest matter... Nothing he said could be take at face value. Even when it suited his purpose to stick close to the facts, his words were infected with falsehood."[8]

In addition to his deception, he was extremely adept at bending people to his will, to essentially enslave people and get them to do what he wanted. This was especially true of his mistresses and wives and of Benjamin and Carrie Pietzel. After Holmes was arrested a multitude of people came forward with stories they had in which they encountered Holmes in some way. Some of the stories were very disturbing. Some of the people had been convinced Holmes was planning their murders. Some people, when they encountered Holmes, had gotten a very bad feeling of dread or evil in the presence of the man. One woman told a story in which Holmes had attempted to swindle her out of money by some deception, but the woman refused to go along with Holmes' proposal after she saw something in him that disturbed her greatly.

"There was something so unsettling in his look[9] that Mrs. Strowers refused to consider the proposition – and never spoke to Holmes about it again.[10]

H.H. Holmes was a brutal, demented killer who slaughtered people, including children, without flinching an eye or displaying one iota of remorse or regret. The fact that he built a castle just for the purposes of killing people in the most horrific ways and also killed three young children who just wanted to see their mother, tells us this man was a true devilish monster. Holmes even confirmed as much when right before he was executed, he said the following:

"I was born with the devil in me. I could not help the fact that I was a murderer, no more than the poet can help the inspiration to sing -- I was born with the "Evil One" standing as my sponsor beside the bed where I was ushered into the world, and he has been with me since."

---

8   Ibid.
9   There is a very similar incident in the life of John Wayne Gacy. One of Gacy's early boyfriends that was living with him became terrified and moved out immediately after seeing something so disturbing in Gacy's eyes that he became terribly frightened.
10   Schechter, *Depraved: The Shocking True Story of America's First Serial Killer*

THEODORE (TED) BUNDY (1946-1989)

> The devil knows when to look attractive. And Ted Bundy was handsome and cultured and charming. Until he was strangling and mutilating his victims, displaying their lopped-off heads in his apartment and sleeping with their corpses until putrefaction made it unbearable. **Then he was simply the devil.** By 1989, when he was executed in the electric chair in Florida at the age of 43, he had confessed to just about 30 murders but there could have been at least four more. He was an insatiable killer.[11]
>
> Well, I'd rather say we've got a very disturbed, sick individual[12]

Ted Bundy is one of America's most prolific serial killers. His crimes saw a level of brutality and depravity rarely seen among men. Ted Bundy confessed to 30 murders in all, however, authorities have speculated the number could be much higher. Bundy was a chronic liar and misled the authorities many times.[13] There are many unsolved homicides from the time and areas he was operating in that have never been solved or accounted for. There are many authorities on the subject that strongly believe Bundy killed at least 50 people and possibly 100 or more. Bundy himself hinted at that fact many times that he had killed over 100 people. The Methodist minister that gave him last rites even commented on the fact that he had the strong impression that Bundy had killed many more than what he actually confessed to.

Ted Bundy was born on November 24, 1946 in Vermont. Right from the beginning Bundy's life seems steeped in scandal. This is because no one knew for sure who Ted's real father was. Bundy's mother claimed he was a sailor in the Navy.[14] Members of the Bundy family however suspected that Ted's true father was his maternal grandfather Samuel Cowell. And Ted did live with the Cowell's for the first years of his life and was told they were his real parents. About Samuel Cowell it is said he was an extremely violent and abusive man. According to one book about Bundy, Cowell was described as a tyrannical bully and racist. It was said he hated blacks, Italians, Catholics, and Jews. Cowell also allegedly beat his wife, the family dog, and shockingly, swung neighborhood cats around

---

11   Howard Chua-Eoan, Crimes of the Century, *Time* Magazine, March 1, 2007
12   Capt. Burl Peacock, Tallahassee Police Department, speaking about Ted Bundy
13   He actually misled and manipulated literally everyone. Even some of the doctors and psychiatrists who interviewed him in prison recounted that Ted was even able to manipulate them at times!
14   It was later discovered that the name of the sailor Bundy's mother had claimed fathered Ted, did not exist in any Navy or Army database, making it likely Ted was born as a result of an incestuous relationship between his mother and grandfather.

by their tails. He is also said to have thrown a girl down a flight of stairs for over sleeping. Another biography of Bundy by Polly Nelson[15] claimed that Cowell spoke aloud to unseen presences and flew into violent rages whenever the issue of Ted's paternity was raised. According to a Time Magazine article, titled, I Deserve Punishment,[16]

> Bundy claimed he spent his early years with a deranged grandfather who assaulted people, tormented animals and had an insatiable appetite for pornography.[17]

According to another biography by Ann Rule[18], Ted apparently displayed very disturbing behavior at a very young age. One incident that is related by Rule is that Julia, who is Bundy's aunt, woke up one day to find herself surrounding by knives from the kitchen that Bundy had placed under her covers. After Ted saw his aunt's shocked expression it is said that he could not stop laughing. This incident occurred when Bundy was only three years old. When Bundy got a little bit older it is said he would get drunk and look around the neighborhood trash bins for pornographic magazines. He was also said to be a peeping tom and look into the windows of neighborhood girls to catch a glimpse of whatever he could.[19]

Bundy was also known to have a very upstanding personality and was of very above average intelligence. He received very good grades when he attended the University of Washington and graduated with a degree in psychology. Bundy then applied to a got into law school with the University of Puget Sound. During this time as well Bundy was deeply involved with Washington State politics, he would become an aide to the states Republican Party chairman and during one campaign, he reported to the governor himself. Ann Rule describes that during this time Bundy was an "imposing figure" in Republican Party politics in Washington State.

According to Ann Rule who wrote *The Stranger Beside Me* something completely changed in Teds countenance and handwriting in 1972. It has been widely speculated by many of Bundy's biographers when he exactly

---

15   Polly Nelson, *Defending the Devil: My Story as Ted Bundy's Last Lawyer*

16   It is very interesting to note that Malachi Martin, while discussing perfectly possessed people claimed that they will often confess to the moral badness of their crimes and say they must be punished and given the death penalty. This is exactly the case with Bundy and Jeffrey Dahmer, and it is entirely possible Martin was referencing Ted Bundy when he wrote what he did regarding perfect possession.

17   Jacob Lamar, I Deserve Punishment, *Time* Magazine, June 24, 2001

18   Ann Rule, *The Stranger Beside Me*

19   Another very interesting story relayed by Ann Rule is that when Rule worked with Bundy at the Suicide Prevention Center she would often bring her dog with her to work. According to Rule, her dog liked literally everyone and never growled or barked, yet whenever the dog would encounter Ted Bundy its hair would literally stand on end and start growling in a deep weird way.

started killing people. There is quite a lot of evidence that he killed an 8-year-old girl in Tacoma, Washington in 1961. Bundy's documented killing spree however, started in 1974 when attractive young women started disappearing in Washington State and Oregon. Bundy's first documented attack occurred when he broke into a house, went to the downstairs room where a 15-year-old girl was living and beat her viciously within an inch of her life. Bundy then broke one of the metal rods off the bed and viciously jammed it into the girl's vagina so violently that it damaged her internal organs. She miraculously survived but endured permanent brain and internal organ damage.[20] Bundy's next victim also lived in a basement room in house that had 3 other young women in it. At some point in the middle of the night Bundy broke into the house, bludgeoned the young woman, leaving blood all over her bed and then abducted her. The only part of Linda Ann Healy that was ever seen again was a skull and mandible bone found on Taylor Mountain. Bundy would go on to kill an additional 8 beautiful young woman in Washington and at least 2 in Oregon.

Bundy's next spree occurred in the states of Idaho, Utah, and Colorado. His method of operation was substantially similar in these new states. Bundy would often dress up with an arm cast or use crutches to make himself look injured and to lure his unsuspecting victims into his car. Thank God Ted Bundy was not always successful in his search for new victims. Many woman that he lured to himself or to his vehicle got a very strange and ominous feeling that caused them to literally run away from Bundy. The story one woman recounted is very disturbing. After asking a young woman to help him carry his books to his car she noticed that the front seat in his Volkswagen Bug was completely removed. Upon seeing the missing seat, she says that,

> Something—she couldn't even say what—had caused the hairs on the back of her neck to stand on end, something about that missing seat.[21]

Ted Bundy strangled, bludgeoned, drowned, and stabbed his victims. His killing spree also included several very young girls under the age of 18 and two girls that were only 12 years old. Bundy would very often keep souvenirs from his victims, even beheading some of them and keeping the skulls in his apartment. One of the most disturbing aspects to the Bundy

---

20   I apologize to my readers for the graphic description, but at least some of it is necessary so you can get a true feel of just how evil and sick Ted Bundy really was. Doing what he did to that girl is just inhuman, its demonic.

21   Ann Rule, *The Stranger Beside Me*

case was the sexual mutilations that occurred during[22] and after the homicides. Bundy would sexually mutilate his victims and then return to the corpse many times to commit necrophilia until putrefaction made the sexual liaisons impossible. This level of sexual depravity takes the Bundy case to a whole higher level of evil. Necrophilia is rare among serial killers, but the ones who do commit this unspeakable atrocity are usually the worst most evil killers in history.

Ed Warren once stated that necrophilia is evil, that its demonic. He made this comment while he was investigating a case of diabolical infestation and oppression in Southington, Connecticut in the 1980's. The house they were investigating was a prior funeral home that a family had moved into after their teenaged son was diagnosed with cancer. The family soon started experiencing very frightening phenomena, including all the crucifixes in the house disappearing. Ed and Lorraine Warren were called in and Lorraine who has the gift of discernment was able to discern that at some point in the house's history necrophilia had been committed on the corpses in the house. This case was so violent that investigators and priests were attacked. John Zaffis, a very experienced investigator, had his most frightening experience of his career in this house when he witnessed a full-bodied diabolical apparition that came after him and attacked him. The house was eventually exorcised during a sanctioned exorcism by the Catholic Church.[23]

Ted Bundy was finally arrested in Utah for the kidnapping and attempted sexual assault of one of his victims that was able to escape. He was convicted of this crime and sentenced to between one and 15 years in the Utah State Prison System. Soon after this Bundy was charged with murder in Colorado. He was extradited to Colorado and housed in the local county jail where he escaped. He was caught a few days later and then miraculously escaped again after losing 35 pounds and squeezing through a passageway he made with a smuggled hacksaw. This time Bundy was not recaptured immediately, and he fled to Florida. This after asking a guard in the county jail he was staying in which state would be the most likely to execute a killer.[24]

---

22   Bundy mostly forcibly sodomized his victims while they were still alive.

23   See In a *Dark Place: The True Story of a Haunting* by Ray Garton and Ed and Lorraine Warren

24   I have noted elsewhere that Malachi Martin said perfectly possessed people will often request to be killed or to be given the death penalty so as to satisfy the Satanist preference of death over life and a fixated desire to join the prince in his kingdom.

Upon arriving in Florida Bundy's murderous spree continued. At approximately 3am[25] on January 15, 1978 Bundy broke into a college frat house and brutally bludgeoned 4 young girls in their sleep and brutally sexually assaulted them, even viciously biting one of them leaving his teeth marks in the poor girl.[26] Two of the girls died from this attack and the others suffered permanent damage. Before leaving the sorority house Bundy entered the room of another young women who has remained unnamed. Earlier that evening the girl had fallen asleep praying the rosary, a devotion she had promised her grandmother she would do. When the girl woke up and saw Bundy standing over her she opened her hand revealing the rosary beads at which point Bundy noticing them, dropped his weapon and fled the scene. Later that day as the girl was in shock she requested to talk to a priest who she relayed her story to, a Monsignor William Kerr who related this story to another priest as well. Later while Bundy was on death row he requested that Monsignor Kerr be his spiritual advisor. Monsignor Kerr asked Bundy about that night and what he related is extraordinary.

> "Bundy explained that when he entered the girl's room, he had fully intended on murdering her; some mysterious power was preventing him."[27]

Bundy then eventually kidnapped a 12-year-old girl from her Lake City Junior High School. Bundy would go on to sexually assault and murder her. Her skeletal remains were later found near a state park.

With Bundy running low on money and the authorities closing in on him Bundy fled west towards the Alabama border where he was pulled over by a Pensacola police officer. Bundy kicked the officer's legs out from under him and took off running. The officer fired a few warning shots and eventually apprehended Bundy. So ended the reign of terror from a monster that took the lives of at least 30 beautiful young woman who held so much promise in life.

While he was on death row Bundy granted many interviews to different psychologists. Bundy attributed his killing to his exposure to his extremely abusive grandfather, his pornography addiction, and something he called "the entity." Bundy said he started viewing porn at a very young

---

25   Known of course as the anti-hour, the hour of the Antichrist as Ed Warren called it, the time when diabolic activity is at its zenith, in direct mockery of 3pm, the hour of mercy.
26   This turned out to be basically the only solid physical evidence at the crime scene as the bite marks left by Bundy matched his teeth pattern exactly.
27   Father Joseph Esper, *With Mary to Jesus*

age but soon started to crave more and more violent forms of it. After he acquired and consumed this violent pornography, he found this still was not enough to satisfy his urges, so he started killing. After he killed his first victim he described it in terms of being possessed.

> Bundy talked of being appalled after his first murder. **"It was like being possessed by something so awful, so alien,"** he said. "But then the impulse to do it again would come back even stronger[28]."[29]

Bundy also spoke of killing his victims in terms of possession as well. Saying that when he killed someone and felt the last breath leave their body and the life disappear from the persons eyes that he felt like God.

> "You feel the last bit of breath leaving their body. You're looking into their eyes. A person in that situation is God!"[30]
> "Murder is not about lust and it's not about violence. It's about possession."[31]
> Women are possessions. Beings which are subservient, more often than not to males. Women are merchandise.[32]

Despite all his admissions and his brutal murders and depraved sexual activity, the best evidence we have that Bundy may have been possessed came from several incidents in which witnesses say he literally changed into a different person and frightened the people he was with. One of Bundy's judges in Florida even called him a changeling after the judge discovered that Bundy's expression could change, and he would look like a totally different person.

> "his expression would so change his whole appearance that there were moments that you weren't even sure you were looking at the same person," said Stewart Hanson, Jr., the judge in the DaRonch trial. "He [was] really a changeling."[33]

Michaud and Aynesworth stated that Bundy had a "chameleon"[34] like ability to somehow look different at will. This was also true of his photographs which became very frustrating to police because they would show

---

28   A perfect example of the theological doctrine regarding sin and its effect on the human will
29   Jacob Lamar, I Deserve Punishment, *Time* Magazine, June 24, 2001
30   Laura Schultz, Hiding in Plain Sight: The Psyche of Serial Killers, *Crime Magazine*, http://www.crimemagazine.com/hiding-plain-sight-psyche-serial-killers
31   *Biographics*, Ted Bundy Biography: Profile of a Serial Killer, https://biographics.org/ted-bundy-biography-profile-serial-killer/
32   *Conversations with a killer: The Ted Bundy Tapes, Season 1, Episode 2*, Netflix documentary
33   Wikipedia, Ted Bundy, https://en.wikipedia.org/wiki/Ted_Bundy
34   Michaud and Aynesworth, *The Only Living Witness, The True Story of Serial Sex Killer Ted Bundy*

photographs of Bundy and people would have a hard time identifying him.

There was also an incident when during Bundy's killing spree he pushed his girlfriend at the time off a raft and into icy water and then made no move to save her. The girlfriend later recounted that Bundy's face had gone completely blank like he was in a trance.

> "About a week before Ted Bundy abducted and killed two girls on the same day in Washington State, his girlfriend thought he seemed odd. He inexplicably pushed her out of a raft into icy water and made no move to help her get out. "His face had gone blank," she later wrote, "as though he was not there at all. I had a sense that he wasn't seeing me."[35]

According to this same article written by Dr. Kathleen Ramsland, Bundy also described to interviewers a kind of entity that would take him over whenever he was tense or drunk.

> To several of his post-arrest interviewers years later (William Hagmaier, Robert Keppel, Steven Michaud), Bundy described a malignant being – an "entity" – that emerged from him whenever he was tense or drunk.[36]

Bundy seemed to describe this entity that inhabited him to a number of different people. One of the more disturbing descriptions comes from Stephen Michaud and Hugh Aynesworth who spent over 100 hours interviewing Bundy at Florida State Prison. Michaud relates that,

> Ted started laying out the history of what he would soon come to call The Entity. It would start as a feeling. The feeling grew and grew until the entity controlled him and he would hear a voice and he did as the entity told him to do.[37]

Polly Nelson also stated that,

> He talked in terms of a voice in his head and this voice would start saying things about women.[38]

35   Dr. Kathleen Ramsland, Bundy's Demon Part 1, Psychology Today, https://www.psychologytoday.com/us/blog/shadow-boxing/201309/bundys-demon-part-i
36   Dr. Kathleen Ramsland, Bundy's Demon Part 1, Psychology Today, https://www.psychologytoday.com/us/blog/shadow-boxing/201309/bundys-demon-part-i
37   *Conversations with a killer: The Ted Bundy Tapes, Season 1, Episode 2*, Netflix documentary
38   Ibid

What is even more interesting is just how deeply the time Michaud and Aynesworth spent with Bundy affected them on a deep level, negatively. Hugh Aynesworth states that

> The last time I saw Ted Bundy or talked with him I was so damn sick of his lies and his denials of what he told us. Sometimes we'd come out of that prison and **we'd be actually sick**. I just was tired of Ted Bundy and what he'd taken of my life really... It was horrendous. Sometimes you wake up at night and think about it.[39]

Steven Michaud notes that,

> I Was heartedly sick of what I was hearing. I'm sick of Ted. I walked out of that prison with an enormous sense of relief... Ted endures in the hearts and minds of those who knew him like a bad cold, he just keeps coming back. **There's a kind of a taint that I can't get rid of.**[40]

Then there were the three incidents in which people who were with Ted Bundy said he completely changed into a different person and even exuded an odor and a negative feeling, vibe or electricity. The first incident is related by Dr Ramsland in the same article about Bundy. This first incident occurred when a defense investigator, Joe Aloi was interviewing Bundy.

> Defense investigator Joe Aloi seemed to have gotten a clear view. While they were talking, he suddenly noticed an odor emanate from Bundy as his face and body contorted. "I felt that negative electricity," Aloi said, "and along with that came that smell." Aloi was suddenly terrified that Bundy would kill him.[41]

The next incident occurred before Bundy was ever arrested for the murders he committed. It occurred while he was with one of his aunts at a darkened train station.

> "a great-aunt witnessed an episode during which Bundy "seemed to turn into another, unrecognizable person ... [she] suddenly, inexplicably found herself afraid of her favorite nephew as they waited together at a dusk-darkened train station. He had turned into a stranger."[42]

39   Ibid
40   Ibid
41   Dr. Kathleen Ramsland, Bundy's Demon Part 1, *Psychology Today*,
42   Polly Nelson, *Defending the Devil: My Story as Ted Bundy's Last Lawyer*; Wikipedia, Ted Bundy, www.wikipedia.org, https://en.wikipedia.org/wiki/Ted_Bundy

The last incident occurred when Bundy was speaking in private to a prison official in Tallahassee.

> Lewis recounted a prison official in Tallahassee describing a similar transformation: "He said, 'He became weird on me.' He did a meta-morphosis, a body and facial change, and he felt there was almost an odor emitting from him. He said, 'Almost a complete change of personality ... that was the day I was afraid of him.'"[43]

These incidents of Bundy having a complete transformation even prompted one psychiatrist to try to label him as a case of multiple personality disorder, known today as dissociative identity disorder. In conclusion, Ted Bundy was a monstrous human being. His crimes go completely beyond the realm of every day crime and are into the realm of a very dark and vicious evil. To kill over 30 young woman in the most brutal fashion and then return to their dead corpses to rape them over and over again speaks to the fact that this was a man most definitely in formal league with the forces of evil. Bundy gave us a hint of the condition of his soul when he said:

> "I'm the most cold-hearted son-of-a-bitch you'll ever meet."

And on another occasion:

> "I'm as cold a motherfucker as you've ever put your fucking eyes on. I don't give a shit about those people."

JEFFREY DAHMER, THE MILWAUKEE CANNIBAL (1960-1994)

> "Jeffrey L. Dahmer's bloody pattern of sexually motivated murder, dismemberment and cannibalism led him to feel that **he was the devil**, his attorney said Thursday."[44]

> "I knew I was sick or evil or both"[45]

> "He is pure evil, but you'd never know it by looking at him"[46]

The crimes of Jeffrey Dahmer are among some of the most depraved and sickening in the annals of serial killer history. At the time they were discovered they dominated front page news and appalled the whole

---

43   Ibid
44   Times Wire Services, Dahmer Believed He Was Satan, Defense Says, *Los Angeles Times*, Jan 31, 1992
45   Jeffrey Dahmer Trial Final Statement, Youtube.com, https://www.youtube.com/watch?v=IkeacWVwROc
46   Bill O'Reilly, *Inside Edition*

world. How could one man engage in such depraved and dark evil people asked. What could have possibly caused this handsome young man to commit such horrific atrocities?

Jeffrey Dahmer killed 17 young men and boys that we know of in the most horrific fashion. He not only killed these promising young men he also cannibalized[47] his victims, tortured his victims, injected acid or boiling water into their brains in an attempt to create living zombies who would be his sex slaves, decapitated them, kept the skulls and used them to masturbate, committed necrophilia on some of his victim's lifeless corpses, and even used some of the body parts and skeletons of his victims to construct a satanic altar in his apartment. His crimes were so horrible the city of Milwaukee condemned the building they occurred in and tore it down. To this day in 2018 the lot sits abandoned and lifeless[48], a testament to the evil that occurred there.

Jeffrey Dahmer was born on May 21, 1960 in Milwaukee, WI. His family had been living in Milwaukee because Jeffrey's father Lionel was studying at Marquette University for a PH. D in chemistry. One very curious fact that is related by Jeffrey's father is that his wife, Joyce Dahmer, had a very difficult pregnancy with Jeffrey. Apparently, she would have these attacks or fits that would be so bad she had to take tranquilizers while pregnant. She also struggled with depression and was hospitalized twice for this. This exchange between Stone Philips and Lionel Dahmer that aired on Dateline NBC is somewhat disturbing.

> SP: Lionel remembers a very difficult pregnancy.
>
> LD: Her jaw would go sideways, and lock and her eyes would bulge, and I know it sort of sounds like epilepsy.
>
> SP: It does sound like a seizure of some kind.
>
> LD: Some type of a fit or seizure, right, but it was not diagnosed as that. The doctor did not say that's what it was, **he did not know what it was.**[49]

After a number of years Jeffrey's family moved to Bath Township, Ohio. Jeffrey was considered an above average student and like many serial killers was very sharply intelligent. He was also described as being very shy and withdrawn in school and was considered a loner. The first indications

---

47   The cannibalism aspect along with the necrophilia is something that takes the Dahmer case to whole higher level of evil. Cannibalism, it should be noted is also part of many satanic rituals.

48   25th Street and Wisconsin Ave, just west of Downtown Milwaukee

49   *Confessions of a Serial Killer*, MSNBC, Stone Philips Interview with Lionel and Jeffrey Dahmer, https://www.youtube.com/watch?v=qZauuAyuA2Y

that things were seriously amiss in Jeffrey Dahmer's life was the fact that he started collecting dead animals on the side of the road and dissecting them and then would masturbate with them. He would also impale animals on sharp poles in a wooded area and leave them out for display. Before these disturbing incidents occurred however, Jeffrey's father relates two incidents from Jeffreys very early childhood in which Jeffrey was spell bound after Lionel had dug up some animal bones under the house. Jeffrey kept picking up the bones and dropping them in a bucket and was mesmerized by the sounds the bones made. Lionel Dahmer also speaks about an incident while he and Jeffrey were fishing and upon cleaning the fish Jeffrey was overly interested in the fish entrails. Upon reaching puberty Jeffrey also discovered that he was gay or was having very strong sexual urges towards other boys his age.

One fact about his childhood that is not commonly talked about is that he had an interest in the occult from a young age. One source about Jeffrey Dahmer describes the fact he had seances and attempted to contact evil spirits.

> It is less well-known that Dahmer had a large interest in the occult going back to his teen years. There was a séance when he was a teenager, where Dahmer talked about wanting to contact "an evil spirit" **that was harassing him and telling him to do things he didn't want to do.** He also announced his intention to contact Lucifer. Dahmer killed animals and dismembered them, as nearly all budding serial killers do. However, unlike most serial killers, these dead animals were found in odd poses or with their heads placed on sticks.[50]

There was also an additional incident that is related by a woman who was Jeffrey Dahmer's prom date in which she attended a party at the Dahmer residence where a séance was held as well.

> A woman said a man who confessed to 17 slayings was polite on their prom date, but she fled from Jeffrey Dahmer's home in 1978 during a seance in which the devil was invoked, a newspaper reported Saturday.[51]
>
> Geiger said it was sometime after the prom in June 1978 that she was invited to a party at Dahmer's home. Geiger said there was "no music, no food or drinks - it was a nerd party. There were seven

50   Serial Killers and Demonic Possession: Is There is a Link, Hubpages.com, June 5, 2015
51   Associated Press Wire, Woman Recalls Experiences with Dahmer At Prom, Seance With AM-Milwaukee Massacre, Bjt, Associated Press, Aug 3, 1991

people at the whole thing. " She said Dahmer and a friend called for a seance. "Then, after we sat down and were situated, the lights went out and one of the kids - not Dahmer - said, 'Let's call Lucifer. ' Then the flame on the candles snapped," she said. She said she was frightened and fled from the house and has not seen Dahmer since.[52]

In addition to outright satanism, according to a psychological report done on Dahmer by Radford University, a school friend remarked that he and Dahmer would often play a game at night called "ghosts in the grave-yard," the same report states that Dahmer also listened to Black Sabbath while in the military.[53]

When he was in high school Dahmer's bizarre behavior[54] increased, so much so that a classmate and friend of his, now Dr. Martha Schmidt stated that she felt frightened around him and was very uncomfortable spending any time at all with him alone. This woman appeared on the documentary *Dahmer on Dahmer* produced by the Oxygen Channel.

When Dahmer turned 18, he committed his first murder. He was living alone at his parent's house at the time because they had been going through a divorce. Dahmer picked up a hitchhiker, brought the young man to his parent's house and then bludgeoned him to death with a weight. Dahmer would later cut his body up and pulverize the bones and hide the body. It is also interesting to note that while Dahmer was disposing of this body he was pulled over by police for driving erratically. Even though he had a green garbage bag in his back seat that stunk like rotting flesh he was somehow able to convince the officer that he was just disposing of some roadkill. This was just the first incident in a long line of incidents in which Dahmer could have been stopped or in which he was somehow able to avoid detection in extraordinary ways.[55]

After this incident Dahmer's father convinced Jeffrey to join the military. In his stint with the military Dahmer raped two fellow platoon members. One of the men he raped was so haunted by the attack that he start-

52   Women Recounts Séance Held at Dahmer House, Newsok.com, Aug 4, 1991
53   Valerie Casey, Liz Clagett, Bo Allen, Lauren Williams, Jeffrey Dahmer, Department of Psychology, Radford University
54   Bizarre behavior included what everyone in his high school called "doing a Dahmer" which included Jeffrey making weird sounds and noises and falling on the ground acting like he was having seizures or acting like he was injured in some way, or even acting like he was mentally retarded.
55   I should also note that this was also common in the case of Ted Bundy, Bundy was able to miraculously avoid being caught, leaving evidence, or even being seen by anyone, a fact that frustrated police greatly. To this day police still do not know how Bundy was able to abduct Georgeann Hawkins who disappeared out of thin air in the last 40 feet leading to her sorority house.

ed drinking heavily and using drugs. He eventually divorced his wife and lived as an addict for many years before finally getting help. The other man Dahmer raped related that Dahmer would tie him up and torture him and then forcibly sodomize him. These allegations did not come out until much later and Dahmer never confessed to them or talked about them. Both victims have relayed their stories on a documentary about Dahmer produced by the Oxygen channel named *Dahmer on Dahmer*.

Dahmer was soon discharged from the military for his excessive drinking and extremely bizarre and erratic behavior around his fellow platoon mates. After getting out of the Army, Dahmer eventually moved in with his grandmother who lived in West Allis, WI. For the first 5 years Dahmer lived there he did not commit any crimes and he even attended church with his grandmother regularly. But then something changed in him after an incident that occurred at a local public library. Dahmer had been sitting at the library when a mysterious man passed him a note offering to have sex with him in the bathroom of the library. Dahmer did not take the man up on the offer, however both Dahmer and Dahmer's father attribute this incident to the start of his killing spree in Milwaukee. Lionel Dahmer also stated that during this time at his grandmother's house Jeff had set up a satanic altar and started dabbling in the occult. This is an exchange between Larry King and Lionel Dahmer:

> LK: Ok, so the spiral starts. He sets up a satanic altar in his house. He dabbles in the occult, right? Your learning all of this, but still no idea of murder?
>
> LD: Right.

After receiving the note at the library and before the killing spree started Dahmer would attend funerals of attractive young men and then later attempt to dig up their bodies so he could have sex with them. When this plan did not work he stole a mannequin from a local department store and slept with it and caressed it on a regular basis. When his grandmother finally found it, she forced him to get rid of it.

Dahmer then started cruising the gay bars and bathhouses of the city of Milwaukee looking for gay partners. During this time, it seems that Dahmer was drugging young males in some of the bathhouses so that he could have sex with their unconscious bodies. He was eventually discovered and had his membership revoked for the bathhouses although shockingly they did not call the police.

Shortly after this Dahmer picked up a young man named Steven Tuomi and brought him to a room at the Ambassador Hotel in Milwaukee. According to Dahmer he had no intention of killing Tuomi, he simply wanted to drug him and then spend the night with him. When Dahmer woke in the morning however he discovered Tuomi lying on the edge of the bed with his chest beaten in and blood coming out of his mouth. Dahmer also related that he had bruises on his forearms and hands. In every interview Dahmer gave to police and the media he consistently swore that he had absolutely no recollection of killing Tuomi. This is simply extraordinary seeing as how the attack must have been very violent, Tuomi was beaten to death. Dahmer experienced some kind of total blackout or loss of time. This frequently happens to victims of partial demonic possession when they go into the crisis state. They very often have absolutely no recollection of what occurred during that time.

After the murder of Tuomi, Dahmer stated that the urge to find submissive sexual partners and kill them became insurmountable. He could not resist the urges to kill anymore.[56] After killing Tuomi he murdered a few other young men before his grandmother finally kicked him out of her home due to a very foul odor emanating from Dahmer's bedroom and the basement. This is when Dahmer moved into apartment 213 in the Oxford Apartments on Wisconsin Ave just west of downtown Milwaukee.

After moving into this apartment Dahmer's crimes rose to a whole new level of depravity and evil. Instead of simply killing his victims and having sex with their corpses, Dahmer started cannibalizing his victims as well. In interviews Dahmer described doing this so that his victims would become a permanent part of him and so that he would gain some type of special powers from it. This apartment is also where Dahmer started experimenting in trying to create living zombies who would be his sex slaves. He did this by drilling into their skulls and then injecting boiling water or acid into their brain. All of the victims he tried this on later died. In addition to these ghastly details Dahmer would also save multiple body parts including skulls of his victims and keep them in his refrigerator. Fellow tenants of the Oxford apartment building constantly complained of a rotting smell coming from Dahmer's apartment. When the landlord confronted Dahmer about this Dahmer was able to convince the man that his fish tank broke and the smell was dead fish. It was also during this time

---

56   He is very clear about this in all of his interviews, he consistently states that the urge to kill and "possess" the bodies of his victims was so strong he was utterly powerless against it. He also stated it was his desire to "possess them permanently." It is important to note that possessiveness is a quality of the diabolic personality and psychology.

that Dahmer started the planning and construction of a gigantic satanic altar in his apartment that when completed would have contained whole skeletons, skulls and other body parts of his victims.[57]

A very disturbing and tragic incident occurred when a 14-year-old boy named Konerak Sinthasomphone escaped from Dahmer's apartment and ran into the street naked, bruised and bleeding from the anus. The police were subsequently called and showed up to the scene at which time Dahmer emerged from his apartment and started speaking with them. Dahmer was able to convince the police that the 14-year-old boy was an adult and that they simply had been having a lover's quarrel. The police thought the boy was drunk because he was unintelligible, yet the reason he was displaying these symptoms is because Dahmer had earlier drilled a hole in his head and injected acid into it. Somehow the police did not notice this and shockingly decided to believe Dahmer's story and turned the boy back over to Dahmer's care. The police were even inside Jeffrey Dahmer's apartment which had a dead body in one of the rooms from his last victim. These police officers were subsequently fired and at trial they could give no explanation of why they thought nothing was wrong. In an interview with the New York Times one of the officers defended himself saying there was no reason to believe anything was amiss. This incident and many others like it in the life of Jeffrey Dahmer show an almost supernatural ability to avoid detection and deceive the authorities.

Dahmer's luck would soon run out however when he would try to kill his last victim, Traci Edwards. Dahmer had invited Edwards up to his apartment for some photographs at which time Dahmer handcuffed his one arm. When Dahmer told Edwards to let him cuff his other hand Edwards did not allow him and at the trial Edwards actually said he felt God or someone else had spoken to him and told him not to allow himself to be handcuffed by this man.[58] At trial Edwards also stated that Dahmer put his head on Edwards chest and then told him he was going to eat his heart. Under questioning from defense attorney Gerald Boyle, Edwards also tes-

---

57   The satanism aspect to the Dahmer case is one that is not often talked about and not very well known because the other gory details of his case overshadow it. But make no mistake, Dahmer was a practicing Satanist throughout most of his life and one of the primary reasons he was killing so many people was for the purposes of using real human skulls and skeletons in the construction of his grand satanic altar he had planned for his apartment.

58   Similar to incidents in the life of H.H. Holmes and Ted Bundy in which people get a deep primal feeling of foreboding or evil around the killer. From a theological standpoint, evil spirits are the true enemy of man from man's first days on earth. I believe God made us with a certain, we will say, antenna to pick up on this danger when it is around us or threatening to destroy us. I think these incidents in the lives of these killers and their interactions with their victims offer us some of the best evidence that these people were perfectly possessed.

tified that he witnessed Dahmer go through multiple different personality changes while he was being held in the apartment which also included episodes of Dahmer chanting some unintelligible gibberish and going into a sort of trance. These changes in personality were especially marked while Dahmer was watching the movie The Exorcist 3 in which a priest becomes possessed. Edwards stated that Dahmer would chant louder and become excited by the diabolic possession being portrayed in the movie. On a side note Dahmer also admitted to authorities that he would watch this movie and Star Wars Return of the Jedi before going out looking for victims. Dahmer said he identified with the Satan character in The Exorcist 3 and the evil emperor character in Return of the Jedi because he felt like he was evil.

It was actually one of these trance-chanting episodes that allowed Traci Edwards to escape from Dahmer's apartment. Edwards then ran into the street still wearing a handcuff and flagged down a police cruiser. When police went into Dahmer's apartment to get the key for the handcuff, they discovered over 80 polaroid photos of Dahmer's victims in various stages of dismemberment. They immediately handcuffed Dahmer and took him into custody. It is also very interesting to note, and I think very significant that Dahmer, during an interview with Inside Edition stated that he had absolutely no memory of the entire incident with Traci Edwards. All Dahmer remembered was the police showing up at his door and him being arrested.[59]

The subsequent search of Dahmer's apartment revealed the full extent of the twisted and sick things that Dahmer had been doing. One of the things officials found was detailed plans for a satanic altar that Dahmer was going to set up in the apartment. Dahmer told investigators this was partially the reason he was saving skeletons and skulls of his victims. The altar was going to include two full skeletons on both sides of the altar as well as human skulls, black linen and burning incense. Investigators also found several human bodies, and body parts in various stages of dismemberment and putrefaction all around his apartment, including finding a human head and heart in his fridge.

The case was front page news all over the country, people were sickened, horrified and appalled. Dahmer plead guilty to all the chargers of murder but also claimed he was insane. Because of his plea a trial was held in Milwaukee to determine his mental competency. Dahmer was eventu-

59   A neighbor of Dahmer's recalls that when he was arrested she heard him howl like a "werewolf."

ally found to be not suffering from any mental disease or defect and he was sentenced to 16 consecutive life terms in prison. In his closing statement to the court Dahmer stated:

> "This was never a case about freedom. I didn't want freedom. **Frankly, I wanted death for myself."[60]**

In *Hostage to the Devil* when speaking about perfectly possessed people Malachi Martin stated that they will often confess to the moral badness of their crimes and even express a desire to die or receive the death penalty.

> "He voices the insistent Satanist preference of death over life and the fixated desire to join the prince in his kingdom."[61]

This is very interesting in the context of Jeffrey Dahmer because in his closing statement he explicitly stated he wanted death for himself. His wish would be granted two short years later when he was brutally bludgeoned to death by a fellow inmate with a weightlifting bar at Columbia Correctional Institution in Portage, WI. The man who killed him was Christopher Scarver a black man serving a life sentence for murder.

What is also very significant is that Scarver being in prison for shooting his boss to death, told investigators that he did this because he started hearing voices. Scarver related that he started hearing the voices of a family including a woman, man, and two children who told him things like that "he was the son of God" and "told him what I'm here for today" and that "everything was going to be all right and was meant to happen like this." Because of these voices Scarver killed his boss. During his trial when officials were trying to determine his competency, in an interview with a court appointed psychiatrist Dr. Crowley, Scarver said that he did not want to go to a mental institution because the doctors would turn him into a vegetable and that the voices he was hearing told him to go to prison instead. And to prison he went, the same prison it turns out Jeffrey Dahmer was housed at. Then by some very unlikely coincidence Scarver was placed on the same work detail as Dahmer. And then by some further very unlikely coincidence they were left unsupervised for 20 minutes, this during a time Dahmer was to have a guard around him at all times, due to threats to his own safety. What this resulted in is Scarver brutally beating Dahmer to death with a metal bar.

---

60   Jeffrey Dahmer Trial Final Statement, Youtube.com, https://www.youtube.com/watch?v=lkeacWVwROc
61   Malachi Martin, *Hostage to the Devil*

Scarver later told investigators and prison officials that God told him to kill Dahmer. This from the Chicago Tribune:

> "God told me to do it," Christopher J. Scarver was quoted by a prison guard as saying shortly after the Nov. 28 murders. "You will hear about it on the 6 o'clock news. Jesse Anderson and Jeffrey Dahmer are dead."… Scarver, who is taller than both Dahmer and Anderson, is quoted as telling investigators he did not plan the acts or discuss them with anyone else. He said he attacked the two men because "the spirit" came upon him "right there."… Investigators at the prison said Scarver told them that, in killing Dahmer and Anderson, he "was simply submitting to the will of God and that he was simply a tool used by the spirit," they wrote.[62]

Needless to say, I do not think all these facts are simply a coincidence. Jeffery Dahmer, a man very likely perfectly possessed, expressed his explicit desire to die. Not two years later he is brutally murdered in prison by an inmate who is hearing voices ordering him to kill people. This incident is just one of many very suspicious and seemingly preternatural occurrences in the life of Jeffrey Dahmer.

Before Dahmer was killed however, he granted several interviews to various tv programs. In one of the interviews and in similar fashion to Ted Bundy, Dahmer related that he killed his victims because he wanted to possess them permanently. This is very significant in that this is what devils seek to do to people, they seek to possess people permanently, so for Dahmer and Bundy to be talking like this, in terms of permanent possession, I think is very profound.

> "I had these obsessive desires and thoughts wanting to control them, to – I don't know how to put it – possess them permanently."[63]

According to Dahmer he also dehumanized his victims and did not even look at them as human beings. His wanting to possess them permanently and his dehumanization of his victims makes sense in the context of Dahmer being fully possessed. This is also what demons do to people. Demons wish to possess people permanently and they constantly seek and do dehumanize their victims. In fact, this is mostly true of all serial killers, they all dehumanize their victims, some to a lesser extent, some

---

62   Rogers Worthington, Inmate Charged In Dahmer Killing Says God Ordered It, *Chicago Tribune*, Dec 16, 1994
63   Jeffrey Dahmer, *Inside Edition*

to a much greater extent. Dahmer also related in multiple interviews that the compulsion to kill people and do the things he did was impossible to resist and completely took him over.

In addition to all the grisly details I have related thus far, possibly the best evidence we have of Dahmer's probable diabolical possession come from his own words right before his death.

> "I have to question whether or not there is an evil force in the world and whether or not I have been influenced by it."[64]
>
> "Am I just an extremely evil person or is it some kind of satanic influence or what? I have no idea. I have no idea at all, do you? Is it possible to be influenced by spirit beings? I know that sounds like an easy way to cop out and say that I couldn't help myself, but from all that the bible says, there are forces that have a direct or indirect influence on people's behavior. The bible calls him Satan. I suppose it's possible because it sure seems like some of my thoughts aren't my own, they just come blasting into my head. These thoughts are very powerful and very destructive, and they do not leave. They're not the kind of thoughts that you can just shake your head and they're gone. They do not leave."[65]

ROBIN GECHT AND THE CHICAGO RIPPERS

> CHICAGO -- A judge ordered 120 years in prison for 'devil' Robin Gecht, convicted of the kidnap, rape, mutilation and attempted murder of a teenage prostitute. '**Only a devil would do these things**,' Cook County Criminal Judge Francis J. Mahon told Gecht in sentencing him Wednesday. 'An animal would not do these things. A monster would.[66]'

The crimes of Robin Gecht and his crew of rippers are just as bad if not worse than those of Jeffrey Dahmer. Just as bad because they both contain elements of brutal murder, torture, sexual mutilation of bodies, necrophilia, cannibalism, and all being done in the context of ritualistic Satanism. Worse, because in the case of the Chicago rippers it was 4 people committing these sick crimes instead of just one like in the case of Dahmer. Crews of serial killers are fairly rare among serial killer history.

---

64   David Arkyn, Music Industry Exposed Part 2 – The Agenda to Promote the Dark Side, *The Conscious Reporter*, https://consciousreporter.com/war-on-consciousness/music-industry-exposed-agenda-to-promote-dark-side/
65   Ibid
66   UPI Archives, A judge ordered 120 years in prison for 'devil'..., UPI, https://www.upi.com/Archives/1983/12/15/A-judge-ordered-120-years-in-prison-for-devil/6522440312400/

We know this was the case with the Son of Sam, David Berkowitz who was operating in tandem with a satanic cult that was responsible for the killings and it is also very probable this was the case with John Wayne Gacy who most likely did not operate alone either.[67]

What makes this case even more disturbing is the fact that three of the men, Edward Spreitzer, Andrew Kokoralis, and Thomas Kokoralis, were completely under the control and dominion of the fourth man, Robin Gecht. This case highlights an aspect sometimes present in cases of perfect possession, that was not really present in the previous three I detailed. That is, some people who are perfectly possessed have an uncanny ability to control other people, enslave other people, and get other people to do their bidding. Additionally, the people who are under the control of the perfectly possessed person very often swear the controller has some type of special powers, or ability to control them; that or they are completely terrified of the controller. Even more disturbingly some of them believe their controller to be divine, to be God, to have supernatural powers; or to be some type of savior, messiah, or guru.

Some of these aspects are present in this case as the 3 co-defendants were seemingly completely beholden to Gecht. In initial interviews with police, all 3 co-defendants said Gecht was the ringleader of this murderous cult and in fact a satanic high priest to boot. In addition, all 3 co-defendants were completely terrified of Gecht and were also convinced he had special powers to harm them and control them. Thomas Kokoralis even warned people not to look into Gecht's eyes because it was through these means he would control people. When the 3 co-defendants were brought into the police station they started talking about how Gecht forced them into murder and other terrible activities. Then when the police told the 3 men that Gecht was also in the police station, they became terrified, immediately clammed up and changed their story so as not to implicate Gecht. The fear they had of Gecht and their belief that he had special powers ran so deep that they all completely refused to testify against him even though such an action could have easily led to reduced sentences for all of them. This was also the primary reason that Gecht himself was never actually convicted of a murder.

---

67   There is evidence to suggest John Wayne Gacy, who is suspected of 33 murders did not act alone. When he was brought in to the police station after getting arrested he asked the police if they had his co-conspirators in custody. Additionally, Gacy was out of town on work when some of his victims initially disappeared. He also had several other younger men living with him at the time of the murders.

And killing is not the only thing Gecht has these other 3 men take part in. There were also satanic rituals in the addict of Gecht's home that included masturbation into the cut off breasts of murder victims and then the subsequent cannibalization of the breasts. There were also readings from the satanic bible[68], Gecht of course acting as the high priests through all of this.

What the Chicago Ripper Crew actually was therefore was a 4-member self-styled satanic cult, led by Gecht that practiced murder and human sacrifice, necrophilia, torture, and cannibalism. Robin Gecht is not the first murderous cult leader that has enslaved other people. I will be profiling a few more in the next chapter.

An additional very curious aspect of the case of Robin Gecht is that he was at one time a sub-contractor for John Wayne Gacy. Yes, that John Wayne Gacy, the one who's basement crawl space contained the murdered bodies of over 30 young men and boys. As I briefly stated above Gacy is widely believed to have had co-conspirators in his murderous killing spree. This is a fact not known to many. Gacy himself was not even in the Chicago area when many of the victims actually disappeared. It is just very curious to me that Gacy is believed to have had accomplices and Gecht at one time did work for the man. John Wayne Gacy was executed in an Illinois prison in 1994 and remained completely unrepentant and defiant all the way to the end. His last words were "kiss my ass."

Robin Gecht had a fairly normal childhood it seems except for the fact that he grew up with his grandparents and without a father. This seems to be a common theme in many of the people I am profiling, lack of a fatherly figure. The devil it seems is good at replacing fathers and being a father himself although obviously not a good one. Jesus himself even says that the devil was the "father" of the pharisees trying to kill him. One disturbing aspect of Gecht's young life which is at the least a very unhealthy obsession and at the worst the possible original diabolic entry point, is the intense **obsession** with breasts he developed. Gecht even told one interviewer later that this obsession with breasts is trans-generational. Meaning his grandfather and his grandfather's father were all obsessed with large breasts. There are reasons to believe trans generational obsessions or sins like could have a demonic root. An even more obvious diabolic component is that this intense obsession with breasts was so intense for Gecht

68   Very likely not the satanic bible penned by Anton LaVey, but probably an ancient grimoire of some type.

that he actually cut off the breasts of many of his victims and had sex with the wounds or masturbated into the breasts and then cannibalized them.

It is also known that from a fairly early age Gecht developed an interest in the occult in general and satanism in particular. He also possessed from an early age a copy of the satanic bible. If the breasts obsession was not the original demonic entry point into Gecht's life, then his satanic practices certainly was.

Gecht was also married at a fairly young age and subjected his wife to his sick breast fantasies. In fairly short order he had his wife under his control and started pricking her breasts with pins, this among other sick, demented and sado machoistic behavior. It is unbelievable to me that Gechts wife would not only allow him to subject her to this sadist behavior but also be obedient to him and then even defend him when he was arrested for attempted murder. His wife still supports him to this day, has proclaimed his innocence, and is waiting for the possibility he may be paroled. It seems sick to a normal person why Gechts wife would stick with him through all this, but I can tell you that the hold some perfectly possessed people have on others is very powerful.

Gecht met his accomplices sometime in the late 1970s and started to slowly move them toward being involved in the murders. In one documentary it is stated that Gecht and one of his accomplices was driving around Chicago when Gecht suddenly told the accomplice that they were going to pick up a prostitute and kill her. I think the accomplices were at first involved very unwillingly, but as Gechts control over them increased they became a much more substantial part of the crimes.

We do not know a lot of exact details about these crimes because a lot of what some of the men confessed to was later recanted. What is known is that 18 young women disappeared from the greater Chicago Metropolitan area in the early 1980's. The bodies of the women then started turning up in various places around Chicago. The story was always the same, the woman had been abducted, beaten, tortured, raped, sexually mutilated in indescribable ways, and had their left breasts cut off. Upon realizing all of the victims had their left breast mutilated in some way the police immediately believed they had a serial killer on their hands.

It is not known exactly how many victims were murdered in Gechts van and how many were murdered in Gechts addict. Some victims were killed in the back of Gechts van and in wooded areas. Some of these women, especially one in particular, a young Asian Immigrant was sexually mutilated in such a despicable way it is just too sick to detail here. It seems at least 7 were actually murdered in Gechts addict in the satanic chapel. The details of these human sacrifices are really sick indeed. Gecht would read from the satanic bible while the other men would torture, mutilate and rape the victims. At some point Gecht himself would cut off the left breast, masturbate into it and then all the men would eat it as a form of "communion." The reason I am highlighting these things is so the reader can get an idea of just how violent, cruel, and brutal these men, but especially Gecht were. These crimes show a clear hatred and loathing for the human person. This is one of the reasons I link crimes like this to the diabolic. Because the diabolic spirits have a hatred beyond imagining for humans, and if given the chance they do everything they can to dehumanize and desecrate and kill the bodies of men, woman, and children. That is why I believe many people who are perfectly possessed eventually take part in some form of murder or suicide.

The last victim that the Ripper Crew would abduct was Beverly Washington. Washington was a prostitute and so Gecht was able to pick her up under the auspices that he wanted her for a trick. Gecht drove the woman to a desolate area at which point his accomplices got out of the back of the van and viciously attacked the woman. They beat her, tortured her, raped her, stabbed her multiple times and cut off her left breast. Thinking she was dead, they then dumped her body on some railroad tracks. Miraculously she survived and was able to provide a description of Gecht and the van the men were driving. This led police to Gecht and the other men. The police brought all the men in for questioning at which point they immediately started spilling the beans about Gecht being the ringleader as I described earlier. Even though the men tried recanting their original statement, they talked enough to incriminate themselves and all three of them were charged, convicted, and sentenced for murder. 2 of the men were even given the death penalty. One of those death sentences was however commuted to life imprisonment. Only Andrew Kokoralis was actually executed by the state of Illinois. As I stated earlier Gecht himself was never convicted of murder, only attempted murder, and rape of Beverly Washington. He was given 120 years in prison and will be eligible for parole in 2022.

There are 3 additional things about Robin Gecht that I think are significant in this case. As I will detail in a later chapter, death and destruction often follow in the wake of the perfectly possessed. Many people who associate themselves with the perfectly possessed sometimes die violent deaths, or end up insane or have any number of terrible things happen to them. In the case of Gecht it was his mother, sister, and 2-year-old nephew who all died in a very violent traffic accident, sandwiched between 2 semi-trucks, immediately after visiting Gecht at the Menard Correctional Center.[69] Diabolic spirits are bringers of death and destruction. If they are fully in control of a person, they still effect the environment around the person and people who come into contact with that person. I am not saying the devil killed Gechts mother, sister, and 2-year-old nephew. It is just curious that they died such a violent death, immediately after visiting Gecht.

Another significant aspect is that Gechts son has also been convicted of murder. David Gecht was convicted of shooting to death a man named Roberto Cruz in an unprovoked attack. I think this is a highly significant factor in this case. It is known Gecht was a Satanist and one of the things serious Satanists like to do is consecrate their children to Satan. Moreover, it is a very common belief among exorcists that demonic affliction can be generational. So, it is very possible indeed that the spirits possessing Robin Gecht, latched on to his son and influenced his life in an unknown way, that led him to commit murder just like his father.

A third person associated with Robin Gecht that experienced severe misfortune after coming into contact with him was the lead detective for the Chicago Police Department who was investigating the Ripper murders and who with his partner is credited with ultimately solving them. Shortly after solving the ripper murders, detective Philip Murphy in short order divorced from his wife of 20 years, suffered a debilitating stroke which left him permanently disabled, and then in 1989 shot his ex-wife to death and then turned the gun on himself and took his own life.

In the case of Robin Gecht, we have a man who started life without a father and with an intense obsession with breasts, moved into satanic worship at a young age and practiced sadism on his wife shortly after getting married. We see he was involved in some of the most brutal sadistic crimes imaginable committed against woman. We also see how all this was committed in the context of ritualistic satanism, which also included elements of necrophilia, torture, and cannibalism. Further we see how Gecht had complete control of many different people in his life, his accomplices and also his wife and how he manipulated them to accept his abuse and commit unspeakable acts against women. Moreover, Gecht is still alive and remains as defiant as ever. He has never repented in any way whatsoever for anything he has done. In fact, it is known he has bragged

---

69   Adam Ramos, Ten 10 Haunting Facts About Chicago's Cannibalistic 'Ripper Crew'

to fellow inmates about his murderous behavior. We also have the aspect of the death and destruction that seems to follow Gecht around like a toxic cloud that infects everything it touches. Death and destruction that took the lives of 18 innocent women, destroyed their families, death and destruction that took the lives of 3 of his relatives, death and destruction that ruined his son's life who also is a murderer, and death and destruction that took the lives of the lead detective on the case and his wife. The number of people who have met a violent end after associating with Gecht is remarkable. When we look at the life of Gecht as a whole and put all these things into perspective it paints a very dark diabolical picture of this man's life. There is very clear evidence indeed of some kind of evil and powerful influence at work in this man's life that affected some of the people around him a great deal. And as if all that were not enough, in similar fashion to Ted Bundy, Gecht also displayed different personalities.

> Gecht was said by behavioral experts to exhibit multiple personalities, perhaps as a ruse. For example, in their discussions with him he wandered. His voice changed. He would speak as a small child, a teenager or a businessman… ``Definitely on the squirrelly side,`` one investigator said of Gecht. ``But if you saw him on the street, you`d never think he was dangerous at all. ``Gecht`s magic was his apparent ability to draw people to him who were loners and in need of jobs and friendship, like his fellow attackers… Spreitzer testified at his trial that he tried to get away from Gecht after the first killing but that Gecht cajoled and pestered him to come back for more. Prosecutors likened Spreitzer and the Kokoraleis brothers to followers of Charles Manson, the California murderer/guru who, like Gecht, gave orders to kill. Thomas Kokoraleis said in his statement to police: ``Robin told us to bring a breast back to the house. He told me to do this to please him.`` His statement is replete with references to the fact that **Gecht`s three companions did what they did** ``**to please Robin.**``[70]

Conclusion:

H.H. Holmes, Ted Bundy, Jeffrey Dahmer, and Robin Gecht are certainly not the only serial killers that I suspect to have been possessed. I earlier mentioned David Berkowitz who made the explicit statement that he believed he had a demon living in him since birth that was controlling him. There just have been so many brutal killers over the past 100 plus years it defies comprehension. And not all series of serial slay-

---

70   Edward Baumann and John O`Brien, Trail's End, *Chicago Tribune*

ings have been solved either. Four in particular that I know of that are known for their horrific brutality and diabolic evil are the Jack the Ripper Murders, the Cleveland Torso Murders, the Villisca Axe Murders and the Black Dahlia murder all of which remain unsolved to this day.

The Cleveland Torso Murders saw an unidentified suspect behead, dismember, and castrate up to 20 victims in the mid to late 1930's during the height of the Great Depression. It is said that all of the victims were still alive when they were beheaded. This case was never solved despite the fact that famous law man Elliot Ness made this case a top priority. In one documentary I watched it said Ness had one suspect that he was sure committed these crimes but he could never prove it. The person in question (Dr. Francis Sweeny) was committed to a mental asylum at some point and after this the killings mysteriously stopped. Not only this but after Sweeny was committed he sent threatening postcards to Ness and his family all the way into the 1950's mocking him for failure to solve the case. It is said this case in particular haunted Elliot Ness for the rest of his life.

Just as brutal and diabolic were the Whitechapel murders committed by Jack the Ripper. This killer slashed the throats of five woman (that we know of) with one swipe of the knife almost beheading all the victims, he also dismembered them in various sickening ways. The man who found the body of the ripper's last victim said it looked like a devil had done the grisly murder. The violence associated with these attacks speaks to the fact the killer knew exactly what he was doing, was very strong, and was filled with an implacable hatred for his fellow humans but especially woman. There has even been plenty of speculation that the murderer was a practicing Satanist and the murders were done as part of a black magic ritual. The aspect of the case that I found most disturbing, besides the violence associated with it, is the infamous "from hell" letter to police. The "from Hell" letter is the only letter police believe to be a genuine correspondence from the actual killer.

One of the victims of the ripper had had one of her kidneys expertly removed, shortly after this, police received a stinking package with a part of the kidney. Also, in the package with the kidney was a letter to police that was headed as "from hell." The killer said in the letter that he had cannibalized the other part of the kidney and that he had enjoyed it. I still remember the first time I saw this letter and saw the "from hell" heading I just got a sick feeling in the pit of my stomach that whoever this killer was and whoever sent that package to police was completely possessed by the devil. Despite the fact that Jack the Ripper has never been identi-

273

fied, the best suspect is a man named Aaron Kosminski. A polish Jew who started exhibiting psychotic behavior in 1885, 3 years before the murders took place. Kosminski was known to experience auditory hallucinations, otherwise known as hearing voices, and also engaged in some form of perverted sexual activity. It is also said that Kosminski displayed a marked hatred of women and homicidal tendencies. The murders took place in 1888 and also stopped in November of 1888. Kosminski was committed to a lunatic asylum in 1891 and died in 1919 as an inmate of the asylum.

The Villisca axe murders took place in the early morning hours (between midnight and 3am) of June 10, 1912. During the evening of June 9, 1912, the Moore family had been attending a church service. At some point during the day or night an unknown assailant entered the Moore household, waited in the addict till everyone was asleep and then brutally murdered all 8 people living in the house, including 6 children. Even more sickening is the fact that after the killer initially killed his victims he then returned to their corpses and mutilated the faces and heads with an axe so terribly it left them completely unrecognizable. It was said the murders were so violent that the ceilings above where the murders were committed bore axe marks from the upswing of the axe. The killer also draped sheets over all the mirrors in the house[71] and covered the bodies with sheets as well. No one was ever brought to justice for these crimes and the house these murders occurred in stands to this day.

One of the primary suspects however, that was arrested twice and confessed thrice, but later recanted, for this crime was a traveling preacher who was known to be a very disturbed individual. In one of his confessions the preacher stated that a dark shadowy figure had handed him the axe and commanded him to commit the murders. The jury felt these confessions were fabricated and the imaginings of a deranged man and so the man was never convicted of these crimes. This house has been a favorite for paranormal investigations and it is thought by many that this house is completely infested with diabolical forces. Paranormal investigators have reported hearing loud growls, banging's, and experienced various emotional and physical disturbances. Many evp's have also been captured on the premises including both demonic voices and children's voices. Then on November 12, 2014 a man from Rhinelander, WI who had paid to sleep in the house along with a few other people, stabbed himself in the chest in one of the rooms in the house at roughly 12:45am, a time widely believed the murders took place.

---

71   This fact makes it very likely that the killer had at least some knowledge of the occult.

In my opinion, the most disturbing aspect of the Villisca axe murders is the fact that it is extremely likely these 8 murders were not the only axe murders the killer perpetrated. From September 1911 to December 1912 there were approximately 10 separate incidents occurring in Washington, Illinois, Colorado, Kansas, Iowa, and Missouri in which up to 30 people were brutally murdered by an axe wielding madman. Many of these cases bore striking similarities, so much so it would be unreasonable to assume they were not committed by the same person. For example, in at least 8 of the cases, including Villisca the axe was found abandoned at the scene. In 7 of the cases there was a railway line in very close proximity to the killings. In 3 of the cases the murders were committed on a Sunday night. In four of the killings the murderer had covered the victims faces and in 3 of them the murderer had washed himself off at the scene. And the most profound similarity, in at least 3 of the killings, those at Villisca, IA; Paola, KA; and Ellsworth, KA, the homes in which the murders took place had been lit by lamps in which the chimney had been cast aside and the wick bent downward. The main suspect in all these slayings, identified by Agent Matthew McClaughry of the Bureau of Investigation (forerunner of the FBI) was a man named Henry Lee Moore who was convicted for the axe murders of his own family in Missouri in December of 1912. Moore was sentenced to life in prison but was eventually released in 1949. In the end all of the axe murders committed in 1911 and 1912, except for the Missouri ones Moore was actually convicted of, remain unsolved to this day.

In more modern times there have been plenty of brutal serial killers who have been associated with the diabolic in some way. We all are well aware of the Night Stalker, Richard Ramirez, who killed 13 people in the greater Los Angeles area and later San Francisco areas in the mid 1980's. Ramirez was an avowed Satanist. He often left pentagrams and other satanic paraphernalia at the crime scenes. In court one day he yelled out "Hail Satan" as he was leaving the court room revealing a pentagram tattoo he had on his hand. At his sentencing Ramirez claimed that "Lucifer dwells within us all." Ramirez was sentenced to death and showed absolutely no care in the world for that sentence. I believe he remarked something to the effect of that he would see us at Disneyland when he was sentenced to die. Ramirez died of cancer before he was to be executed and he remained completely unrepentant all the way up to his death.[72]

---

72   It should also be noted that in his recent book about diabolic activity, Jesse Romero states that he met Ramirez many times while working as a correctional officer in Los Angeles and that he considered him an example of someone who is perfectly possessed.

There is also the case of Peter Sutcliff, also known as the Yorkshire ripper who before he started killing worked in a graveyard. Sutcliff told investigators that while working in the graveyard he began hearing voices that identified themselves as God. He said the voices eventually ordered him to start killing prostitutes, which he did in the most brutal fashion imaginable. There is also Henry Lee Lucas who I briefly profiled in an earlier chapter who Bob Larson was absolutely convinced was completely possessed and controlled by Satan.

Then we have the BTK killer (bind, torture, kill), Dennis Rader who killed 10 people in Kansas. Rader is one serial killer who readily admitted that he was possessed and controlled by the devil and he has made some very profound statements to that effect. In addition, Rader's long-time pastor at the Lutheran Church that Rader was a leader at believed Rader was possessed as well. Rader actually had a name for the force that possessed him, he called it "Factor X." In an interview with Harvard neuropsychologist Robert Mendoza, Rader said:

> "Factor X is probably something I'll never know. I actually think it may be possessed with demons. **I can't stop it … it controls me, you know, it's like in the driver's seat**. That's probably the reason we're sitting here. You know, if I could just say, no I don't want to do this, and go crawl into a hole. **But it is driving me.**"[73]

Also, in an interview with KAKE-TV, Rader said:

> "I just know it's a dark side of me. **It kind of controls me**. I personally think it's a ---- and I know it is not very Christian--- but I actually think it's a demon that's within me… At some point and time, it entered me when I was very young."[74]

And finally,

> "I actually think I may be possessed with demons; I was dropped on my head as a kid."[75]

Considering everything I have written thus far about perfectly possessed people being completely under the dominion and control of the devil, Rader's statements are very profound indeed. With his statements,

73   Dateline NBC, Secret Confessions of BTK, NBC News, https://www.nbcnews.com/id/wbna8917644

74   Associated Press, BTK Sorry for Murders, Blames 'Demon', Fox News, https://www.foxnews.com/story/btk-sorry-for-murders-blames-demon

75   Astrid Mc Clymont, Top 10 Serial Killer Quotes, Listverse, https://listverse.com/2012/09/04/top-10-serial-killer-quotes/

Rader has confirmed the whole premise of this work. That is, that there are in the world perfectly possessed people who are completely under the slavery of the devil and commit unspeakable and evil acts against their fellow human persons. In previous chapters I described perfect possession as a kind of slavery to the devil, where a human being is completely and totally possessed and under the dominion of an evil spirit. For some people this may be difficult to believe and leave some folks incredulous, yet when Dennis Rader, who murdered 10 people, including children, and who has admitted being possessed, says things like "I can't stop it… it controls me, you know, it's like in the driver's seat" and "It kind of controls me." It should give all of us in the faith great pause. In Dennis Rader we have a genuinely perfectly possessed person speaking openly about his condition, a very rare occurrence indeed.

Rader also believed that all serial killers have this "factor X" and he actually drew a picture of what it looked like. This illustration can be found in the photo section in the middle of this book. Rader's pastor, The Reverend Michael Clark of Wichita's Christ Lutheran Church who also believed Rader was possessed stated:

> "The person I heard in the courtroom was not the real Dennis. There was someone else speaking from Dennis that day. I personally think we're dealing with some kind of possession. From all that I've seen and the people I've talked with who have dealt with demonic possession, I feel there was something working there. When I go back to the beginning when Dennis made his first statement to the public about his condition in the 70's he, 'there's a monster inside of me that I can't control.'"[76]

At the time this book is being finished and edited a new American serial killer has been discovered, one that may hold the infamous title of Americas worst serial killer. On Sept 12, 2012, Samuel Little was arrested at a homeless shelter in Louiville, Kentucky after DNA evidence had linked him to a series of slayings that took place in the greater Los Angeles area in the 1980's. After this he started to be investigated for "dozens" of murders across various states. In 2018 Little was extradited to Texas to face trial for another series of murders. Under questioning from the Texas Rangers, Little, then confessed to 93 murders across various U.S. states. If true this would make him the deadliest serial killer, that is known about, in United States history. As of the time of this writing the FBI has positively linked his confessions to over 60 known unsolved homicides. In a chilling interview, one of the Texas homicide investigators who has been interviewing Little said that Little was "Evil in its purest form"[77], even more disturbing and diabolic is the fact that when asked why he had committed so many murders, Little's reply was that "God put me here to do this"[78].

Herbert Mullin is another brutal serial killer who murdered 13 people because he heard voices telling him to commit human sacrifices to avert a California earthquake. It should be noted that one of Mullins victims was a Catholic priest who Mullin brutally stabbed to death immediately after the priest had heard his confession.[79]

Another very recent arrest of an absolutely infamous serial killer was the 2018 arrest of the Golden State Killer who had eluded police for decades. The man who was arrested, Joseph DeAngelo, who is an ex-police officer, committed 150 burglaries, 50 rapes and 13 homicides. The Golden State Killer was one of the most infamous series of serial slayings that had never been solved, right up there with the Zodiac killings. When a 75-year-old DeAngelo finally sat down with police and was asked why he had done this he said that it was an alto ego part of him he could not control, that he heard voices ordering him to kill.[80]

> DeAngelo, 74, did not cooperate with authorities. But he muttered a confession of sorts after his arrest that cryptically referred to an alter ego named "Jerry" that he said forced him to commit the wave of crimes that appeared to end abruptly in 1986… "I didn't have the strength to push him out," DeAngelo said. "He made me. He went with me. It was like in my head, I mean, he's a part of me. I didn't want to do those things.[81]

Lastly, one of the most prolific killers in United States history is a man named Richard Kuklinski, otherwise known as the "Ice Man." Kuklinski was a professional contract killer, or a hitman for the Mafia in New Jersey and New York. He was ultimately convicted of 6 murders, it is widely believed by law enforcement however that he killed many, many more,

77   Carson Chambers, 'Evil in the purest form': Confessed serial killer Samuel Little blames God in killings of 90 women, ABC Action News Tampa Bay
78   Ibid.
79   Vernetta Watts et al., Serial Killer Timeline Herbert Mullin, Radford University Department of Psychology
80   Arthur Shawcross is yet another serial killer who during an interview said he had some kind of monster inside of him that he listened to and could not control, that was responsible for his slayings.
81   Stefanie Dazio et al., 'I Did All That': Inner Person Drove the Golden State Killer, Prosecutor Says, CBS 13 Sacramento

possibly hundreds. Kuklinski himself, when asked how many people he killed admitted the number was over 100. For the investigators tasked to investigate and bring Kuklinski to justice, the Ice Man, as he was called by investigators, was nothing short of a diabolic, ruthless, professional killer.

> "The consensus of the federal, state, county and local law enforcement agencies that were involved in this investigation is that Richard Kuklinski is one of the most dangerous criminals we have ever come across in this state. Further, it's our feeling that he is of such a diabolical, methodical type of killer that it's very possible that when all is said and done, we may never know how many people he has actually killed."[82]

To answer the question of why the perfectly possessed commit these murders all one has to do is look to the scriptures and listen to the words of Our Lord who explicitly stated that Satan is a murderer and a murderer from the beginning. That when people murder, they are fulfilling the desires of their master or specifically their *father* who is the devil. It is a mystery of evil of why these murders take place. You would think Satan would want to stay hidden as best as possible so as not to attract attention. Serial Killings and mass killings definitely get the attention of people and people just naturally associate such activities with evil or the devil. Who does not think the holocaust and the millions of people killed by the Nazi regime was not evil and diabolically inspired, the same can be said of all the other genocidal episodes in the history of mankind but especially over the last hundred years. The fact is that Satan is a murderer and he and the other demons enjoy murdering people in the most brutal ways imaginable.

Theologically it is probably because Christ, the son of God, took on human flesh. This goes all the way back to dawn of time and the fall of Lucifer and the other angels. In chapter one I described how many modern theologians believe the reason for the fall to be that they rejected Christ generally and the incarnation specifically, meaning they rejected Jesus taking on human flesh. Lucifer believed if Jesus was going to become incarnate it should be through his nature, not human nature. Based on this we know Satan is intensely jealous of human beings and their material bodies. Because God himself, clothed himself with this human flesh, Satan now seeks to destroy and desecrate this same human flesh by inspiring the murder of untold people. And this has been going on for thousands of years. Cain was the first murderer, inspired by Satan, and there have been servants of the devil committing murder all the way up to the present day. The blood-soaked lands of Rwanda, Iraq, Syria, Mexico and places like Chicago showcase the murderous desires of the devil and his servant's willingness to carry it out, all too well in modern times.

CHAPTER 9

EVIL ON A WIDER SCALE

In this chapter I am going to profile three people who have committed various forms of evil and have had a lasting negative impact on mankind. Some of the people I am going to profile in this section are not as well-known as some of the others. I am briefly going to talk about Hitler, because there is overwhelming evidence for his being totally controlled by evil forces, but I am also going to profile people like the Reverend Jim Jones and Aleister Crowley who are not spoken about as much as people like Hitler. The three people I am going to showcase here have all committed evil on a much greater scale than the serial killings talked about in the last chapter. Some of the evil that these people committed remains to this day and is still affecting the world and corrupting souls. A prime example is Aleister Crowley whose voluminous works on various aspects of occultism continue to inspire practitioners of the dark arts to this very day. All of the people I am profiling here have displayed various indications of being fully possessed and being under the dominion of the powers of darkness. All of them have actively led other people into evil as well. Whereas in the case of some serial killers, who just commit murders themselves, the people I will be writing about in this chapter actively and intentionally lead others to evil and lead others to commit evil acts. This is done through various means, deception being the foremost but also fear and intimidation, coercion, manipulation, and various other forms of control and slavery these people exercise over their fellow man.

Some people might think that labeling the control these people have over their followers as slavery is taking it a step too far, I disagree. As I showed in the article from the Chicago Tribune at the end of the section on Robin Gecht, Gecht's accomplices were so beholden to him that they committed these terrible acts just to "please Robin." As I will show in this section, the followers of some of the people I will be profiling were so enslaved to the controller that they committed just unspeakable acts at the behest of their master. The case of Jim Jones and Adolf Hitler are two of the best examples. Hitler obviously controlled a much larger group of people that committed many more murders, however Jim Jones had no less a hold on his followers who voluntarily murdered their own children when Jones ordered this to occur. Satanic slavery is a terrible and frightening thing, but it happens, and it is a part of how evil works and acts in the world. Enslaving other people and leading other people into perdition is one of the hallmarks of someone who is perfectly possessed. As I stated in the introduction of this book, perfect possession is one of the primary ways that the devil is able to attack mankind on a larger scale and cause major events to unfold in the course of human history. He does this not by appearing personally but acting through his servants, the perfectly possessed.

Jim Jones and the People's Temple

> There's only one hope of glory; that's within you! Nobody's gonna come out of the sky! There's no heaven up there! We'll have to make heaven down here![1]
>
> "I could see his eyes over the top of his dark sunglasses he had on. What I saw scared the daylights out of me, and I jerked my hand back. There was something very strange and frightening about what I both saw and felt… I understood that what I sensed was pure evil, but as a kid, I had no idea what my feelings were. All I knew is that this was a strange man… I know that without a doubt, that what I saw and felt as a child, was in fact, pure evil.[2]

"If you see me as your God, I will be your God" and "I am God" Jones screamed to a group of his followers during a sermon in the early days of the People's Temple when it was still in San Francisco. This kind of messianic and ultimately blasphemous rhetoric from the Rev. Jim Jones paired with Jones's claims that he had special and supernatural powers demonstrated by fraudulent and diabolical pseudo miracles, and also along with systematic financial, emotional, sexual, spiritual, and physical abuse and mind control, led to his complete control of over a 1000 people who believed he was the messiah, called him father and who ultimately followed him to their deaths in the Guyanese jungle in one of the largest acts of mass murder and loss of American life before Sept 11, 2001.

Jim Jones was born in 1931 in Lynn, Indiana. His father was a disabled World War 1 veteran and also a violent alcoholic who abused Jones.

---

1   *American Experience.* 2007. Jonestown: The Life and Death of Peoples Temple
2   Experience of man who met Jim Jones as a child, Alternative Considerations of Jonestown & Peoples Temple by San Diego State University Department of Religion

EVIL ON A WIDER SCALE

Jones's mother was usually never around the home because she was forced to work outside the home to support the family due to her husband's alcoholism. Jones's father displayed absolutely no interest in the young Jones and showed him no love or tenderness whatsoever. Based on this and some other factors it is safe to say Jones was raised in an extremely dysfunctional and unloving family. Childhood friends have said that he was pretty much left to his own devices.

According to these same childhood friends Jones began to display disturbing and abnormal behavior at a very young age. In one documentary it is said that from a very young age Jones was obsessed with religion and death. So much so that he would kill animals and then proceed to conduct funeral services for them in which he was the presiding minister.[3]

In his teenage years it became very clear that Jones had a dark side, a very dark side. Not only did he continue to kill animals he also abused a classmate named Donald Foreman by locking him in an attic and shooting him with a bb gun on several occasions. It seems Jones took pleasure in inflicting fear and pain on others. When Jones would abuse Donald Foreman, Foreman noticed that Jones's facial expression changed a great deal. Whenever Jones would hurt him Jones would get this eerie smirk on his face that disturbed Foreman greatly, Foreman described it as "a really strange look."[4] There was also another incident like this when Jones as a very young adult was working as an orderly at Reed Memorial Hospital in Richmond. One of his co-workers at the hospital recalled a very disturbing incident in which Jones asked him to dry shave a patient in traction. Jones's co-worker grabbed all of the necessary tools and started to lather the mans face at which time Jones became furious, grabbed the razor away from the co-worker and wiped the lather off the man's face at which time he snarled "I didn't mean like that, I'll show you what I meant." Jones then proceeded to drag the razor along the poor patients face until the patient had tears streaming down his face. Jones's colleague stated that it was extremely clear that the man was in a great deal of pain at which time Jones turned to his colleague and gave him this sick smirk or smile. The look on Jones's face frightened the co-worker so much that he quit his job at the hospital 2 weeks later.[5]

---

3   *Jonestown: The Life and Death of Peoples Temple*, directed by Stanley Nelson (2006 Tribeca Film Festival, Firelight Media 2006)
4   *Biography Jim Jones: Journey Into Madness*, Created by David Wolper (1998 ABC News Productions & A&E Television Network)
5   Ibid.

At some point in Jones's late teens or early adulthood he started studying Marxism and Communism and became completely obsessed with the idea of infiltrating the Christian Church with these doctrines. His wife at the time, a woman named Marcy, recalled a time when Jones slammed the bible down on his table yelling "I've got to destroy this paper idol"[6]. This display of blasphemy and religious desecration would be a foretaste of some of the things that would come later when Jones was head of the People's Temple in San Francisco.

When Jones became a young adult, he became a member of a Presbyterian Church in Indianapolis. In very short order Jones became disillusioned with mainstream churches because of what he claimed were elements of segregation and racism issues. This is what he told others his problem with mainstream churches was. However, knowing Jones was a Marxist, it could be that he was never really a true Christian or believer in Jesus Christ and the only reason he had been a member of a Christian church was to infiltrate it and destroy it from the inside. This theory has precedent because when Jones started his own church this is exactly what he did. He started off by preaching genuine classic Christianity and slowly introduced elements of Marxism, until the foundational Christian teachings were completely warped and unrecognizable.

In 1955 Jones founded the People's Temple as an independent congregation in Indianapolis. In the early 1960's the People's Temple affiliated itself with another mainstream church, the Disciples of Christ and then in 1964 Jim Jones was ordained as a minister. In the early days of the People's Temple Jones mainly preached on ideas that "a just society that could overcome the evils of racism and poverty"[7] was something to work towards. Jones consistently preached about inclusivity and integration. This preaching flew in the face of some of the preaching of the day that was very negative towards the concepts of integration. As a result of this preaching from Jones he attracted a very large number of African American members. In fact, most of his congregation was made up of black folks.

During the later years of the People's Temple's existence in Indianapolis Jones preached about an "us versus them" mentality. Carefully quoting both Marx and scripture to plant the seeds of communism in his listeners hearts. Even though Jones would quote bible passages to fit his personal theology, he would very often viciously attack the rest of scripture.

6   Robert Lindsey, Jim Jones— From Poverty To Power of Life and Death, *New York Times*, Nov 26, 1978
7   The People's Temple, *Encyclopedia Britannica*

He would also tell his members to abstain from sex, all the while himself engaging in multiple adulterous relationships with multiple woman and men from his congregation. The other thing that was slowly introduced in the time right before the move to California was that Jones was some type of messianic figure or Christ like figure, he also started preaching about full religious communalism in which members would give Jones all of their personal possessions including financial resources in exchange for the People's Temple providing for all their needs. What this really was however was the beginning of a systematic campaign of cult abuse and mind control, to make, essentially, slaves out of his followers.

In 1961 Jones claimed that he saw a vision of the city of Chicago coming under an intense nuclear attack from the Russians. This vision and his further preaching about an imminent nuclear holocaust would eventually lead him to move his church to Redwood Valley, California.

In 1965 Jones moved the People's Temple to Redwood Valley and also established locations in San Francisco and Los Angeles. He told his followers this was due to his belief in a nuclear attack on middle America and also due to the fact that California was much more accepting than the conservatism of the heartland. The move to California really seemed to accelerate Jones's descent into evil. This was when he started to actively alienate his members from the rest of their families. Nevertheless, membership at the People's Temple seemed to explode with the move to California. Jones now started telling his people that the Holy Spirit was with them but because he displayed special healing abilities meant that he was a manifestation of what he called "Christ the revolution"[8]. It should be noted that these supposed special healing abilities were either fraudulent, meaning Jones would have a prearrangement with someone in the congregation who would fake a sickness or injury and then be healed miraculously by Jones; this or they were what are known as diabolic imitation of miracles. The devil does not have power to enact an actual miracle, but he does certainly have power to do things in the preternatural realm that look to us to be miraculous.

The actual authenticity of Jones's healing ability is a topic of great disagreement between surviving members of the people's temple. There are some, understandably who are certain he possessed no genuine abilities whatsoever. However, there are others who swear to this day that Jones had numerous paranormal abilities, both healing abilities and psychic powers. One previous member of the People's Temple notes,

"I can 'testify' that Jim's ability to heal, to reveal the future and to fathom the depths of one's personal and our own collectively karmic pasts was evident a dozen times in any particular meeting and not open to question – public or private – by anyone I know of at the time."[9]

Another former member named Don Beck also writes that,

the fact remains, he had a gift. Whether you wish to call it faith-healing or a paranormal faculty or an extra-dimensional power or a metaphysical consciousness, he had it, and it worked.[10]

Beck then goes on to relate several personal experiences that he had with Jones in which Jones healed him of a fever and on two separate occasions knew where Beck was, what he was doing, what he was wearing, and even what he was thinking! Needless to say, this is a clear and classic sign of diabolical possession, in this case perfect possession.

With the move to California also came the beginning of Jones's subjection of his people to various forms of abuse and mind control techniques. People sometimes wonder how someone could get involved in a cult, how they could not detect something was very wrong. In my study of Jim Jones, all these things were done over a very long period of time. Jones's hold over his followers grew very slowly, but it still grew sure as ever. These people were basically enslaved to Jones slowly but surely over a period of time, which enslavement then led to their deaths and the deaths of their children.

After the People's Temple moved to California Jones became extremely hostile to mainstream Christianity and the scriptures. He started saying very disturbing things like that the bible was a white man's justification to dominate women and enslave people of color. This despite the fact that Jones himself was using the scriptures to enslave his members, most of whom were people of color. Jones would say that the bible contained beliefs about only a "sky God," "spook God" or "buzzard God"[11] who he thought was no God at all. Jones even went so far as to subject the scriptures to a physical assault. During his sermons Jones would violently throw the good book down on the floor and scream blasphemies like "this

---

9   Did Jim Jones Have the Power to Heal, Alternative Considerations of Jonestown & Peoples Temple, San Diego State University
10   Ibid.
11   David Chidester, Jonestown and the People's Temple, encyclopedia.com, https://www.encyclopedia.com/environment/encyclopedias-almanacs-transcripts-and-maps/jonestown-and-peoples-temple

black book has held you people down for 2000 years. It has no power"[12]. Jones even once told his followers that they should use the pages of the bible as "toilet paper"[13]. Jones would also commonly distribute a pamphlet that contained his blasphemous attacks on the scriptures. These attacks from Jones were clearly directed more to his African American followers.

Jones then took his show on the road so to speak and commenced long road trips in which the people's temple would take multiple busses all over the country trying to recruit followers. They would also conduct the fraudulent healing services in different cities to deceive people into joining the temple and moving to San Francisco. Jones would have a pre-arranged plant in the crowds of people he was preaching to who would come up and be miraculously healed of some non-existent injury or illness. All of this was occurring in the early to mid-1970's and during this time members of the Peoples Temple, including children were subjected to sexual abuse and physical abuse. Really all of the members were subjected to some form of abuse and control. Jones continued his multiple sexual liaisons with People's Temple members, and the Temple's financial dealings were also known to be very shady indeed. There was just a massive amount of cult like control and abuse going on that the outside world was not really privy to. But some people did leave the People's Temple and then tried warning police and other authorities of what was going on there.

By 1976 the facade of Christianity that Jones had initially used to gain loyal followers fell away completely. Jones now openly proclaimed that he was an atheist. His attacks on the scriptures and other religious doctrines increased in ferocity to a truly diabolic level. He continually physically assaulted the scriptures, often stomping on the word of God, trampling it under his feet, or tearing it to pieces like a possessed animal. In doing this he would even issue direct mocking challenges to God, telling his members after he violated the scriptures "did you see lightning come down from heaven and strike me dead"[14]. According to one source apparently Jones even very often blasphemed the Holy Virgin Mary, calling her a whore and saying Jesus was an illegitimate child.

Due to Jones's preaching and systematic indoctrination his followers literally went from believing in God and Jesus Christ to eventually believ-

12   Kinsolving, Lester. "SEX, SOCIALISM, AND CHILD TORTURE WITH REV. JIM JONES." *San Francisco Examiner*. September 1972.
13   Did people have Bibles in Jonestown? Alternative Considerations of Jonestown and People's Temple, San Diego State University
14   Kinsolving, Lester. "SEX, SOCIALISM, AND CHILD TORTURE WITH REV. JIM JONES." *San Francisco Examiner*. September 1972.

ing that the God of the bible did not exist and that Jim Jones was God and messiah. When one analyzes the preaching of Jim Jones and the events and circumstances in the final years of the People's Temple it becomes clear that it is breathtakingly Satanic in nature. Members of the People's Temple were systematically dehumanized and abused financially, spiritually, sexually, in their relationships and physically and ended up in complete slavery to Jim Jones. Jones often preached that not only was he God but that all his followers were also God's and that there was no such thing as heaven and so it was their responsibility to make a heaven on earth.

Jones's preaching on sexual matters also became extremely perverse and twisted. Jones would preach that he was the only heterosexual on the planet and that all of his members were either gay or lesbian. Through his satanically inspired preaching Jones gave himself license to have sex with any of his followers at any time for any reason. Even more disgusting is the stories of past members who said that Jones would go around to his male followers and tell the men that he would gladly "fuck them in the ass"[15] if that's what they wanted. Tim Carver is one such previous member who was propositioned in this way by Jones. And it seems Jones did go through with this and sodomized many of his male followers.

All of the constant deception and abuse of People's Temple members led them to be in complete thralldom to Jones, in the literal sense of the word. In addition, it also led to greater media scrutiny and the beginning of various investigations into the people's Temple. These investigations came as a result of many people who had left the Temple and had told authorities about some of the horrors that people were being subjected to. In 1978 an increasingly paranoid and delusional Jones moved the People's Temple to Guyana, South America to a commune far out into the jungle many, many miles from any civilization. It seems that about 1000 people followed Jones to Guyana, the rest stayed in the states. The decision by these people to follow Jones to Guyana would be the final step in the diabolical process of separating them from the rest of society so as to eventually systematically destroy them. It seems in cases like this diabolical evil is almost contagious. Meaning Jones was clearly possessed, but in the end so might have been many of his followers who engaged in depraved sex acts with him and who followed through on orders to kill and then kill their children and themselves.

---

15   *Jonestown: The Life and Death of Peoples Temple,* directed by Stanley Nelson (2006 Tribeca Film Festival, Firelight Media 2006)

Jonestown is a stunning example of the concept Father M talked about at the Mundelein Conference in 2005 and 2006. Specifically, that many people get into trouble with "demonic stuff" as he called it when they separate themselves from their families and other meaningful loving relationships. Jonestown was in the middle of nowhere in the Guyanese jungle, far away from any influence these people's families could have possibly had on them. This was all by diabolical design of course. Once the people arrived in Jonestown they discovered the final stage of their slavery was complete and they could not leave, even if they wanted to.

The cult of the People's Temple was their new family and Jim Jones was their diabolic version of a father. And despite the fact that Jonestown was full of nuclear families and even extended families (many entire families lived at Jonestown, including husbands, wives, children, grandparents, etc.), it did not matter because the atmosphere at Jonestown was one of fear betrayal, and control. Jones so deceived and enslaved these people that fathers would turn in their children to Jones for minor infractions, wives would report on their husbands and children would tell on their parents. The loving familial relationships and bonds that normally protect people from the demonic were completely destroyed at Jonestown by Jim Jones and the diabolical preaching and slavery he exerted over his people. These loving familial bonds were so thoroughly and completely destroyed and perverted that in the final act of diabolic victory parents were actually killing their own children with cyanide laced Kool-Aid at the request and behest of the Reverend Jim Jones.

The move to Jonestown would prove to be the ultimate undoing of Jones and his followers. As I stated earlier, the move to the jungle would ultimately seal their doom. I strongly suspect that Jones and his diabolical masters had planned it this way all along. When the people actually did move to Jonestown all the forms of cultic abuse continued and in fact now intensified. People were not allowed to leave the compound and if they expressed a desire to leave to anyone, they would be informed on to Jones who would then severely humiliate and punish the person who said they wanted to leave the compound. Jones's voice would be broadcast 24 hours a day from the loudspeakers in the compound and followers would be rousted out of bed in the middle of the night for emergency drills. According to one survivor, Eugene Smith, things were much worse around the compound when Jones himself was actually present. In the documentary, Jim Jones: Journey into Madness, Smith states:

When Jim Jones wasn't there things tended to be a little bit lighter. You know people would be dancing and singing there would be music in different cottages. **But when Jones was present it was very dark. It was almost like a dark cloud.**[16]

Back in the states relatives of people in Jonestown became extremely concerned. They started a letter writing campaign to members of congress and the media. Finally, these letters caught the attention of one Congressman, Leo Ryan, who organized a trip to Jonestown to see for himself what was going on down there. The delegation traveling to Jonestown would include the congressman and his aide Jackie Speier, along with media members from NBC, a cameraman and concerned family members. They arrived in Jonestown on November 17, 1978. The first evening of their visit seemingly went very well until one of the Jonestown residents passed the NBC reporter a note saying to effect, "please help us get out of here." In one documentary, Jackie Speier stated that that is when the delegation knew something was seriously amiss at Jonestown.

Night came and turned into morning in Jonestown. It was now Nov 18, 1978. One of the Jonestown survivors who said he was one of the first to wake up that day said that he felt something very strange in the air that morning, that things just did not feel quite right and that despite it being a perfectly sunny day. At some point during the day it became clear that not only did the note passer, a man named Vernan Gosney, want to leave, but multiple other people wanted to leave the compound as well. When this news got around Jonestown and got to Jim Jones the atmosphere at Jonestown changed completely and for the worst. People described it as sensing something in the air like electricity, or evil. According to Tim Carter, a Jonestown survivor:

Literally out of nowhere this storm came rolling in. The sky turned black, the wind came up and it just... torrential rain. But what I personally felt was that evil itself blew into Jonestown.[17]

As some of the defectors were getting loaded up onto a truck to make the long trek to the airport, Congressman Ryan, who during this whole time was completely calm and confident in his safety and was going to wait at Jonestown for the next load of people, was attacked by a follower of Jones. The man who attacked the congressman was trying to kill him and

---

16   *Biography Jim Jones: Journey Into Madness*, Created by David Wolper (1998 ABC News Productions & A&E Television Network)
17   *Jonestown: The Life and Death of Peoples Temple*, directed by Stanley Nelson (2006 Tribeca Film Festival, Firelight Media 2006)

the congressman did receive a wound albeit a minor one. Leo Ryan then blood all over his shirt and became very shaken and began to fear for his life, so much so that he momentarily panicked and hopped on the load of people that was leaving for the airstrip. Some of the other people on the truck were also very scared because before this incident they had taken solace in the presence of the Congressman to provide safety. Apparently seeing him be attacked and seeing blood all over his shirt totally destroyed any hope of safety that they had.

The people on the truck then started the long journey through the jungle to the air strip. One survivor recalls feeling terror the whole ride there. He was convinced gunman were going to come out of the jungle and shoot them all to death. His fears would be well founded. When the truck got to air strip, they started boarding 2 different planes. At that moment another truck pulled up at the air strip with 5 men in the back of it. The men got out of the truck and immediately started shooting at all the people being loaded onto the planes. Complete terror and panic ensued, some tried running into the jungle, only a few were successful at getting away. In all 5 people were gunned down on orders from Jim Jones. Among the dead were the congressman, Leo Ryan, and the NBC reporter Don Harris.

At the same time this murderous spree was going on at the airstrip, back at the compound Jones called one his "white night" emergency sessions. This meant that everyone in the compound was required to come to the main pavilion and listen to Jones speak. There is a final recording on this dialogue that exists, it spans about 45 minutes and it contains the voice of Jones urging his followers on to suicide and murder. The tape also contains the voices of some dissenters who were definitely in the minority, who were trying to convince Jones, unsuccessfully, to not go through with the mass suicide.[18]

I spent 5 years in the Wisconsin State Prison System, I have battled a lifelong opiate addiction and have experienced and seen many of the horrors related to drug addiction, I have seen and heard many disturbing things. In addition, I have studied demonology for the last 10 years and have certainly seen, read and listened to some very disturbing and frightening things. I can safely say that the recording of Jim Jones, urging and cajoling his enslaved followers to suicide and murder, and then urging the parents to kill their children and saying that the children will feel no

18   Jim Jones, "Transcript of Recovered FBI tape Q 42." Alternative Considerations of Jonestown and Peoples Temple. Jonestown Project: San Diego State University.

pain, all the while in the background of the recording you hear children screaming and moaning, and then you hear adults screaming and wailing in pain because their children are dying; is by far and away the most disturbing, heart rending, and evil thing I have ever listened to. When I listened to this while conducting research for this book and was watching the documentary that has this recording and then shows the dead bodies of over 900 men, women, and children laying in the jungle, I started sobbing and could not stop until I turned it off. The very feel you get from this, in listening to Jones speak, in hearing the children wail and scream in terror, in seeing the dead bodies, and seeing the metal vats filled with the poisonous Kool aid, is one of pure evil. The hairs on the back of your neck almost stand up and you know this unfathomable tragedy was inspired directly from the perverse and twisted mind of the devil.

In all 909 people lost their lives that day, almost 300 of which were small children of various ages, including infants. Four of the people that lost their lives were not even at Jonestown but in the capitol city of Georgetown, where Jonestown resident Sharon Amos slashed the throats of her children before killing herself. Sometimes this event is called the greatest mass suicide in modern recorded history. There was absolutely suicide, no question about it, but many of the people were also murdered, especially the children. Many of the adults as well who refused to take the cyanide were forcibly injected with it including Marceline Jones, Jim Jones's wife who objected to the killing of the children.

Many studies have been conducted of this event trying to answer the question of why. Was Jim Jones just a malignant narcissist and sociopath who became suicidal and homicidal, that was able to deceive a great many people and eventually lead them to their deaths. This is undoubtedly true. However, the reader knows what my position is on this matter. I firmly believe there was a diabolical component to this as well. There is much evidence for this. I think Jim Jones was completely and totally perfectly possessed by the devil. His very presence was malignant. Above, I stated how one survivor of Jonestown said that when Jones was around there was like an oppressive atmosphere around, like a black cloud he said. Just the general amount of malignancy, death, destruction, and blasphemy that followed in the wake of Jones is proof positive for my assertion. In closing I will leave the reader with 4 very profound quotes that seem to confirm my suspicions, the last of which is very disturbing considering a passage written by Malachi Martin in Hostage to the Devil, where he stated that perfectly possessed people often request to be put to death or display an attitude of wanting to die so as to join the prince in his kingdom.

> "Jim Jones had the deepest darkest eyes and if you would watch him and listen to him, he could convince you of a lot of things. He had a strange power."[19]
>
> – Donald Foreman, schoolmate of Jim Jones

> "He said there was no Jesus, there was no God; that he was the only God. I think he got possessed of the devil."[20]
>
> – Hyacinth Thrash, Jonestown Massacre Survivor

> "Mr. Jones was a slave of a diabolical supernatural power from which he refused to be set free."[21]
>
> – Rev. Billy Graham

> "To me death is not a fearful thing. It's living that's cursed."[22]
>
> – Jim Jones

ALEISTER CROWLEY

> "The King of Depravity"
>
> "A Wizard of Wickedness"
>
> "The Wickedest man in the World"[23]
>
> "Before Hitler was, I AM"[24]
>
> – Aleister Crowley

Aleister Crowley is easily one of the most infamous and powerful occultists of modern times. It is commonly thought that he attained the magical rank of ipsissimus, one of the highest ranks one can attain throughout the world of the occult, magic, and devil worship. His writings, directly inspired by the devils, have had a profound effect and have influenced many people. The influence that they have had, I can safely say has been completely negative. Crowley's life and writings have influenced many, many people to dabble in the occult, to experiment with darkness, and so has led many people to destruction, death, possession, and madness.

---

19   *Biography Jim Jones: Journey Into Madness*, Created by David Wolper (1998 ABC News Productions & A&E Television Network)

20   Ghost of Jonestown Haunts Survivor, *New York Times* Archives, Nov 18, 1988

21   Billy Graham, on Satan and Jonestown, *New York Times* Archives, Dec 5, 1978

22   Excerpts From Transcript of Tape Describing Final Moments at Jonestown, *New York Times* Archives, March 15, 1979

23   *John Bull Magazine*, 1923

24   Cristiani, *Evidence of Satan in the Modern World*

Even while Crowley was alive he left a wake of destruction, ruin, and perversion. It is thought Crowley was even responsible for the death of MacGregor Mathers the head of the secret society, The Order of the Golden Dawn. It is thought Crowley summoned the high devil, Beelzebub, and sent the demon after Mathers. In addition to Mathers very many of Crowley's wives, disciples, and mistresses either ended up mad and in insane asylums or committed suicide, or experienced other life changing ruinous events. Crowley called himself the "Great Beast," the real significance of which initially escaped me[25]. He traveled the world practicing black magic mixed with unfettered debauchery. He sacrificed animals to a plethora of pagan deities and demonic forces, killed people via black magic, caused people to go insane, caused the houses he lived in to become completely infested, put curses and hexes on people, ate human excrement, left people to perish on a mountain, crucified a frog, injected heroin, and engaged in the most depraved sex magic acts known to man. Crowley died alone, a hopeless heroin addict in 1947 at the age of 72. In examining the life of Aleister Crowley it is very easy to see the exact point at which he turned away from Christianity. What is more difficult is to pin down the moment when the diabolic entered his life. I suspect it occurred at a very young age. A short review of his life will suffice.

Aleister Crowley was born in 1875 in Leamington spa, Warwickshire, England, to wealthy parents. Aleister's father made a small fortune in the ale brewing business, a fortune Crowley would later inherit and use to finance his debauched escapades. Crowley was raised very strictly as a Christian. His parents were members of the Plymouth Brethren, a very strict protestant sect. His childhood days were filled with bible readings and church. According to two separate biographies of Crowley he genuinely looked up to his father calling him "my hero and my friend."

The major turning point in Crowley's life came at age 11 when his father passed away of tongue cancer. Instead of choosing modern medicine, Crowley's parents and the Plymouth Brethren chose more natural and faith-based means. This led to the death of Crowley's father who did not receive proper medical treatment. This absolutely infuriated Crowley and he never forgave the Plymouth Brethren or wider Christianity for that matter. Here begins his descent into a life of absolute depravity. In chapter 5 when I discussed the why's of perfect possession, I stated that some people have something bad happened to them that they then use to blame

---

25   I initially thought he called himself this as a kind of joke or to gain attention. However when taken in the context of his possible perfect possession, the meaning of this gains a far deeper level of understanding.

God for and live a life completely separated from him. This seems to be what happened to Aleister Crowley. Crowley became so bad and sinful after his father's death that his mother called him the great beast from the book of Revelation, a title by all accounts, he relished in.

Crowley's sexual urges then became insatiable, losing his virginity to a household maid on his mother's bed. There were also other signs in his youth that pointed to some dark force in his life. One incident occurred when Crowley killed and mutilated a cat, attempting, as he described it, to take all of it's 9 lives. During this time, he also attempted to sexually seduce another boy at the school he was attending.

Crowley finally ended up at Cambridge University where he wrote pornographic poetry, engaged in various sexual activities with men and woman even contracting gonorrhea from a prostitute, and also started his fascination with and involvement in the occult. His interest in the occult was peaked by reading the book of Black Magic and Pacts by Edward Arthur Waite and The Cloud Upon the Sanctuary by Carl von Eckartshausen. According to Rosemary Ellen Guilly:

> "In his first volume of poetry published in 1898, Crowley foreshadowed his occult excesses with his statement that God and Satan had fought many hours over his soul. He wrote, 'God conquered'---- now I have only one doubt left--- which of the twain was God"[26]

We can see from what occurred in the remainder of Crowley's life who clearly won the battle for his soul. During his time at Cambridge Crowley travelled very often while on break, endeavoring to climb mountains in his free time. It was on one of these trips in the winter of 1896 that Crowley had his first mystical experience in Stockholm, Sweden. Laying in bed one night, the time close to midnight, Crowley suddenly realized that,

> "he had found something in his nature hitherto hidden, a magical gift or talent for magick, a kind of knack: 'I was awakened to the knowledge that I possessed a magical means of becoming conscious of and satisfying a part of my nature which had up to that moment concealed itself from me."[27]

This would be the first of many mystical experiences that Crowley had, these experiences clearly being produced through preternatural diabolical means.

After leaving Cambridge without a degree Crowley moved into an apartment in Chancery Lane, London. During this period in Crowley's

---

26   Guilly, *Encyclopedia of Demons and Demonology*
27   Tobias Churton, *Aleister Crowley: The Biography*

life he was introduced to a man named George Jones, who was a member of the Hermetic Order of the Golden Dawn. Crowley, being very interested in such matters, asked to join the secret society and was accepted. His initiation took place in November of 1898 by the societies leader, a man named Samuel Liddell MacGregor Mathers. As I mentioned above it is believed by many that Mathers' eventual demise came at the hands of Crowley through magic rituals meant to harm Mathers.

Once initiated into the outer order of the Golden Dawn, Crowley proved to be an extremely skilled and adept magician rising through the ranks of the magical order very quickly. While he was a member of the Golden Dawn and living in Chancery Lane Crowley began to get involved in the practice of black magic very heavily. Crowley practiced these dark arts mostly in secret because black magic and explicit satanic rituals were frowned upon by the other members of the Golden Dawn. According to Crowley's *Confessions*, one day a fellow member of the Golden Dawn and respected occultist, Allan Bennett came up to Crowley and accused him of meddling with the forces of evil, an accusation Crowley denied. As I said it is was against the code of the Golden Dawn for any member to practice black magic and practice evil for evils sake. A few days after this accusation from Bennett, Crowley showed up on the doorstep of Bennett's very meager apartment and invited Bennett to come and live with him in his much nicer flat in Chancery lane. Bennett accepted with the understanding that he would show Crowley and teach him all he knew about black magic.[28]

Crowley then constructed two black magic temples in two separate rooms of his flat, both of which contained very large pentagrams painted on the floor. In one of the temples was contained a blood-stained real skeleton that was seated right in front of the altar in the temple. Crowley would actually feed this skeleton blood, small birds, and beef tea in an effort to revive it. The two men (Crowley and Bennett) then began on a very regular basis to practice black magic rituals. During this time George Jones who had introduced Crowley to the Golden Dawn was also a regular visitor at the flat and also partook of the black magic with Crowley and Bennett. In addition to trying to revive the skeleton, there were animal sacrifices and sex magic that was also practiced. The flat was said to contain an absolutely rotten stench at all times that filled the air and smelled like rotting meat. As a result of the constant practice of the dark arts and frequent invocation of powerful diabolic entities and pagan deities, the

---

28   Aleister Crowley, *The Confessions of Aleister Crowley*

flat at Chancery Lane became completely infested with diabolical forces. Rosemary Ellen Guilly states:

> "One of his flat neighbors claimed to be hurled downstairs by a malevolent force, and visitors said they experienced dizzy spells while climbing the stairs or felt an overwhelmingly evil presence"[29]

In his *Confessions* Crowley admitted that after practicing this black magic at the Chancery Lane flat the home became infested. Crowley stated:

> "As we went out, we noticed semi-solid shadows on the stairs; the whole atmosphere was vibrating with the forces which we had been using. We restored order and then observed that semi-materialized beings were marching around the main room in almost unending procession"[30]

Crowley also admitted in his Confessions that two moving men who came into the flat to move Crowley's belongings became completely overcome by the evil presence in the flat and fled in absolute terror. Crowley also details in The Equinox how he was attacked on an almost nightly basis by a succubus and how a woman visitor to the flat became possessed by an evil spirit who inhabited Crowley's skeleton. The flat at 67 Chancery Lane had many issues for many years even long after Crowley moved out. As late as 2006 a human skull, candle, and pentagram made out of sticks was found in the basement of the building that contained Crowley's flat. One of the workers who discovered these occult objects apparently became very frightened.

During the time Crowley was living at 67 Chancery Lane and practicing all of this black magic he started to get a reputation as being a very powerful magician indeed. Sometimes Crowley would emit a powerfully foul odor from his person, or people would see a "ghostly light" surrounding him. I have read claims that horses in the street reared at his approach and that there was an occasion when his coat mysteriously burst into flames. Crowley also had very dark and mesmerizing eyes which frightened some people and seduced others, especially women.

During the first few years in the Golden Dawn Crowley was introduced to an ancient book of black magic named "*The Sacred Magic of Abra-Melin the Mage.*" This manuscript was translated by MacGreger Mathers who thought the book was bewitched and had some kind of entity living in

---

29   Guilly, *Encyclopedia of Demons and Demonology*
30   Aleister Crowley, *The Confessions of Aleister Crowley*

it. In his *Confessions* Crowley claimed that translating the Abra-Melin was the ultimate thing that led to Mather's demise. Crowley claimed that while translating, Mathers "met with so many bicycle accidents that he was driven to go on foot"[31]. Crowley also stated:

> "Other misfortunes of every kind overwhelmed Mathers. He was an expert Magician and had been accustomed to use the Greater Key of Solomon with excellent effect. He did not realize that Abra-Melin was an altogether bigger proposition. It was like a man, accustomed to handle gunpowder, suddenly supplied with dynamite without being beware of the difference. He became the prey of the malignant forces of the book, lost his integrity and was cast out of the order of which he had been the visible head."[32]

The Abra-Melin book of black magic prescribed a 6-month ritual in which the magician, who was expected to fast, would gain the favor of their guardian angel and through this power be able to completely control the powers of darkness to have them do the bidding of the magician. According to the ritual in order to accomplish this the magician must summon "the 12 kings and dukes of hell." Crowley himself put it like this:

> "it is necessary, first, to call forth the four great princes of evil of the world, next their eight sub-princes; and lastly the three hundred and sixteen servitors of these."[33]

The book also prescribes that the 6-month ritual take place at a very secluded location, free from interruptions. Based on this, Crowley, who decided to undertake this ritual, purchased the Boleskine House in 1899 on the shores of Loch Ness in Scotland. According to the documentary *Aleister Crowley: The Most Wicked Man in the World*, this ritual was very dangerous and no magician had dared attempt it for centuries. The consequences of not completing the ritual as prescribed would be that the demons who are evoked in the ritual would then control and completely possess the magician.

> "The aim of the 6-month ritual is to master demons but it is considered extremely dangerous. If the ritual went wrong, it was believed the evil spirits could be set loose and take possession of the magician."[34]

---

31   Crowley, *Confessions*
32   Ibid
33   Ibid
34   Documentary, *Aleister Crowley: The Most Wicked Man in the World*

Crowley began the ritual in 1900 and from the very beginning things stared to go awry. There was a lodgekeeper, a man named Rosher who spent a mere few weeks at Boleskine House before becoming terrified and fleeing without so much as a word to Crowley. There was another lodge-keeper that then apparently went mad and attempted to kill his whole family. In his Confessions Crowley stated:

> "One day I came back from shooting rabbits on the hill and found a Catholic priest in my study. He had come to tell me that my lodge-keeper, a total abstainer for twenty years, had been raving drunk for three days and had tried to kill his wife and children."[35]

Crowley then got an old Cambridge associate to take Rosher's place, but according to Crowley "he too began to show symptoms of panic fear."[36] There was also a local butcher who accidentally cut off his own hand while reading one of Crowley's notes. Another lodgekeeper of Bole-skine house, a man named Hugh Gillies suffered personal tragedy when 2 of his children died very unexpectedly. All of Crowley's dogs died and the property became infested with beetles which the local museum could not identify. Years later when Crowley would return to the house, this time with a wife, a local man Crowley had hired for general labor also went insane and tried to kill Crowley's wife.

Crowley never did finish the diabolic ritual because he was called away for a meeting with Mathers in Paris. Shortly after leaving for Paris how-ever, the locals began to murmur about the dark black clouds hanging in the skies around the Boleskine House. One documentary even stated that the clouds hanging over the house had a decidedly negative effect on people in that it frightened them a great deal. When Crowley returned to the house, he found that his Cambridge associate had fled and Crow-ley himself even noticed a drastic change within the house. He speaks in one of his journals about certain rooms in the house becoming pitch dark even in the middle of the day time and also him seeing dark shapes flitting about the house. Crowley wrote:

> "It was a darkness which might almost be felt. The lodge and ter-race, moreover, soon became peopled with shadowy shapes, suffi-ciently substantial as a rule, to be almost opaque. I say shapes; and yet the truth is that they were no shapes properly speaking. The phenomena are hard to describe. It was as if the faculty of vision

---

35   Crowley, *Confessions*
36   Ibid

suffered some interference as if the objects of vision were not properly objects at all. It was as if they belonged to an order of matter which affected the sight without informing it."[37]

Even after Crowley moved away from Boleskine House it remained severely infested with diabolic forces all the way up to and through Jimmy Page's (Led Zeppelin Guitarist) ownership of the house and up to the present day. Notable incidents include British film star George Sanders starting a pig farm on the property which failed spectacularly; his partner was jailed and all the animals staved to death. There was also a retired Army Major who committed suicide via shotgun blast to the head in Crowley's old bedroom. Jimmy Page, a Crowley devotee and occultist, purchased Boleskine House in the early seventies. Page spent very little time at Boleskine House and so he left it mostly in the care of a man named Malcolm Dent. When Dent took over the house it was in complete disrepute and there had even been a mysterious fire there. Dent had a very frightening experience one night in which he heard wild animals snorting and banging outside his bedroom door. Dent said about this experience that "whatever was there was pure evil"[38] and he also said that he felt whatever was outside his door was "huge and very very evil"[39]. Apparently, a friend of Dent stayed there one night and claimed to have been attacked by some kind of devil. Another friend of Dent a man named Dougie Corrance spent quite a few nights at the house in which he would wake up at 2 or 3 am and feel extremely uncomfortable and sense a very strong evil presence that he felt was "trying to get into you"[40]. There were also additional phenomena "such as chairs switching places, doors slamming open and closed for no reason and carpets and rugs rolling up inexplicably"[41].

In the late 1990's a film crew from BBC Scotland filmed a documentary about Boleskine House. The crew had asked a priest to bless their project because of the rumors and events surrounding the house. Apparently, this film crew was attacked by a plague of beetles, suffered repeated equipment failures and experienced strangely similar nightmares about Crowley. Numerous series of photographs taken by the crew show a ghostly fog and were ruined. During one shoot late at night in the graveyard that is located opposite the house, the crew were showered with glass when lights exploded, fuses burned out and camera stands fell over. In a fitting end to the evil that took place at Boleskine House, the house mysteriously

37   Crowley, *Confessions*
38   Mick Wall, *When Giants Walked the Earth: A Biography of Led Zeppelin.*
39   Ibid
40   Ibid
41   Ibid

caught fire while the owners were away in 2015. The house was gutted in the fire and has been abandoned ever since.

After abandoning the Abra-Melin ritual Crowley traveled to Paris to see Mathers to lend him his support regarding some dealings with the Order of the Golden Dawn. From there Crowley traveled to Mexico, India, and Paris and eventually was married to Rose Edith Kelly. The next significant event in Crowley's life occurs in 1904 in Cairo, Egypt. While on their honeymoon, Crowley began to invoke ancient Egyptian deities. During one of these sessions his wife Rose went into a kind of trance and kept repeating "they are waiting for you." On one of the following days Crowley attempted to invoke Thoth, the God of wisdom when Rose went into another one of her trances and muttered "it is all about the child"[42] and "All Osiris." Finally, Rose revealed that the deity whom she had been receiving messages from was the ancient Egyptian deity Horus. Rose pointed out a statue of the deity at a museum in Cairo, which display was incidentally marked as exhibit 666. The actual communication Rose was receiving was from a messenger of Horus that called itself Aiwass. According to Rosemary Ellen Guilly:

> "The communicating messenger, Aiwass, was an imposing entity described by Rose as an emissary for the Egyptian trinity of Horus, Osiris, and Isis. Crowley envisioned Aiwass as a male entity and one distinctly different and more unfathomable than other entities he had encountered."[43]

This is very surprising considering Crowley had already supposedly invoked the 12 princes of hell in the Abra-Melin ritual. It seems Aiwass was of a stature and class of devil far higher than what Crowley had encountered thus far. This is not surprising considering the long-lasting impact the evil perpetrated by Aiwass through *The Book of the Law* would have upon the world.

Aiwass commanded that Crowley's Cairo apartment be turned into a temple and that he enter the temple at precisely noon for 3 straight days to take 3 total hours of dictation (1 hour each day) from the entity. This started on April 8, 1904 and ended on April 10, 1904. Crowley always heard the voice of Aiwass over his left shoulder and described the voice as

42   Symonds, *The Great Beast*
43   Guilly, *Encyclopedia of Demons and Demonology*

"a rich tenor or baritone, deep timbre, musical and expressive, its tones solemn, voluptuous, tender, fierce or aught else as suited the moods of the message."[44]

Crowley also received a visual impression of Aiwass's form which Crowley described as

"a body of fine matter or astral matter, transparent as a veil of gauze or a cloud of intense smoke. He seemed to be very tall, dark man in his thirties, well knit, active and strong, with the face of a savage king, and eyes veiled lest their gaze should destroy what they saw."[45]

Crowley also said of Aiwass,

"We are forced to conclude that the author of the book of the law is an intelligence both alien and superior to myself yet acquainted with my inmost secrets; and most important point of all, that this intelligence is discarnate."[46]

Crowley went on to say that Aiwass was an "immensely superior intelligence." What this entity, who was in fact a very high ranking and powerful devil, dictated to Crowley was what Crowley would call "The Book of the Law," the whole of which is the infamous statement "do what thou wilt shall be the whole of the law." This book became the basis for Crowley's new religion and law Aiwass called Thelema. After receiving these messages from Aiwass, Crowley saw himself as a new messiah of a new coming era that was about to come upon the earth.

When one reads the book that was dictated to Crowley by the spirit it becomes very clear it originated from a purely diabolical source. Instead of saying that this is the era of Jesus Christ, it says this is the aeon of Horus, among other diabolical garbage. Crowley in his Confessions says of this new Aeon:

"We may then expect the new Aeon to release mankind from its pretense of altruism, its obsession of fear and its consciousness of sin… it will be utterly conscienceless, cruel, helpless, affectionate and ambitious without knowing why."[47]

Besides *Magick in Theory in Practice*, *The Book of the Law* is Crowley's most important work. When we examine the contents of the book of the

---

44   Crowley, *Confessions*
45   Ibid
46   Ibid
47   Crowley, *Confessions*

law, how it was dictated, who the source claims to be (Horus & Aiwass), the outrageous blasphemies contained within it, and the immensely negative and wide spread effect it has had on thousands if not millions of people, we can come to the easy conclusion that the ultimate source is of course the devil. These are the kind of spirits Crowley was in league with, these are the spirits he served, these are the spirits he was in slavery to and perfectly possessed by. It should also be noted that the book of the law is not the only book Crowley claimed to have received from what he thought was a supernatural source. There were others, all of which he called "the holy books of Thelema."

There were two additional major events in the life of Aleister Crowley that I would like to briefly highlight. These episodes really just give more evidence for the assertion that Crowley was perfectly possessed throughout most of his life. The first occurred in the desert of Algeria in 1909. According to Tobias Churton, Crowley was again contacted by Aiwass who was calling him into the desert south of Algiers to perform Enochian Magic. This would entail animal sacrifices, gay sex magic with poet Victor Neuberg, and Enochian magic rituals. What the rituals consisted of was the evocation of 19 calls or keys called Aethyrs. Each Aethyr contained some occult force that was to be invoked by the magician. Ill note that despite the magic claiming that angels are being evoked, it is really the devils who are being evoked. This magic if followed through with will almost certainly result in the diabolical possession of the magician. Despite the fact that I strongly believe Crowley was already fully possessed by this point, people around him did notice a change in him after he performed the Enochian magic in the desert. It is possible that Aiwass commanded Crowley into the desert to perform these rituals so that Crowley would be possessed by higher level and more powerful devils and also complete the possession and make it perfect. Crowley summed up these Aethyrs and its ultimate effect on the magician and what the magician must do in his Confessions. I would like to quote it here because it is extremely relevant to our discussion of perfect possession and what that means. Crowley said of the 17th Aethyr:

> "I understood that every disturbance implies deviation from perfection. It is for this reason that my individuality (which distinguishes me from all other beings) involves the idea of injustice. Therefore, to penetrate beyond the Abyss, where iniquity cannot exist, **my personal selfhood must be annihilated.** The sixteenth Aethyr showed me how this might be done. **My being must be dissolved in that of the infinite."**[48]

---

48   Crowley, Confessions

What Crowley says here is very profound and so relevant to our discussion on what perfect possession consists of from the viewpoint of someone who was actually perfectly possessed. Clearly the goal of this Enochian magic and really all magical practices for that matter is the eventual dissolving of the personality and will of the individual so that can be replaced with one of a diabolic nature. I quoted earlier the words of David Berkowitz who confirmed as much when he said "my personality was dissolved." I'm not saying that the persons will and personality would cease to exist, it would just be so under the control and absolute slavery of a diabolic force that you would not be able to tell the difference between the two. Like I wrote in a previous chapter, Father M, called this "seamlessness" and called it "integral possession." Where the human personality and diabolic personality can no longer be told apart. The reader can also remember what I wrote in chapter 3 regarding what Crowley thought "perfect magic" consisted of.

> "Perfect magic is the complete and total alignment of the will with universal will or cosmic forces. When one **surrenders** to that alignment, one becomes a **perfect channel for the flow of cosmic forces**."[49]

The key words here being "surrenders," meaning the magician, intentionally and with full intention of will, explicitly allows themselves to be taken over by cosmic forces (diabolical forces) so as to become a "perfect channel for the flow of cosmic forces," meaning they are now perfectly possessed by these forces and the forces are able to perfectly (work without hindrance) through the magician and introduce evil into the world. Perfect alignment of a persons will with that of cosmic forces is literally the very definition of perfect possession.

On December 3, 1909 Crowley entered the 14th Aethyr of Enochian Magic, at which point he received a command from some discarnate entity that he must construct a magic circle and altar made of stones. The altar was so that he could sacrifice himself, involving an act of sodomy with Victor Neuberg, in which Crowley would take the receptive role. This would be done as an act of worship to the pagan deity Pan. One book about Neuberg said that Neuberg received an image in his mind of what Pan looked like, the book says this image terrified Neuberg and haunted him for the rest of life. This ceremonial magic ritual was supposed to ele-

---

vate Crowley to the higher magical grade of "Magister Templi." According to a biographer of Crowley, Tobias Churton,

> "The grade of Magister Templi suddenly made sense to him; it was the gateway to service of humanity. He had become as a little child, a true babe of the Abyss entering a state of childlike **receptivity**."[50]

According to Churton the ritual proved insufficient to secure Crowley's magical progress. Churton stated, "He would have to experience the Abyss itself. The ritual risked disintegration of mind." The new ritual would involve the evocation of the spirit of the abyss, personified as the demon Choronzon. On December 6, 1909 Crowley and Neuberg attempted the ritual to summon Choronzon. This is how Tobias Churton describes the scene:

> "The blood of three pigeons provides energy for visible evocation. There is a triangle in which the spirit may manifest, and a circle outside of it for the protection of the magicians. Crowley is probably, dangerously, in the triangle. Neuberg is in the circle taking notes, or trying to. A materialization of the evoked forces appears. Neuberg fights a naked demon that penetrates the circle. The savage threatens to tear Neuberg apart."[51]

According to another biography of Crowley, Crowley most definitely stepped outside the circle of protection (the circle does not provide any actual protection, the magicians are completely deceived) and into the triangle used for the materialization of the demon. Many authors who have a background in magic who have commented on this episode have said that Crowley most probably was possessed by Choronzon as a consequence of stepping outside the circle of protection. This same book claims that this ritual and this battle with the demon left both men broken.

> "It was the magical experience that taken its toll. Those who knew them said that Neuberg 'bore the marks of this magical adventure to the grave', and that Crowley, shattered psychologically, never recovered from the ordeal."[52]

After the episode in the desert in 1909, Crowley attempted another major ritual in 1918 in New York City called the Almalantrah. This ritual

---

50   Churton, *Aleister Crowley: A Biography*
51   Ibid
52   Alex Owen, *The Place of Enchantment*

was another sex magic ritual that led to the summoning of another diabolic force that called itself Lam. According to Rosemary Ellen Guilly,

> The working created a portal in the spaces between stars, through which the entity Lam was able to enter the known physical universe. Since then, other entities are believed to enter through this widening portal, and to be the basis for numerous contact experiences with UFO's and extraterrestrials."[53]

Aleister Crowley believed that Lam was the soul of a dead Tibetan lama from Leng, between China and Tibet. Lam was apparently supposed to complete the work through Crowley that was initiated by Aiwass. A very significant aspect of this is that Crowley drew a portrait of what Lam looked like, which is very eerie. You definitely get a feeling of evil from looking at this portrait. The entity in the portrait also looks identical to what modern Ufologists call "greys" or extraterrestrials. I believe this is very significant considering the ritual that summoned Lam into the world occurred in 1918, some years before the whole UFO and alien abduction phenomena started. In another book I am currently working on I devote a chapter to UFO's and extraterrestrial phenomena. My thesis is that these unexplained phenomena have a diabolic source, for which there is a great amount of evidence, but way beyond the scope of this book.

The last major event in Crowley's life that I would like to touch on briefly is his founding of the "Abbey of Thelema" in Sicily, Italy in 1920. Crowley's goal in founding this abbey was to make a center of occult knowledge and learning for his disciples, and a place to live out his law of Thelema, to "do what thou wilt." Crowley and what he called his "scarlet woman" of the time, Leah Herzig moved there in 1920 and founded the Abbey of Thelema. Soon Crowley's disciples started arriving and partaking of all manner of debauchery. The Abbey of Thelema was in operation from 1920-1923. During this time all manner of perversion and depravity was practiced there. Animal sacrifices, sex magic, group sex and orgies that included gay and lesbian sex, worship and invocation of pagan deities and demonic forces, and liberal drug use during rituals are just some of the things that went on there. All of these things occurred while children were living at the Abbey and Crowley even impregnated two separate women, one of which had a miscarriage, while living at the abbey. The walls of the abbey were covered in murals painted by Crowley of various

---

53   Guilly, *Encyclopedia of Demons and Demonology*

occult symbols and demonic faces. Looking at photographs of the walls there as they are today gives one a sense of foreboding and evil.

In 1923 the abbey was forcibly shut down by Mussolini's government. Crowley and all his supporters were deported after a Crowley disciple Raoul Loveday died after drinking the blood of a sacrificed cat in a satanic ritual. After the group left the abbey it remained abandoned and has not been occupied since, except for the occasional teenage or self-styled Satanist performing rituals there and tagging the walls with satanic graphitti. It seems the locals are frightened of the place and believe that it is evil.

Aleister Crowley left the Abbey a worn-down heroin addict, an addiction he would have until the day he died. Crowley spent his final years in a combination of places such as Tunisia, Paris, Berlin, and London. Crowley finally ended up at Hastings in Sussex and lived his final years at the Netter wood boarding house. Crowley died on December 1, 1947 of chronic bronchitis and myocardial degeneration. Crowley died as an old, sad, degenerate heroin addict. It is said he cursed his doctor to die before his death because the doctor refused to give him more morphine. The doctor actually died 18 hours after Crowley

Crowley's last words were "I am perplexed." Perplexed at what we can only imagine and shutter at. I don't even want to think about what this wicked man saw when he crossed over to the other side.

What I have detailed here in the life of Aleister Crowley is just a very small portion of the total wickedness this man practiced throughout his life. When one examines the life of Aleister Crowley, reads his numerous biographies by Symonds, Sutton, Kaczynski, and Churton and his own Confessions and other various writings, one comes to a very easy conclusion that this was a man who spent most of his natural life in complete slavery to and possession of the diabolic realm. He was a true servant of the devil in the highest sense. He took diabolical writings (the book of the law and others) and introduced them to the public as a new religion and way of life, one without Jesus Christ and the Church. His whole life was literally filled with perversion, debauchery and depravity and this was coupled with a complete hatred of Christianity and zero desire to repent or amend his life in any way. He remained completely in the grip of absolute depravity to the last moments of his life (cursing his doctor who then died). He engaged in a lifelong practice of very advanced forms of ceremonial magic and devil worship that included elements of animal sacrifice and gnostic masses (black mass). He was a high-level member of at least 3 secret societies (Hermetic order of the Golden Dawn, Ordo

Templi Orientis or OTO, and Freemasonry. He claimed to have been initiated as a 33rd degree mason in Mexico). He was also the founder of one secret society, the A, A, or the Argentium Astrum. He had summoned and had personal, direct contact and communication with multiple diabolical entities (the 12 princes of hell, Aiwass, Horus, Choronzon, Lam). He partook of some of the most depraved sex acts known to man in the context of ritual magic. Many people regarded him as a very powerful magician possessed of supernatural abilities. His writings (diabolically inspired) and life have had a profoundly negative impact on many thousands of people inspiring them to start dabbling in some form of the black arts and inspiring many modern musicians (Led Zeppelin, The Beatles, Ozzy Osbourne). At least 4 of the places he lived throughout his life became completely infested with diabolical forces even possibly resulting in the death of a man (Major Edward Grant). He had a very mesmerizing personality and eyes for that matter and had a unique ability to control people and get them to do what he wanted, including to participate in demonic sex magic rituals. And finally, his life and influence had a totally ruinous effect on many people who associated with him. A profound number of Crowley's wives, mistresses, and disciples ended up insane, institutionalized in mental asylums, addicted to drugs and alcohol, or committed suicide. The man simply left a path of ruin, death, destruction, scandal and infamy in his wake, everywhere he went.

> "Crowley left behind a trail of devastation when it came to the women in his life. Alcoholism, insanity, and suicide followed in his wake."[54]

When we examine all these things about his life its leads me to the certain conclusion that Aleister Crowley was indeed completely controlled, in slavery to and perfectly possessed by a very powerful diabolic spirit or spirits, if not Satan himself. Aleister Crowley's life was completely and totally dedicated to serving evil and furthering the interests of the diabolic kingdom. A service that continues to plaque society to this very day. I said I was going to try and give the reader the clearest examples of people who were possibly perfectly possessed. Crowley is one of the clearest examples I know of if not the clearest. There is just a veritable mountain of evidence to suggest very dark and powerful evil forces were at work in this man's life. Even so the next person I will be profiling had an even more negative effect on humanity.

54   Alex Owen, *The Place of Enchantment*

Adolf Hitler and the Nazi Regime

> "He had conjured up the fearful idol of an all-devouring Moloch of which he was the priest and incarnation."
> — *Winston Churchill, speaking about Adolf Hitler*

> "I believe one can see that he was taken into the demonic realm in some profound way, by the way in which he was able to wield power and by the terror, the harm, that his power inflicted"
> — *Pope Benedict XVI on Adolf Hitler*

> "I am convinced that the Nazis were possessed by the devil," he said. "If one thinks of what was committed by people like Stalin or Hitler, certainly they were possessed by the devil. This is seen in their actions, in their behavior and in the horrors they committed."
> — Father Gabriel Amorth

Adolf Hitler is probably the best example I can give to my readers of someone who was perfectly possessed and who as a result of their being perfectly possessed caused inestimable damage to humanity. This is going to seem like an obvious choice to many people, and indeed it is. The list of eminent minds that have labeled Hitler as possessed by the devil is very long. People like Father Gabriele Amorth, Father John Struzzo, Father Malachi Martin, Winston Churchill and Pope Pius XII who is even rumored to have attempted a long-distance exorcism of Hitler. This fact is actually significant as the reason any exorcism of Hitler would have been unsuccessful is because the person being exorcised must desire to be free of their diabolical masters. Denis de Rougemont, speaking of Adolf Hitler stated:

> "Some people believe, from having experienced in his presence a feeling of horror and an impression of supernatural power, that he is the seat of 'Thrones, Dominations, and Powers', by which Saint Paul meant those hierarchical spirits which can descend into any ordinary mortal and occupy him like a garrison."[55]

Many of Hitler's fellow Nazi's even believed he was completely possessed. Adolf Hitler has been called the evilest man in history by many people. The moral evil of killing 6 million plus Jews in ovens and gas chambers is completely overwhelming, clearly demonic, and should sicken all of us.

> "The Holocaust was so monstrous that it could only have been satanic."[56]

---

55   Ravenscroft, *The Spear of Destiny*
56   Carr, *The Twisted Cross*

Under this though is a far deeper evil, a theological evil as Father M called it. This evil basically consisted of the satanic plan to completely undermine and subvert God's plan for the salvation of the world. If we read Romans 11, we know that God's plan of salvation includes the Jews or Israel as Paul calls them. God is not finished with Israel, he has not abandoned them and still has a plan for them. God still has a totally valid covenant with the Jews.

The holocaust was in effect a satanic effort to undermine and destroy God's plan of salvation for the whole world, which will include the Jews in some way. Adolf Hitler and the other top Nazi's completely cooperated in this evil campaign and set it in motion and almost accomplished it. This in my opinion is the greatest indication Hitler and many of the other top Nazi's were perfectly possessed (Himmler, Goering, Goebbels, Heidrich, Eickmen, Philipp Bouhler, Mengele). Hitler, Himmler, Goering, Josef Goebbels, and Philipp Bouhler all committed suicide; Goebbels even killed his whole family including his little children before killing himself. Heinrich Heidrich was assassinated, Eickman was executed in Israel and Josef Mengele lived out the rest of his life performing abortions in South America.

Even though I strongly suspect diabolical influence in all of these men's lives, and really diabolical influence in the whole of Germany during this period, I will concentrate on Hitler for the sake of brevity. Really a whole book (many have been written) would need to be written to fully investigate these Nazi's and their lives and the way diabolic evil intertwined itself through their lives and into the whole of Germany eventually effecting the whole world in the form of the most deadly war in world history. The moral and theological evils that were committed by Hitler is evidence enough he was a slave to diabolical forces, however, there is additional indications throughout his life that point in this direction as well, it is these I will be concentrating on in this section.

Adolf Hitler was born in 1889 in Austria and grew up near Linz. Hitler's mother was by all accounts a good woman and a good mother to Hitler. Hitler's father on the other hand was known to be vicious and very abusive towards Hitler. Hitler has this in common with many of the other people I am profiling, especially Jim Jones and Ted Bundy. The Hitler family had 3 children before Adolf was born and all 3 died very young. The child born after Hitler also died. Alois and Klara Hitler had a total of 6 children, only 2 of which survived, Adolf and his sister Paola. Hitler's parents were blood relatives and childhood friend of Hitler August

Kubizek speculates this is the reason so many of the Hitler children died so young. It should also be noted that even though Adolf survived he was plagued throughout his whole life with poor health and his sister Paola almost died young as well.

Hitler was born and baptized as a Catholic, however according to Percy Ernst Schramm he displayed a marked aversion to Christianity from a very young age. Hitler's mother was devout, and she wished for Hitler to become confirmed. Hitler was confirmed at the Linz Cathedral in 1904 but Hitler biographer John Toland recalls a very disturbing scene. Toland writes:

> "Of all the boys Emmanuel Lugert had sponsored 'none was so sulky and surly as Adolf Hitler. I had almost to drag the words out of him… It was almost as though the whole business, the whole confirmation was **repugnant** to him, as though he only went through with it with the greatest reluctance."[57]

The next very significant episodes in the life of Adolf Hitler are related to us by a very close childhood friend of his, August Kubizek. Kubizek wrote a book titled *The Young Hitler I Knew*. To read this book and some of the accounts of a young Hitler from the prospective of the one friend that knew him the best, especially in the light of the holocaust gives one the chills. Kubizek talks about a young Hitler in many different negative respects. He paints a picture of a young boy that is very odd, that is far too serious for his age, that loses his temper at a simple whim, that hates people for no good reason and that is moved by a force external and separate from himself.

When speaking about Hitler's view of school and schooling Kubizek stated:

> "He **hated** the teachers and did not even greet them anymore, and he also **hated** his schoolmates whom, he said, the school was turning into idlers."[58]

For such a young person to be filled with such hate, I think is unusual and his schoolmates and teachers were not the only people a young Hitler felt hatred for. Kubizek also talked at some length about how Hitler would lose his temper over very trivial things, things that seemed to Kubizek to not matter at all. Kubizek states:

57 John Toland, *Adolf Hitler*
58 August Kubizek, *The Young Hitler I Knew*

"Adolf was **exceedingly violent** and high strung. Quite trivial things, such as a few thoughtless words, could produce in him **outbursts of temper** which I thought were quite out of proportion to the significance of the matter."

"There was no end to the things, even trivial ones, that could upset him."[59]

Kubizek stated that when Hitler would lose his temper that:

"Sometimes he seemed to me almost **sinister**"

And

"His face assumed a **truly threatening** aspect"[60]

In addition to Hitler being filled with hatred and having an extremely short fuse he also apparently had virtually no sense of humor and very rarely laughed or even smiled. Kubizek stated of Hitler:

"There was in his **nature something firm, inflexible, immovable, obstinately rigid**, which manifested itself in his profound seriousness and was at the bottom of all his characteristics. Adolf simply could not change his mind or his nature. Everything that lay in these rigid precincts of his being remained unaltered forever."[61]

This statement from August Kubizek is very profound when one considers some of the well-established and well-known signs theologians have enumerated as signs of the presence of a diabolic spirit in someone's life. For example, Father Jordan Aumann in his *Spiritual Theology* gives a list of 15 signs that would alert us to the presence of a diabolic spirit. Sign number 4 states:

"Obstinacy. One of the surest signs of a diabolical spirit."[62]

Father Royo Marin also lists obstinacy as a sure sign of a diabolical spirit. From all accounts even a young Hitler was stunningly obstinate, so much so that Kubizek actually states that this trait was the basis of his whole personality and character. Hitler was so obstinate that, according to Kubizek,

59   August Kubizek, *The Young Hitler I Knew*
60   Ibid
61   Ibid
62   Aumann, *Spiritual Theology*

"Once he had conceived an idea, he was like **one possessed**"[63]

To paint a further dark picture of a young Hitler, Kubizek also relates an event in which Adolf, having a crush on a local girl named Stephanie, planned to kill her and then commit suicide if she rejected him. Hitler went so far as to plan this in every minute detail even enlisting his friend August Kubizek for help. When one reads Kubizek's book it becomes clear this event greatly disturbed him, he even states in the book that he had nightmares as a result of this.

In addition to Hitler being obstinate, hateful, wrathful, and sinister he also had a marked ability from a very young age to convince people to do things and also to frighten people. Kubizek recalls an incident in which a young Hitler was able to convince his father to allow him to travel to Vienna with Hitler. Kubizek recalls this instance as being somewhat extraordinary based on the fact that Kubizek thought there was no way his father would allow this. Hitler had an even more profound effect on Kubizek's mother. Kubizek relates that despite the fact Hitler was always in poor health and did not have really any extraordinary bodily features, one feature did stand out and those were his eyes. His eyes were apparently so intense that they frightened Kubizek's mother. Mr. Kubizek writes:

"For in this countenance the eyes were so outstanding that one didn't notice anything else. Never in my life have I seen any other person whose appearance – how shall I put it – was so completely dominated by the eyes. They were the light eyes of his mother, but her somewhat staring, penetrating gaze was even more marked in the son and had even more force and expressiveness. It was uncanny how these eyes could change their expression, especially when Adolf was speaking. To me his sonorous voice meant much less that the expression of his eyes. In fact, Adolf spoke with his eyes, and even when his lips were silent one knew what he wanted to say. When he first came to our house and I introduced him to my mother, she said to me in the evening. 'What eyes your friend has!' And I remember quite distinctly that there was **more fear** than admiration in her words. If I am asked where one could perceive, in his youth, this man's exceptional qualities, I can only answer, 'In the eyes.'"[64]

This observation and statement from Hitler's childhood friend becomes even more profound when we consider the well-known saying that "the eyes are the windows to the soul." Even more disturbing is the fact that Hitlers piercing eyes are something he holds in common with many of the other people I am profiling in this study which I have detailed fully in the next chapter.

Hitler's sinister and threatening countenance paired with his ability to be very persuasive is strikingly similar to how a young Jim Jones was described. And in addition to Hitler's dark and piercing eyes and sinister countenance, his voice has also been described by Robert Waite as "strangely guttural."

Despite all of these disturbing revelations by Kubizek there is an even still more disturbing event and really events he witnessed, and these occurred whenever Hitler would give a speech for the benefit of Kubizek alone. Kubizek stated that he was often "startled" when Hitler would make a speech to him accompanied by vivid gestures. Kubizek relayed that it seemed as if a "volcano" were erupting out of Hitler and that,

> "It was as though something **quite apart from him** was bursting out of him."[65]

Kubizek writes about one incident in particular that was so profound he remembered it the rest of his life. I think it is worth quoting at length. Kubizek recalled an incident in which he and Hitler had just watched a Wagner opera. When August asked Hitler what he thought about the opera Hitler,

> "Threw me a strange, **almost hostile** glance. 'Shut up' he said brusquely... He looked almost **sinister**, and **paler** than ever. His turned-up coat collar increased this impression. I wanted to ask him, 'where are you going?' But his **pallid face looked so forbidding** that I suppressed the question. As if propelled by an **invisible force**, Adolf climbed up to the top of the Freinberg. And only now did I realize that we were no longer in solitude and darkness, for the stars shone brilliantly above us. Adolf stood in front of me; and now he gripped both my hands and held them tight. He had never made such a gesture before. I felt from the grasp of his hands how deeply moved he was. His eyes were feverish with excitement. The words did not come smoothly from his mouth as they usually did, but rather **erupted, hoarse and raucous**. From his voice I could tell even more how much this experience had shaken him. Gradually his speech loosened, and the words flowed more freely. Never before and never again have I heard Adolf Hitler speak as he did

in that hour, as we stood there alone under the stars, as though we were the only creatures in the world. I cannot repeat every word that my friend uttered. I was struck by something strange, which I had never noticed before, even when he had talked to me in moments of the greatest excitement. **It was as if another being spoke out of his body and moved him as much as it did me**. It wasn't at all a case of a speaker being carried away by his own words. On the contrary; I rather felt as though he himself listened with astonishment and emotion to what burst forth from him with **elementary force**. I will not attempt to interpret this phenomenon, but it was a state of complete ecstasy and rapture… It was an unknown youth who spoke to me in that strange hour. He spoke of a **special mission** which one day would be entrusted to him, and I, his only listener, could hardly understand what he meant. Many years had to pass before I realized the significance of this enraptured hour for my friend. His words were followed by silence. We descended into the town. The clock struck **three.**"[66]

As I said previously, all of these revelations and observations about a young Hitler are to me very disturbing when looked at in the light of Hitler's rise to power and the murderous episodes of the Holocaust and World War 2. These are not the only incidents that occurred in Hitler's life however that would lead one to conclude he was under the influence of diabolical forces. Before I continue, I would like to make one last note about August Kubizek's observations about Adolf Hitler. Kubizek did note that in his book that despite the fact Hitler's mother Klara was a devout Catholic and wished Hitler to be that too Hitler never attended mass, ever. The only time Kubizek witnessed Hitler attend mass was for Klara's funeral mass. Moving to Hitler's time in Vienna, it is widely known that Hitler never attended mass there either. Kubizek writes:

> "As long as I knew Adolf Hitler, I never remember his going to church… his mother was also a religious woman, but nevertheless he would not let her drag him to church."[67]

It was in the spring of 1906 that Hitler moved to Vienna and it is in Vienna where Hitler was introduced to the occult. It was here that according to historian Alan Bullock that Hitler read books on,

---

66   August Kubizek, *The Young Hitler I Knew*
67   Ibid

"Ancient Rome, the Eastern Religions, yoga, occultism, hypno-
tism, and astrology"[68]

This is very significant because Hitler's deep study of the occult is most
certainly where his world view was formed and where the holocaust originated from. Hitler's time in Vienna was very significant in that a very large
portion of it was devoted to the study of the black arts, Hitler then goes on
to say that it was this period that formed the basis for everything he did.

"Vienna was and remained for me the hardest, though most thor-
ough, school of my life ... In this period there took shape within me
a world picture and a philosophy which became the granite foundation of all my acts.[69]

The philosophy he speaks of is most certainly occult based and therefore diabolically inspired. The idea of Aryans being a pure and almost superhuman race, is an occult idea that originated from a very famous occultist Helena Blavatsky, she gleaned the idea from what she called "the
Great White Brotherhood," which is what Aleister Crowley called "the
Secret Chief's," known to us as devils. Dr. Walter Stein also confirms this
fact about Hitler because Stein had personally witnessed Hitler attain-
ing "higher levels of consciousness" by means of drugs and a penetrating
study of medieval occultism and ritual magic.

Hitler's descent into the blackness of the occult did not occur however
until he was a proven and miserable failure in really all his endeavors in Vienna. He had failed to be accepted into art school and not one soul would
even look at his architectural sketches that contained grandiose plans for
mega structures of brilliance to hearken Germany back to its former glory,
thus were the early fantasies of Hitler. In absolute disgust at himself and
his situation he one day roamed into the Hapsburg Treasure House and
discovered for the first time a mystical object that legend says whoever
possesses, will decide the destinies of many and which legend also says
the object (a spear) pierced the side of Jesus Christ while he hung on the
cross.

"According to the legend associated with the Spear of Longinus,
the claimant to this talisman of power has a choice between the
service of two opposing spirits in the fulfillment of his world-his-
toric aims – a Good and an Evil Spirit."[70]

68   Ravenscroft, *The Spear of Destiny*
69   Adolf Hitler, *Mein Kampf*
70   Ravenscroft, *The Spear of Destiny*

It would be the evil spirit, the anti-Christ spirit of the spear that Hitler would follow and be totally possessed by. His first meeting with the Spear of Destiny remained uneventful, but he remained intrigued and returned to view and study the object day after day. According to Trevor Ravenscroft one day Hitler was shown a vision, a precognitive vision of the future. Hitler talked about this event in his autobiography, Mien Kampf, but he never revealed exactly what he saw that day. This would not be the first time Hitler displayed an ability for prophecy or precognition. I already quoted the passage by August Kubizek in which Hitler, seemingly moved by an invisible force and with hoarse and raucous voice proclaimed that he had to fulfill a grand mission to the German people. This incident with the Spear of Longinus would be just one of many times Hitler was seemingly privy to information about the future. This may confuse some readers who are familiar with demonology and who know as a general principle that the devil cannot tell the future, that this is the domain of the supernatural, the divine, not the preternatural or the demonic. While this is true it comes with caveats. It is true and widely taught that the devil cannot tell the future based on the free future actions of God and man, however, everything else is open to him based on his natural intellectual abilities. In one of the best books about the angels ever written, Jesuit Father Simon Augustine Blackmore writes:

> "For all future events may be known either in themselves or in their causes, and these are of three kinds. To the first class of causes may be ascribed all those that always and necessarily produce their effects. If such effects can be foreknown by men of science, as astronomers, who predict future eclipses, they certainly are not hidden from the angels. For excelling man in more perfect knowledge of the nature of such causes and their activities they possess a broader vision and certainty of predetermined effects. The second class of causes comprises those which, while generally producing their effects, yet do not do so of necessity. Their action may be so counteracted by one or more conflicting causes as to make the effect wholly contingent upon the presence or absence of such a conflict. Hence these contingent effects cannot be predicted with certainty, but only with reasonable conjecture, as when the weatherman foretells a local rain with more or less probability. Angels, on the contrary, know such effects with certainty. Gifted with a more universal knowledge, and actually comprehending not only the hidden powers of nature, but also the force of every natural cause and its correlation, they can compare one with the other, and see

317

for certain whatever future effect will result from such conflicting causes. In like manner a physician with perfect knowledge of his art can in some cases, diagnose with certainty the nature and cause of his patient's malady, and by virtue of known efficacious remedies, can foretell his recovery."[71]

The last class of causes is of course those that are totally dependent upon the future free choices and actions of men, angels and God. These causes the diabolical spirits cannot determine with absolute certainty. However, even this class of causes could be guessed at correctly based on the diabolical spirits extensive knowledge of human nature, history, and cause and effect. The diabolic spirits would be especially likely to be able to predict the future actions of men and woman who are possessed and enslaved to the devil. Finally, it would be the very highest of diabolical spirits, those that were probably involved with Hitler, based on their more universal knowledge, to be much better disposed to be able to correctly guess at what might happen in the future. It is in this context that Adolf Hitler having precognitive visions of the future that seemed to come true must be discussed.

In hindsight it is very clear that Adolf Hitler's rise to power was not just some fluke, not just a series of events, all unrelated that came together to help this man rise to the pinnacle of power. This was a coordinated dia-bolical plan, possibly hundreds of years in the making, that allowed Adolf Hitler to rise to lead Germany and then unleash a campaign of evil and destruction completely unprecedented in the history of humanity. Many have used this argument for why Hitler must have been possessed. How could an awkward, angry, and totally unremarkable youth, rise to power in Germany like he did, against all odds. How could an obscure youth, a total failure in all his early endeavors, do what he did, and unleash the evil that he did.

I firmly believe he had diabolical assistance, whether he knew it or not, and there is actually some evidence to suggest Hitler did know he had some kind of assistance as early as his teen years even though he may not have known the exact identity of the source. We know that Hitler unequiv-ocally knew he had help as early as his time in Vienna, and also during his service in World War 1 when he heard disembodied voices ordering him to move so as to avoid bomb blasts. Suffice it to say for now, one of the best evidences for Hitler's possession is the fact that not only was he shown visions of the future through very dubious occult means, but that

71   Blackmore, *The Angel World*

these visions actually came true. Additionally, that he clearly had diabolical help, that probably disguised itself as divine, to allow him to rise to the pinnacle of power which resulted in a release of evil upon mankind that was blatantly devilish.

I earlier mentioned Dr. Walter Stein as the person who was witness to some of Hitler's encounters with the spear of destiny and I will relate those experiences, however even before Dr Stein witnessed these disturbing events he had a disturbing encounter with Adolf Hitler which was the first time the two men met. Dr Walter Stein describes in vivid detail his first encounter with Hitler. Stein had wandered into a Vienna coffee shop and had located a bookshelf with a book on it that seemed to be separated from the rest. The book was a worn copy of Parseval, by Eschenbach. As Dr. Stein started paging through the worn copy of Parseval he became extremely disturbed. It seems someone had made copious notes on all the pages in the worn copy. Handwritten notes that were extremely dark, from a dark, disturbed and hateful mind. Dr. Stein felt the notes written in the book were blatantly evil. Ravenscroft relates the story:

> "the more he read the more disturbed he became. This was no ordinary commentary but the work of somebody who had achieved more than a working knowledge of the black arts! The unknown commentator had found the key to unveiling many of the deepest secrets of the grail, yet obviously **spurned the Christian ideals of the knights and delighted in the devious machinations of the Anti-Christ**. It suddenly dawned on him that he was reading the **footnotes of Satan**! In contrast to a genuine facility to interpret the whole sequence of 'Adventures of Parseval' as initiation trials on a prescribed path to the heights of transcendent awareness, **there were endless crude, vulgar and, in many cases, obscene comments.** A theme of racial fanaticism and an **almost insane worship of Aryan blood lineage** and Pan-Germanism ran throughout the commentary, which was pervaded with **loathing and contempt** for the Jews who were blamed for all the evils in the world and all the suffering of mankind."[72]

As Dr. Walter Stein was reading this diabolic commentary from an unknown author he looked up from the book and saw Adolf Hitler for the first time in his life. The experience was burned into his memory. Ravenscroft writes:

72   Ravenscroft, *The Spear of Destiny*

"Walter Stein looked up from the book and out through the trays in the showcase window into the most **arrogant face and demoniacal eyes he had ever seen**... Of course, he did not know that he was looking into the eyes of the man who would far outstrip the terrible prophecies associated with Klingsor, the man who would inspire a satanic reign of terror and cold-blooded butchery outstripping in savagery and bestial cruelty all previous ages of oppression in the entire history of mankind."[73]

Walter Stein finished reading the notes and then purchased the book. Upon getting up to leave he noticed the young man with "hypnotic eyes" was outside selling postcard size watercolors to passing tourists. Stein being intrigued bought three of the paintings, one of which was a portrait of the spear of destiny. It was at this point Dr. Stein noticed the name on the portrait, it was the same name he saw on the inside cover of the tattered copy of Parseval, Adolf Hitler!

It is significant to note that the man who owned the coffee shop in which Dr. Stein bought Adolf Hitler's copy of Parseval, was a man named Ernst Pretzsche. According to Trevor Ravenscroft, Dr. Stein, when he first met Pretzsche got the feeling that the man was evil. Ravenscroft writes:

"Pretzsche was a malevolent-looking man... The **moist black eyes** looking out at him from a sallow bloodless face seemed **to exude evil**"[74]

Ravenscroft makes it clear that Pretzsche was an active practitioner of the black arts and also a member of a cult led by a man named Guido von List, who was an infamous black occultist, very similar to Aleister Crowley, who operated a cult in Germany in the early 1900's. Even more significant it seems that Pretzsche was a mentor to Adolf Hitler from Hitler's earliest years in Vienna. It is believed by Stein and Ravenscroft that Pretzsche played a very large part in introducing Adolf Hitler to the occult. According to Pretzsche's own words,

"I am considered in some quarters to be a great authority on occultism," Pretzsche told him. "Adolf Hitler is not the only person to whom I give assistance and advice in these matters.[75]

This is a theme that will also come up later when I detail a man named Dietrich Eckart, who was also a mentor of Hitler. It seems Hitler had a

73   Ravenscroft, *The Spear of Destiny*
74   Ibid
75   Ravenscroft, *The Spear of Destiny*

slew of evil and diabolical personalities mentoring him and directing him throughout his life as well as a number of authors who were inspirations to him, people like Friedrich Nietzsche and Houston Stewart Chamberlain, Nietzsche being a person who inspired untold evils through his evil and blatantly blasphemous writings. Chamberlin, who himself admitted that he believed his writings were of a diabolic origin and who also believed he was haunted by demons and also claimed to actually see demonic beings on a regular basis. People like former monk von Liebenfelds who's racist and blasphemous "Ostara" magazine surely had an influence on a young Hitler while he lived in Vienna.

After the initial encounter with Adolf Hitler at Ernst Pretzsche's coffee shop, Dr Stein decided to investigate further who Adolf Hitler was. His first stop was to go back to the coffee shop and talk to Pretzsche, who informed Stein that he supported the poor Hitler by allowing Hitler to pawn some of his books and sell Pretzsche some of his substandard paintings. Stein noticed in Pretzsche's back office a photo of Guido von List, the previously mentioned black occultist as well as numerous drawings portraying occult and astrological symbols. It was at this meeting that Pretzsche informed Stein he had been mentoring the destitute Hitler in the ways of the occult. Pretzsche went on to direct Stein about where Stein could find Hitler and after the two men formally met it was these encounters between Stein and Hitler having a common interest in the spear of destiny, that would provide some of the most direct and stunning evidence of Hitler's diabolical possession.

There is one episode that stands out particularly. On an occasion when both Dr. Stein and Adolf Hitler had gone to the Hapsburg Treasure House to view the spear together, Hitler seemingly went into some kind of trance. What Dr. Stein witnessed that day, leaves absolutely no doubt that Hitler was a person under complete and total diabolical possession. Moreover, I believe this incident occurred, as a direct diabolic mockery of Stein's faith. When the two men had walked into the treasure house and viewed the spear, Stein had been deeply moved by the love of Christ. Stein related that he had thought about what the spear meant, that this very spear pieced the side of Jesus Christ, the savior of mankind. Stein had been almost overwhelmed with emotions of deep reverence for Christ and his sacrifice when he looked over and witnessed Hitler having a similar but reverse reaction to the spear. Hitler, or rather the spirits within him were delighted with joy and euphoria at viewing the spear, the spear that had dealt the final death blow to the Son of God, that had pierced his flesh and spilt his blood. Ravenscroft relates the incident:

> "Walter Stein found that he was not the only one moved by the sight of this historic Spearhead. Adolf Hitler stood beside him like a man **in a trance**, a man over whom some dreadful magic spell had been cast. His face was flushed, and his brooding eyes shone with an **alien emanation**. He was swaying on his feet as though caught up in some totally inexplicable euphoria. **The very space around him seemed enlivened with some subtle irradiation, a kind of ghostly ectoplasmic light.** His whole physiognomy and stance appeared transformed **as if some mighty spirit now inhabited his very soul**, creating within and around him a kind of evil transfiguration of its own nature and power. The young student recalled the legend of the two opposing spirits of good and evil associated with this spear of world destiny. Was he a witness of the incorporation of the spirit of the anti-Christ in this deluded human soul? Had this tramp from the dosshouse momentarily become **the vessel of that spirit which the bible called Lucifer?**"[76]

In a description that sounds strikingly similar to what perfect possession is, Dr Stein recounted the incident further:

> "It appeared to me that Hitler was in so deep a condition of trance that he was suffering almost complete sense-denudation and a total eclipse of self-consciousness"[77]

Even more extraordinary and quite disturbing is the fact that Dr. Stein talked to Hitler about this incident and Hitler apparently described the episode from his perspective to Dr. Stein. If this account is true, and I have no reason to doubt the veracity and credibility of Dr. Stein, it very well could have been the very moment when Hitler fully consented to the diabolic and actually became perfectly possessed. Quoting Hitler, Ravenscroft writes:

> "The air became stifling so that I could barely breath. The noisy scene of the Treasure House seemed to melt away before my eyes. I stood alone and trembling before the hovering form of the Superman (obermensch) – a Spirit sublime and fearful, a countenance intrepid and cruel. In holy awe, I offered my soul as a vessel of his Will."[78]

76   Ravenscroft, *The Spear of Destiny*
77   Ibid
78   Ravenscroft, *The Spear of Destiny*

And a later quote from Hitler,

"I move like a sleep-walker where providence dictates"[79]

We obviously know what providence he was speaking of. Not the providence of God, but the providence and will of Lucifer, who was using this man to complete his ends on this planet among men.

These passages from *The Spear of Destiny* by Trevor Ravenscroft are simply breathtaking. And profound. The last sentence of the last quote goes to the very depth of what perfect possession is, the consent, full consent given to a diabolic spirit. "I offered my soul as a vessel of his Will," is **exactly** how one becomes perfectly possessed. It appears this is the case with Adolf Hitler. Readers may be confused about the timeline of events in the life of Hitler because Hitler did in fact display signs of being possessed before he ever moved to Vienna. I have said elsewhere in this book that all forms of diabolical possession are usually a long process taking place over a period of time. I believe Hitler was initially possessed at a very young age, I don't believe he was perfectly possessed until much later however. There are many varying degrees of diabolical possession and a person can be partially possessed for many years and experience relatively little problems in their life, especially if they are consensual, it is only when the person gives full and unequivocal consent that they become perfectly possessed. It is important to note that after Hitler moved from Vienna he began to meet the people who would eventually contribute to him rising to power.

And as if this were not enough, Dr. Stein has additional information that is very useful for us to further our determination on whether Hitler was perfectly possessed. This further information is corroborative to some of August Kubizek's testimony. Dr. Stein relayed to Trevor Ravenscroft that when Hitler would get excited and give some kind of speech that it seemed as if another being took Hitler over. This is exactly how August Kubizek describes Hitler's speaking, and it will not be the last either. Further on in Hitler's life many others described this phenomenon as well. Ravenscroft writes:

"When Hitler was elated, his normal halting awkward style of speaking was transformed into a magical flow of words, delivered with spellbinding effect. On these occasions it was as though Hitler himself was listening to the extraneous intelligence which had temporarily taken over his soul. Later he would sit back exhausted, a solitary figure cast down from the heights of orgiastic ecstasy and utterly stripped of that charismatic quality which moments before had given him such a masterful command of himself and his audience. The strange transformation which Stein was witnessing in its early beginnings would later be described by others who saw this Luciferic possession take place yet more concretely as Hitler rose step by step to the very pinnacle of power."[80]

I mentioned earlier that Hitler had served in World War 1 and that while serving in the war had a number of significant experiences that were of a mystical nature. Hitler moved to Munich in 1913 and was accepted into the German war effort in 1914. The first mystical experience would come while he was fighting on the line during battle. He had been carrying messages to the front line and speaking with some fellow soldiers when a voice told him to run! And then further to turn left. Immediately after this a massive bomb exploded right where he had been, killing everyone he had just been speaking with. According to Robert Waite in *The Psychopathic God*, this incident along with many other incidents of seemingly close calls where Hitler's comrades were left dead and maimed and Hitler totally unscathed led to Hitler believing that he had divine help and further implanted the idea into his mind that he had a great destiny to fulfill for the German people.

The second incident occurred while Hitler was recovering from a wound in a hospital in Pasewalk. Apparently, Hitler had lost his sight, and this had been diagnosed as hysteria. According to Joseph Carr in *The Twisted Cross*, Hitler had been hearing voices also in the hospital telling him he was the German messiah and diabolically informing him that the Jews must be exterminated. Carr writes:

> "Something happened to Hitler at Pasewalk. He was temporarily blinded, and his doctors diagnosed the problem as 'hysteria'. During his hospitalization Hitler claimed to have heard 'voices', which he likened to those heard by Joan of ark. **Those voices told him that he had been selected by God to be Germany's messiah** and would save Germany from the claws of international Jewry."[81]

These mystical experiences in Hitler's life in which he heard and listened to diabolical voices, would prove to be decisive in the life of Adolf Hitler. It was because of these experiences that Hitler ultimately decided to enter politics.

80   Ravenscroft, *The Spear of Destiny*
81   Carr, *The Twisted Cross*

After the war Hitler would be reenlisted in the Army as a spy. It was during these spying missions that Hitler first encountered the German Workers Party, which would eventually be renamed as the National Socialist German Workers Party, otherwise known as the Nazi Party. Hitler quickly joined this group of racist's and occultists and was soon recognized by many in the group as having great potential. One personality in particular took notice of Hitler and that was the previously mentioned Dietrich Eckart.

When one looks at the life and works of Eckart it becomes very clear this man was a diabolical servant of the highest order. Eckart not only was ingratiated with many wealthy and influential people in Germany, people who were crucial in the rise of Adolf Hitler to power, but he was also a dedicated Satanist, as Ravenscroft calls him, and a member of the Thule Society. The Thule society being a powerful black magic cult that was fully expecting the coming of a German messiah that would hearken Germany back to its former glory before it lost World War one. The Thule society was a very powerful satanic cult that counted as its members some of the most powerful people in Germany. Ravenscroft describes the Thule as being full of rich and powerful people, he writes:

> This powerful Occult circle included among its members and adepts, Judges, Police-Chiefs, Barristers, Lawyers, University Professors and Lecturers, Aristocratic families including former members of the royal entourage of the Wittelsbach Kings, leading Industrialists, Surgeons, Physicians, Scientists, as well as a host of rich and influential bourgeois like the proprietor of the famous "Four Seasons Hotel" in Munich.[82]

Eckart himself is known to have said many times that he and others felt the presence of this messiah but could not see him. After Eckart met Hitler in 1919 he became convinced that Adolf Hitler was in fact the prophesied messiah. Eckart then proceeded to essentially take Hitler under his wing, mentoring him in politics and most probably the occult, introducing evil and racist ideas to him, as well as introducing him to influential people in German society, many who were members of the Thule cult that would be crucial for the future rise to power of Adolf Hitler. Eckart had such a massive influence on Hitler that on his deathbed Eckart uttered:

> "Follow Hitler! He will dance, but it is I who have called the tune!
> "I have initiated him into the 'Secret Doctrine', opened his centers

---

82   Ravenscroft, *The Spear of Destiny*

in vision **and given him the means to communicate with the Powers**. "Do not mourn for me: I shall have influenced history more than any other German."[83]

I bring all this up in the life of Adolf Hitler because it is important to understand what types of people and organizations Hitler was surrounded by before he rose to power. It is clear from the sources I have listed and many others for that matter that Hitler was surrounded by and helped by purely diabolical people. Occultists and racists, powerful satanic cults made up of rich and influential people. When one considers the fact that the Thule society and Dietrich Eckart in particular had been given a kind of "satanic annunciation" as Ravenscroft calls it, proclaiming the coming of a German messiah, which messiah was then provided in the form of Adolf Hitler, who then went on to lead Germany to utter evil and destruction, it becomes clear there was a profound amount of diabolical interference and coordination in all these events.

When one examines just how this satanic annunciation proclaiming the coming of a German messiah was brought about the whole scenario becomes even more appalling. It seems that Eckart and small group of Thule members conducted spiritualistic seances in which a medium, possessed by diabolical forces, proclaimed in foreign tongues that there would come a man to lead Germany to glory and exterminate European Jewry. Trevor Ravenscroft relates the scene,

> "In deep trance this simple hulk of a woman emanated from her vagina ectoplasmic heads and shrouds which manifested as in some ghostly birth from the nether world. It was not the emanations which were of importance to the circle of occultists who so wickedly exploited this poor wretch of a woman, but the voices which rang forth as she spoke in almost poetic form from deep unconsciousness in numerous foreign tongues. Dietrich Eckart was the master of ceremonies at these regular seances, but it was another significant character, Alfred Rosenberg, a German refugee from Moscow, who took it upon himself to question the ever-changing spirits which briefly occupied and possessed the medium. And it was Alfred Rosenberg, too, the prophet of the Anti-Christ of the "Protocols of Zion," who dared to call forth the presence of the Beast of the Revelation— the Luciferic Leviathan which had taken over body and soul of Adolf Hitler. According to Konrad Ritzier, one of the earliest members of the Thule Group and later the lit-

erary editor of its secret publications, all those present were terrified by the mighty powers which they had unleashed. The air in the
room became stifling and unbearable and the naked body of the
medium became translucent in an aura of ectoplasmic light. Rudolf
Glaucr, the founder of the Thule Gesellschaft, began to run from
the room in panic but Eckart grabbed hold of him and threw him
down to the floor.[84]

I quote this disturbing scene so that my readers can get the full picture
of just what kind of evil was at work here and what kind of evil would
ultimately be in full and total control of Adolf Hitler and the Nazi regime.
In addition to Dietrich Eckart, another evil man that would have a great
deal of influence on Hitler was the just mentioned Alfred Rosenburg who
Ravenscroft calls the prophet of the Protocols of Zion, a diabolical and
racist document that had a great deal of influence on the early Nazi's and
definitely contributed to the holocaust. The document was a forgery, pur-
porting to show evidence of a worldwide Jewish conspiracy to take over
the world. Eckart, Rosenburg, Hitler and the earliest Nazi's took this as
fact and used it to justify their virulently racist and murderous attitude
towards the Jews.

∞

The diabolical kingdom, through the mouth of a possessed medium,
during a spiritualistic séance had proclaimed the coming of a German
messiah, a complete mockery of the real annunciation by the great Archangel Gabriel 19 centuries earlier! The proclamation would come true
in its totality in 1933 when President Paul Von Hindenburg appointed
Hitler as Chancellor and also passed the Enabling Act, basically ensuring
Hitler could exercise power dictatorially without interference.

I have necessarily skipped over a large part of Hitler's rise to power
which occurred in the 1920's. As I said in the beginning, I would be briefly
highlighting his life and space does not allow to go over every incident
that is significant. The 1920's saw Hitler and the Nazi's gain in popularity
from a small party to one of national importance. Hitler, Eckart and the
early Nazi party attempted a coup in 1923, named the Beer Hall Putsch
in which a small group of Nazi's attempted to take over the government.
They failed miserably, many were killed, and Hitler was jailed. While in
jail Hitler penned possibly one of the evilest books in the history of humanity, Mein Kampf, or in English, My Struggle. This book would be-

84   Ravenscroft, *The Spear of Destiny*

come an immediate bestseller and was in effect the Nazi bible. This book was required reading in German schools and was used as a means of indoctrination of the German people. As the 1920's went on violent incidents between Nazi brownshirts and rival political parties would spiral out of control leading to much bloodshed on German streets. The Nazi's essentially took power, they were not given it, they took it by force and by murder, another calling card of the diabolical masters Hitler and his inner circle served.

After Hitler was named Chancellor in 1933, he went about methodically gathering full power for himself on the one hand and on the other hand murderously eliminating all political competition. The stories from this time of the Gestapo, visiting pollical dissidents and then said political opposition disappearing never to be heard from again are notorious. The 1934 Night of the Long Knives is especially notorious as anywhere from 100 to 1000 very prominent political rivals to Hitler, including Catholic leaders, were summarily executed by Gestapo and SS soldiers, some extremely gruesomely, like Gustav Ritter von Kahr who was found hacked to death by pick axes in a German forest.

After the death of President Hindenburg in 1934, Hitler combined the positions of Chancellor and President and had full unequaled power as the leader of Germany. Slowly but surely him and his inner circle of Nazi's would start to lay their devilish plans for the whole of Germany. This would include the start of the persecution of the Jews, the total elimination of anyone critical of the Nazi's, including Catholics, the total indoctrination of the German people with an idea that a superior Aryan race was Germany's birthright and that the Third Reich would rule the world for 1000 years.

Due to Hitler's ability to completely enrapture an audience he was speaking to, coupled with the work of his propaganda minster Joseph Goebbels, the German people became totally convinced of Hitler's power and plan for the German people. They became essentially possessed by the satanic idea that they were superior, that the Jews were sub human and must be eliminated. Hitler's ability to convince an entire nation to buy into his diabolical plans are one of the greatest indications of his perfect possession. I have said elsewhere that perfectly possessed people are sometimes able to convince and deceive great multitudes of people, and the reason is because it is really the evil spirit speaking through the perfectly possessed person. These spirits have intelligence that we cannot possibly comprehend, far superior to ours. If a person listens to this evil, they will inevitably be deceived. That is how powerful these diabolic lies, ideas and arguments can be. This is precisely the reason an exorcist is very sternly cautioned against engaging a diabolic spirit in conversation.

Nazi Germany was seduced by these diabolic lies coming out of the possessed mouth of Adolf Hitler and modern society is full of the same. The only protection from this pervasive evil is the bosom of the church and her teachings and doctrine regarding faith and morals. It could also be said that not only did Hitler convince the great majority of Germany to go along with his plans but he also in a way had a kind of hold over them. This is another sign of his probable possession. To show just how tight of a hold Hitler had over Germany we can look to the last days of the war when the elderly and children were tasked to defend Berlin to the very bitter end, and died for a totally lost cause they believed in. Additionally, the amount of suicides in Germany in the final days are also an indication of rampant diabolical activity in Germany during this time. There was an estimated 7000 suicides in Berlin alone during this time and possibly many more going unreported due to the chaos of the war. And that is just in Berlin, there were many more suicides in many other places all around Germany. Whole families slaughtered themselves, with parents killing their own children and husband and wives killing each other. In a final show of diabolical power by the Nazi regime it is thought many of these suicides were the result of Nazi propaganda urging Germans on to suicide rather than be captured by the Red Army or Allied forces.

In addition to what has already been written concerning the diabolical possession of Adolf Hitler the question can be asked if there are additional indications. One indication that I already touched upon is the fact that Hitler seemed to have inordinate good luck when it came to avoiding death. This was not only true of his service in World War 1 where he miraculously survived many times, when close comrades were blown to pieces. I have already listed the fact that Hitler heard voices directing him on where to go to avoid being killed. Even after the war however Hitler seemed to be under the protection of some force that saved him multiple times from certain death.

The previous mentioned Beer Hall Putsch is one such example. This incident saw many of his fellow coup seekers die violent deaths. When Hitler gained full power there was many different assassination attempts with Hitler somehow escaping, sometimes at the last possible second. The reason this contributes to the possibility of his perfect possession is because Hitler was being used to complete a diabolic plan, and his early death would not have suited those plans. Trust me, diabolic spirits love to see wholesale death and destruction and had Hitler not been the prophet and vessel of a larger diabolic scheme he most likely would have died violently many years earlier. In the end however he did still die a violent death, as many perfectly possessed people do. Taking his own life with a single shot to the head on the eve of Walpurisnact 1945.

Another well-known fact about Hitler is that he had many different fears and obsessions, and these fears and obsessions when looked at in the light of his perfect possession seem to make more sense than if they were simply isolated incidents. The first is his ordinate fear of the dark and nighttime. It is related in many different sources the fact that Hitler would often wake up in the middle of the night, between midnight and 3am in an absolute terror-stricken state, and not only that but that he would cry out and be adamant there was some kind of shadow in his room. Hitler's fear was so great he would often not go to sleep until well after 4am and up until that time every single possible lighting source around him would be kept fully lit to fend off some unknown darkness. One trembles to think if this inordinate fear of the dark was really a fear of what he surely knew awaited him when he died and spent all eternity in "outer darkness"

In addition to his inordinate fear of the dark, Hitler also had an obsession with destruction, blood and fire. Author Joseph Carr notes in his book, The Twisted Cross in chapter 3, *Was Hitler Demon Possessed*, that Hitler's

> "fear often bubbled to the surface in the form of morbid fascinations, such as fire, destruction and human blood."[85]

From the perspective of someone who is perfectly possessed these fascinations and really obsessions would seem to make perfect sense. The reason for the diabolic fascination surrounding blood is twofold. On the one hand the scripture teaches that the life is in the blood and the Jews held the blood as absolutely sacred. The image comes to mind of the Blessed Mother mopping up the blood of Christ after his scourging in that powerful and dramatic scene of Mel Gibson's film. The demonic of course despises human life and so they do what they can to corrupt and mock the sacred nature of human blood.[86] This is part of the reason why satanic cultists will drink the blood of other people in their rituals. This is

85   Carr, The Twisted Cross
86   The Nightstalker Richard Ramirez once stated ""I love to kill people. I love watching them die. I'd shoot them in the head and they would wiggle and squirm all over the place and just stop. Or I'd cut them with a knife and watch their faces turn real white. I love all that blood."

the reason Hitler was obsessed with blood and obsessed with the fact that pure Aryan blood was corrupted by the Jews and used this in part as justification for the slaughter of the Jews and other people thought to have tainted blood lines. This is also the reason Hitler apparently offered to open up his arm and let his followers drink his blood near the end of the war, in what Joseph Carr calls a total mockery of the Catholic sacrament.

The second reason for the diabolic obsession with blood has to do of course with the blood of Christ which redeemed all of mankind. In the end it was human blood, the blood of Jesus Christ, fully man and fully God that completely and utterly destroyed Satan's reign on this earth.

The compulsion surrounding fire and destruction also make perfect sense in the context of Hitler's possession by diabolical forces. How many times is it clearly stated in the scriptures that hell, the home of Satan and the diabolical kingdom contains a fire that never dies. We know for sure, based on the words of Jesus Christ himself that Satan and the rest of the damned, angelic and human will spend eternity in the lake of fire and brimstone. We also know that fire plays a very large part in the doctrine of Satanists. They use fire in their rituals and also use fire to destroy things. One little known fact about the previously mentioned Son of Sam, who was a member of a very dark and dangerous Satanic cult is the fact that before the murders started in the summer of 1976 that Berkowitz committed on estimate a couple hundred arson's all-around New York City. According to Joseph Carr Hitler had wanted the whole city of Paris burnt to the ground and he many times ordered wholesale destruction seemingly for destructions sake. Destructiveness is a well-known diabolic trait, they are destructive entities, they love to destroy. They love to destroy almost anything they can. In fact, the best-known way to discern between a human and diabolic haunting of a physical premises is to determine whether or not the haunting is destructive, destruction being indicative of the presence of one or more evil spirits.

Lastly, I would like to talk about something in the life of Adolf Hitler that is not well known and not often talked about. That would be his totally perverted sex life and as an extension to that the fact that many of his mistresses killed themselves or attempted to kill themselves. The sex life of Adolf Hitler has been a topic that has been hotly debated by many historians. Coming across actual historical facts regarding this matter proves to be somewhat difficult. The reason for this is because Hitler created a public persona for himself that he was essentially celibate, that he was married to Germany and totally committed to her instead of to any women. Furthermore, some of the possible evidence of Hitler's sexual deviance was most probably destroyed by him and his henchman during the years of his rule, this would include records from the first world war as well as arrest records from Munich possibly showing his arrest for sodomy and pedophilia. I will say that it in no way surprises me that there are many substantial rumors of Hitler's sick sexual perversions, he would only have this in common with every single other person I have profiled in this book.

There are various sources that allege Hitler was a homosexual and had many gay relationships with many different men throughout his life. These reports come from various sources including Nazi's of Hitler's inner circle as well as from American and British intelligence reports from the war. Hermann Rauschning is one such source as he claimed to have seen Hitler's records from the first world war which included an arrest for pederasty or pedophilia as well as alleging that Hitler was found guilty in Munich of violating the law against homosexual practices. While there is no direct evidence of these claims, this is not all that surprising as we can be sure that if these records did indeed exist, they would have almost certainly been destroyed by Hitler or his allies shortly before or shorty after Hitler gained power in Germany. Hitler also did associate with many different known homosexuals throughout his life up until the night of the long knives. German general Ernst Rohm is one such example. There is one source that claims the motivation for the night of the long knives and Hitler's subsequent persecution of homosexuals was an attempt to cover up his previous homosexual activity. Suffice it to say that where there is smoke there is fire and in the context of someone perfectly possessed, they almost always lead a totally depraved sex life which usually includes homosexuality, pedophilia, bestiality, rape, sexual sadism, necrophilia and various other forms of depraved sexual acts.

One of the sickest forms of sexual perversion Hitler has been alleged to have engaged in is the practice known as coprophilia. This is where a person becomes aroused through the use of human excrement during sex. There are multiple sources, the most believable coming from American and British intelligence reports that claim Hitler was an "Impotent Coprophil" and forced his nice Geli Raubal to perform these sick sex acts on him. In addition to these sick perversions, there is also evidence Hitler did carry on a number of heterosexual relationships with multiple different women. Even these however were marked by total perversion and destruction when almost all of the woman Hitler was supposed to have been sexually involved with either committed suicide successfully or attempted suicide. The sources differ on the actual amount of suicides committed by Hitler lovers, but suffice it to say, a conservative estimate is 4-woman total that either committed suicide or attempted it and some sources place the number far higher at 8 women. It is known for sure that Geli Raubal, Eva Braun and Unity Mitford all committed suicide successfully after having sexual encounters with Adolf Hitler, and a fourth woman Maria Reiter attempted suicide. Hitler has this trait in common with Aleister Crowley, who saw many of his lovers and associates commit suicide or attempt it.

For me, this final piece of evidence in the life of Adolf Hitler is conclusive. When a person who has shown the indications Adolf Hitler has throughout his life, that I have recorded thus far, and then in addition to that the people closest to him start killing themselves, it is a profound indication of someone totally and entirely in the grip of diabolical forces. I have said clearly that perfectly possessed people almost always leave a trail of destruction in their wake, no case presents this better than the case of Adolf Hitler who left a trail of destruction through mankind that was not seen in the history of mankind up to that point and has yet to be duplicated up to the present day.

There have also been possession cases, Anneliese Michel being the primary in which the demons present claimed they were Hitler. In *Mary Crushes the Serpent* the anonymous exorcist and author of this book says the demons who claim to be Judas are really the demon who was possessing that historical person while they were alive, therefore it is possible that the demon who claimed to be Adolf Hitler who was possessing Michel may have been the actual demon that was in control of Hitler for most of his life.

There was also multiple people who seemed to sense a deep foreboding around Adolf Hitler, including Joseph Goebbels. Lastly, in addition to Hitler having a strange control over the people of Germany, Hitler held the same power of control over his own Generals who vehemently disagreed with many of his military decisions. Cardinal Ratzinger before he was Pope Benedict even talked about Adolf Hitlers relationship to the diabolic and one of the things he mentioned was the fact that Hitlers generals when they would come into Hitlers actual presence would lose their courage. In an article for the National Catholic Register Cardinal Ratzinger stated,

Cardinal Ratzinger answered: **"On the one hand, Hitler was a demonic figure**. One only need read the history of the German generals, who time and again made up their minds, just for once, to tell him to his face what they really thought, and who were then yet again so overcome by his power of fascination that they did not dare to.[87]

CONCLUSION

The three people I have profiled here are certainly not the only three I could have. History has been full of world leaders, cult leaders, and diabolical apologists that very likely were perfectly possessed. These people have all inflicted various forms of evil upon mankind. In addition to the Rev Jim Jones I could have profiled people like Warren Jeffs, David Koresh, Marshall Applewhite, Jeff Lundgren, Charles Manson and Brother 12. All 5 of these people displayed some of the very same indications of diabolical involvement that Jim Jones displayed. All 5 claimed in some way to be a messiah, savior, or more blatantly blasphemous, Christ or God himself, which from a demonological perspective is very significant and very telling when it comes to discernment of involvement with diabolical forces or possession. All 5 of these people left significant amounts of destruction and ruinous evil in their wake. The murderous and suicidal episodes perpetrated by Koresh, Applewhite, Lungren, and Manson are all well-known and infamously evil. Associates of Brother 12 even claimed to have seen a hooded specter surrounding the cult leader at certain times. I believe all five were to varying degrees heavily involved with diabolical forces.

In addition to Aleister Crowley I could have profiled people such as Madame Helena Blavatsky the founder of Theosophy who claimed to be in intimate contact with the Great White Brotherhood, who were supposed to be 12 ascended master spirits who sought to lead mankind. From a Catholic demonological perspective these entities are devils. In fact, Brother 12, the cult leader I just mentioned got his name from the 12th of these spirits who he claimed to be in contact with. I also could have profiled people like L. Ron Hubbard the founder of the Scientology cult which has a lot of sway in todays Hollywood. Based upon my research I am confident in making the assumption that Hubbard was possessed. He himself, like many other of the perfectly possessed, believed he was the devil. He was also deeply involved with the practice of black magic and

---

87   Edward Pentin, Vatican exorcist: Hitler Knew the Devil, *National Catholic Register*

one Jack Parsons, an infamous Crowleyan black occultist who was deeply involved with America's rocket propulsion research.[88]

In addition to Adolf Hitler I could have profiled any number of world leaders throughout history that I believe to have been servants of the devil and possessed by him. People like Joseph Stalin, who may be the only other person in history who could come close to being responsible for as many deaths as Adolf Hitler. Stalin's own daughter Svetlana believed he was possessed by a "terrible devil" and after the magnitude of evil committed by him, intentionally killing millions of people through various means including starvation, is there any doubt to her assessment? I could have profiled people like Mao Zedong, the communist leader of China, who also rivals Hitler and Stalin and may even exceed them as far as mass murder goes. I could have profiled numerous murderous dictators like Sadam Hussein, Pol Pot, Hirohito, Talat Pasha, Kim Il Sung, and Idi Amin the homicidal maniac leader of Uganda who not only murdered hundreds of thousands of people but also was an active practitioner of black magic.

I could have profiled many people who through their satanic ideas and writings have inspired many evils in the course of history. People like Carl Marx who was a blatant devil worshiper and inspired the one form of government that has claimed more lives than any other in the history of humanity. People like Friedrich Nietzsche who as spokesman for his master, the devil, famously said "God is Dead." People like Margaret Sanger, the founder of Planned Parenthood, a eugenicist and evil racist, who helped change the culture in the U.S. from one of life to one of death and who said diabolical things like:

> "The most merciful thing that the large family does to one of its infant members is to kill it."

I could have profiled numerous other people as well who have been prophets and purveyors of doom, evil and destruction. People like Osama Bin Laden, Ayatollah Khomeini, Anders Behring Breivik, Abu Bakr Al-Baghdadi, Pablo Escobar, El Chapo and many others too numerous to list here.

I could have even gone back farther in history and profiled monsters like Herod, Nero, Diocletian, Caligula, Henry VIII, Vlad the Impaler, Rasputin, Elizabeth Bathory, Gilles de Rais, and Thug Behram, a mem-

---

88   The connection between Aleister Crowley, Jack Parsons (who was said to be brilliant) and America's rocket propulsion program, which eventually allowed human beings to go into space but also made it possible to annihilate all of humanity in the form of ICBMS is very interesting indeed.

ber of the Thugee cult, a murderer of up to 900 people and a worshipper of the diabolic entity Kali. I could have profiled people such as Robespierre, Ivan the Terrible, Ghencas Kahan, and Attila the Hun who murdered Saint Ursula and her companions after she refused to marry him.

Finally, all the people I have profiled in the last 3 chapters are just the people we know about that have either shown evidence of being perfectly possessed or have acted in a way that would lead us to believe they are in league with the devil. One of the most disturbing aspects of the phenomena known as perfect possession is the fact that there are many people out in the world in various positions and levels of society that are in fact totally dedicated to the devil who operate in secret that we know nothing about and will know nothing about until judgement day. Father Euteneuer is totally correct on this point when he states in his little section on perfect possession that there are many more possessed people out in the world than we will ever know, and we speak of freely chosen possession.

CHAPTER 10

SIGNS AND SYMPTOMS OF PERFECT POSSESSION

*"Joseph Stalin remains one of the most polarizing figures in Russia's history, reviled as a **mass murderer** by some, praised as a **savior** by others."*[1]

*"They say when the Russian dictator Joseph Stalin entered a room, the whole place was **palpably transformed**, and not in a good way. Everyone was suddenly **very afraid.**"*[2] *Spiritdaily.com*

*"Behind his bland **dark eyes**, the "man of steel" had a hard-mechanical brain that never hesitated at mass murder in its driving ambition to **dominate the world.**"*[3]

*"Stalin's secret police (GPU, predecessor of the KGB) also went to work waging a campaign of **terror** designed to **break the people's will.**"*[4]

*"By the end of 1933, nearly 25 percent of the population of the Ukraine, including three million **children, had perished**. The Kulaks as a class were **destroyed**"*[5]

*A "criminal on the worldwide political scene" might very well be possessed… he would display an **unusually great capacity for work, unusual energy,** and a **virtually uncanny feeling for interrelations and dangers in his daily activities**… Such a man might **command uncanny suggestive powers; his knowledge** and his **grandiose plans** might well be **impressive**. He could exercise nearly **irresistible power**-and yet, all his actions would lead to **destruction and death.**[6]*

I have said elsewhere in this book that perfect possession is qualitatively different than traditional or partial diabolic possession. I have said that people who are perfectly possessed, do not display the traditional

1   Stalin: feared and revered, RT, Dec 21, 2009, https://www.rt.com/news/stalin-anniversary-purge-leadership/
2   Michael Brown, Spiritual Atmosphere, Spirit Daily, Jan 9, 2019, https://spiritdailyblog.com/spiritual-warfare/spiritual-atmosphere
3   Josef Stalin was one of the most ruthless and cold-blooded leaders in recorded history., UPI Archives, March 6, 1953, https://www.upi.com/Archives/1953/03/06/Josef-Stalin-was-one-of-the-most-ruthless-and-cold-blooded-leaders-in-recorded-history/7420410824161/
4   The History Place, *Genocide in the 20th Century: Stalin's Forced Famine 1932-1933 7 Million Deaths*, http://www.historyplace.com/worldhistory/genocide/stalin.htm
5   Ibid
6   Rodewyk, *Possessed by Satan*, 1975, P.185

"crisis" state of the partially possessed. Speaking in languages previously unknown, superhuman strength, occult knowledge, paranormal phenomena (levitation, dematerialization, etc.) and an intense aversion to the sacred are generally considered to be the traditional signs of demonic possession. While it is true perfect possession displays some of those signs[7], it also does display some of its own signs and symptoms or better put, people who I believe to have been perfectly possessed have many things in common amongst themselves.

Just as in a case of partial possession a genuinely possessed person may speak fluent Latin but not levitate, cases of perfect possession do not display *all* of the signs and symptoms I am about to list. Some people only display a few of the signs and some display many of them. What they for sure do not display is the traditional crisis state of diabolic possession which as I said in a previous chapter, the reason for is because the perfectly possessed are people totally at peace with the deal and collaboration they have entered into with the devil or a devil. Rather than being victims of attack from diabolical forces they are willing collaborators and allies with these same diabolical forces. I have repeated this point time and time again because it is the most important aspect of what we are speaking about and also very important to understanding the true nature of perfect possession and how evil works in our world.

From a theological perspective most of these signs and symptoms I am about to list are really hallmarks of the diabolic psychology and personality. When an evil spirit in is complete control of a person and possessing them totally, some of these very same traits of the diabolic psychology and personality start to show through.

The following are signs and symptoms I have observed in people who may have been perfectly possessed.

1. LACK OF FAMILY, ESPECIALLY A FATHER AND LACK OF MEANINGFUL LOVING RELATIONSHIPS.

> "As he was getting into the boat, the man who had been possessed pleaded to remain with him. But he would not permit him but told him instead, "**Go home" to your family**" Mark 5:18-19

Most of the people I profiled in this book, especially in chapters 11 and 12 seem to have this trait in common. In fact, the only person

7 I noted above how both Jim Jones and Adolf Hitler displayed at least one of the traditional signs of possession, (occult knowledge)

338

I profiled here that had a loving father that was present during childhood was Jeffrey Dahmer, however, even Dahmer did not have a totally normal childhood as his parents did divorce when he was a young boy and family disfunction was the order of the day in the Dahmer home due to his mother Joyce's mental illness. The rest of these people either did not have a father at all or they had a father that was either an alcoholic or extremely abusive. Take Ted Bundy for example, Bundy never knew who his real father was and in fact grew up believing his grandfather was his actual father. In addition to that, Bundy's grandfather Samuel Cowell, was known to be extremely abusive and was possibly possessed himself. Jim Jones's father was an abusive alcoholic, Crowley's father died when he was very young, Hitler's father was vicious and abusive towards him. I also previously mentioned two cases from the literature, that of Gary Lyttle in the book *The Dark Sacrament* and that of Jamsie Z in *Hostage to the Devil*, both of whom grew up largely without a father. Lastly, Richard Kuklinski, the mafia hit man I mentioned at the end of chapter 11, also had a father that was an abusive and violent alcoholic, in addition to this and in similar fashion to Robin Gecht's son being a convicted murderer, Kuklinski's brother is also a convicted murderer and rapist.

When someone grows up without a family, father or meaningful familial relationships it leaves a significant void in their lives, a void diabolical forces will seek to exploit. From the perspective of perfect possession, a person that has no meaningful familial relationships will be much more prone to enter into meaningful relationships with evil spirits and accept those relationships as a supplant to their lack of family. This is the reason why cults, gangs, secret societies, and sub-cultures are doorways for the demonic realm. When someone gets involved in one of these activities it is usually because they have no family, or it is to the severe detriment of their family. When someone has no family, or they stray from their family they are much more likely to then get involved in activities which have diabolical involvement.

I will give the reader two examples. The first comes from the scriptures and the possession and exorcism episode at Gerasa. After Christ had exorcised the man, the man being very grateful wanted to follow Christ, Christ instead tells the man to go back to his family. This is extremely significant because it was most probably his separation from his family that led to his initial possession. Secondly in the movie *Eyes Wide Shut*, the Tom Cruise character, Doctor Bill Hartford, finds himself involved in a very high-end cult, only after he separates from his wife for the night after she tells him she almost cheated on him with a sailor during a family vacation. The important point being, Dr. Hartford only got involved with a destructive and evil practice after separating himself from his family.

One last note on this a lack of family. It can also happen that family members themselves are totally corrupted and possessed by evil spirits which then leads to subsequent diabolic involvement of other family members for generations. This can happen in a number of ways the foremost example being multi-generational cults, which take many forms. It can also happen however in the context of pedophilia and sexual abuse where generations of family members are sexually abused as children who then abuse their own children. For an example of this the reader can consult the book, *The Dark Sacrament*, Chapter 10, Devilry on the Dingle Peninsula.

2. SEXUAL PERVERSIONS AND DEPRAVITY

> "The practice of this perversion represents the lowest depths of degradation."
>
> – Dr. Walter Langer on Adolf Hitler's Coprophilia

> "My whole life revolved around just pleasing these men and keeping Ghislaine and Jeffrey happy. Their whole entire lives revolved around sex… This man couldn't take a 2-hour flight without ejaculating, that's how sick he was."[8]
>
> – Virginia Roberts Giuffre, Epstein victim

> (According to allegations in court documents, Epstein claimed that, because of his **demigod biology**[9], he needed "at least three" orgasms a day.)
>
> – Los Angeles Times

This is the one trait that every single person I profiled here has. Almost without exception, people who are perfectly possessed engage in any number of seriously depraved and dehumanizing sexual aberrations. These range from orgies, pedophilia, rape, and sex magic to things like necrophilia, coprophilia, bestiality, sodomy and sadism. People who are perfectly possessed do not have what would be considered normal and moral sex lives. They either engage in the activities I listed above or are

---

8   *Filthy Rich*, Netflix Documentary
9   This type of thinking on the part of Epstein is so utterly satanic it is frightening. This kind of confirms what I knew to be true and that is that not only was Epstein a monster but he was a card carrying Satanist or luciferian. The belief that one is a God is satanic doctrine going back hundreds if not thousands of years. Additionally, the belief that one is a God is a fundamental part of the diabolic psychology, and shows clearly this psychology at work in Epstein.

strangely and unnaturally a sexual. The greatest examples of this are of course the serial killers I profiled, some of whom engaged in the totally depraved practice of necrophilia, which is having sex with a corpse. Jeffrey Dahmer even committed necrophilia with both animals, in his younger years, and people in his adult years.

We also see this present in the Rev Jim Jones who sodomized many of his followers and taught this as being ok and normal. We see this in cult leader Warren Jeffs who was an infamous pedophile and polygamist. We see it in the depraved sex magic rituals of Aleister Crowley and in the supposed coprophilia practiced by Adolf Hitler and see it especially in the life of Jeffrey Epstein. In one documentary about Epstein, one of his victims talks about the sadistic sexual abuse and rapes she and others were subjected to at the hands of Epstein, Sarah Ransome stated,

> He did things that no man should ever do to a woman, and he did them all the time.[10]

Another Epstein victim described similar abuse at the hands of Epstein.

> Alison also told Recarey that Epstein got so violent with her that he ripped out her hair and threw her around. "I mean," she said, "there's been nights that I walked out of there barely able to walk, um, from him being so rough."[11]

In one of Ed Warren's books, titled Satan's Harvest[12], the possessed man and subject of the book, Maurice Theriault, initially became possessed after engaging in bestiality at the behest of his father, who may have been perfectly possessed.[13] We even see it in the recent case of Matt Lauer, a famous NBC Newsman who has been exposed as being a total monster. According to one victim Lauer forcefully raped her anally.

There are numerous theological reasons why this is the case. One of the reasons is because all of the aforementioned sexual practices are all extremely dehumanizing to both the victims and perpetrators. Evil spirits absolutely hate and despise human beings, even the human beings who are on their side and seek to serve and collaborate with them. They seek to do anything possible to totally corrupt the body and especially the souls

---

10   *Filthy Rich*, Netflix Documentary

11   Maureen Callahan, The 'sex slave' scandal that exposed pedophile billionaire Jeffrey Epstein, *New York Post*, October 9, 2016

12   Warren, *Satan's Harvest*

13   Another Warren case that occurred in Southington, Connecticut occurred because necrophilia had been practiced in the house which was previously a funeral home.

of all humans and such degrading sexual practices do just that. As an extension to this it can also be said that all the above mentioned depraved sexual practices are all extremely sinful and most importantly, all of them are extremely offensive to God which is partially the reason perfectly possessed people engage in them.

Secondly, evil spirits are jealous of our sexuality as humans and the fact we can actively participate in the creative power of God through the creation of new life through love. Lucifer, who wanted to be like God, was never granted such a privilege and so he and his angels seek to destroy, corrupt and pervert our sexuality in any number of ways. Thirdly, evil spirits are non-sexual beings and when they are in complete control of a human being through a perfect possession, one of the ways this shows through is through extremely degrading and depraved sexual practices. Whereas the good angels always seek to teach man how to live morally when it comes to sexual matters (Raphael), the bad angels (Asmodeus) seek to totally pervert and corrupt it and by doing so pervert and corrupt human hearts and souls.[14]

The reader can again consult *The Dark Sacrament* Chapter 8, Mr. Gant and the Neighbor from Hell, and Chapter 10, Devilry on the Dingle Peninsula to see concrete examples of perfectly possessed people engaging in sexual depravity. I would also remind the reader that in Malachi Martin's book, *Hostage to the Devil* it was said about Jay Beedem, the perfectly possessed radio station manager, that some of the woman at the station had slept with him, but never more than once.

3. They Are Feared By People, They Cause Widespread Fear Around Them Or Cause People To Become Terrified In A Deep Primal Way.

"As soon as I saw Smith the hairs on the back of my neck went up. I tried everything I could to get Kelly Anne away from him."
– Margaret Bates, Mother of Kelly Anne Bates, who was brutally tortured and murdered by James Patterson Smith

"That couple, they emanated pure evil"
– Jodi Foster, speaking about dream she had of Cameron and Janice Hooker

With each unpredictable outburst, Sam boxed the city farther into a prison of fear.[15]

---

14   See the book of Tobit
15   Simone Wilson, Son Of Sam: This Summer In 1977, An NYC Serial Killer Is Taken Down By

There was something about Ted Bundy that so terrified some of the women who got away from him at the last minute. They "smelled" danger early enough to scream, fight, or run. For years, they could not even talk about their encounters with him.[16]

Perfectly possessed people are often feared by other people or they cause widespread fear around themselves. As an extension to this, sometimes people feel a certain foreboding around them or sense some kind of evil emanating from them. There are multiple examples of this that I could cite, one of the best being from the section on the Rev Jim Jones. Right at the beginning of that profile of Jones I quoted a man who as a young teen met Jim Jones for the first time and sensed some kind of pure evil around the man. I also quoted one of the documentaries about Jones when one of the previous residents of Jonestown stated clearly that things were a little bit lighter around Jonestown when Jones himself was not physically present, but when he was present it was like an oppressive "dark cloud" had arrived. Additionally, when Jones was around there was an atmosphere of fear, people were terrified of breaking the rules of the Jonestown compound lest they be physically and psychologically broken. I could highlight any number of stories about Charles Manson in which people felt very uncomfortable or sensed a certain doom or evil around the man. Many of Manson's followers also totally feared him. In fact, Terry Melcher feared Manson so much that he had to be given a tranquilizer before testifying at his trial.[17] In an article about Charles Manson that appeared on Spirit Daily and in which Michael Brown speculates he may be perfectly possessed; Brown said the following about Manson:

"those who have met him have spoken of the truly dark and awful gravity ("charisma") in and around him"[18]

This was also the case with H.H. Holmes. One of Holmes possible victims had had a very bad feeling of foreboding around him which actually saved the woman's life as she chose not to have any involvement with him. One of the greatest examples of this is the case of the Chicago Rippers. The three other suspects besides Robin Gecht totally feared Gecht and did anything he asked them to do, which included murder and the sexual mutilation of woman. In the section on Ted Bundy, I related two episodes

A Parking Ticket, *The Patch*, Aug 10, 2017
16   Rule, Ann; Rule, Ann. *The Stranger Beside* Me. Estate of Ann Rule in conjunction with Renaissance Literary & Talent. Kindle Edition.
17   Bugliosi, Helter Skelter
18   Michael Brown, The Manson Mystique, SpiritDaily.com, Jan 5, 2017

of people being afraid of him after sensing some type of evil, the incident with Joe Aloi being the best example, with Aloi clearly stating that he was afraid of Bundy. I also noted that some of Bundy's intended victims got very frightened around him, sensing some kind of evil, one girl even having the hairs on the back of her neck stand up. In an incident similar to that of Ted Bundy and Joe Aloi, serial killer Samuel Little and an unnamed Texas Ranger also had an encounter that led the Texas investigator to sense that Samuel Little is "Evil in its purest form."

Of all the serial killers I have studied, even though they are all different people, have different victim profiles, killed differently, operated in different geographical areas, they all have one thing in common which is that the area they are operating in, once it has been discovered there is a killer on the loose, becomes terrified, and fearful, often changing their lives and daily habits as a result of this fear. The fear felt around Washington State and Tallahassee College campuses during the Ted Bundy saga was palpable. The fear felt in New York City during the summer of Sam was the same. Even the fear felt around Virginia and Maryland during the reign of the D.C. Sniper was very intense. The widespread fear around the greater Los Angeles area during the reign of the Nightstalker was very great. The fear people had to go on airplanes after 9/11, I could give many examples in which perfectly possessed people and the evil they commit causes widespread fear.

The stories of Adolf Hitler's generals fearing him are also well known as are the people who said they felt an overwhelming sense of evil around Aleister Crowley. I could again mention Jay Beedem who Malachi said was either "despised or feared"[19] around the radio station. One relatively unknown fact about Jeffrey Epstein is that he was known to be absolutely ruthless and was feared by people in some of his early positions as a hatchet man before he started his own hedge fund. In addition to that almost all of Epstein's victims totally feared him and this is partially the reason he was able to get away with his evil for so long, because his victims, through absolutely no fault of their own[20], totally feared Epstein. Attorney Brad Edwards, an attorney for some of Epstein's victims stated,

> Everybody feared him and fear was his greatest asset, that's what gave him his power[21]

---

19   Martin, *Hostage to the Devil*
20   One Epstein victim stated that she routinely overheard Epstein talking on the phone and actually threatening to kill people and torture them.
21   *Filthy Rich*, Netflix Documentary

The stories about both J.P. Morgan and John D. Rockefeller and in modern days Carl Icahn and George Soros being totally feared in the world of finance are also well known. And finally one of the most disturbing examples of all and one that I cited earlier in this book is the fact that Virginia Tech Shooter Seung-hui Cho, gave off an aura of evil so strong it led to many teachers not wanting to have anything to do with him and one English teacher in specific to get the feeling that Cho was evil.

I really could go on and on. If one reads the biographical accounts of the people I have profiled, there is inevitably at least one episode somewhere in their lives where people feel some kind of deep foreboding, evil, or sense of doom around them or people fear them in some way.

4. Able To Manipulate and Control People and Get People To Do Their Bidding.

"Robin was the leader of the Crew; he had a strange power over his younger accomplices."[22]

"Joseph Goebbels manipulated and deceived the German population and the outside world"[23]

"Essentially, his family was doing Manson's bidding when they killed on his behalf and in compliance with his orders."[24]

This is kind of an extension to No. 3 in the sense that many of the people I profiled were extremely skilled at manipulation and getting people to do what they wanted, and this occurred sometimes through fear, but not always. Sometimes the manipulation occurred through outright deception and things like false miracles like in the case of Jim Jones. Perfectly possessed people are extremely persuasive and have an uncanny ability to manipulate people into engaging in all kinds of evil and destructive activities. This was one of the biggest factors present in the life of Jeffrey Epstein, who was able to manipulate people with unbelievable ease. He not only manipulated the victims of his sadistic sexual abuse but also manipulated many of his business partners, including Les Wexner. Steven Hoffenberg, former CEO of Towers Financial Corporation, had this to say about Epstein,

---

22   Sean Reveron, The Grim Story of the Chicago Rippers, www.cvltnation.com, Jan 26, 2017
23   United States Holocaust Memorial Museum
24   Scott A. Bonn Ph.D., If Not a Serial Killer, Then What Is Charles Manson? A fanatical cult leader, Manson ordered his followers to kill., *Psychology Today*, https://www.psychologytoday.com/us/blog/wicked-deeds/201403/if-not-serial-killer-then-what-is-charles-manson

> He's got a gift that's extraordinary where he controls the people he meets and manipulates them totally with his charisma. You can't grasp the magnitude of this controlling effect. Jeffrey Epstein was able to control and manipulate people in an extreme method. That was typical Jeffrey Epstein.[25]

This was definitely the case with many of the serial killers I profiled who had no problem manipulating their victims into compromising situations which would ultimately lead to their deaths. H.H. Holmes was especially skilled at manipulation and getting people to do his bidding, especially Benjamin Pietzal. Ted Bundy's charisma helped him to manipulate his victims into feeling sorry for him so as to get the woman to get near his car where he would bludgeon them and kidnap them and eventually murder them. Robin Gecht was easily able to manipulate his three associates into murder, torture, sexual mutilation, and devil worship. Additionally, very many of the serial killers I have written about here and others I have not have stated on many occasions that their killing had a lot to do with their desire to completely control other people, or completely "possess" them as both Jeffrey Dahmer and Ted Bundy stated so clearly.

The greatest examples of this however come from the cult leaders I profiled as well as Adolf Hitler. Even Aleister Crowley was able to gain many followers through manipulation and brainwashing who he led into the darkness of black magic and depraved sex magic rituals. The ability of Jim Jones to manipulate his followers was very profound, so profound that in the end, the majority of his followers freely killed themselves and their own children on his orders. A larger scale example of this is of course Adolf Hitler who basically hypnotized a whole nation into going along with his diabolical plan of mass murder. I sometimes think about all the Nazi officials involved in the Holocaust; the number was in the thousands. All of these people were basically convinced that what they were doing was the right thing and if not, they were just too fearful of the repercussions to speak up. I think it is safe to say that the vast majority were true believers in the Nazi cause and this is very frightening when we consider just how easily these people were deceived and manipulated by Adolf Hitler and his diabolic masters. Very many of these Nazi's were Catholic for goodness sakes, they grew up with the sacraments and mass and the catechism. Yet they willingly and enthusiastically engaged in the most depraved forms of mass murder and human degradation imaginable.

Perfectly possessed people sometimes gain large followings of people who they then intentionally deceive, manipulate, control and lead astray. I already mentioned Adolf Hitler, who is probably the greatest example of this concept. When I was profiling Hitler, I mentioned the fact that he was such a gifted orator that he was able to hold his audiences "spell bound" and hanging on his every word. I also see this concept at work in people like Margaret Sanger who had quite a large following and was able to manipulate woman the world over that abortion and birth control were not only not evil, but morally necessary! Turning evil into good and good into evil is one of the clearest signs that a diabolical intelligence is at work.

There are also people like Oprah or Sylvia Browne who lead modern day society astray into evil and new age style religious teachings. There are people like Lennon, Marx, Fidel Castro, Fredrich Nietzsche, Martin Luther, Mohammad, Joseph Smith, Arius and the list goes on and on of people who have manipulated and deceived large groups of people and led them into various forms of evil. Not one of the people I have listed lead others to truth, but instead to error and deception and primarily away from the protective embrace of the Catholic Church. Making evil good and good evil was also at work in the life of Martin Luther who labeled the holy Catholic Church as evil and corrupt and the vicar of Christ, the anti-Christ. Who then promoted his false and destructive heresies as divine truth. For good reason the popes of that time correctly labeled Martin Luther as a true Anti-Christ. I am not saying that every person who has a large following is perfectly possessed, however it is definitely one of the signs of a perfectly possessed person that they are easily able to manipulate and deceive varying groups of people and lead them into sin, error, false teaching, and the ultimately hell and eternal damnation. This concept will be one of the primary characteristics of the Anti-Christ, as we know he will lead a good portion of humanity astray.

5. Enslavement

"A few hundred years ago they started to develop a banking structure system which would control the human race to **enslave** them."
– Ronald Bernard

Epstein and Ghislaine Maxwell fed **sex slaves** iced tea and fruit to keep them 'prepubescent-thin'[26]

---

26   Jon Lockett, FORCED TO STARVE Epstein and Ghislaine Maxwell fed sex slaves ice tea and fruit to keep them 'prepubescent-thin', Virginia Giuffre claims, The U.S. *Sun*, September 21, 2020.

As for the other family witnesses, Squeaky, Sandy and the others, "all of them sounded like a broken record on that witness stand. They all have the same thought, they use the same language, each one was a carbon copy of the other. They are all still totally **subservient and subject** to Charles Manson. They are his X'd-out **slaves.**[27]

This is related to some of the other signs I have listed already, specifically fear and manipulation. However, enslavement or better put subjugation goes a step farther than manipulation, coercion or having people fear you. What I can say about this is that perfectly possessed people have a unique ability to enslave people and they can often be found to engage in this activity. According to Webster's the definition of subjugation is "the action of bringing someone or something under domination or control." In the context of perfect possession this can take many different forms. What it basically entails is that the perfectly possessed are able to bring people completely under their control and in various different ways.

Some of the things the serial killers have done would qualify as enslavement, such as kidnapping people and forcing them to do various evil things before their ultimate demise. What is portrayed in the movie The Silence of the Lambs would be a great example where serial killer buffalo bill abducts woman, enslaves them in an old dried out well and then murders them. The case of Elizabeth Smart or even the recent case of Jaymie Closs, both of who were young girls who were kidnapped, and enslaved by their captors, but both eventually finding freedom. Those cases are just one form this can take, physical enslavement.[28] One of the best examples of diabolic physical enslavement that I could cite comes to us from the scriptures. I am of coarse speaking here of the Israelites, Gods own chosen people, being totally enslaved by the Egyptians. The good book makes it fairly clear what the mysterious power working behind the scenes on Pharaoh's behalf is, it is demonic in nature.

The much more disturbing form is when someone's soul is enslaved. This was almost certainly the case of the followers of Jim Jones and Charles Manson. Jones's followers underwent a long process of enslavement that culminated with the move to Jonestown in Guyana. Once Jones followers made that decision to follow Jones down there it basically sealed their fate. Really no one was allowed to leave Jonestown and even

27   Bugliosi, *Helter Skelter*
28   Jeffrey Epstein keeping sex slaves for himself and also seemingly always being surrounded by a harem of young beautiful woman who were likely enslaved to Epstein in various ways.

if anyone wanted to, they were too terrified to speak up to their desire. Jones's followers were so enslaved to him that the vast majority did not hesitate when Jones ordered the mass suicide. Neither did Charles Manson's followers hesitate when he ordered them to slaughter Sharon Tate and multiple other people in an effort to start a race war Manson called Helter Skelter. Neither did Marshall Applewhite's followers hesitate when he ordered that diabolic mass suicide.[29]

Who can doubt that a great part of Nazi Germany was enslaved to Adolf Hitler? Adolf Hitler enslaved the hearts and minds of the people of Germany with the erroneous notion that he was their messiah and would lead them to greatness in the form of a 1000 year Third Reich. In reality he led them to ultimate destruction both physically and spiritually. In order for those Nazi's to commit the atrocities they did under orders from Hitler and Himmler, they would have had to of been totally enslaved to their masters. The process of enslavement of Nazi Germany did not happened overnight either, this was a long process of Adolf Hitler slowly gaining more and more power over time coupled with his fiery speeches, huge open air demonstrations, and diabolic propaganda.

Really the same concept can be found in numerous other murderous world leaders who enslave their people under various forms of oppressive government. Communism being the best example by far of this concept. The oppressive control of communism, the religious persecution, the lack of free press, controlled movement, etc., was all meant to bring the people of a country under the total slavery of the state.

There are also many forms of modern slavery that I could cite, and this is in addition to the older forms of slavery where human beings were literally bought and sold and forced into hard labor. Believe it or not forced labor slavery is still a problem in the world, it still goes on to this day. People are still bought and sold and treated as sub-human, like animals. I will quickly note that this is one very important aspect to understand. The bringing of human beings down to the level of animals through various means, slavery being among them, is utterly diabolic in its nature.

There are two additional forms of modern-day slavery I would like to cite, the first is something called debt-based slavery. This can also take various different forms. It can take the form in third world countries of someone having to borrow money from a wealthy person only to be enslaved as indentured servants until the money is paid back, which was also a common

---

29   Almost without exception cult leaders are able to enslave their followers in various ways which eventually leads their destruction.

practice in ancient times. But it can also take the form of being enslaved to debt with no way out, which is a very common and widespread phenomena in modern westernized countries, especially the United States. It can be people opening up multiple credit cards with huge interest rates and being enslaved by the temptation to continue spending with no way out in sight or it can look like buying a car with a huge interest rate so that it takes many years to pay off, all the while that extra money could have gone to much more worthwhile and holy things. Even the United States itself is essentially enslaved in debt, over 100 trillion of unfunded liabilities are essentially unpayable. Debt based slavery is very insidious and is not even thought about as slavery by many people, however if you really look at the effects of going deep into debt and what it does, how there is often no way out except to ruin one's credit and declare bankruptcy, it becomes clear this is a form of enslavement. Modern student loans that young people are enslaved by is another great example. Enslavement to drugs is another great example.[30]

The other disturbing modern-day example I wanted to cite is something called human trafficking or sex trafficking. It is when people are totally enslaved by a captor and then sold into forced sex labor, or another type of labor, but most often it is done for forced prostitution.

There are people out there who are responsible for these types of enslavement. Suffice it to say, when one human being voluntarily and purposely acts to intentionally enslave or subjugate another human being so as to de-humanize them and kill their spirit, it is a great indication of diabolic activity and intelligence at work.

6. They Are Viewed As Messiahs, Saviors, and Gods Or They View Themselves This Way.

"I think at one point I really believed he was Jesus Christ,"[31]

"I happen to know I'm the Messiah… I know that I am God the Messiah"

– Rev Jim Jones

"I am the embodiment of God. I am divinity and humanity combined."

– Cult Leader, Wayne Curtis Bent

---

30   The drug cartels and drug dealers the world over count on enslavement to make money. In fact, the whole drug business is based on enslavement. People who become addicted to drugs, especially heroin, crack and meth are essentially enslaved to the drug and as a result enslaved to the drug dealer.

31   Leslie Van Houten, member of Manson Cult who participated in the murder of Sharon Tate

This is perhaps one of the greatest and clearest indications of perfect possession, mental illness notwithstanding.[32] This trait is present in a remarkable number of people that I profiled in this book. The previously mentioned Ted Bundy is a clear example and even though he did not claim to be God or a messiah, he stated in the clearest terms possible that when he killed people it made him feel like God and that this was a primary reason for his murderous spree. What Bundy states here is blatantly diabolic and runs as follows,

> "You feel the last bit of breath leaving their body. You're looking into their eyes. A person in that situation is God!"[33]

When you pair up the two concepts of wanting to be like God or claiming to be God or feeling like God and murder, it is the clearest indication of diabolic intelligence possible. I also mentioned in an earlier chapter that a man named Samuel Little who has confessed to upward of 90 murders said he committed these atrocities at the behest of God. This is also the case with the so-called Yorkshire Ripper, Peter Sutcliffe who claimed to hear the voice of God commanding him to kill prostitutes. When serial killers claim to be doing the work of God and claim to hear the voice of God we can be just about assured that this is diabolic activity. It also makes the serial killer seem to be some type of prophet or messiah like figure doing the work of God. I cannot stress to the reader just how blasphemous and diabolic it is for someone to claim to be working at the behest of God or claim to be God while violently murdering people, this phenomenon is indeed a clear sign of perfect possession.

Even though this trait is present in some of the serial killers I profiled, there are no greater examples of this than the cult leaders and some world leaders. As I said in the conclusion of the last chapter many cult leaders view themselves as messiahs and savior's or even God and their followers view them this way also. The example of Jim Jones proclaiming that he was God and messiah is one of the best examples. However, Charles Manson, Marshall Applewhite, Jeff Lundgren, Warren Jeff's, David Koresh, and L. Ron Hubbard all claimed to be some sort of messiah, savior, prophet or God himself. I believe Charles Manson claimed to be both God and the devil and L Ron Hubbard is venerated to this day as a God

---

32   What I mean is that very many people suffering from mental illness and delusions sometimes claim to be God or Christ.

33   Adriana Belmonte, 12 of the most despicable quotes attributed to the world's most notorious serial killers, Insider, https://www.insider.com/disturbing-infamous-serial-killer-quotes-2018-6

like figure in the cult of scientology. I also quoted the LA Times above in which according to unsealed court documents Jeffrey Epstein believed himself to be a demigod.

On a larger scale we see this at work glaringly in the life of Adolf Hitler who from a very early age believed himself to be the savior of Germany and later in life had other people and eventually a whole nation believing he was the savior and messiah of Germany. We also see this in people like Margaret Sanger who many people believed was some kind of a messiah or savior for a woman's supposed right to choose death for the baby's in their wombs. This was even present in a particular way in the life of Aleister Crowley who was viewed as a type of messiah or prophet for the new age of Horus that he proclaimed through his *Book of the Law*.

The theological reason why this is the case in the lives of people who may have been perfectly possessed is fairly clear from the scriptures. Despite the fact that theologians differ widely among themselves as to the ultimate reason for the angelic fall from heaven, scripturally it is clear that the entity named Satan or Lucifer in some way desired to be God or be like God. There are many examples of this the first coming right away in the book of Genesis where the serpent tells the woman that Adam and Eve would "be like Gods knowing good and evil"[34]. Then we have the commentary in the books of Isiah and Ezekiel, commentary which Tertullian, Origen, Jerome, and Augustine thought referred allegorically to Lucifer.

The book of Ezekiel starting in verse 1 states

> The word of the LORD came to me: Son of man, say to the prince of Tyre: Thus, says the Lord GOD: Because you are haughty of heart, you say, **"I am a god!** I sit on a god's throne in the heart of the sea!"[35]

Similarly, the book of Isiah states,

> How you have fallen from the heavens, O Morning Star, son of the dawn! How you have been cut down to the earth, you who conquered nations! In your heart you said: "I will scale the heavens; Above the stars of God* I will set up my throne; I will take my seat on the Mount of Assembly, on the heights of Zaphon. I will ascend above the tops of the clouds; **I will be like the Most High!"**[36]

34   Genesis 3:5, NAB, USCCB, https://bible.usccb.org/bible/genesis/3
35   Ezekiel 28:1-2 NAB, USCCB, https://bible.usccb.org/bible/ezekiel/28
36   Isiah 14:12-14 NAB, USCCB, https://bible.usccb.org/bible/isaiah/14

Then we turn to the Gospel of Luke where Satan offers Christ all the kingdoms of the world and all their glory if he will just bow down and worship him, the key word being worship. This verse especially shows that Satan desires to be worshipped as a God. Finally, we see it in the very name of the Archangel Michael, translated into Latin as Quis Ut Deus, meaning Who is like God. The very name of Michael is very widely believed to be a question or a rebuke to Satan from Michael because Satan wanted to be like God. The scripture is also chalk full of warnings that false messiahs and false Christs, totally in league with Satan will come upon the scene and have already come upon the scene and who can really doubt that when the final Anti-Christ does come, the one totally under the control of the devil that he will claim to be God or Christ himself.

Lastly, we see this concept at play in the absolute plethora of false God's that are talked about in both the old and new testaments. The scripture is clear that the actual entities behind these false deities are diabolic in nature. This also demonstrates that it is a foundational part of the diabolic psychology and nature that in some way they wish to be Gods, be like Gods and are desirous of worship, homage and sacrifice.

7. THEY DISPLAY MANY OF THE SIGNS OF PSYCHOPATHY, SOCIOPATHY, OR ANTI-SOCIAL PERSONALITY DISORDER.

"They knew. They knew the taxpayers would bail them out. **They weren't being stupid; they just didn't care.**"
— Mark Baum, The Big Short

"I've never felt sorry for anything I've done… I'm not looking for forgiveness and I'm not repenting."
— Richard Kuklinski, the Ice Man, Mafia Hitman

"I don't feel guilty for any of it. I feel less guilty now than I've felt at any time in my whole life… I am in the enviable position of not having to feel any guilt.
— Ted Bundy

This is a sign and symptom that is going to contain many subcategories as psychopathic personality disorder displays many signs and symptoms in itself. Perfectly possessed people usually display all the classic signs of what is known as anti-social personality disorder, or what used to be called psychopathy. What this comes down to is the perfectly possessed have a complete lack of empathy, or a callous unconcern for the feelings and pains of other people. Another way to describe this would be to say that the perfectly possessed display extreme cold-heartedness, or a total and complete lack of any love or warmth. I could also say that the perfectly possessed are very often mean, **cruel** and abusive, sexually, physically, and emotionally, to their fellow human beings, but especially to children and the elderly.[37]

Displaying signs of psychopathy also means the person would have a compete lack of guilt or personal responsibility when they harm someone and also a sense of ruthlessness, narcissism, and selfishness. An ability to compulsively lie and deceive without the least hint of feeling any guilt for this. Also, a general lack of emotion, embarrassment, shame, and a complete lack of genuine love and tenderness. The "PCL" or psychopathy checklist describes psychopaths as emotionally shallow. Malachi Martin in writing about Jay Beedem stated that Jamsie,

> "had never seen Jay Beedem display an emotion. Nothing from inside. He had never even seen him really laugh."[38]

When you take away empathy, guilt, fear, warmth and other emotions you are left with a disgusting sense of inhumanness. The ability to feel empathy and love and also feel bad (guilt) when we hurt someone are things that make us uniquely human and psychopaths generally lack these things in totality. To sum it up I could say that perfectly possessed people show signs of inhumanness. The diabolic entities of course have no empathy and no love. They did at one time and the good angels do now, the demons however have completely corrupted themselves and are now filled with implacable hatred. Not only are they filled with hatred, but they also take pleasure in the destruction of human beings, a trait we see very clearly in some serial killers, cult leaders, and murderous world leaders. Psychopaths are also often described as not being capable of feeling fear in situations where normal human beings would be fearful. This is also generally true of the fallen angels although there are exceptions. The fallen angels are known to show dread fear when they are confronted with the fact of their inevitable eternal punishment in the fires of hell and they also can show fear when faced with rebuke from God himself or by the likes of the Virgin Mary or St. Michael the Archangel. There have also been many exorcists who have stated that generally it is the demons who fear them, not the other way around.

---

37   Cruelty is an absolute hallmark of the perfectly possessed, they all display this trait whether in public or private.

38   Martin, *Hostage to the Devil*

A sense of inhumanness has also been described in other ways One of the best ways I have heard this described is that the perfectly possessed have a certain alienness to them, this being the way Malachi Martin used to describe them when being interviewed by Art Bell on Coast to Coast AM. Martin once said that the perfectly possessed "breath alienation" and that he avoids them like the pest. In other places this has also been described as a coolness, or total lack of warmth or discernable love. For example, an article on diabolical phenomena on fisheaters.com, a Catholic web site, describes them like this:

> "there is the even more frightening phenomenon of those who are "perfectly possessed," people whose bodies have not only been overtaken by the Evil One or his minions, but who've consciously, of their own free will, given over their souls to him. They typically appear generally normal to the eye, but the sensitive can detect an "otherworldly" quality to them, a **darkness** about them, a **coldness**, a **lack of true charity** and **true warmth**. They may not be even able to name what is wrong, but just have a **sense of trepidation or fear**, or experience an **inner "chill"** when encountering the perfectly possessed.[39]

The examples I could give of this concept from the people I profiled are numerous, but probably one of the most chilling and appalling statements for that matter that's shows a clear lack of empathy and a callous disregard for human life came from Ted Bundy who said

> "I'm as cold a motherfucker as you've ever put your fucking eyes on. I don't give a shit about those people."[40]

This is basically the essence of what we are talking about here, and the reader can be sure that all the serial killers I profiled as well as Jim Jones, Aleister Crowley and Adolf Hitler basically felt the same way about their fellow humans, and this is the way the diabolic entities feel about human beings. To quote Bundy, they don't give a shit about those people, or about us, they only seek our total ruin and destruction, during this life and in eternity.

This is also a trait that was most certainly present in the life of Jeffrey Epstein. One of Epstein's victims' attorneys, a man named Spencer Kuvin had this to say about Epstein,

39   Tracy Tucciarone, *Oppression, Obsession, and Possession*, Fisheaters.com
40   Berit Brogaard D.M.Sci., Ph. D, The Making of a Serial Killer Possible social causes of psychopathology. *Psychology Today*, Dec 7, 2012, https://www.psychologytoday.com/us/blog/the-superhuman-mind/201212/the-making-serial-killer

"He was a narcissist; he had no ability to feel empathy and saw himself as the master of puppets"[41]

Even more disturbing than this quote is what one of Epstein's victims said about him. In the documentary Filthy Rich, Epstein abuse victim Sarah Ransome states,

"I was trapped from the very first day. I think I was in such shock because I think the more he saw you being damaged the more he enjoyed it, the more it excited him."[42]

Jeffrey Epstein being excited by and enjoying the fact that he was psychologically and sexually damaging his victims is the absolute definition of cruelty, ruthlessness and evil.

The previously mentioned Jimmy Saville is also another example of someone who was very likely perfectly possessed who displayed very many signs of being a psychopath. It has been confirmed from hundreds of victims that Saville brutally sexually assaulted and raped them and it also has been confirmed by different victims in different places that Saville was most certainly a Satanist. When a psychological profile of Saville was done after his many depravities came to light the diagnosis was psychopathy,

His behavior — mania, dissociation with his victims, split personalities evinces something psychologists call a "dark triad of personality characteristics." Psychologist Oliver James wrote that Savile was likely afflicted with **psychopathy**, Machiavellianism and narcissism. "Such people often are able to slide effortlessly between personas. ... Savile must have had a fantastical inner life — grandiose, wild and desperate."[43]

Whenever we see a totally callous disregard for human life, like we see in the lives of the people I profiled that is paired with a total lack of guilt and indifference towards human life and an almost glee for their murderous attitude and actions, it is a definite sign of diabolic activity and intelligence at work. Whenever we see a total lack of empathy, love, and genuine warmth, and instead see a total lack of emotion when they hurt or kill someone and even a marked hatred in place of empathy, it is a sure sign of diabolic intelligence at work in the person displaying these traits.

41   *Filthy Rich*, Netflix Documentary
42   Ibid
43   Terrence McCoy, How BBC star Jimmy Savile allegedly got away with abusing 500 children and sex with dead bodies, *Washington Post*, June 27, 2014

I would however like to make one final note and that is that I am in no way postulating that every person who displays signs of sociopathy or psychopathy is perfectly possessed. There is a very real possibility that psychopathy is a real psychiatric disorder caused by defects in a certain part of the brain or caused by environment. In these cases this needs to be treated by professionals like any other mental disorder. Where a problem comes along, theologically that is, is the belief that God has created every human being with a conscience, a built-in conscience that they can know right from wrong, good from evil. What psychiatrists tell us however is that people with genuine psychopathy have no conscience, no guilt. I guess I have a bit of an issue with this from a theological perspective. I think every case of this needs to be looked at singly. I think there could be cases in which a defect in the brain or growing up in a violent environment could leave a person lacking some vital emotions and in this case I believe they can be treated. I also believe however that there are people who are born totally normal, who from a very young age decide for whatever reason to choose evil, and they continue to choose evil throughout their whole life. Then when they commit some atrocity and take pleasure in it they are labeled as a psychopath. In reality, they are simply evil human beings that have intentionally chosen evil over good, who have chosen to align themselves with the devil despite knowing this was wrong, it is these people who are the perfectly possessed.

8. Sometimes They Are Extremely Sophisticated, Brilliant, and Smart, People.

> "Sometimes his intelligence is astonishing… miraculous political intuition, devoid of all moral sense, but extraordinarily precise."
> – OSS Report on Adolf Hitler

> "His unique mind is what attracts the world's smartest people to his home," said one Epstein dinner guest, which could be put another way: I thought Epstein was brilliant because he associated with me.
> – Los Angeles Times

> Bundy's brilliant mind made him a master predator, with his abductions being as well planned as a military action.[44]

Perfectly possessed people can sometimes be extremely sophisticated and intelligent people. This is a concept we see at work in some of the

---

44   Biographics, Ted Bundy: Profile of a Serial Killer, Jan 10, 2018, https://biographics.org/ted-bundy-biography-profile-serial-killer/

serial killers, Ted Bundy is a good example, but also people like Edmund Kemper, who has displayed many signs of being possessed and who has an IQ on par with that of a genius.[45] I could again mention Jay Beedem who Malachi Martin said was an extremely talented salesman, speaking many languages. Even Jeffrey Dahmer was his IQ was tested came to a score of 145, very high indeed.

As the quote states above Adolf Hitler was known to be very intelligent, sometimes preternaturally so. So intelligent that he was able to come from nothing and rise to the height of power, almost taking over the whole of Europe. Cult leaders sometimes display this trait as well although it is related to many of the other traits I have listed thus far. Cult leaders are intelliugent enough to gather for themselves large followings of people who they are then able to subjugate, and part of this has to do with the fact that they are intelligent enough to be able to manipulate and control people with ease, which was mentioned in no.4.

Why this is the case theologically is fairly clear. Diabolical entities have an angelic nature and it is clear from theology that these beings have an intelligence and intellect that far exceeds our own. They are able to process information in the blink of an eye, at the speed of thought. They can take in whole areas of information and learn them at once, that is if they do not already know it from it being infused into them upon their creation. The way their intellect works is they have what are called co-natural infused intelligible species or forms. These species or forms contain whole areas of knowable things. The angels can access *all* of the information contained inside one of these species all at once, knowing all there is to know in them all at once. The higher the angelic nature the less forms or species they have and the more knowledge is contains in one form. So the higher angels know more and can think about more and do more all at once. Additionally, because of their knowledge of the universe, cause and effect, human nature ect theyv are sometimes able to accurately predict what will happen in the future as I explained in an earlier chapter.

When one of these entities has totally enslaved and possessed a person it comes out in their personality and their interactions in everyday life. That is why it seems that some perfectly possessed people are extremely

---

45   Edmund Kemper was an exceedingly evil individual. From a very young age he displayed signs of extremely high intelligence, but his mother subjected him to severe abuse, locking him in a dark basement all alone for many nights. At age 15 he killed both his grandparents and was sent to a California state hospital for the criminally insane. When he got out, he killed 6 hitchhiking co-eds, decapitating them, then having sex with their dead bodies. He would save the severed heads of his victims and have sex with these as well. His spree ended when he killed his own mother and her friend on Good Friday, 1973 and subsequently turned himself in.

intelligent, because it is really the personality and intellect of the diabolic entity coming through, which shows in their higher intellect and intelligence.

9. They Are Sometimes Extremely Wealthy, Successful, and Powerful.

"I had information from various sources that judges, law enforcement, prosecutors, attorneys, doctors and many many prominent individuals including actors, actresses, professional football and baseball players are involved in this type of activity."[46]

This is a trait that is certainly not present in every perfectly possessed person but is present in some of them. Father M, Malachi Martin, and Father Steffon were very clear on this point.

I already spoke about this in great detail in a prior chapter, so I will not delve too much into it now except to say that it is important to understand that this is partially the case because perfectly possessed people are sometimes placed in positions of great power and wealth so as to influence societies towards evil. Below I will profile a quote about the 2008 financial crisis. I think many Americans are under the impression that the root cause of this crisis was greedy bankers and while this may be partially true, it does not tell the whole story.

When one really sits down and thinks about the financial crisis it becomes clear that this event caused a great deal of destruction to the global financial system and societies in general, *destruction* being the key word. One of the clearest calling cards of the diabolic is destruction, and at it core this is what the 2008 financial crisis was all about. It was about very powerful people in the global banking system, that very well may be perfectly possessed causing destruction the world over and destroying countless lives, financially. This is just one example I could give.

The truth is that there are perfectly possessed people who are wealthy and powerful not only in the financial sector but in many other facets of society as well. The entertainment industry, the healthcare industry, the judiciary, the political world and even in religion. I can look at any of these industries and point out to you the reader specific instances of destruction and evil caused by powerful people in these industries. This is all done in coordination and at the behest of the devil.

---

46   Ted Gunderson, former head of the FBI field office in Los Angeles

Malachi Martin, while he was being interviewed by Art Bell on Coast to Coast AM once said that all perfectly possessed people are successful in one way or another, but only because they have entered into a contract with diabolical forces and for the specific reason to influence society towards evil.

10. THEY SOMETIMES ADMIT THEY ARE IN LEAGUE WITH THE DEVIL AND POSSESSED BY HIM.

"it felt like being possessed by something awful and alien."

– Ted Bundy

"I am beyond good and evil. I will be avenged. Lucifer dwells within us all"

– Nightstalker, Richard Ramirez

"I think I may be possessed by demons."

– Dennis Rader, BTK killer

This is present in many of the people I profiled and wrote about in earlier chapters. We have H. H. Holmes declaring that he was born with the devil in him. There was Jefferey Dahmer who admitted to his attorney that he felt like the devil and questioned whether or not it was an evil force that caused him to commit his crimes. There is Ted Bundy who told many of his interviewers about some kind of "alien" entity inside him that possessed him.[47] There is of course BTK killed Dennis Rader who clearly said he was possessed by demons and also The Son of Sam, David Berkowitz who also said he was possessed.[48] We also see this at work in people like Richard Ramirez who said he was a servant of the devil and Henry Lee Lucas who said the same. The recent arrest of the Golden State killer confirms this concept as he told investigators that he had something inside of him that forced him to kill. The recent case of Samuel Little who told investigators God had put him on earth to kill people.

Charles Manson also at one time said he was the devil as did one of the people who helped kill Sharon Tate, declaring that he was there to do the devil's work. Railway killer Angel Hernandez also said he allowed the devil to rule his life. Sometimes this takes the form of the person declaring that they are a monster or have a malevolent force within them that is unidentifiable. Arthur Shawcross said this exact thing when he declared he had something inside of him that made him kill. I could give the reader many more examples.

---

47   Bundy also once said, "Sometimes I feel like a vampire and I like to kill"

48   Berkowitz, in one of his letters to the police also wrote "I am a monster."

Why this is the case is I admit a mystery to me. On the one hand many perfectly possessed people are totally hidden in society, so as to better work their evil, on the other we have some serial killers who committed horrific crimes fully admitting that they are possessed and in league with the devil which definitely seems to be a contradiction in the nature and way diabolic activity of this sort works in the world. The only two ideas I have to answer this perplexing question are that the devil is just too proud of his handy work to not admit this was his doing, that or some mysterious decree of God has said that we as a society must be warned as to the true nature and intelligence that is behind some of these diabolical killers, so as to better combat it with prayer and actions of the church.

11. THEY ARE COMPULSIVE LIARS AND MARKED BY FALSITY.

"because there is no truth in him. When he tells a lie, he speaks in character, because he is a liar and the father of lies."
– John 8:44

In no 4 I said one of the signs of perfect possession is the ability to easily manipulate, coerce and get people to do their evil bidding. While this is clearly true, and this is sometimes accomplished through deception I would go further and say perfectly possessed people very often have their whole lives marked with deception and lies. They compulsively lie for no other reason than to lie and deceive people so as to lead them to destruction. If they tell the truth it is usually only a half truth and this to better deceive further down the line. I have personal experience with a person who was like this, although I don't believe this person was perfectly possessed, he was a compulsive liar. I would catch him in lies about the most mundane and inconsequential things. Things there was no reason to lie about, yet he did. This person was a salesman, and very often would lie to and deceive his customers and prospective clients. The man through and through was just a liar, he lied about everything. The disturbing thing that went along with this is that if anyone decided to call him out on a lie you would feel this tension in the room and see him get flustered and lie even further to get out of the original lie.

This is the way perfectly possessed people are, they lie and lie and then lie some more and have absolutely no qualms about doing so. The examples of this are myriad in the people I profiled. When one looks at the life of the

Rev. Jim Jones you hardly cannot find one iota of truth anywhere. All one must do is turn on C Span and watch any number of congressional hearings where various government officials and politicians are lying through their teeth about crimes they have committed and then looking smug and arrogant about it. I can think of one very powerful political couple that has been around for a long time that displays this type of lying very prominently. As I said earlier the lying done by the perfectly possessed can be of the most mundane kind, yet it can also be of the most sophisticated kind. Perfectly possessed people can weave extremely elaborate deceptions that are very powerful and believable. This is another sign of what I am speaking about, the fact that the lies they tell seem to have some kind of power behind them, some kind of force so that you almost have to believe them.

The lies and deceptions that are present in modern society that have infected our minds have largely come from perfectly possessed people in entertainment, politics, the media, and the judiciary. A woman's right to choose death for her baby is one such very powerful lie. A person right to choose their own gender is another one, as is the supposed right of two homosexual people to get married. I could pick out any number of lies and deceptions that have been told over the past hundred years that have caused untold destruction, and evil.

From a theological perspective this sign is present in the perfectly possessed because the evil entities controlling these people are themselves through and through liars. Our Lord Jesus Christ labeled Satan as a liar and said there is no truth in him. Exorcists are warned not to engage in conversation with these entities precisely because of the danger of being deceived and exorcists can also attest to the fact that these entities are liars. Even in the literature on certain possession cases we see some possessing demons making proclamations and prophecies that have certainly not come true. It is no surprise then that the people who have totally chosen to serve the devil and do his work and are consequently perfectly possessed are total liars. These people lie and deceive for the purpose of leading mankind astray into sin, error and eventual destruction.

12. THE EYES ARE THE WINDOWS TO THE SOUL.

"Some have reported that at their first meeting Hitler fixated them with his eyes as if to bore through them."

– OSS Report on Hitler

"He turns around and looks at me and he came walking over and stuck his face up in my face and his eyes got like a snake's."
– Actor Jeff Fenholt on encounter with Charlie Manson

"I will never forget those eyes and that stare as long as I live.[49]

Before I list the last of the signs and symptoms of perfect possession, I would like to list the one physical symptom that is sometimes present in the perfectly possessed. That would be the fact that sometimes their eyes give away the true nature of the state of their soul and who they are possessed by. How this manifests itself is the fact that sometimes their eyes are unnaturally black or dark, lifeless, emotionless or even red in the center.

From the literature and many other sources I have read and researched there are multiple instances of truly evil people and possibly perfectly possessed people that there is something wrong or off or unnatural about their eyes. I keep bringing up Jay Beedem because this is really the only person in the literature that has been positively identified as being perfectly possessed and I think we can learn a great deal from this. It should be noted Jay Beedem is a real person who Malachi Martin actually knew and interacted with. In addition, many of the things Malachi Martin wrote and observed about Jay Beedem or John Beedem as he called him an interview with Art Bell, I have observed in some of the other people I have profiled. In the case of Jay Beedem, Jamsie Z's very first impression of Beedem's eyes and personality was a negative one, Martin writes:

> Jamsie concluded that his boss's eyes were completely closed to him. Jay Beedem laughed, glanced, conveyed meanings, and questioned him with his eyes, but all this seemed to be as revealing as images skipping across a film screen. There is no feeling there, thought Jamsie to himself. No real feeling. At least, I can't see any. Each smile and laugh was only on Beedem's mouth. He did not seem really smiling or laughing.[50]

And in an even more disturbing passage Martin writes,

> Beedem's eyes were blank. Really blank. No metaphor. They could have been made of colored glass, except that, unlike glass, they did

---

49   Rule, Ann; Rule, Ann. *The Stranger Beside Me*. Estate of Ann Rule in conjunction with Renaissance Literary & Talent. Kindle Edition. One of Bundy's almost victims describing a terrifying encounter in which Bundy almost killed her roommate in a dark alley.

50   Martin, *Hostage to the Devil*

not reflect the office or the objects around them or the light from the windows.[51]

Despite the fact that Jamsie could detect no feeling or warmth in Beedem's eyes, the one thing he did eventually detect there was a simmering hatred,

> Beedem was looking through him, Jamsie thought. Was that a look of hate and sneering contempt in Beedem's eyes?[52]

Aleister Crowley has been described many times as having dark and mesmerizing eyes and viewing certain photographs of him confirms this. I'll mention again that the accomplices of Robin Gecht warned police not to look into his eyes because he had the ability to control people through a simple glance. Jim Jones was described by childhood friend Donald Foreman as having "the deepest, darkest eyes." Jeffrey Dahmer's father Lionel Dahmer described Jeffrey Dahmer's eyes as being "dead." This incident occurred in 1978 after Dahmer killed his first victim in Ohio. Dahmer had been home alone during the killing and when Lionel came home after Dahmer had killed a young man, Lionel said Jeffrey's eyes looked dead.

The character of Ed O'Gribben in the previously mentioned book, *The Dark Sacrament*, who very likely was perfectly possessed was described as being,

> "a man with eyes so dark and penetrating that her immediate impulse was to reverse the car swiftly and flee the scene."[53]

From the same book Gary Lyttle who I spoke about earlier was described by Canon Lundrum as having a disturbing "old" or ancient look in his eyes. Serial killer David Allan Gore who brutally murdered 6 people in Florida and who was executed by lethal injection was described as having eyes that looked like the devil's eyes. Prosecutor Bob Stone who had direct contact with the killer said this about Gore,

> "I looked in his eyes. If the devil had eyes, that's what they'd look like, said former prosecutor Bob Stone who stood next to the serial killer as police dug up the bodies. **They were red in the center.** It was like a fire had come out of his eyes. **You could see all the way through em.** That was the strangest sight I ever saw. If there is a human that's got the devil in him, he's it."[54]

51   Ibid
52   Ibid
53   Kiely and McKenna, *The Dark Sacrament*
54   Daily Mail Reporter, 'He had devil eyes': Florida serial killer who preyed on women for his abusive sexual fantasies set to die, *Mail* Online, April 12, 2012

Even looking at photographs of people like Sung Cho, Charles Manson, Aleister Crowley, Richard Ramirez, Adam Lanza, Eileen Wiernoz and many others gives one the creeps, there is something dark and evil present in each one of these persons eyes that it easily confirmable by viewing their photographs. One very disturbing example of this that I discovered comes from a journalist named Stephen Michaud. Michaud along with Hugh Ayensworth spent months in the Florida State Prison interviewing Ted Bundy. The conversations between Michaud, Ayensworth and Bundy provide some of the most disturbing examples and proof of Bundy's possession, some of which I already quoted in the section on Bundy above. In the documentary produced by Netflix titled Conversations with a killer: The Ted Bundy Tapes, Michaud and Ayensworth note a very disturbing phenomena relating to Ted Bundy, they stated that whenever Bundy would start talking about the murders and really get going that his eyes would go absolutely black. Steven Michaud states,

> When he really got going his eyes went absolutely black. He had very blue eyes, but his eyes would go black.[55]

In the documentary "Have you seen Andy" which is about the disappearance of a .ten year old boy named Andy Puglisi from Lawrence, Massachusetts on August 22, 1976 it is said that one of the witnesses who saw the suspect and had an encounter with him described the suspect as having something very strange about his eyes. Additionally the filmmaker who made the documentary also went to see the suspect in prison and also said there was something very strange about the suspects eyes. I am of course talking about Wayne Chapman who was the primary suspect in Andy Buglisi's disappearance and was also a convicted child rapist and likely a child murderer. Viewing a mugshot of Chapman confirms this as there is something dead looking about his eyes, very similar to many of the other people I have mentioned.

Bundy's eyes also were described by some of his victims who survived his attacks as "eyes and face of stone."[56]

Lastly I would like to talk about a person who I learned about as a child, a story that I never forgot and that disturbed me for many years. In fact me learning about this man as a child was one of the reasons I decided to write this book, I took it as a sign, this one among many that I was supposed to write a book about this topic. The man I am speaking about

---

55   *Conversations With a Killer: The Ted Bundy Tapes*, Netflix Documentary
56   Laura Schultz, Hiding in Plain Sight: The Psyche of Serial Killers, *Crime Magazine*, June 10, 2010, http://www.crimemagazine.com/hiding-plain-sight-psyche-serial-killers

almost nobody has heard of yet he is a brutal child killer and an evil man. His name is Andrew Pixley and he raped, viciously beat, murdered and cannibalized two young girls aged 12 and 8. Pixley was found covered in the blood of his victims and claimed to not remember anything of the murders. Andrew Pixley was tried and convicted of murder and given the death penalty in the state of Wyoming. His attorneys attempted to file an appeal but Pixley refused and said he preferred to die. When he was sentenced to death, he laughed out loud in the court room. Shortly before he was executed Pixley renounced the Catholic faith. Andrew Pixley holds the record for the amount of time taken by an inmate to die in Wyoming's gas chamber. Whereas all other inmates were dead within 3 minutes or less, it took Pixley a full 6 minutes to die in the gas chamber. When one looks at Pixley's mug shot you can see that this man has very dark if not black eyes, a fact that thoroughly frightened a prison historian doing research late at night near the prison's gas chamber. In the tv series Ghost Stories narrated by Patrick Macnee, the prison historian states,

> "my flashlight drifted over, and I caught the **black eyes** of Andrew Pixley. As I looked deep into his eyes for the first time, I thought there is something different about this guy. I never thought about it before, ah, something evil, possessed, demonic. The instant I thought that, I swear to you I heard something, I didn't recognize it at first but behind me I heard the faint sound of crying. Not just crying, young girls crying and the sound of crying was coming from the gas chamber. I was scared to death."[57]

13. MURDER AND SUICIDE

> "You belong to your father the devil and you willingly carry out your father's desires. He was a murderer from the beginning."
> – John 8:44

> "For she had been given in marriage to seven husbands, but the wicked demon Asmodeus kept killing them off"
> – Tobit 3:8

One of the clearest signs of perfect possession is the presence of murder and suicide. Sometimes these are both present and we have a person commit some act of murder and then subsequently kill themselves as well. This is a symptom that is basically present in every person I profiled in chapters 11 and 12. All 4 serial killers I profiled murdered numerous people in the most brutal and horrific fashion imaginable. The number of victims attributable to U.S. serial killers varies widely. Some serial killers are responsible for only a few deaths and some are responsible for truly staggering numbers of murders. Ted Bundy for example was thought to have killed at least 30 people, but many believe the number is many more. Even more staggering is people like Gary Ridgeway and Samuel Little who both have murder victims that number above 50. It is easy to get desensitized to these numbers, however when you really stop to think about the evil committed by these people and the individual suffering of each one of their victims, it becomes horribly clear the true nature of the evil present in these murderers' lives.

In addition to traditional serial killers we have several other types of murderers present in this country. The first is the mass shooting killer of which we have many examples. People like Adam Lanza, Stephen Paddock, Nicholas Cruz and Omar Mateen, who murdered 49 people in an Orlando nightclub. Needless to say, I strongly suspect diabolical involvement in all of these cases.

Another type of murderer present in this country is one known as the professional contract killer. The most disturbing thing about these people is that many of them truly are professionals and have not been caught and are hence out there in society among us. The best example of this type of killer is the Ice Man, Richard Kuklinski who is believed to have killed upwards of 100 people. As I stated elsewhere in this book Kuklinski was a brutal and diabolical killer of the highest order. Law enforcement sources claimed he was one of the most dangerous people the state of New Jersey ever saw. What makes Kuklinski so diabolical is that this was a man who held a regular job and lived a totally normal family life and existence, yet according to law enforcement he is perhaps the most stone cold, ruthless, diabolical killer in la cosa nostra history. As I said the disturbing thing about this type of professional killer is there are many of them out there in society, as I write this, that you would not be able to know them if you passed them on the street, and I guess the same is true of serial killers as well. The FBI estimates that there are at any one time 25-50 active serial killers present in the United States.

In another chapter I already mentioned the fact that it is very possible for abortionists to be perfectly possessed. Performing an abortion is absolutely no different than killing an adult and in some respects, it is worse because the crime is committed against the most innocent and helpless among us, infant children. One abortionist I will mention who is known for his horrific crimes is Dr. Kermit Gosnell, a diabolical monster who found pleasure in snipping the spinal cords of new born infants and then storing their body parts in various places of his office. Ann McElhinney was one of three people who decided to investigate this case and subsequently wrote a book and produced a movie about Gosnell. Before doing this investigative work McElhinney was pro-choice and hadn't prayed in years. The evil of Dr. Gosnell disturbed her so much that she became pro-life and started praying again. This from an article in the Christian Post,

> "It made us sick to our stomach, made us nauseous, because of how evil, how dehumanized, how banal the evil was," McElhinney recalled. "In that circle of Hell that [Gosnell] created, people were laughing, people were jovial, people joked around, and there's something uniquely macabre, something uniquely diabolical about that." "I have definitely reengaged spiritually as a result of this case," she added. "It has brought me back to Jesus, to prayer, to the Bible, and to my faith. It is very much because of the absolute darkness of this story."[58]

Lastly, as far as serial murderers go there is another type that is also present in our country and other westernized countries and that is what is known as the trans-generational satanic cult. These cults are present in just about every state of the continental U.S. They are underground, meaning they completely blend in with society, they are not out there wearing dark makeup and performing rituals in the local cemetery. These are your serious and dedicated devil worshipers who have been brought into this religion by their parents or grandparents. These cults ritualistically sacrifice many people, including children. These cults are very often made up of professionals and these people are very rarely if ever brought to justice. The people they murder come from various sources which include runaways, homeless people, migrants, baby breeders, and abducted children.

Just about every single cult leader I mentioned was involved in murder as well, the darkest example of this coming from Jim Jones who ordered the murder and suicide of 900 some people and then took his own life at the end of it. The Charles Manson murders are well known for their horrific brutality as are the murders committed by Jeff Lungren and his followers. Marshall Applewhite's cult, Heaven's Gate, saw 39 people, including Applewhite commit suicide and the Branch Davidians led by

---

58   Brandon Showalter, Kermit Gosnell's 'House of Horrors' Abortion Crimes Exposed in New Book on 'America's Most Prolific Serial Killer', *Christian Post,* Jan 26, 2017

David Koresh lost 76 people in total, many of which died as a result of an intentional fire set to the Mt Carmel Center by cult members during an FBI siege, as well as an additional 6 federal agents that were shot and killed by cult members.

The evil and perfectly possessed world leaders are the people that have the potential to cause the most damage to mankind. Clear examples of this abound, the greatest obviously being Hitler. However, I also mentioned many other names in a previous chapter, total monsters like Stalin, Pol Pot, Mao, Saddam Hussein, Bashar Al Assad, Emperor Hirohito, and many more too numerous to list.

Theologically this is a very clear indication of diabolic activity, the desire to murder is of a thoroughly satanic nature. Jesus told us very clearly that the devil is a murderer and that his desire is to murder. The fact is that he hates human beings and wants to murder them, he who wanted to be like God wants to have the prerogative to take human life, which is what all murder really is, its about deciding to play God. Its about stealing away the right of God to give life and take it away and depute such rights for oneself. The quote from Ted Bundy in this respect is so significant,

> "You feel the last bit of breath leaving their body. You're looking into their eyes. A person in that situation is God!"

This statement from Bundy is so utterly satanic in its nature on so many different levels that it is breathtaking.

14. A DIABOLICAL FORCE IS LET LOOSE AFTER A PERSON DIES

> "It was as if, with the news of the priest's death, something dark and malefic was loosed."[59]

This is a fairly rare symptom but there are clear examples of it in the literature and in the accounts of cases of diabolical attack. I earlier mentioned the case of Andrew Pixley, who died in Wyoming's gas chamber, it seems now for years after his death there has been very strange phenomena around the prison where he was housed as well as in his cell and the gas chamber where he died. The reader can also consult the book the Dark Sacrament, Devilry on the Dingle Peninsula; Paranormal Witness, Episode 3: Rain Man; and The Haunted, Episode 19, Relative Evil. I will give a brief synopsis of each so the reader understands what this exactly entails.

---

59   Kiely and McKenna, *The Dark Sacrament*

Devilry on the Dingle Peninsula centers around something called generational evil. In this case the O'Gribben family and generational pedophilia. The story starts when a young woman meets Ed O'Gribben who is described as having "too dark, eyes," they eventually get married and the woman (Erin) moves into the O'Gribben family house on the Dingle Peninsula in Ireland. Also living in the house is Ed's mother who is extremely *cold* and *cruel* to Erin. Erin starts noticing very strange things around the house such as weird smells coming from Martha O'Gribben's room and the fact that the whole house seemed to be unnaturally cold despite having central heating. Soon old Martha passes away, and the paranormal activity around her room gets worse. Now Erin can smell raw sewage coming from the room as well as seeing black shadows around the house and having visitations in the middle of the night. In addition, when Erin goes into Martha O'Gribben's room she finds the windowsills filled with dead black flies, some of which have been torn apart.

This is the first example of this concept, Martha O'Gribben, from what is written about her in the book seems to have been a thoroughly evil person. Not only was she cruel, cold and mean to Erin, she also allowed all of her own children to be molested and raped as youngsters, sometimes by their own father. It is very possible this woman was perfectly possessed.

> "There was no discernable warmth in the woman. Her manner was as cool as the hand she offered in greeting. At first Erin felt sorry for her, interpreting the hostility in the old woman's eyes as resentment of her new daughter in law. Yet as time wore on, she was to discover that the woman's hatred went deeper- deeper by far than anything she could have imagined."[60]

We see that after she died, the demonic phenomena in the house intensified. Almost as if now that she is dead a force has been let loose.

> "When she died… well, it was then that all those strange things started happening."[61]

The story continues with the local parish priest, Father Lyons, who according to Erin is a very strange character who she gets a sick and uneasy feeling from sometimes. It seems that Ed O'Gribben and Father Lyons have a very close relationship, too close for Erin's liking. This culminates when one night she sees Ed and Father Lyons passionately kissing in the driveway of her home. When she confronts Ed about this, he acts like

60 Kiely and McKenna, *The Dark Sacrament*
61 Ibid

nothing is wrong at all and that it is perfectly normal, telling Erin that he has been gay lovers with Father Lyons for many years. It is further revealed by Ed that not only are he and Father Lyons lovers, but they are partners in crime in a massive child molestation ring. Ed tells Erin that he and Father Lyons have been molesting and raping children for years, the same children that they have been coaching on the local Gaelic football team which contains boys younger than 12. Even more appalling, Erin finds out later after she leaves Ed that Father Lyons, Ed, and Ed's brothers were all molesting Erin's child, 6-year-old Quentin, who Erin gave birth to a few years after marrying Ed.

What can we attribute this appalling level of evil too? The priest who eventually helped Erin be free of the demonic infestation gave the following opinion,

> "Father Ignatius McCarthy believes that Erin's case is a classic example of generational evil. He believes that, at some point in the families past, an unholy thing entered the O'Gribben line and persisted down the generations, tainting and corrupting all those born into that benighted house"[62]

When Erin questioned Ed about why he has been molesting children he states that it all began when his own father started "raping" him in the room that old Martha would eventually die in. Ed also states that when he got older his father then raped his 2 brothers and sister. After Ed's father died, Ed's mother, Martha would have "gentlemen callers" over to the house to have paid sex with all the O'Gribben children. Somewhere along this demented line Father Lyons entered the picture and became enmeshed in this evil as well. Erin being so disgusted with Father Lyons calls him a "travesty of a priest."

Shortly after Ed reveals the truth of all this evil to Erin she moves out of the old O'Gribben home and into a new home in County Donegal. One day she gets a call from her attorney who is working on a divorce settlement with Ed. The attorney informs her that Father Lyons has just been killed in a car accident. After Erin gets this news of Father Lyons death is when the diabolic infestation of her house and life takes a new and intense turn.

> "It was as if, with the news of the priest's death, something dark and malefic was loosed. Erin's lovely home, her retreat from the bleak past, was to become the focus of an evil presence."[63]

---

62   Kiely and McKenna, *The Dark Sacrament*
63   Ibid

Father McCarthy, the priest who helped Erin even confirmed himself that the paranormal activity occurring in Erin's home was a sign the priest was possessed. In talking to Erin about the black shadowy mass she had been seeing around her house Father McCarthy stated:

> "Yes. But it wouldn't be the priest himself, you understand. It's whatever it was that got into him while he was alive. It still has him in its clutches, you see."[64]

The second story comes from the show Paranormal Witness, Episode 3, Rain Man. This story has also appeared in many other places such as the show Unsolved Mysteries. The story centers around a young man named Don Decker and his recently deceased grandfather. Don Decker states that his grandfather was an exceedingly mean and cruel man who apparently physically and sexually abused Don Decker throughout most of his life. In the Paranormal Witness Episode, Don Decker states:

> "My grandfather was a very bad person. He was very, very abusive. He hurt me when I was growing up, and I was glad he was dead."[65]

Don was in the county jail when his grandfather passed and was released to attend the funeral. Decker subsequently stayed at the house of a family friend during this time, the home of Bob Kiefer. On the first evening that Don was in the Kiefer house, after he had attended his grandfather's funeral, he was attacked in the bathroom by a diabolical force. Decker reports that he went up to the bathroom to wash up for dinner when the atmosphere in the room completely changed and got cold, the lights also started to malfunction. Decker was then overcome by a feeling of fear and shortness of breath, which he describes as feeling all the air being sucked out of the bathroom and feeling like he was in a vacuum. It was at this time that he witnessed a vision of an old man, that he says looked like "the devil" that resembled his grandfather, and that was also wearing a crown on its head.

When Don Decker went downstairs to join the Kiefer's for dinner, Bob Kiefer noticed that Donnie had 3 very large scratches on his wrist. Shortly after this the whole atmosphere in the Kiefer house changed and water subsequently started pouring down the walls. Not only did water start pouring down the walls but it started raining down from the ceiling and then started to defy gravity and go upwards from the ground as

64   Ibid
65   *Paranormal Witness*, Season 1, Rain Man

well as travel horizontal throughout the house. During the course of the evening the Kiefer home would be the scene of some of the most intense paranormal activity ever recorded. Not only was it literally raining inside the Kiefer house but Don Decker, in the presence of at least 5 witnesses was levitated in the air and then thrown violently against the kitchen wall. It was after this incident that Decker says a "King's Crown" was gouged into his forearm. It should be noted that this demonic activity was not only witnessed by Bob Kiefer and his wife but also by Ron Van Wey, the landlord, and numerous police officers. All those present who witnessed these things stated that they were frightened and that they genuinely felt that they were in the presence of pure evil.

After this night at the Kiefer house Don Decker returned to the city jail to complete his sentence. It seems the phenomena surrounding Decker moved with Decker from the Kiefer and into the jail where it was witnessed by the warden and multiple correction officers. Don even had to be housed alone because one of his cell mates had become terrified while in the presence of Donnie. This story concludes when jail staff enlist a Rev. Blackburn, who I believe is or was a Catholic priest, to conduct an exorcism on Donnie. In the episode of Unsolved Mysteries that profiles this case Rev. Blackburn states that when he confronted Donnie and accused him of hoaxing this whole affair, the atmosphere in the room changed to one of pure evil. Additionally, it became cold, an extremely foul stench of rotting flesh permeated the room and it also started raining in the small room. Rev. Blackburn called it "the devil's rain." Thankfully the exorcism was successful, in this case I think because the possession of Decker was not very deeply rooted. Decker's grandfather however was an entirely different matter, and I believe, based on the available evidence that he was perfectly possessed by a very powerful devil, possibly Satan himself. Decker himself also believes this whole episode was caused by his grandfather, at the end of the episode he states,

> "I think my grandfather caused all this, so um, he hurt me when I was growing up, tried to hurt me after his death."[66]

The last story I would like to highlight to the reader comes from the show The Haunted, Episode 19, Relative Evil. This story centers around a family, Kimberly and Marc and their daughters who live in Connecticut. This story starts with all the traditional signs of a demonic infestation. It starts when Kimberly is meditating, and she sees a black form rush at her in her meditation. Subsequent phenomena include one of their children talking to an imaginary friend and their animals' acting strange as if someone is attacking them. Kimberly and Marc then decide to call in a well-known Connecticut paranormal investigator whose name is Bob Baker as well as a physic medium. When the medium comes to the house, she says she senses a very angry and mean old man. When Kimberly sees the medium mimicking some of her recently deceased grandfathers arm movements, Kimberly realizes that her grandfather has something to do with the infestation of her house.

Marc then reveals that Kimberlie's grandfather had recently passed away and that he passed away on Halloween of 2005. It is then revealed that just like Don Decker's grandfather, Kimberlie's grandfather was exceedingly mean and cruel. Kimberly and Marc have this to say about Kimberlie's grandfather:

> "My grandfather wasn't a very nice person. He was an abusive person and intimidated people into respecting him … Even to this day in his death, his children are still afraid of him."[67]

I earlier mentioned that sometimes perfectly possessed people are mean and cruel and that they are also feared by others, it seems this was the case with Kimberlie's grandfather. The subsequent things that are revealed about the grandfather however are far more disturbing when all of this is looked at in the same context, that of perfect possession. Kimberly then goes upstairs and says she felt something pulling her to her jewelry box which contained many pieces of jewelry handed down to her from her grandmother. When she looks at her grandmother's old jewelry, she is shocked to find an evil looking piece with a pentagram on it which immediately makes her feel sick like she wants to vomit. Kimberly then recalls certain peculiar things about her childhood and specifically the behavior of her grandparents. She recalls that there were areas of their grandparent's house that were totally off limits and also that one of her cousins saw a very large statue of a goat with horns in one of her grandparents rooms. This is coupled with the fact that Kimberly remembers her grandparents having larger groups of people over for so called parties, which had definite ritual overtones. Kimberly then went about talking to cousins and relatives and everything she suspected was confirmed. The conclusion being that her grandparents were deeply involved in a satanic cult, with her grandfather possibly being the high priest of said cult. The diabolic

---

67   *The Haunted*, Episode 19, Relative Evil

infestation of Kimberlie and Marc's home was only put to a halt by the actions of Bob Baker and Bishop Robert McKenna.

There is also a case that is detailed in the book "An Army in Heaven" by Kelley Jankowski. Jankowski is a hospice nurse and has had many very strange and supernatural encounters while working in Hospice. One of the most disturbing related by her is the case of an old woman who was very likely perfectly possessed. It should be noted that several exorcists as well as Ed Warren have stated that when they come across cases of very elderly people who are possessed that these are mostly cases of perfect possession, that the elderly people who are possessed have likely been possessed for most of their lives and the only reason the possession is sometimes discovered is during the process of death. Which brings me back to the story that Jankowski related in her book.

She relates the story of a very elderly woman who was dying in hospice. A different hospice nurse who was an atheist apparently had some very frightening encounters with the woman, including chairs moving across the room, lights flickering and her having the feeling that there "was a terrible presence in the room" so much so that she asked Jankowski to bring holy water to work and also asked for a priest to come. When the priest arrived and started doing the last rights the woman started screaming so loud that the entire hospice could hear it. Upon hearing the screaming Jankowski and the other nurse went running from the nurses desk into the room to see why she was screaming. Upon entering the room the woman had stopped screaming but was cold and clammy to the touch. The two nurses went back to the nurses station and the priest joined them about 5 minutes later.

When the priest joined them he informed the two nurses that the woman had passed away, at which time the nurse who was the atheist went to the room to check to make sure she had passed. The priest then showed the remaining nurse his crucifix which he had used to bless the woman. The crucifix had been inexplicably bent forward to give the impression that the figure on the cross was bowing forward, bowing to the woman or whoever was in the women. Upon hearing that little tidbit of information suddenly the intercom from the room in which the woman had just died turned itself on and a horrible deep and guttural voice boomed from the intercom screaming "Get your hands off of her, I'm not done with her yet!"

The other nurse who had been in the room came running back to the nurses station in tears and promptly left her shift. The nurse literally quit that day and never returned to the hospice, not even to get he personal effects. Needless to say the hospice kept the room in which the old woman had died vacant for quite some time because even after the womans body had been removed very strange phenomena continued to plague that room, which was room 12. The intercom and call bell would turn on at all hours of the day and night, there was a foul smell that permeated the room, furniture would be rearranged and the chairs would be stacked. This went on for months until another priest that was visiting the hospice did a minor exorcism in the room which apparently seemed to put an end to the diabolical phenomena. This story is just one more instance in which some kind of evil force is let loose after a person who was very likely perfectly possessed dies.

Because of the nature of this sign or indication of possible perfect possession, one can only make a determination after a certain person has died. Like I said at the beginning, this is a fairly rare sign and is not seen that often, despite the fact that there are concrete examples of this from the literature and case histories of diabolic activity. The reader will notice a common theme in the four people I mentioned (Martha O'Gribben, Father Lyons, Don Decker's grandfather, Kimberlie's grandfather), they all seemed to be thoroughly evil and cruel people, causing much suffering, fear, and pain for the people who had the displeasure of knowing them.

15. They Leave A Trail of Destruction, Evil, Sin, Suffering, and Death In Their Wake.

"they become highly **destructive** in society, almost a kind of insidious hard to put your finger on, but whatever that guy does, somethings up there."
— Father M, Mundelein Conference

The criminal activity Guzman allegedly directed contributed to the death and **destruction** of millions of lives across the globe through drug addiction, violence, and corruption.
— Attorney General Eric Holder

"He could exercise nearly irresistible power-and yet, all his actions would lead to **destruction** and death."[68]

"In my experience, these persons do not ever receive peace, and they leave behind them a trail of sorrow, solitude, and death."
—Father Gabriel Amorth

This is in effect, possibly the clearest indication of perfect possession. I will direct my readers to the very beginning of this book, in the introduction when I stated that this book is at its core about evil on a wide scale. I said that the people that are the primary topic of this book have perpetuated some very grave evils upon mankind, destruction on a wide scale. There is no greater example of this than the just mentioned El Chapo Guzman, leader of the Sinaloa drug cartel. Mr. Guzman, according to former Attorney General Holder is directly responsible for the destruction of millions of lives spanning the globe. This is what true evil looks like, this is what true diabolic activity looks like, this is what perfect possession looks like. I would urge my readers, if you want to learn about demonic activity and how it works in the world, read a book about the Mexican drug wars over the last 15 years and forego reading the latest book about possession and exorcism.

We could think about the serial killers I profiled and wrote about and the destruction that they were responsible for. Of course, they were responsible for the murder of dozens of people, but they also caused destruction in the lives of many other people as a result. The families of the victims and the ruination and fear they experienced, the sadness, heartbreak and even unforgiveness that goes along with that. The trial of Jeffrey Dahmer and the victims' family's statements at the end bring this aspect out clearly for any one with thick enough skin to watch these poor families break down and even become hysterical in open court. The whole community as well being paralyzed with fear at the thought of a demented killer on the loose. I often think about the summer of 1977 in New York, nicknamed the "Summer of Sam," in which terror and fear was the order of the day.

The last 3 people I profiled caused even more widespread destruction than the serial killers. Think about all of the families that were negatively impacted by the Jonestown massacre. Much more frightening to think about is the spiritual consequences and eternal consequences of those who chose to follow Jones to the end. Those who had a hand in the massacre, who killed other people and injected children with cyanide. Jim Jones himself did not murder all 900 people, in the end he turned many of his followers into murderers and murderers of children. Think about how they must answer for this upon their deaths by suicide. When one looks at the widespread destruction, evil, and death that followed Jim Jones around it becomes truly staggering.

Aleister Crowley is no different, he also caused widespread destruction, evil, and death, albeit in a different form. It is truly extraordinary how many of Crowley's wives, mistresses, and followers ended up dead, committed suicide or ended up insane and institutionalized. Then think about all the people the world over who have had negative consequences due to Crowley's occult teachings, how many have been sucked up into the blackness of the occult and have lost their souls as a result.

In the case of Hitler, I ponder the sheer despair of those in the death camps, families that were separated and then killed in ovens or gas chambers. Think about all the lives that were ruined or ended as a result of World War 2. Think about all of the women in Hitler's life who committed suicide after being involved with him and also the thousands of suicides in Nazi Germany during the end of the war. And again, most frightening in my opinion is to think of the eternal state of the souls who chose to follow Hitler, who were deceived by him, who carried out his diabolical designs and murderous machinations. The amount of destruction, ruin, and evil that followed in Hitler's path is profound and unrivaled in the history of humanity.

In addition to the people I profiled in this book there are many others who I see this concept active in. People like Margaret Sanger, who has a profound amount of blood on her hands in regards to her work in ushering in a culture of death in this country. When I think about the trail of destruction left by Sanger, I think about the million and millions of infants that will never live and have never been born. Who will never know the joy of having loving parents, who will never know the euphoria from a first kiss or first love, who will never have children of their own and experience that profound joy. I think of all the mother's lives who had abortions, how wounded they become, their spiritual and eternal consequences for taking the lives of their own children. I think about all those who participate in the abortion industry, the doctors, nurses, executives, judges who legalized it, and politicians that advocated for it and continue to protect it. So-called Catholic politicians who are really travesties of Catholic's and who make a total mockery of the faith[69] and God by doing all they can to protect and enshrine the culture and cult of death in this country. This whole filth pot of evil, a lot of it can be attributed to Margaret Sanger and the tireless work she did in promoting evil.

I think about the previously mentioned banking executives who profited from the housing bubble and subsequent crash, and all the destruction this caused to normal everyday people. Not only the financial ruin that came to millions but also the appalling number of suicides directly attributable to the financial crisis.

---

69   The two foremost on my mind are Nancy Pelosi and Andrew Cuomo

"Researchers from the University of Oxford compared suicide data from before 2007 with the years of the crisis and found more than 10,000 "economic suicides" associated with the recession across the U.S., Canada and Europe."[70]

I think about people like Friedrich Nietzsche and Carl Marx[71] and all the destruction, deception, and evil caused by these men's diabolical doctrines. I think of Martin Luther, John Calvin, Jimmy Swaggert, and Arius and all the people who were separated from the bread of life due to their false and misleading doctrine. I think about the Roman emperors and the innumerable Christians they murdered in the most gruesome ways.

We can look to many Hollywood executives and pornography producers for the same exact concept. How many people's souls have been ruined and how many people have fallen into hell because of the production of pornography? How many people have fallen into mortal sin and especially deception because of the filth that is produced in Hollywood? Filth that promotes sin, normalizes sin, glamorizes sin and makes Christians look stupid, irrelevant and archaic. Think about all the young people who have been corrupted by the demonic doctrines present in modern music, the music executives and musicians responsible for this. Think about the politicians who advocate for diabolic laws and breed total corruption. Think about the politicians who have run up a 22 trillion-dollar national debt and unsustainable entitlement programs, that if left unchecked will cause a massive debt crisis and possible hyperinflation which will *destroy* the hard-earned money of million and millions of people.

At the beginning of this section I mentioned the drug cartels in Mexico, think about all the evil that is originating in Mexico with these cartels. Think about the millions of lives that have been totally destroyed due to the thousands of metric tons of heroin, cocaine and meth that are trafficked by these cartels on a yearly basis. Think of the thousands of brutal murders in Mexico, Central and South America that have been perpetrated by these cartels. Even more sickening is some of the other stories that we hear coming from Mexico in relation to the cartels; mass killing fields and mass graves, people lined up and beheaded sometimes with chain saws, human heads and headless corpses found throughout the country, people hanging from bridges and dismembered, the kidnap and murder of Catholic priests including a Cardinal, the worship of Santa Muerte and

---

70   Melanie Haiken, More Than 10,000 Suicides Tied To Economic Crisis, Study Says, forbes.com, Jun 12, 2014

71   Karl Marx also had people close to him commit suicide, I believe 3 of his own daughters all committed suicide.

related human sacrifice, the curses and spells put on drug loads so as to ensure the addiction and subsequent destruction of addicts and even the numerous stories of cannibalism practiced by the cartels. The fact is that there are very specific individual people responsible for this overwhelming and appalling evil.

Think about the Illuminati, Luciferians and high-level Satanists that are at work in the world behind the scenes and pulling strings on the world stage from the shadows. Think about all the unknown evils perpetrated by these people and the destruction it causes. Financial destruction, destruction from unnecessary wars and conflicts, destruction from bad laws and treaties that are passed, destruction from hunger, immigration policies, sicknesses and disease, etc., etc. It is widely believed in many quarters that the eventual goal of these elite Satanists is the killing off of a good part of humanity so that the planet will be sustainable for the elites to rule over for generations.

I could go on and on giving examples of people who have had an absolutely malignant effect on the people and societies around them. People who have left paths of destruction throughout the world. History is full of these people and modern society has its fair share of them, they have always been with us and always will. From the high priests of ancient Canaan who sacrificed babies to Moloch to the modern-day Hitler's Stalin's and Pablo Escobar's of the world, they will always be with us. They are the totally evil, servants of the devil and his kingdom, the perfectly possessed. Anytime a person is responsible for tearing a hole in the economy of salvation which numerous people fall through and into eternal hell and that have had a totally evil effect on the people and societies around them, and also have affected history in a negative and demonic way, we can be gravely suspicious that these people are in direct league with the devil, that they are either directly or indirectly serving him and are perfectly possessed.

16. They Sometimes Have Seemingly Preternatural Powers.

A "criminal on the worldwide political scene" might very well be possessed… Such a man might command **uncanny suggestive powers**; his knowledge and his grandiose plans might well be impressive. He could **exercise nearly irresistible power**-and yet, all his actions would lead to destruction and death.[72]

72   Rodewyk, *Possessed by Satan*

"The ones who have given themselves to Satan, who are in league with Satan, **have awful powers**."

— Father Gabriel Amorth

The last concrete sign, symptom or trait I would like to highlight that is present in some people I suspect of being perfectly possessed is that they sometimes claim to have special powers or people believe they have special powers or supernatural abilities or they really do seem to have such powers. A great many people I profiled in this book and people I research privately have this trait. For example, during the height of H. H. Holmes's diabolical activities he was viewed as a character of almost supernatural evil and abilities. Jeffrey Dahmer believed that he had special powers and also believed he would gain additional special powers through setting up his ritual altar and also by consuming his victims. Based on the testimony of the Chicago Ripper Crew we know for sure the 3 accomplices of Robin Gecht most definitely believed he had special powers and an ability to control them and make them do his bidding, with even something as simple as glance and look into his eyes. In fact, Thomas Kokoralis warned police investigators not to look into Gecht's eyes because he had special powers to force people to do his bidding. This is even the case in the life of Ted Bundy who himself believed he had speciel powers. In an interview with Steven Michaud and Hugh Ayensworth, Bundy, speaking in the third person stated,

> "I think we can say that he felt almost as if he was immune. From detection as if he were in a dimension that he just kind of like could walk through doors. That he had some supernatural **powers**."[73]

In addition to the serial killers I mentioned both Jim Jones and Aleister Crowley attributed special powers to themselves, in the case of Jones, supernatural healing ability. In the section on Jim Jones I quoted different people who knew Jim Jones and swore that he really did have some kind of special powers, powers to both heal people and tell what people were thinking. In the case of Crowley he attributed to himself magical abilities and powers and it is very likely he really did possess these because of how deeply involved he was with diabolical forces. It has been the testimony of many exorcists that genuine magicians or sorcerers do in fact possess some special abilities or powers that have been given to them by the devil and because they are totally in league with the devil, I quoted Father Amorth above demonstrating this fact.

---

73   *Conversations With a Killer: The Ted Bundy Tapes*, Netflix Documentary

Even in the life of Jeffrey Epstein we see this at work. Epstein was able to get away with so much for so long and amass such a massive fortune because of his special powers of charisma, manipulation and brilliance. However, the case of Epstein is a good example of the concept that God will not be mocked indefinitely and people who serve the devil will eventually meet a violent demise, like Epstein, in this life and in the next.

The life of Adolf Hitler presents one of the best examples of this concept. It is clear that Hitler had some type of special abilities, miraculous political intuition, the ability to keep large crowds absolutely spellbound and hanging on his every word. His ability to seemingly tell the future, his ability to somehow know he would rise to power as Germany's leader demonstrated by his words to August Kubizek as I detailed in depth on the section on Hitler. Hitler's ability to sense danger and miraculously escape from it. The incidents of his service in World War 1 and the many failed assassination attempts against him bare this out pretty clearly.

Lastly, I would like to mention the well-known fact about Vincent Bugliosi and his encounter with Charles Manson in court one day. Bugliosi relates in his book, *Helter Skelter* that one day in court he had been looking to see what time it was and noticed that his watch had stopped at which point he looked at Manson who was looking at him and his watch and grinning. Bugliosi was apparently "spooked" by the event. There is also another incident that occurred in the courtroom in which Manson attempted to kill the Judge and in doing so literally lept 10 feet across the courtroom to harm the judge. The curious bailiff measured the distance that Manson leapt and measured it at 10 feet. The bailiff tried doing this himself and could not even come close. It is also noted by Bugliosi that after this incident when the deputies took Manson from the courtroom it took 4 large deputies to finally restrain him and get him in cuffs, Manson was not a large man.

I would also like to mention the case of a man named Adolfo Constanzo because it illustrates this concept so well. Constanzo was a drug trafficker and was the man responsible for the murder of a young American man named Mark Kilroy. Kilroy and several of his friends had gone down to Matamoros, Mexico for a weekend of partying during spring break. Sometime during the partying Kilroy disappeared and was never seen again. This story exploded into the headlines because of the fact that Kilroy was an American who had disappeared in Mexico, and the case further exploded into the headlines when it was discovered what had happened to Mark Kilroy.

Kilroy had been kidnapped by a gang of drug dealers lead by the afore-mentioned Adolfo Constanzo. In addition to being a major drug trafficker Constanzo was also deeply involved with Brujeria or Mexican Witchcraft and also Santeria. Needless to say Constanzo had murdered Kilroy as part of a human sacrifice. When authorities discovered the farm outside of Mattamores what they found was absolutely horrific. Authorities found multiple sets of human remains in various stages of putrefaction including sets of human remains inside of barrels full of acid. Mexican police and the DEA also found much evidence of witchcraft including a cauldron, also with human remains inside it.

Upon further investigation it was discovered that Constanzo was the leader of a faction of drug traffickers that also trafficked in black magic and witchcraft so that they would be protected from the police. Constanzo had himself ordered the killings of many people including Kilroy and had himself participated in the human sacrifices. Lastly it was discovered through intensive investigations and interviews that Constanzo was very much feared by the people working under him. Constanzo's fellow gang members were absolutely convinced that he was a figure of supernatural abilities and that Constanzo possessed magical powers and supernatural abilities because of his practice of black magic and witchcraft.

The primary reason this trait is present in the perfectly possessed is because the demons they are possessed by are preternatural beings, they are angels, although fallen they still retain many of their natural powers that were bestowed upon them by God upon their creation. This is the fundamental reason the ritual of exorcism lists some of these special powers as indications a person may be possessed, because all of these things are totally beyond the natural power of a human being. Speaking in languages unknown to oneself is an indication of another intelligence working, a diabolical one. The same thing goes for occult knowledge and superhuman strength[74]. Generally, these things are beyond what a normal human can do. The reason the perfectly possessed sometimes display powers that are

---

74   There is wide debate among exorcists as to just how efficacious the signs and symptoms laid down by the ritual really are. Many argue that someone could recall a language they once heard long ago and had long forgotten. Some also argue that abnormal human strength can be produced by pathological states, and this is indeed true. Obviously, this needs to be looked at on a case-by-case basis and common sense must be used. For example, the exorcism case that took place in Gary, Indiana featured a young child walking backwards up a wall, obviously completely beyond the ability of a human being even in a severe pathological state. If a person is speaking languages unknown, are they just repeating words and phrases they once heard which is easily replicable or are they speaking in fluent Aramaic, a language only a handful of people in the world can speak fluently. Common sense must be used, and a priest can never be too incredulous and ready to believe.

beyond the capacity of a human nature is because they are possessed by and in league with evil spirits who exercise their powers when they are in complete control of a human being.

CONCLUSION:

I want to say that just because a certain evil person may display some of these signs and symptoms does not mean they are necessarily possessed. As I stated in an earlier chapter, not all evil people are possessed or perfectly possessed. At the end of the day diabolic possession whether partial or perfect remains a rare phenomenon and probably always will remain a rare phenomenon, we have Christ to thank for that.

This section is not meant for people to obsessively look at and then try to constantly label people as perfectly possessed. Please avoid the temptation of doing so. In the end there is not a whole lot one can do about a perfectly possessed person if they are so identified. The only thing faithful Christians can do is pray for their soul and try and somehow oppose the evil they bring into the world. Our Lord has been very clear with us that there is a certain power working behind the scenes that is spiritual and satanic, it should come to no surprise to any of us that there are people out there who are totally in league with the devil. What will not be helpful is obsessing over this topic and trying to determine who is and who isn't. All we can do is pray, oppose evil, and bring the love of Christ out into the world, and by doing this we very well may encounter those servants of the devil who will oppose us, just as the apostles and early Christians did and just as Christians of every generation have.

Despite the fact that I listed 16 individual signs and symptoms of perfect possession, I did not include some of the more obvious ones that I already covered heavily in earlier chapters. For instance, I noted in an earlier chapter that many of the perfectly possessed are wealthy and powerful and I covered that extensively and the reasons why that is.

One of the more obvious signs of perfect possession would be to organizationally oppose the work of the church, the preaching of the gospel and the sacraments. This is activity that many of the perfectly possessed engage in and much of this has been covered in previous chapters.

Another sign or symptom I could have listed would be to make good into evil and evil into good. Richard Cavendish notes,

> Satanists believe that what Christians call good is really evil, and vice versa"[75]

Again, I covered this extensively in earlier chapters and so did not feel the need to list it as an individual symptom, however many perfectly possessed people display this trait.

Sometimes the perfectly possessed can be people of unbelievable narcissism and pride, which could be included under psychopathic personality disorder. I noted above that many of the perfectly possessed display all the classic symptoms of psychopathy and narcissism and pride is definitely a symptom of that disorder. Additionally, pride is one of the primary characteristics of some diabolic personalities, although according to exorcists, not all. Apparently, their personalities and temperaments vary greatly.

CHAPTER 11

CAN A PERFECT POSSESSION BE REVERSED?

"Finally, I am often asked if wizards can go back to the Faith. Wizards-like exorcists, even if obviously on the completely opposite side, touch the invisible world with their hands. When a true wizard sells himself to Satan, his reasoning is no longer his own, and normally he does not have the strength to liberate himself. **For this reason, I believe that it is difficult, if not impossible, to convert back to God. God will seek to redeem him, even to the end**, as He does with all His children."[1]

"For this reason, it is necessary to think of the consequences of such a choice, **which is often irreversible or at least very difficult to reverse.** I know persons who have left, but only after an **enormous struggle,** and often while being threatened by the followers. Even more, they always remain marked in their psyche and in their body, often enduring **years and years of exorcisms** in order to be liberated from the devil and the diabolical possessions on their backs."[2]

The short answer is that ultimately yes it can be reversed, however it is extremely unlikely and it would only be through great difficulty and danger to those involved and only by direct miracle of God and furthermore only through purely supernatural means, meaning prayer, sacrifice, fasting, masses, rosaries, visits to the blessed sacrament, and eventually when some separation has occurred between demonic personality and human, exorcism, possibly for years.

Before I explain why it is possible to be free of a perfect possession I would like to state that there are two authors that, based on what they have written about this topic would lead one to believe that they do not believe this is a reversable state, that it is in fact permanent, that once someone is perfectly possessed, they will remain in that state forever. What these

---

1   Amorth, *An Exorcist Explains the Demonic*
2   Ibid

authors write is the exception, not the rule. One of the authors that I am referring to is of course Malachi Martin who wrote this about the perfectly possessed Jay Beedem. Martin wrote that Jay Beedem in his perfectly possessed state was,

> "immune to any touch of therapy, isolated from any saving intervention, trussed, mummified, and locked away safely by the evil power that possessed him perfectly."[3]

Even in all of the interviews that Martin did with Art Bell on Coast to Coast A.M. back in the late 90's, he very clearly said that when he comes in contact with the perfectly possessed, he runs the other way, he wants absolutely nothing to do with them. In one interview he stated:

> "The most extreme state is 'perfect possession', when the demon has taken complete control. The perfectly possessed person is totally lost. There is nothing I can do," says Father Martin."[4]

Similarly, Father Euteneuer wrote:

> "These individuals are the walking damned, and they cannot be helped, nor will they come for help from the exorcist, except perhaps to test him or persecute him. Exorcists will do well to "test" all spirits in turn when they suspect that they are in the presence of such a person and dismiss all such insidious individuals as soon as they are exposed for what they are."[5]

> "more than anything we should pray to be protected from them"[6]

REASONS WHY PERFECT POSSESSION IS A REVERSABLE STATE:

I will note that right before Father Euteneuer made the last statement regarding praying for protection from them, he also stated that it is important to pray for these individuals. Similarly, I earlier quoted Father Royo Marin in which he states that people who voluntarily give themselves to devil will be very difficult to liberate. He stated:

> "The unfortunate ones who dare to do this voluntarily give themselves to the devil, and as a just punishment from God it will be

---

3   Martin, *Hostage to the Devil*
4   http://www.tribulation-now.org/2009/08/06/perfect-possession-father-malachi-martin/
5   Euteneuer, *Exorcism and the Church Militant*
6   Ibid

most difficult to liberate them. Such persons place themselves in great danger of eternal damnation"[7]

Most difficult to liberate them does not mean impossible. I also quoted Father Amorth at the beginning of this chapter who said some of the same things, namely that these people can be liberated, albeit with grave difficulty. Father Amorth even goes so far as to say that these cases are "often irreversible" and "if not impossible" to liberate.

This is where great discernment is needed, we must distinguish 3 factors in this regard and also remember that the word "perfect" as in "perfect possession" should not be thought to mean "permanent." It is true that human beings have free will, we are completely and totally free. So free that if we want to, we can give ourselves over to the devil, body and soul, for all eternity. This choice is made somewhere in a person's life or over a period of time and sometimes results in the state known as perfect possession. As I stated multiple times throughout this book, while the perfect possession is active these people are completely at peace with their state and their decision, they do not desire to change. However, due to multiple different factors, including the nature of our will as compared to angelic will, the freedom of will humans have up until the moment of death, and also the mercy of God and intercession of other people, it would seem, theologically, that a perfect possession could theoretically be reversed, albeit unlikely and with great difficultly the reasons for which I will also give.

Human persons are not angels, our intellect and will do not operate in the same fashion as an angel. An angel decides or chooses with their will, with the fullest possible amount of knowledge, making their decisions essentially final, they also do not experience time in the same fashion as we humans do. When an angel makes a decision, he sees everything related to that decision, all aspects of the choice before him. This is why the devil can never repent, he already made his decision to reject Christ with full knowledge and with the full force of his will. He cannot then, millions of years later just decide to change his mind. The reason why I mentioned the factor of time is because angels do not experience time in the same way humans do and for this reason the angelic choice is always present in the present to the angelic will and intellect. It is not as if an angel makes a choice and then 100 years later can change its mind due to the passage of time and the erosion of the original choice made, the choice they make is always present to them as if it occurred in the here and now.

7   Royo Marin, *The Theology of Christian Perfection*

Human beings on the other hand do have this ability. Sometimes in the literature, some authors give the impression that perfect possession happens because of one choice made at some time and this choice is forever permanent. I do not believe this is the case. Human beings live in a continuity of time and we do not make decisions with full knowledge. That is exactly why in chapter 3 when describing the explicit form of perfect possession, I said that these people desire to sell their souls and invite possession with full knowledge but with the caveat that it is "to the extent that human nature and state in life allows." That last part is an important distinction. A human cannot make a decision with full knowledge, but only full knowledge to the extent human nature allows, which really is not full knowledge in the same sense as an angel. What this means is that even if a human being made a decision to fully give themselves to the devil at some point in time, there is nothing in human nature that would preclude them from changing their mind at a later point in time, based on the fact that the original decision for selling oneself to the devil was not made with "full knowledge." This would be the first reason it is possible for a perfect possession to be reversed.

The second reason has to do with the fact that a human being has freedom of will everyday throughout their lives which constitutes a certain span of time. A human being must choose to remain in their state of life every day in order to remain in that state. For example, a priest gets up every morning and decides with his will to continue being a priest of Jesus Christ, at any time he could choose to leave the priesthood as many do. Therefore, in order for a perfect possession to continually be effective the human person must continually choose to belong fully to the devil. Father Euteneuer writes:

> "Furthermore, he is a person who is perfectly aware of the eternal consequences of his decision and **perseveres in that state** with full knowledge and consent of the will."[8]

The key word being "perseveres." If a human being must constantly affirm the decision to be perfectly possessed in order for the perfect possession to continually be effective, then this can also work in the opposite fashion. Meaning if a human being has enough freedom of will left to continually affirm perfect possession, then they also have enough freedom of will left to change their mind. This is in short, the second theological reason why a perfect possession is never permanent, it is only permanent

---

8   Euteneuer, *Exorcism and the Church Militant*

if the human person, with their will, wishes it to continually be so up until their death. Theologically, it has been the constant church teaching that a human beings *will* remains free up until the very moment of death. So, Malachi Martin is correct that these people are "totally lost" if they so choose to be, but he is not correct in the sense that they could change their mind at some point later on.

The third reason is the mercy of God, which is completely and totally unfathomable and also the intercession and love of other people. I earlier quoted a story from Father Vince Lampert in which he spoke about a man who he claimed was perfectly possessed whose family was very concerned about him, whose family asked Father Lampert to talk to the man, which is a form of intercession. Now in a case like this it could be that the family who loves this man takes action and storms heaven for his conversion. Meaning they make heroic sacrifices and acts of prayer to effect a change of heart. It should be noted that these acts of love on the part of this man's family will not go totally unnoticed by God. God is fully capable of choosing to reach into this mans will, however so slightly in only the way God can and move it towards the good. Now the man then can choose to respond to this grace or not, but if he chooses to respond to it, then he has his family to thank and also the ultimate mercy of God. In the end God wants each one of us to be saved, he paid way too high a price (Christs death on the cross) to give up on us. Additionally, he created us and loves us more than we can ever fathom. It follows that God then will use almost anything, any act of love, done by us or on behalf of us by those who love us, to save our souls. This is where I would like to take the time to quote Father M and what he had to say at the 2008 Mundelein Conference on this topic because it has great bearing on what was just written. Father stated:

> "over to the point of what's called, so called **perfect possession**, where the demonic spirit no longer manifests itself apart from or distinct from the human personality but instead the two have become inseparably one. That's the point where a real choice has been made. **And its not a point however, as long as they're still alive, it is not a point where God can not intervene. Where his love cannot touch them, where mercy cannot reform them, where they cannot see truth, where something may change them. As long as we're alive change is possible.** However, you and I know certain kinds of relationships are very difficult to break apart once they reach that spot. And when someone reaches that

spot where the demonic no longer shows itself independently, so we can distinguish, or we can see struggle or there are indications of freedom, one against the other. When that happens its very hard to see if there's anything wrong at all. Because it all goes into hiding. Its very subtle. It perfects itself as a force in the world disguised as something else. Very difficult, very sad, for these people we must always pray very hard."[9]

Reasons Why it is Unlikely For Perfect Possession to Be Reversed or Why it Would Be So Difficult to Do So:

In the above quote Father M states the church's theological position which is that as long as a person is alive, change is possible. He follows this however by stating the practical side of things, which is that some demonic relationships, specifically perfect possessions, are "very difficult" to break apart when they reach a certain level. This is in addition to all the other authors I quoted above who said things like "most difficult to liberate them" and "if not impossible" and "often irreversible or at least very difficult to reverse." The question must be asked, just how difficult is it? The best answer comes from Father Royo Marin, he states:

> "**The conversion of one of these persons would require a miracle of grace greater than the resurrection of the dead in the natural order.** The only method to be used with them is the strictly supernatural: prayer, fasting, tears, constant recourse to the Blessed Virgin. This requires a true miracle and only God can do it. And God will not always perform the miracle in spite of many prayers and supplications. It could be said that these unfortunate ones have exhausted the patience of God and are destined to be for all eternity the living testimony of inflexible and rigorous divine justice, because they have abused divine mercy."[10]

We find supplemental answers in the writings of Father Amorth who stated that sometimes these people can be found to be "often enduring years and years of exorcisms." So, the question remains why. Why is it so difficult to liberate those who are perfectly possessed, who have sold their souls to the devil and given their whole being over to Satan? There are four main factors that need to be considered here, the fourth probably

---

9   Father M, *Mundelein Conference on Healing, Deliverance and Exorcism*, 2008
10   Royo Marin, *The Theology of Christian Perfection*

being the most significant. I will list them in the order of significance that I believe they constitute.

The first factor we need to consider is diabolic action. In this regard Father Euteneuer writes:

> "The Devil does not allow his servitors to have easy conversions without a fight, and this is why they need the prayers of all Christians to bring them out of their slavery to the darkness."[11]

Even though it is theoretically possible for a human being to change his/her mind and exercise free will at any time, the possessing evil spirit is going to do everything in its power to not allow this. In the case of Jamsie Z this took the form of extremely painful attacks on the body. If Jamsie even thought about resisting Ponto, he would be attacked by being subjected to stifling pains all throughout his body that would not relent until he consented to Ponto. The same was true for Gary Lyttle, except in this case it took the form of fear and the threat of harm. When one reads the account of this case it becomes clear that this 10-year-old boy is completely terrified of the entity Tyrannus. The book states:

> "Answer me this, Gary: do you want to be free of this evil?" "Yes, Mr. Lendrum. I do. But Tyrannus doesn't want that. He says if I don't do what he says he'll make me feel so bad that I'll want to kill myself."[12]

Another form this can take is the fact that if the person was part of a coven or cult, the other cult members very well may seek to retaliate against the person seeking liberation. This was portrayed very well in the movie Eyes Wide Shut, where Doctor Bill Hartford received gravely threatening letters and was followed, all after taking part in the Satanic orgy. I already quoted Father Amorth who stated:

> "I know persons who have left, but only after an enormous struggle, and often while being threatened by the followers"[13]

Dr. Richard Gallagher has also spoken about a case like this. He named the woman in question Julia to protect her identity. Dr. Gallagher was involved with a team of people, including 2 exorcists, trying to help this woman. Unfortunately, the team was ultimately unsuccessful in liberating her despite multiple exorcisms. According to the Dr, Julia was a "avowed

---

11   Euteneuer, *Demonic Abortion*
12   Kiely and McKenna, *The Dark Sacrament*
13   Amorth, *An Exorcist Explains the Demonic*

and prominent Satanist" who was also part of a coven and who apparently was the high priestess of said coven. There were many reasons this team was unable to help Julia, including the fact that Julia herself, despite originally asking sincerely for help, was not on the "up and up" as Dr. Gallagher noted. Dr. Gallagher speculates that she may have liked being part of the cult because of the social and sexual aspects of her involvement. In the end, it seems one of the most significant reasons they were unable to successfully liberate her was because of the constant harassment from the demons possessing her and also harassment from her fellow coven members to coerce and harass her back into compliance, which also included harassment of Dr. Gallagher who was followed and harassed via a phone call to his wife. Dr. Gallagher notes:

> "She eventually dropped out. **She at some point seemed to prefer the cult**, she also may well have been **afraid that the cult would harm her**."[14]

I would also like to note that Julia had confided in Dr. Gallagher that when she made the decision to go through with the exorcism ritual, she was punished by Satan with what she called "hell fire." Julia apparently described this as extremely painful. With painful attacks like these in tandem with harassment from her cult, is it any wonder she was not delivered. This case is a perfect example of the fact that once a person is in deep into the satanic underworld, it is extremely difficult to get free and may never happen. These cases are true tragedies in every sense of the word and also present for a dire warning to anyone considering getting involved in such things. The truth is that there is a point of no return, a point at which getting out is all but impossible. It is in this context I hearken back to a quote I highlighted in the Introduction from Father Bamonte. In citing the opinion of Father Candido Amantini, Father Bamonte writes,

> "According to some exorcists (among them the Servant of God Candido Amantini, who died in the odor of sanctity in Rome on September 22nd, 1992), sorcerers and Satanists can reach a point in which **conversion is impossible**, becoming something akin to slaves of Satan who find it impossible to turn back."[15]

In addition to fear, painful physical attacks, and harassment from cult members, the most severe form this can take is when the person considering renouncing their pact or seeking liberation is then subjected to all

---

14   Dr Gallagher, *Mundelein Conference on Healing, Deliverance, and Exorcism*, 2011
15   Bamonte, *Diabolical Possession and the Ministry of Exorcism*

393

the normal terrors of diabolic infestation, oppression, and possession. In chapter 4 I quoted many authors who all gave the same opinion that people who are perfectly possessed do not display the crisis state that partially possessed individuals do. This is true because the will of the human person is perfectly aligned with the will of the demonic spirit, there is no struggle or resistance on the part of the human person. This would not be the case however if the person makes an act of will to want to be free or makes a move to renounce the pact entered by them. Father Bamonte, Father Amorth, and Father Ripperger all state that once a person makes some act to try and get free from the subjugation, they will be visited with all the horrors of demonic attack. They essentially go from willing collaborators of the devil to victims of his attack. This attack is of course meant to beat the person back into submission to the diabolic force. Father Bamonte writes:

> "the consecrated Satanist undergoes neither the crisis nor manifests the symptoms of those who suffer the extraordinary action of the devil. In fact, as long as he remains the way he is, the devil does not torment him with the usual vexations of the obsessed or possessed. **Yet, should that pact be threatened through a renunciation, Satan will immediately command that all the torments of vexation, obsession, and diabolical possession be visited upon that person so as not to lose one who has voluntarily subjected himself to him. By tormenting the person, he hopes to convince the person to reaffirm the pact he made.** This is confirmed by many exorcists who have been confronted with problems of this kind."[16]

Likewise, in the section on Diabolical Subjugation and Dependence written by Father Chad Ripperger in his book *Introduction to the Science of Mental Health* he states:

> "If a psychologist discovers this in his directee, he must immediately counsel the breaking of the pact or subjugation. This is normally done through saying the words voluntarily which reject the pact and then he should get to Confession immediately. **However, it may not end there. The demons will seek to take dominion over their "property" and so they will adversely affect the directee in the ways described above.**"[17]

---

16   Bamonte, *Diabolical Possession and the Ministry of Exorcism*
17   Ripperger, *Introduction to the Science of Mental Health*

Father Ripperger states that the demons will adversely affect the directee in the ways described above, meaning all the forms of extraordinary diabolic attack he described previously, which he lists as external pain, diabolic possession, diabolic oppression, diabolic obsession, and diabolic infestation. Meaning that if a person who has entered into a pact with diabolical forces seeks to terminate the pact or get help in some way, they will be subjected to an extraordinary attack from evil spirits designed specifically to stop any possible liberation.

One last note I would like to make is that it is also possible for the diabolical spirits in control of a perfectly possessed person to not only harass and attack the person who is possessed but also attack any person who even thinks about helping them. Meaning priests, friends, family members, etc. They will do this as a warning to back off essentially making a statement of ownership on the person and violently protecting that ownership by whatever means necessary. In conclusion, the devil is not going to just give up a person that has been his, the evil spirit is going to visit all manner of pain and misfortune upon the person until the person relents and re-affirms the diabolical pact.

The second factor that we need to consider is the justice of God. While it is true that God is merciful, he is not always going to show that mercy, especially when a person has continually abused his mercy and mocked him. In the passage I quoted from Father Royo Marin he clearly said that God will not always bring about this type of miracle because these persons could be said to have exhausted the patience of God and they have "abused" his divine mercy. This is true even though many people may have prayed for the person in question. There comes a point when even God knows, because he sees all things, that there is no hope left for an individual because that individual will not change, hence why Christ made no attempt to liberate Judas Iscariot from the possession of Satan himself.

I think that this is the reason that thoroughly evil people who harm other people and introduce much evil into the world sometimes die very early and violent deaths. Father Fortea spoke about this at the 2005 Mundelein Conference and what he had to say was controversial indeed. Father speculated that when a person reaches the point where even God sees there is no hope left and all the person will do is bring more evil into the world if allowed to continue living, then it is at that point their lives end, sometimes violently. I do not have an opinion on whether or not Father Fortea is correct in this matter, what I do know however is that some people who are evil seem to die early and violent deaths, whether or not this has anything to do with the action of God must be left open.

Personally, my favorite attribute of God is his mercy, his mercy makes me want to love him more and not commit sin precisely for the reason he is so merciful. When we concentrate on his mercy, we often forget that God is equally just. Meaning sometimes perfectly possessed persons have committed evil on such a magnitude that God will not bring about the miracle of their conversion based purely on his justice. What perfect possession really comes down to is hatred of God. For someone to end up in this most deplorable state completely belonging to the devil, they must have hated God and his mercy. Based on his justice, God is not going to allow for the conversion of a person that actively hates him. To bring out just how clear and appalling a crime it is to hate God I would like to quote from the Catholic Encyclopedia.

> "When by any conceivable stretch of human wickedness God himself is the object of hatred the guilt is appallingly special. If it be that kind of enmity which prompts the sinner to loath God in himself, to regret the divine perfections precisely in so far as they belong to God, then the offense committed obtains the undisputed primacy in all the miserable hierarchy of sin. In fact, such an attitude of mind is fairly and adequately described as diabolical."[18]

Likewise, Father Garrigou Lagrange notes:

> "hatred of God manifests the total depravity of the will"[19]

This hatred of God becomes even more sickening when we consider just how much of a loving father God really is. When we consider the beautiful planet he created for us, the laughter of our children, the love and death of Christ, etc. All perfectly possessed people are perfectly possessed because they have so hated and despised God and because God is perfectly just in all his dealings with us, makes it very likely the previously mentioned type of person will not be delivered but will instead continue belonging to the devil, whom they wanted to serve and worship. Furthermore, intercourse with the devil, in addition to being a harbinger of someone hating God is also a great and blasphemous insult of God. When a human being decides to actively serve and worship the enemy of God and hold intimate relations with the devil it is a grave insult and mockery of God. Father Thomas Slater states:

---

18   Joseph Delany, Hatred, *Catholic Encyclopedia* Vol 7
19   Garrigou Lagrange, *Life Everlasting: A Theological Treatise on the Four Last Things*, P.121

"Divination is mortally sinful, **for it is a great insult to God to hold intercourse with and seek aid from the devil, his bitter enemy**, and besides, it is most dangerous to the parties concerned. He is wont gradually to insinuate himself until he has his victim within his power, and then he works on him his evil will."[20]

It is very clear from the scriptures and the teaching of the church and the saints that God is merciful, more merciful than we can ever comprehend, however he will not allow himself to be actively mocked, insulted, and hated, he furthermore will not help to bring about the conversion of such a person.

The third factor we must consider is the human will and just how sacred, free and powerful it really is. I asked the reader above to consider the fact that a person who is perfectly possessed could have friends and family praying unceasingly for them. While it is true this theoretically could lead to the eventual conversion and liberation of a person, it will most certainly not if the person obstinately chooses to not change. In fact, this was the exact case with the article I had mentioned involving Father Vince Lampert. The man who Father Lampert speculated was perfectly possessed basically acknowledged that his family was concerned about him and praying for him, he just didn't care. Father Lampert notes,

"He told me that throughout his life he had cultivated relationships with demons and with Satan and that when he died it was his desire to spend eternity with these demons. He said, 'I know my family is concerned about me, but this is the free choice that I make'"[21]

Here we can see very clearly that despite his family's effort he is not going to change. It is true this itself could change at a later date after the man is possibly given some special grace, but it is unlikely. Our human *will* is inviolable, meaning despite prayers, supplications, tears, sacrifices, and even the grace of God, we can still choose to obdurately reject all these things and choose evil continually. People who are perfectly possessed are in that state because they wanted to be, they desired to be, they willed it. There was something inside them, some unique part of their specific human personality and will that chooses this and likes it. It stands to reason then they probably will continue to like it and want it, and as long as their heart is hard, and they are intractable in their choice, no change is possible.

20 Slater S.J., *A Manuel of Moral Theology*
21 Rachael Ray, Leading US exorcists explain huge increase in demand for the Rite – and priests to carry them out, www.telegraph.co.uk, Sept 26, 2016

The fourth and final reason it would be unlikely or so difficult for a case of perfect possession to be reversed is because of the Catholic doctrine regarding "sin" and the affect it has on human nature, intellect and will. The basic doctrine states that mortal sin essentially damages the soul, it inflicts a wound upon the soul and as an extension the will and intellect which are faculties of the soul. What occurs as a result of this is the will gets more damaged and more warped over time with every mortal sin committed. Further, with every mortal sin committed it conditions the will to commit further sin, deeper and darker levels of sin, inclines the will towards the practice of evil and also clouds and darkens the intellect as to what is good and what is evil. This process can progress so severely that in the end the person not only believes that evil is good and good is evil, but they also find it near impossible to stop sinning, the will undergoing a confirmation in the practice of evil. Regarding this doctrine one author who is a very respected German theologian even goes so far as to say that free will may essentially be extinguished if this process is allowed to progress enough.

Regarding this doctrine the *Catholic Encyclopedia* states:

> "other effects of sins are, an inclination towards evil. As habits are formed by a repetition of similar acts; a darkening of the intelligence, and a hardening of the will."[22]

Likewise, the *Catechism of the Catholic Church* states:

> "Sin creates a proclivity to sin; it engenders vice by repetition of the same acts. This results in a perverse inclination which clouds conscience and corrupts judgement of good and evil. Thus, sin tends to reproduce itself and reinforce itself."[23]

James Bellord, in his, *Meditations on Christian Dogma* writes:
> "When sin grows into a habit deliberately persevered in, then it becomes a most fruitful source of further sin and the greatest obstacle to salvation."[24]

And from a different perspective also, the practice of the occult, which is of course mortally sinful, does the same thing. This sin is particularly dangerous because the practice of the occult leads to far deeper levels of the occult and almost certain bondage to diabolical forces. Peter Haining, in *The Anatomy of Witchcraft* writes:

---

22   A.C. O'Neil, Mortal Sin, *Catholic Encyclopedia* Vol 14
23   *Catechism of the Catholic Church*, No. 1865
24   Bellord, *Meditations on Christian Dogma*

"The will weakens, moral values become obscured, the senses blunted. Habits, motives and actions which would previously have appeared grotesque or revolting now appear amusing and desirable, or worse still are taken in deadly seriousness as being a means of obtaining the favor of the powers of darkness."[25]

Lastly, I would like to quote the author that I mentioned previously who when describing the affect mortal sin has on the soul used extremely strong language. What I am about to quote is the best passage I could locate to really show clearly this principle at work and show clearly to you the reader just why it is so unlikely, even though theoretically possible, for a person perfectly possessed to be liberated. In a classic work of Catholic Theology based off Joseph Scheeben's work, titled *A Manuel of Catholic Theology*, the author writes,

"The perpetuity of habitual sin does not necessarily imply a continuation of actual sin, or even the impossibility of a conversion of some kind. **Yet, if such conversion be wanting, a continuation of actual sin is naturally to be expected, and, with it, a stronger inclination towards sin and a greater unworthiness of Divine grace, until a stage may be reached in which conversion is all but impossible, except by miracle.** Such is particularly the case with sins against the Holy Ghost, direct and formal contempt of God's truth and grace, which blind the sinner's intellect and harden his heart."[26]

"An effect common to mortal and venial sin in the natural and supernatural order, is the production of an inclination of the will towards evil. The frequent repetition of sinful acts bends the will in a wrong direction and hampers it in avoiding evil and doing good. From the will the difficulty extends to the intellect, inclining it to judge falsely of things moral; and in man it may even affect the sensitive appetites. **The perversity thus engendered may render the difficulty of doing good insuperable, and may for all practical purposes, extinguish free will."**[27]

There you have it, the greatest reason why it is exceedingly rare or unlikely for a case of perfect possession to be remedied and end with the salvation of the person. I stated above in an earlier chapter that perfectly possessed people have often spent whole lives committing crime on top of crime and moral perversions heaped one upon the other. These are

25   Haining, *The Anatomy of Witchcraft*
26   Wilhelm-Scannell, *A Manuel of Catholic Theology*
27   Ibid

people utterly devoted to the practice of evil. As a result, their wills and intellects have been hardened and darkened to the point where freedom of choice is almost nonexistent. They are so conditioned to the practice of evil, which is all they know, and are devoted to it that it follows they will continue to act this way, making conversion extremely unlikely.

I often think about the serial killers in this regard. People who are obviously confirmed in the practice of evil. Some of them have said very clearly that the compulsion to kill became so strong they felt powerless to resist it. This was especially the case after they killed, meaning the compulsion and desire to murder people became greater and stronger every time they killed. This concept was especially at play in the lives of both Jeffrey Dahmer and Ted Bundy. In interviews done by both men, they related how their killing sprees progressed. Both men, well before they were ever serial killers were committing sexual sins like masturbation and viewing pornography. For both of them this became inadequate to satisfy their deepening desires. This progression of sin to darker and darker levels of sin, ultimately ending in murder, torture, and necrophilia for both men is a prime example of this doctrine at work in two people who were evil and very likely perfectly possessed. In one interview with Steven Michaud, Ted Bundy even noted that he knew it was unreasonable for him to believe that his urge to kill would be satisfied after killing, yet he continued to kill, believing with each murder that his stronger and stronger desire to kill would somehow be satisfied until he of course simply could not control the urge to slaughter people whatsoever.

CONCLUSION

In conclusion, we do need to realize that perfectly possessed people can be extremely dangerous. With that said, if a person is suspected as such we should make an effort to pray for that person. It is true conversion is unlikely, very unlikely, but not impossible. The question must be asked as to what remedies would be the most effective in this regard? I would say with Father Royo Marin, the strictly supernatural; prayer, fasting, tears, having masses said for the person, rosaries in front of the blessed sacrament, and probably the most powerful, entrusting the person constantly to the immaculate Heart of Mary. In the end I think the tears of a mother, especially our Blessed Mother are the most powerful weapon we can use to try and affect the conversion of a person. This is how I was converted, and I was a confirmed sinner, criminal, convict and drug addict who wanted absolutely nothing to do with God whatsoever.

And what if by some miracle the person has a change of heart and makes some move to try and get help? Well, as I described it is likely this is where the real battle will ensue. It is even possible the person may never be fully liberated, they may die in a state of possession but with their soul in a state of grace. Father Amorth noted sometimes these people must endure years and years of exorcism and even then, they will always be marked or wounded somehow. Father Malachi Martin made a similar comment as to those people who attend black masses, he said a black mass is so evil that anyone who attends loses some part of themselves, as if some part of their soul permanently withers. Meaning, even if they are liberated from the possession, the practice of satanism and devil worship will leave lasting wounds that they may never recover from and may never be healed except by God himself after they die.

I would like to end on a positive note and say that it is also possible that there could be a complete and total conversion and liberation with no exorcism being necessary at all. It seems this is the case with the infamous and previously mentioned David Berkowitz, the Son of Sam. David Berkowitz, who has admitted freely he was possessed by the devil and deeply involved with satanic cults; who helped gun down 13 people and terrorize the whole city of New York; who Malachi Martin identified as perfectly possessed after meeting him in person- now calls himself the Son of Hope and is a devoted Christian who evangelizes his fellow inmates. He now says the Son of Sam moniker was evil, that it came from a demon and he has seen the light, the light of Christ which he tries to introduce to his fellow inmates. In closing I would like to quote a passage from his spiritual testament, a truly extraordinary story and a testament to the absolute and almighty power of God to change our lives and bring us out of the deepest and darkest bondage imaginable. Berkowitz writes:

> Ten years into my prison sentence, when I was feeling despondent and without hope, another inmate came up to me as I was walking the prison yard one cold winter evening. He introduced himself and began to tell me that Jesus Christ loved me and wanted to forgive me. Although I knew he meant well I mocked him because I did not think that God would ever forgive me or that He would want anything to do with me. Still this man persisted, and we became friends. His name was Rick, and we would walk the yard together. Little by little he would share with me about his life and what he believed Jesus had done for him. He kept reminding me that no matter what a person did, Christ stood ready to forgive if

that individual would be willing to turn from the bad things he was doing and would put his full faith and trust in Jesus Christ and what He did on the cross--dying for our sins. He gave me a Gideon Pocket Testament and asked me to read the Psalms. I did. Every night I would read from them. It was at this time the Lord was quietly melting my stone-cold heart.

A New Life Begins

One night I was reading Psalm 34. I came upon the 6th verse which says, "This poor man cried, and the Lord heard him, and saved him out of all his troubles." It was at this moment, in 1987, that I began to pour out my heart to God. Everything seemed to hit me at once--the guilt of what I had done and the disgust at what I had become. Late that night in my cold cell I got down on my knees and began to cry to Jesus Christ. I told Him that I was sick and tired of doing evil. I asked Jesus to forgive me for all my sins. I spent a good while on my knees praying to Him. When I got up it felt as if a heavy but invisible chain that had been around me for so many years was broken. A peace flooded over me. I did not understand what was happening. In my heart I just knew that somehow my life was going to be different.

∞

Appendix A

Multi-Generational Perfect Possession

"Possession of the real diabolic kind is generational, its generational. It's passed on by training and it's a dreadful thing when somebody comes in who is perfectly respectable, good, noble, American family and they have reared their children to be Satanists and to accept possession and they would unless they're stopped, themselves pass it on to their children and it's been going on for well over 200 years."
— Malachi Martin, Coast to Coast AM

Multi-Generational perfect possession can essentially occur in a number of ways. What it entails is that certain members of a family at some point in the family's history become possessed and then this possession is passed on down through generations, sometimes lasting hundreds and hundreds of years. The possession is passed on through various different means the biggest obviously being the practice of evil, which can take a few different forms. I earlier mentioned the story Devilry on the Dingle Peninsula, where generations of family members were in bondage to diabolical forces because of the practice of incestual pedophilia for generations. The generational perfect possession is basically carried on by the current family member who is possessed and who then inflicts some evil on subsequent generations who also subsequently inflict it on subsequent generations. Like the above story it can take the form of horrific forms of sexual abuse where a father rapes and molests all his children, said children growing up and doing the same thing to their children.

This can take the form of other things too like generations of family members all being involved in murder, I listed a few examples of this in the book, the example of Robin Gecht and his son being the best example.

The most prominent form this takes however and the one I want to concentrate this appendix on is when generations of family members are involved in satanic cults and devil worship. This is a very dark area indeed. There are many people out there who say these underground familial cults do not exist, that there is no evidence of their existence going back hundreds of years, Special Agent Kenneth Lanning and the FBI being one of the critics. Many exorcists, and other professionals would highly disagree.

When we break down the overall practice of satanism it essentially takes five forms.

1. The first is what I would call religious satanism, which actually can be atheistic or theistic. Atheistic satanism means the adherents do not believe in Satan as an actual entity, a spiritual person. They instead hold the belief that Satan represents all of the forbidden desires and sensual urges of man. Theistic satanism means the adherents do believe Satan is an actual entity and they worship him as such within the confines of the law. These are groups that are well known and out in the open practicing satanism like it is a religion. Many of these groups are recognized by the government as being religions. The most prominent examples are the Church of Satan founded by Anton Szandor LaVey in 1966 and also the Satanic Temple, which has been in the news many times as of late. Out of all the forms of satanism, this is the least dangerous form.

2. The second form is what has been called the teenage dabbler. The teenage dabbler is the teenager who gets involved in satanism mostly for the rebellion aspect and also for the thrills, drugs, and sex. These are people who begin by listening to hard core rock music or being introduced to it through movies, friends at school or role playing games like Dungeons and Dragons. The teenage dabbler usually wears dark clothing and lets it be known they are Satanists. They do this for shock value mostly. Sometimes the teenage dabbler can be part of a small group of other high school age kids all involved in the same activities. They almost always get their satanic theology from Anton LaVey or Aleister Crowley. They very often commit crimes and are usually into drugs and alcohol. The teenage dabbler can be dangerous. I know of many cases where teenage Satanists have committed horrific crimes and brutal murders, usually their parents being the victims.

3. The third form is called the "self-styled satanic cult."[1] This can also take many different forms but is certainly a step above the teenage dabbler. These are people who are now in early adulthood or sometimes much older who are much more serious about their

---

1   Two very dangerous examples would be The Process Church of the Final Judgement and The Order of Nine Angles.

satanism and devil worship. Sometimes they use the satanic theology of LaVey and Crowley, but sometimes not. Sometimes these groups make up their own beliefs and practices and sometimes they use ones that have been around, making use of older magical grimoires and similar texts. Self-styled satanic cults have been known to engage in all manner of crime and violence. These groups very often practice animal sacrifice and even human sacrifice occasionally. For instance, it was a self-styled satanic cult responsible for the above-mentioned Son of Sam killings. These groups can have varying numbers of people, some having only a few, some 12 or 13, and some many more. These cults usually center around a charismatic leader who acts as the high priest of the cult. These groups recruit in varying ways and once someone is initiated into the cult it is very difficult to get free.

4. The fourth form is what I would call "power satanism." This form of devil worship is usually not generational but instead involves some of the richest, most powerful people on the planet. This is the primary form I discussed in chapter 8. One very prominent form this takes is called Luciferianism. These groups can vary in size and shape. In reality they are all over the globe probably in every major city worldwide, or at least every major city in westernized countries, especially Europe and the U.S. where this is very prominent. I earlier mentioned New York City, Chicago, Los Angeles, Paris, Washington D.C., Brussels, Sydney, and London. The people involved in this form of satanism are there for the power and money they gain. The Illuminati is the most well-known of these groups. These people are respectable businessmen, politicians, entertainers, artists, dancers, investors, judges and bankers. They are out there on the world stage serving their master, the devil, and reaping the material benefits. As I said in chapter 8, despite the fact that these groups are very deep underground and very secretive, we sometimes catch glimpses of their activity.

5. The fifth form is called generational satanism. Satanism which is generational can take several different forms. There can be generational witchcraft covens, which have also been called "Multi-Generational Fertility Cults." There can be generational devotion to Lucifer in the form of luciferianism. There can be generational occultism that has elements of Nazi and Hitler worship. And generational satanism proper which does not always find its adherents worshipping Satan. Sometimes these groups can be dedicated and devoted to some other devil in hell rather than Satan or Lucifer. For instance, a family could be devoted to the service and worship

of Baal or be dedicated to the devil Leviathan. This being done at some point in the family line possibly going back centuries.

This form of satanism is extremely dark and disturbing and for various different reasons. First, these groups are almost always involved with the sexual abuse, torture, mind control, cannibalism, and murder of children and adults. These groups perform "bizarre rituals" in which both animals and humans are sexual abused, tortured, and sacrificed to the devil they worship in the cult. Secondly, these groups, to acquire people for their rituals use various means including baby breeding and kidnapping. Every year in the United States and Europe many children go missing that are never heard from or seen again, I suspect some of these are the victims of such cults. Third, these groups practice mind control, which includes torture, on children so as to condition them to become part of the cult and accept diabolical possession. Fourth, these cults are extremely secretive and underground. They blend in with regular society and you would never suspect them as being involved with a satanic cult. Fifth, these groups are utterly devoted to the devil and the practice of evil, and as a result I believe many of the people that are members of these cults and are active participants are perfectly possessed.

These are just some of the reasons I find this particular form of devil worship very disturbing. The exact theology of these cults is known to a certain extant in that prior members of these cults have escaped and told their stories. The theology is obviously going to varying depending on which type of generational group it is. I earlier mentioned these groups can include witchcraft elements, Nazi-Hitler worship, lucifer worship, satanism, and specific devil worship. For instance, a group practicing generational witchcraft is going to have a totally different theology than a group that is dedicated to a specific devil. For anyone who wants to delve into this topic more and study what these groups do believe, the foremost expert on this matter is a man named Steve Ogilvie. I will also give a list sources at the end of this book.

Just based on the nature of these groups and how secretive and underground they are, direct evidence of their existence is sometimes hard to come by. I would say the greatest evidence of their existence comes from cult members who have escaped the cult and seek help from members of the church. There have been many Catholic exorcists who have assisted people in this regard and many of these exorcists have testified as to the existence of these cults. There are many additional people as well who have either written about these cults or talked about their existence.

Additional evidence of these cults is wholly circumstantial and secondary. It either comes from first person eye witness accounts, or other pieces of evidence that when pieced together paints a whole picture, a very dark picture. One overlooked piece of evidence of these cults is the phenomena known as cattle mutilation. This has been going on at least since the 1940's and probably much earlier but went unreported. Starting in the 1950's cattle all around the U.S. but especially in the Midwest and western United States started turning up dead with pieces of their body's being surgically removed. These phenomena have been blamed on many different things, including ufo's and extraterrestrials. When one looks at all the evidence however, including the dates on which these things happen as well as the fact that most of these cattle mutilations involve the complete draining of all the blood of the animal, it leads to the easy conclusion that this is being done by professional satanic cults. I say professional because nobody has ever been caught, arrested or prosecuted for these crimes. Whoever is doing this, knows what they are doing, and it is being done with a level of sophistication and professionalism rarely seen in crimes of this nature.

Some of the most prominent states where cattle mutilations have occurred are Idaho, Montana, Colorado, Oklahoma, Kansas, Wyoming and Nevada. As I said, these cattle are often found with sexual organs expertly removed with surgical precision and all the blood drained from the animal without even so much as a drop found on the ground. It is speculated that advanced veterinary equipment is being used to harvest the blood. Lastly, there has been multiple investigations of the cattle mutilation phenomenon, but without them ever being solved and not one single person ever being arrested. In one of the investigations tissue samples from mutilated cattle were found to contain drugs and sedatives that would be used to incapacitate the animal before mutilating it.

Rarely there have been cases where members of these cults have been arrested and charged with child molestation, pedophilia, and incest. In these cases, the victims often tell police of the ritual and cult overtones of the abuse. A very recent case and example of this was discovered in Seattle, Washington. In this case three elderly brothers who had been living together their whole lives were found to be in possession of mountains of child pornography. Additionally, their house was searched and revealed many pieces of evidence suggesting these brothers were involved in satanic worship and were possibly responsible for multiple child murders and abductions. An internet search will reveal many disturbing aspects of this case for anyone who wants to delve deeper. The reason I suspect multi-generational satanism in this case is because it awfully peculiar for all four brothers to all have the same proclivity for abusing young girls in a ritualistic fashion. This tells me most likely the brothers were abused themselves as children by their own father and or grandparents and this has probably been going on for generations. The police in this case also confirmed that the brothers themselves had abused multiple generations of their own family members. On the outside this may look like a simple case of pedophilia. However, we need to consider the evidence of satanism found in the house, including detailed journals, possibly grimoires, detailing the sacrifice, rape and murder of children for the purposes of ritualistic satanism.

There was a very curious case that occurred on Long Island, New York that was portrayed on the show, Paranormal Witness. This was an episode in season three entitled "The Long Island Terror." In this story, the Myrum family moved into a Long Island home in the small town of St. James. Upon renovating the house it was discovered that there was a very prominent and professional looking upside down pentagram etched onto the basement floor. There was also discovered multiple carvings and other satanic imagery in the forest behind the house including animal bones. Most disturbing, a journal was found in one of the walls that was dated from 1927 in which a small girl of about 12 years named Christina, detailed horrific ritualistic abuse she suffered at the hands of her father. According to Janet Myrum, the journal detailed the fact that the girl's father was a member of a satanic cult that met at the house in St. James and performed sexual abuse and torture of children, animal sacrifice and possible human sacrifice. Keep in mind the journal was dated from 1927, so the exorcists and others who have all claimed this sort of thing has been going on in this country for hundreds of years are indeed correct. Needless to say, the Myrum family experienced a fairly violent infestation of the home they moved into and the house needed to be eventually exorcised.

Additional evidence comes in the form of eyewitnesses who have come across various ritual sites and seen disturbing things. Space does not allow me to detail all the evidence out there, but it is common to hear stories of people coming upon cults deep in the woods or even forest rangers finding ritual sites deep in the woods. These are most likely not the work of teenage dabblers but rather serious Satanists who wish to keep their identity and activity completely secret.

When all the evidence is put together in totality it becomes clear that multi-generational Satanists and witches do in fact exist. There is just too much evidence to ignore it or claim that they do not exist. The reason I bring this topic up is because these specific types of Satanists can be well respected members of the community or be from very rural areas but in all cases their identity as Satanists is kept completely secret. They function completely normally in society. We can be certain that at least some of these people, who engage in ritualistic abuse of children, torture, murder, animal sacrifice, gross sexual perversion, and the direct invocation of diabolic entities are possessed. Their possessions, because they have intentionally given themselves over to the devil, because they worship and serve him, because they are completely consensual to such activities and show no sign of traditional possession are almost certainly perfectly possessed. Malachi Martin once said that one of the hallmarks of this form of satanism is that generation after generation teaches or conditions their heirs to "accept" possession. Meaning the diabolic entity or entities that are in charge of these cults and families have been nourished and kept by these families for generations and in complete possession of the family members that are consensual to this.

That does not mean that all familial cult members are possessed in this way. Very often members of these cults escape the cult and wish to be free of their possession and the cult. This can occur for many reasons and Adam Blai in his two books lists a number of them. Needless to say, these people almost always require extensive exorcisms, therapy, and care to heal their extensive wounds, both spiritual and psychological.

APPENDIX B

PHOTOGRAPHS
THE FACES OF THE PERFECTLY POSSESSED

Dennis Radar, (Bind, Torture, Kill) BTK Killer

Dennis Radar's drawing of Factor X, the demon he claimed possessed him

Jeffrey Dahmer, the Milwaukee Cannibal

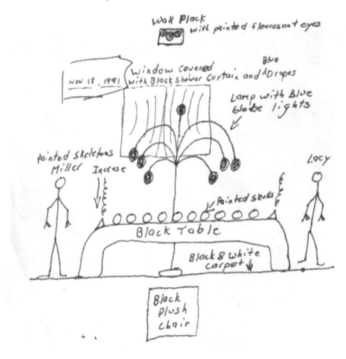

Jeffrey Dahmer's drawing of Satanic altar he was going to set up in his apartment using his victim's skeletal remains.

Ted Bundy   Charles Manson   Andrew Pixley

The Chicago Rippers, from left to right, Edward Spreitzer, Robin Gecht, Thomas Kokoraleis, Andrew Kokoraleis

Gecht's attic where satanic rituals took place, note the red cross still visible on right hand side

413

"I looked in his eyes. If the devil had eyes, that's what they'd look like. They were red in the center. It was like a fire had come out of his eyes. You could see all the way through `em," Stone said. "That was the strangest sight I ever saw. If there is a human that's got the devil in him, he's it." Prosecutor Bob Stone on encounter he had with David Allen Gore as authorities were digging up his murder victims in a Florida orange grove

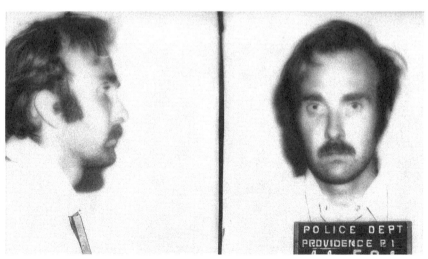

Wayne Chapman, serial child rapist and child murderer whom several witnesses described as having very strange evil looking eyes.

Aleister Crowley   Aleister Crowley dressed in ceremonial garb

Marshall Applewhite, leader of Heaven's Gate cult

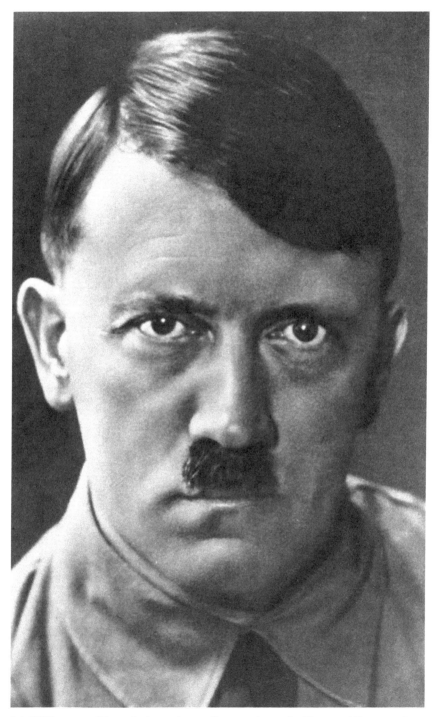

Adolf Hitler, one of the evilest men to ever live, murderer of millions and the man who a childhood friend remarked of him "It was as if another being spoke out of his body and moved him"

Hitler, a mesmerizing public speaker, addressed political meetings in Munich calling for a new German order to replace what he saw as an incompetent and inefficient democratic regime. This New Order was distinguished by an authoritarian political system based on a leadership structure in which authority flowed downward from a supreme national leader.

In the new Germany, all citizens would unselfishly serve the state, or Volk; democracy would be abolished; and individual rights sacrificed for the good of the führer state. The ultimate aim of the Nazi Party was to seize power through Germany's parliamentary system, install Hitler as dictator, and create a community of racially pure Germans loyal to their führer, who would lead them in a campaign of racial cleansing and world conquest. Caption from: https://www.nationalww2museum.org/war/articles/how-did-adolf-hitler-happen

417

Bundesarchiv, Bild 183-H08447
Foto: o.Ang. | 1. Juli 1938

Himmler laying a wreath in Wewelsburg Castle

Wewelsburg Castle foundations date back to the Middles Ages. As the site stands today, the castle design dates to the 17th century. The castle is located near the Teutoburg Forest. It is believed to be the site where Arminus, a Germanic tribe leader defeated the Roman Army which in part lends the castle to ancient fantasy. For the last 75 years the castle has exuded a dark fascination luring Satanists and Neo-Nazi's alike drawn in by pagan symbology and Nazi occultism making this site a kind of sadistic pilgrimage.

Much of the pseudo-religious mystery that has surrounded this castle since 1945 of torch-lit ceremonies, ancient Nordic and pagan rituals and the mythos of the Ancient Aryan is all fake.

Much of the rumours stem from Himmler's own delusional understanding and interpretation of Germanic and Nordic mythology. He was fascinated by prophecy, magical power and the belief that the Aryans were a super race. The SS was designed to be the very embodiment of this belief.

Himmler desperately wanted a facility where he could drum these values into future SS leaders. Acquired in 1934, Himmler leased the property for 100 years at the symbolic rental price of 1 Reichsmark per year. Initially he planned to turn the facility into a leadership school for SS officers', but this later changed, and it was designed as a meeting point for the SS elite. Caption from: https://onthefront.com/blog/2020/6/23/nazi-temple-of-doom-the-real-castle-wolfenstein

Left: In the zenith of the vault there is a swastika. Right: A sun wheel–shaped ornament, called the "Black Sun" in the SS Generals Hall

On the evening of Feb. 20, 1939, the marquee of New York's Madison Square Garden was lit up with the evening's main event: a "Pro American Rally." The organizers had chosen the date in celebration of George Washington's birthday and had procured a 30-foot-tall banner of America's first president for the stage. More than 20,000 men and women streamed inside and took their seats. The view they had was stunning: Washington was hung between American flags — and swastikas.

The rally was sponsored by the German American Bund, an organization with headquarters in Manhattan and thousands of members across the United States. In the 1930s, the Bund was one of several organizations in the United States that were openly supportive of Adolf Hitler and the rise of fascism in Europe. They had parades, bookstores and summer camps for youth. Their vision for America was a cocktail of white supremacy, fascist ideology and American patriotism. Caption from: https://www.npr.org/sections/codeswitch/2019/02/20/695941323/when-nazis-took-manhattan

Nazi parade in New York City, 1939.

419

The Rev Jim Jones just hours before his death and the death of all his followers.

Above: Jones levitating. Below: Notice the strange lights around Jones

White lights around Jones?

The aftermath, 900 dead, 300 of them children.

Double Headed Eagle with a crown on the top of the High Priests Throne Chair which depicts the 33rd Degree of Freemasonry.

33rd Degree of Freemasonry symbol.

Jeffrey Epstein, serial rapist and abuser of woman who believed he had a "Demigod" Biology which caused him to have to have at least three orgasms a day.

Is it just a coincidence that Epstein's temple resembles the same symbol, the 2 eagles with a crown in the middle? It should be noted that these were not the only occult symbols on Epstein's Island. According to witnesses the island was littered with gargoyles and devil figures with stars on them as well as statues of pagan Gods and goddesses.

423

Engraving of Faust's pact with Mephisto, by Adolf Gnauth (circa 1840)

BIBLIOGRAPHY

A.V. Miller, O.S.C. 1908. Sermons on Modern Spiritualism. St. Louis: B. Herder.

Africa, National Prosecuting Authority of South. 2010. Tsireledzani: Understanding the Dimensions of Human Trafficking in South Africa. Research Report, Republic of South Africa.

Alexandria, Athanatius of. 2003. The Life of Antony. Kalamazoo: Cistercian Publications Inc.

Allen, Thomas. 1993. Possessed: The True Story of An Exorcism. New York: Doubleday.

Amorth, Gabriel. 2016. An Exorcist Explains the Demonic. Manchester: Sophia Institute Press.

—. 2002. An Exorcist More Stories. San Francisco: Ignatius Press.

—. 1999. An Exorcist Tells His Story. San Francisco: Ignatius Press.

—. 2014. Get Out Satan. Manilla: St Paul's Publishing.

—. 2020. Mary and Satan. Manilla: St Pauls Publishing.

—. 2014. Memoirs of an Exorcist. Milan: Piemme.

—. 2017. My Battle Against Satan. Manchester: Sophia Institute Press.

—. 2019. The Devil is Afraid of Me: The Life and Work of the Worlds Most Famous Exorcist. Manchester: Sophia Institute Press.

—. 2018. We Will Be Judged By Love: The Devil Can Do Nothing Against God's Mercy. Manilla: St Pauls Publishing.

Aradi, Zsolt. 1956. The Book of Miracles. New York: Farrar, Straus and Cudahy.

Arintero, John. 1979. The Mystical Evolution in the Development and Vitality of the Church. 2 vols. Rockford: Tan Books.

Aumann, Jordan. 2006. Spiritual Theology. London, New York: Continuum.

Avila, Teresa of. 1988. The Life of Saint Teresa of Avila by Herself. Translated by J. M. Cohen. Penguin Classics.

Ayensworth, Stephen Michaud and Hugh. 1999. The Only Living Witness: The True Story of Serial Sex Killer Ted Bundy. Irving: Authorlink Press.

Baglio, Matt. 2009. The Rite: The Making of a Modern Exorcist. New York: Doubleday.

Balducci, Corrado. 1959. Gli Indemoniati. Roma Coletti: Generico.

—. 1990. The Devil Alive and Active in Our World. Statan Island: Alba House.

Bamonte, Francesco. 2017. Diabolical Possession and the Ministry of Exorcism. Translated by CE. PLXIIIIP.

—. 2019. The Rebellious Angels: The Mystery of Evil in the Experience of An Exorcist. PLXIIIIP.

—. 2018. The Virgin Mary and the Devil in Exorcisms. PLXIIIIP.

Barron, Bishop Robert. 2018. "The McCarrick Mess." Word On Fire. August 9. Accessed August 10, 2018. https://www.wordonfire.org/resources/article/the-mccarrick-mess/5873/.

Bellord, Rev. James. 1906. Meditations on Christian Dogma. Callan: Convent of Mercy.

Bernard J Kelly, C.S.Sp. 1950. God, Man and Satan. Westminster: The Newman Press.

Beyersdorf, Eunice. 1975. A Manual of Exorcism Very Useful for Priests and Ministers of the Church. New York: Hispanic Society of America.

Blackmore, Simon Augustine. 1924. Spiritism Facts and Frauds. New York, Cincinatti, Chicago: Benziger Brothers.

Blackmore, Simon Augustus. 1927. The Angel World. Cleveland: John W. Winterich.

Blai, Adam. 2017. Hauntings, Possessions, and Exorcisms. Steubenville: Emmaus Road Publishing.

—. 2014. religousdemonology.com. Accessed May 3, 2019. http://religiousdemonology.com/questions.html.

Blann, Nelson Pacheco and Tommy. 1994. Unmasking the Enemy: Visions Around the World and Global Deception in the End Times. Arlington: Bendan Press Inc.

Blatty, William Peter. 1971. The Exorcist. New York: Bantam Books.

Bolobanic, Msgr. Milivoj. 2013. An Exorcist Speaks: How to Recognize and Protect Oneself From the Snares of the Evil One. Notre Dame: Ave Maria Press.

Brennan, Betty. n.d. "Trappings of the Occult." Saint Joseph Communications.

Brennan, Father Joseph. 1989. The Kingdom of Darkness. Lafayette: Acadian House Publishing.

Brennan, Robert, ed. 1942. Essays in Thomism. Freeport: Books For Libraries Press.

Brittle, Gerald. 2013. The Demonologist: The Extraordinary Career of Ed and Lorraine Warren. Los Angeles, New York: Graymalkin Media.

—. 1983. The Devil in Connecticut. New York City: Bantam Books.

Bryant, Nick. 2009. The Franklin Scandal: A Story of Powerbrokers, Child Abuse & Betrayal. Walterville: Trine Day.

Bugliosi, Vincent. 2001. Helter Skelter: The True Story of the Manson Murders. New York, London: W.W. Norton & Company.

Capua, Blessed Raymond of. 2011. The Life of St Catherine of Sienna. Charlotte: Tan Books.

Carlin, Paolo. 2017. An Exorcist Explains How to Heal the Possessed. Manchester: Sophia Institute Press.

Carr, Joseph. 1985. The Twisted Cross: The Occultic Religion of Hitler and the New Age Nazism of the Third Reich. Shreveport, Lafayette: Huntington House.

Cavendish, Richard. 1967. The Black Arts. New York: G. P. Putnam's Sons.

Cervinara, Fr. Tarcisio of. 1994. The Devil In The Life of Padre Pio. Edited by Father Alessio Parente. Translated by Geraldine Nolan. Foggia: Leone Editrice.

Chetwood, Thomas. 1928. God and Creation. New York: Benziger Brothers.

Churton, Tobias. 2014. Aleister Crowley: The Biography: Spiritual Revolutionary, Romantic Explorer, Occult Master and Spy. London: Watkins Publishing.

Cochem, Martin Von. 1899. The Four Last Things: Death, Judgement, Hell, and Heaven. New York: Benziger Brothers.

Collins, James. 1947. The Thomistic Philosophy of the Angels. A Dissertation. Vol. The Catholic University of America Philosophical Studies Volume 89. Washington D.C.: The Catholic University of America Press.

Connell, Janice. 2004. Queen of the Cosmos. Brewster: Paraclete Press.

Conrad, Barry. 2009. An Unknown Encounter: A True Account of the San Pedro Haunting. Pittsburgh: Rose Dog Books.

Corte, Nicolas. 1958. Who is the Devil. First. Edited by Henri Daniel-Rops. Translated by D.K. Pryce. Vol. 21. New York: Hawthorn Books.

Cranmer, Bob. 2014. The Demon of Brownville Road. New York: The Berkley Publishing Group.

Cristiani, Leon. 1955. Actualite de Satan. Paris: Centurion.

—. 1974. Evidence of Satan In The Modern World. Rockford: Tan Books and Publishers.

Crowley, Aleister. 1989. The Confessions of Aleister Crowley. New York: Penguin Books.

Cruz, Juan Carroll. 1999. Angels and Devils. Charlotte: Tan Books and Publishers.

Cruz, Rachael. 2018. "Pope Francis says the Italian Mafia is not Christian, 'They carry death in their souls.'" Christian Daily, March 28.

Cuneo, Michael. 2001. American Exorcism: Expelling Demons in the Land of Plenty. New York: Broadway Books.

Curran, Robert. 1989. The Haunted: The True Story of One Families Nightmare. New York: St Martin's Press.

Danielou, Jean. 1957. The Angels and Their Mission. Translated by David Heimann. Westminster: The Newman Press.

Davies, Jeremy. 2008. Exorcism From a Catholic Perspective. London: Catholic Truth Society.

Davis, Henry. 1959. Moral and Pastoral Theology. 4 vols. London, New York: Sheed and Ward.

De Sales, St. Francis. 2013. An Introduction to the Devout Life. Charlotte: Tan Books.

DeCamp, John. 1992. The Franklin Cover Up: Child Abuse, Satanism, and Murder in Nebraska. AWT, Inc.

Deferrari, Roy J., ed. 1954. Early Christian Biographies. Fathers of the Church, Inc.

Delaney, J. 1910. "Hatred." In The Catholic Encyclopedia. New York: Robert Appleton Company.

Delaport, Father. 1992. The Devil Does He Exist and What Does He Do. Rockford: Tan Books.

Devine, Arthur. 1903. A Manual of Mystical Theology. London: R & T Washbourne.

Devivier, Walter S.J. 1908. Christian Apologetics. Vol. 2. New York: Benziger Brothers.

Donaldson, Christopher. 1985. Martin of Tours. Parish Priest, Mystic and Exorcist. Routledge Kegan & Paul.

Ermatinger, Cliff. 2017. The Devil's Role in the Spiritual Life. Padre Pio Press.

Esper, Rev. Joseph. 2010. With Mary to Jesus. Queenship Publishing Company.

Euteneuer, Thomas. 2010. Demonic Abortion. Front Royal: Human Life International.

Euteneuer, Thomas J. 2010. Exorcism and the Church Militant. Front Royal: Human Life International.

F.J. Bunse, Theophilus Riesinger. 1934. The Earling Possession Case: An Exposition of the Exorcism of Mary a Demoniac and Certain Marvelous Revelations Foretelling the Near Advent of the Antichrist and the Coming Persecution of the Church in the Years 1952-1955. Unpublished Pamphlet.

Faith, Congregation for the Doctrine of the. 1975. Christian Faith and Demonology. Boston: Pauline Books and Media.

Faroni, Adolf. n.d. Don Bosco's Experience of the Devil. Manila: Don Bosco Press.

Farrell, Walter. 1941. A Companion To The Summa: The Architect of the Universe. New York: Sheed and Ward.

Ferrari, Giuseppe. n.d. "PHENOMENON OF SATANISM IN CONTEMPORARY SOCIETY." EWTN. Accessed May 26, 2017. https://www.ewtn.com/catholicism/library/phenomenon-of-satanism-in-contemporary-society-6078.

Fishman, Steve. 2006. "The Devil in David Berkowitz." New York Magazine, September 8.

Fortea, Jose Antonio. 2006. Interview With An Exorcist. West Chester: Ascension Press.

Gallagher, Richard. 2008. "Among the Many Counterfeits, a Case of Demonic Possession." New Oxford Review.

—. 2020. Demonic Foes: My Twenty-Five Years As a Psychiatrist Investigating Possessions, Diabolic Attacks, and the Paranormal. New York: Harper One.

Garrigou-Lagrange, Reginald. 1949. God His Existence and His Nature: A Thomistic Solution of Certain Agnostic Antinomies. Translated by Dom Bede Rose. Vol. 1. St. Louis, London: B. Herder Book Co.

—. 1952. Life Everlasting and the Immensity of the Soul: A Theological Treatise on the Four Last Things: Death, Judgment, Heaven, Hell. Rockford: Tan Books.

—. 2015. Reality: A Synthesis of Thomistic Thought. Middletown: Ex Fontibus Company.

—. 1991. The Three Ages of the Interior Life: Prelude of Eternal Life. 2 vols. Rockford: Tan Books.

—. 2015. The Trinity and God the Creator: A Commentary of St. Thomas' Theological Summa. San Bernardino: Ex Fontibus Company.

Garton, Ray. 2014. In a Dark Place: The True Story of a Haunting. Graymalkin Media.

Geiger, Rev. Theodore, ed. n.d. Mary Crushes the Serpent. Translated by O.S.B. Rev. Celestine Kapsner. Collegeville: St Johns Abbey.

Genelli, Christoph. 1871. The Life of Saint Ignatius of Loyola. London: Burnes, Oats and Company.

Germanus, Fr. 2012. The Life of St. Gemma Galgani. Charlotte: Tan Books.

Gilson, Etienne. 1960. The Christian Philosophy of Saint Augustine. New York: Random House.

—. 1966. The Christian Philosophy of St. Thomas Aquinas. New York: Random House.

Glenn, Paul. 1960. A Tour of the Summa. St. Louis, London: B. Herder Book Co.

Gmeiner, John. 1886. The Spirits of Darkness and Their Manifestations on Earth. Milwaukee-Chicago: Hoffmann Brothers.

Goodman, Felicitas. 2005. The Exorcism of Annaliese Michel. Eugene: Resource Publications.

Guazzo, Francesco Maria. 1929. Compendium Maleficarum. Edited by Montague Summers. London: John Rodker.

Guiley, Rosemary Ellen. 2009. The Encyclopedia of Demons and Demonology. New York: Checkmark Books.

Haining, Peter. 1972. The Anatomy of Witchcraft. Taplinger Publishing co.

Heidt, William George. 1949. Angelology of the Old Testament: A Study in Biblical Theology. Vol. Studies in Sacred Theology No. 24. Washington D.C.: Catholic University of America Press.

Henry, A.M. 1954. Theology Library. 6 vols. Fides Publishers Association.

Heredia, C.M. 1922. Spiritism and Common Sense. New York: P.J. Kenedy & Sons.

Hernandez, Isabelle. n.d. "Meet the Man Who Started the Illuminati." National Geographic. Accessed July 2, 2019. https://www.nationalgeographic.com/history/magazine/2016/07-08/profile-adam-weishaupt-illuminati-secret-society/.

Hitler, Adolf. 1998. Mein Kampf. Boston: Houghton Mifflin Company.

Houck, Frederick. 1948. Our Friends and Foes or The Angels, Good and Bad. St Louis, London: B. Herder Book Co.

Husslein, Joseph S.J. 1934. The Spirit World About Us. Milwaukee: The Bruce Publishing Company.

Huxley, Aldous. 1952. The Devil's of Loudun. New York: Harper & Brother's Publishers.

Jesus-Marie, Bruno de, ed. 1952. Satan. New York: Sheed & Ward.

John A. McHugh, Charles J. Callan. 1958. Moral Theology A Complete Course Based on St. Thomas Aquinas and the Best Modern Authorities. London: B. Herder.

Johnson, Kevin Orlan. 1998. Apparitions: Mystic Phenomena and What They Mean. Dallas: Pangaeus Press.

Jose Antonio Fortea, Lawrence Leblanc. 2012. Anneliese Michel: A True Story of a Case of Demon Possession. Self Published.

Kennedy, William H. 2004. Lucifers Lodge: Satanic Ritual Abuse in the Catholic Church. Sophia Perennis.

—. 2006. Satanic Crime: A Threat to the New Millenium. Mystic Valley Media.

Koch, Father Antony. 1928. A Handbook of Moral Theology. 3rd. Edited by Arthur Pruess. Vol. 2 Sins and the Means of Grace. St Louis, London: B Herder Book Co.

Kosicki, Father George. 2003. Spiritual Warfare: The Attack Against the Woman. CMJ Marian Publishers.

Kubizek, August. 1955. The Young Hitler I Knew. New York: Tower Books.

Lampert, Father Vincent. 2020. Exorcism: The Battle Against Satan and His Demons. Steubenville: Emmaus Road Publishing.

Lanning, Special Agent Kenneth. 1992. Investigator's Guide to Allegations of Ritual Child Abuse. Quantico: FBI Academy.

Larson, Bob. 1999. Larson's Book of Spiritual Warfare. Nashville: Thomas Nelson Publishers.

Lawler, Philip. 2018. The Smoke of Satan: How Corrupt and Cowardly BishopsBetrayed Christ, His Church and the Faithful and What Can Be Done About It. Charlotte: Tan Books.

Lea, Henry Charles. 1957. Materials Toward a History of Witchcraft. 3 vols. Thomas Yoseloff.

Lehodey, Dom Vitalis. 1982. The Ways of Mental Prayer. Charlotte: Tan Books.

Lepicier, Alexius. 1906. The Unseen World: An Exposition of Catholic Theology in Its Relation to Modern Spiritism. New York: Benziger Brothers.

Lewis, C.S. 2015. The Screwtape Letters. New York City: HarperOne.

Lhermitte, Jean. 1963. Diabolical Possession, True and False. Edited by Daniel-Rops. Vol. Faith and Fact Books: 57. Londen: Burnes & Oates.

Lieber, William. 1917. Devil & Devilry. New York, Cincinnati, Chicago: Benziger Brothers.

Longenecker, Father Dwight. 2018. "Hostage to the Devil." Fr. Dwight Longenecker. March 2. Accessed October 4, 2019. https://dwightlongenecker.com/hostage-to-the-devil/.

Louismet, Dom S. 1918. Mysticism True and False. New York: P.J. Kenedy & Sons.

Marin, Antonio Royo. 2012. The Theology of Christian Perfection. Eugene: Wipf and Stock.

Marshall, Taylor. 2019. Infiltration: The Plot to Destroy the Church From Within. Manchester: Crisis Publications.

Martin, Malachi. 1992. Hostage to the Devil: The Possession and Exorcism of Five Contemporary Americans. San Francisco: Harper One.

—. 2007. The Kingdom Of Darkness Interview With Malachi Martin. Triumph Communications.

—. 1996. Windswept House: A Vatican Novel. New York: Broadway Books.

Matthew, Laurie. 2002. Where Angels Fear: Ritual Abuse in Scotland. Dundee: Dundee Young Women's Centre.

McAstocker, David S.J. 1946. Speaking of Angels. Milwaukee: The Bruce Publishing Company.

Monden, Louis. 1966. Signs and Wonders: A study of the miraculous element in religion. New York: Desclee Co.

Nelson, Polly. 2019. Defending the Devil: My Story As Ted Bundy's Last Lawyer. Echo Point Books & Media.

Nicola, John. 1974. Diabolical Possession and Exorcism. Rockford: Tan Books.

—. 1976. Is Solemn Public Exorcism A Viable Rite In The Modern Western World? A Theological Response. Washington D.C.: Doctoral Dissertation.

Noort, Msgr G Van. 1957. Dogmatic Theology. 3 vols. Westminster: The Newman Press.

O.C.D., Kieran Kavanaugh, trans. 1987. The Collected Works of Teresa of Avila. Lincoln Road: ICS Publications.

O'Connell, William Cardinal. 1928. Devotion to the Holy Angels. Boston: Pastoral Letter.

Oesterreich, Traugott K. 1974. Possession and Exorcism Among Primitive Races, In Antiquity, The Middle Ages, and Modern Times. Translated by D. Ibberson. New York: Causeway Books.

O'Neil, A.C. 1912. "Sin." In The Catholic Encyclopedia. New York: Robert Appleton Company.

Owen, Alex. 2004. The Place of Enchantment: British Occultism and the Culture of the Modern. Chicago: The University of Chicago Press.

Parente, Pascal. 1946. The Mystical Life. St. Louis: B. Herder Book Co.

Patella, Michael. 2012. Angels and Demons: A Christian Primer of the Spiritual World. Collegeville: Liturgical Press.

Patterson, James. 2016. Filthy Rich. New York: Grand Central Publishing.

Paula, Sister Mary. 1935. Presenting the Angels. New York, Chicago, Cincinnati: Benziger Brothers.

Peck, Scott. 2005. Glipses of the Devil: A Psychiatrist's Personal Accounts of Possession, Exorcism, and Redemption. New York: Free Press.

—. 1983. People of the Lie: The Hope for Healing Human Evil. New York: Touchstone.

431

Peterson, Eric. 1964. The Angels and the Liturgy. Translated by Ronald Walls. New York: Herder and Herder.

Pickman, Debra Lyn. 2010. The Sallie House Haunting A True Story. Woodbury: Llewellyn Publications.

Pius of the Name of Mary, Fr. 1924. The Life of Saint Paul of the Cross. New York: P. O'Shea.

Pohle, Joseph. 1940. God: The Author of Nature and the Supernatural, A Dogmatic Treatise. Edited by Arthur Pruess. St Louis: B. Herder Book Co.

Porteous, Bishop Julian. 2012. Manual of Minor Exorcisms. London: Catholic Truth Society.

Poulain, Augustine. 2016. The Graces of Interior Prayer. Jeffersonville: Caritas Publishing.

Pourrat, Pierre. 1953. Christian Spirituality in the Middle Ages. Vol. 2. Westminster: The Newman Press.

Prummer, Dominic. 1958. Handbook of Moral Theology. Cork: The Mercier Press Limited.

Raphael V. O'Connell, S.J. 1923. The Holy Angels. New York: P.J. Kenedy & Sons.

Ratzinger, Joseph Cardinal. 2002. God and the World: Believing and Living in Our Time. San Francisco: Ignatius Press.

Ratzinger, Joseph. 2011. Jesus of Nazareth Holy Week: From the Entrance Into Jerusalem to the Resurrection. San Francisco: Ignatius Press.

Ravenscroft, Trevor. 1982. The Spear of Destiny the Occult Power Behind the Spear Which Pierced the Side of Christ and How Hitler Inverted the Force in a Bid to Conquer the World. York Beach: Red Wheel/Weiser LLC.

Reiterman, Tim. 2008. Raven: The Untold Story of the Rev. Jim Jones and His People. New York: Tarcher Penguin.

Ribet, M.J. 1902. La Mystique Divine Distinguee Contrefacons Diaboliques Et Des Analogies Humaines. Vol. Tome 3. Paris: Librairie Ch. Poussielgue.

Ripperger, Chad. 2013. Introduction to the Science of Mental Health. Lincoln: Sensus Traditionis Press.

Robbins, Russell Hope. 1981. The Encyclopedia of Witchcraft and Demonology. Prineville: Bonanza Books.

Robert J. Bunker, Ph.D. 2013. "Santa Muerte: Inspired and Ritualistic Killings." LEB FBI. February 5. Accessed Jan 13, 2019. https://leb.fbi.gov/articles/featured-articles/santa-muerte-inspired-and-ritualistic-killings.

Rodewyk, Adolf. 1975. Possessed by Satan: The Church's teaching on the devil, possession, and exorcism. Translated by Martin Ebon. Garden City, New York: Doubleday & Company.

Romero, Jesse. 2019. The Devil in the City of Angels. Charlotte: Tan Books.

Rule, Ann. 2000. The Stranger Beside Me. New York, London: W.W. Norton & Company.

Russell, Jeffrey Burton. 1977. The Devil: Perceptions of Evil from Antiquity to Primitive Christianity. Ithica and London: Cornell University Press.

—. 1976. Witchcraft in the Middle Ages. Carol Publishing Group.

Ryder, Daniel. 1994. Cover Up of the Century: Satanic Ritual Crime and World Conspiracy. Nobelsville: Ryder Publishing.

Sagues, Joseph. 2014. Sacrae Theologia Summa: On God the Creator and Sanctifier, On Sins. Translated by Kenneth Baker S.J. Saddle River: Keep The Faith.

Saudreau, Abbe A. 1907. The Degrees of the Spiritual Life. 2 vols. London: R & T Washbourne.

Saudreau, Auguste. 1921. L'Etat Mystique Sa Nature Ses Phases et Les Faits Extraordinaires De La Vie Spirituelle. Angers: G. Grassin, Richou Freres, Editeurs.

Scanlan, Michael. 1980. Deliverance From Evil Spirits. Servant.

Scannell, Joseph Wilhelm and Thomas. 1906. A Manual of Catholic Theology, Based on Scheeben's "Domatik." 2 vols. New York: Benziger Brothers.

Scaramelli, Giovanni Battista. 1754. Il Direttorio Mistico. Venezia: Appresso Simone Occhi.

Scaramelli, J.B. 2005. Handbook of Mystical Theology. Lakeworth: Nicholas-Hays, Inc.

Scaramelli, John Baptist. 1870. The Directorium Asceticum or Guide to the Spiritual Life. London: Burns and Oats.

Schechter, Harold. 1994. Depraved: The Definitive True Story of H.H. Holmes. New York: Pocket Books.

Scheeben, Mathias Joseph. 2019. Handbook of Catholic Dogmatics. 2 vols. Steubenville: Emmaus Academics.

Slater, S.J. Father Thomas. 1925. A Manual of Moral Theology. 2 vols. London: Burns, Oats and Washbourne.

Smit, Johannes. 1913. De Daemoniacis in Historia Evangelica. Roma: Scripta Pontificii Instituti Biblici.

Spence, Lewis. 2006. An Encyclopedia of Occultism. New York: Cosimo, Inc.

Spirago, Francis. 2020. The Catechism Explained: An Exhaustive Exposition of the Christian Religion. Post Falls: Mediatrix Press.

Sprenger, James & Heinrich Kramer. 1971. Malleus Maleficarum. Translated by Montague Summers. New York: Dover.

Squires, Nick. 2010. "Chief Exorcist Says Devil is in Vatican." The Telegraph. March 11. Accessed October 23, 2019. https://www.telegraph.co.uk/news/worldnews/europe/vaticancityandholysee/7416458/Chief-exorcist-says-Devil-is-in-Vatican.html.

Stang, WM. 1900. The Devil: Who He Is and What He Does. Providence: D.H. Williams & Co. Printers.

Steffen, Father Jeffrey. 1992. Satanism: Is It Real. Ann Arbor: Servant Publications.

Summers, Montague. 1926. The History of Witchcraft and Demonology. London: Kegan Paul, Trench, Trubner & Co.

Sutton, Anthony. 2002. America's Secret Establishment: An Introduction to the Order of Skull & Bones. Trine Day.

Sylvester Joseph Hunter, S.J. 1896. Outlines of Dogmatic Theology. Vol. 2. New York, Cincinnati, Chicago: Benziger Brothers.

Symonds, John. 1973. The Great Beast: The Life and Magick of Aleister Crowley. London: Mayflower Books Ltd.

Syquia, Jose Francisco. 2006. Exorcism: Encounters With the Paranormal and the Occult. Second Edition. Quezon City: Shepherds Voice Publications, Inc.

—. 2013. Exorcism: Encounters With the Paranormal and the Occult, Revised Edition. Makati City: St Pauls Philippines.

—. 2010. Exorcist A Spiritual Journey. Vol. 1. Makati City: St Pauls Philippines.

—. 2012. Exorcist Spiritual Battle Lines. Vol. 2. Makati City: St Pauls Philippines.

—. 2016. Exorcist: Spiritual Warfare and Discernement. Vol. 3. Makati City: St Pauls Philippines.

Szymanski, Dominic. 1974. A Notebook on the Devil and Exorcism. Libertyville: Franciscan Marytown Press.

Tanquerey, A. 1959. Manual of Dogmatic Theology. Translated by Msgr. J. Byrnes. 2 vols. Tournai: Desclee Company.

Tanquerey, Adolphe. 1930. The Spiritual Life: A Treatise on Ascetical and Mystical Theology. Translated by S.S., A.M. Rev. Herman Branderis. Baltimore: St Mary's Seminary.

Terry, Maury. 1987. The Ultimate Evil: An Investigation Into America's Most Dangerous Satanic Cult. New York: Doubleday.

Thomas, Father Gary, interview by Patrick Coffin. 2012. What You Need to Know About Exorcism Catholic Answers, (November 12).

Thurston, Herbert. 1954. Ghosts and Poltergeists. Chicago: Henry Regnery Company.

—. 1955. Surprising Mystics. Chicago: Henry Regnerey Company.

—. 1999. The Church and Spiritualism. Roman Catholic Books.

—. 1952. The Physical Phenomena of Mysticism. Chicago: Henry Regnery Company.

Thyraeus, Petrus. 1598. Hoc Est Daemoniaci. ex officina Mater. Cholini, sumptibus Gosuini Cholini.

Toland, John. 1992. Adolf Hitler. New York: First Anchor Books.

2009. Tribulation Now. August 6. Accessed January 30, 2019. http://www.tribulation-now.org/2009/08/06/perfect-possession-father-malachi-martin/.

Trochu, Francois. 2018. The Cure d'Ars. Jeffersonville: Caritas Publishing.

Tucciarone, Tracy. n.d. Oppression, Obsession, and Possession. Accessed May 31, 2019. https://www.fisheaters.com/praeternaturalworld4.html.

Ullathorne, William Bernard. 1886. Christian Patience The Strength and Discipline of the Soul. New York: Catholic Publication Society.

Vogl, Father Carl. 2010. Begone Satan. Charlotte: Tan Books.

Volken, Laurent. 1963. Visions, Revelations and the Church. New York: P.J. Kenedy and Sons.

Wall, Mick. 2010. When Giants Walked the Earth: A Biography of Led Zeppelin. New York: St. Martin's Press.

Warren, Ed and Lorraine. 1990. Satan's Harvest. New York: Dell Publishing.

Weller, Philip. 2007. Roman Ritual: Christian Buriel, Exorcisms, Reserved Blessings. Vol. 2. Boonville: Preserving Christian Publications.

Wilkinson, Tracy. 2007. The Vatican's Exorcists: Driving Out The Devil In The 21st Century. New York: Warner Books.

William Murphy, Francis Cunningham, et al. 1958. College Texts in Theology: God and His Creation. The Priory Press.

Winkelhofer, Alois. 1961. Traktat Uber Den Teufel. . Frankfurt: J. Knecht.

Zerbolt, Gerard. 1908. The Spiritual Ascent: A Devotional Treatise. London: Burns & Oats.